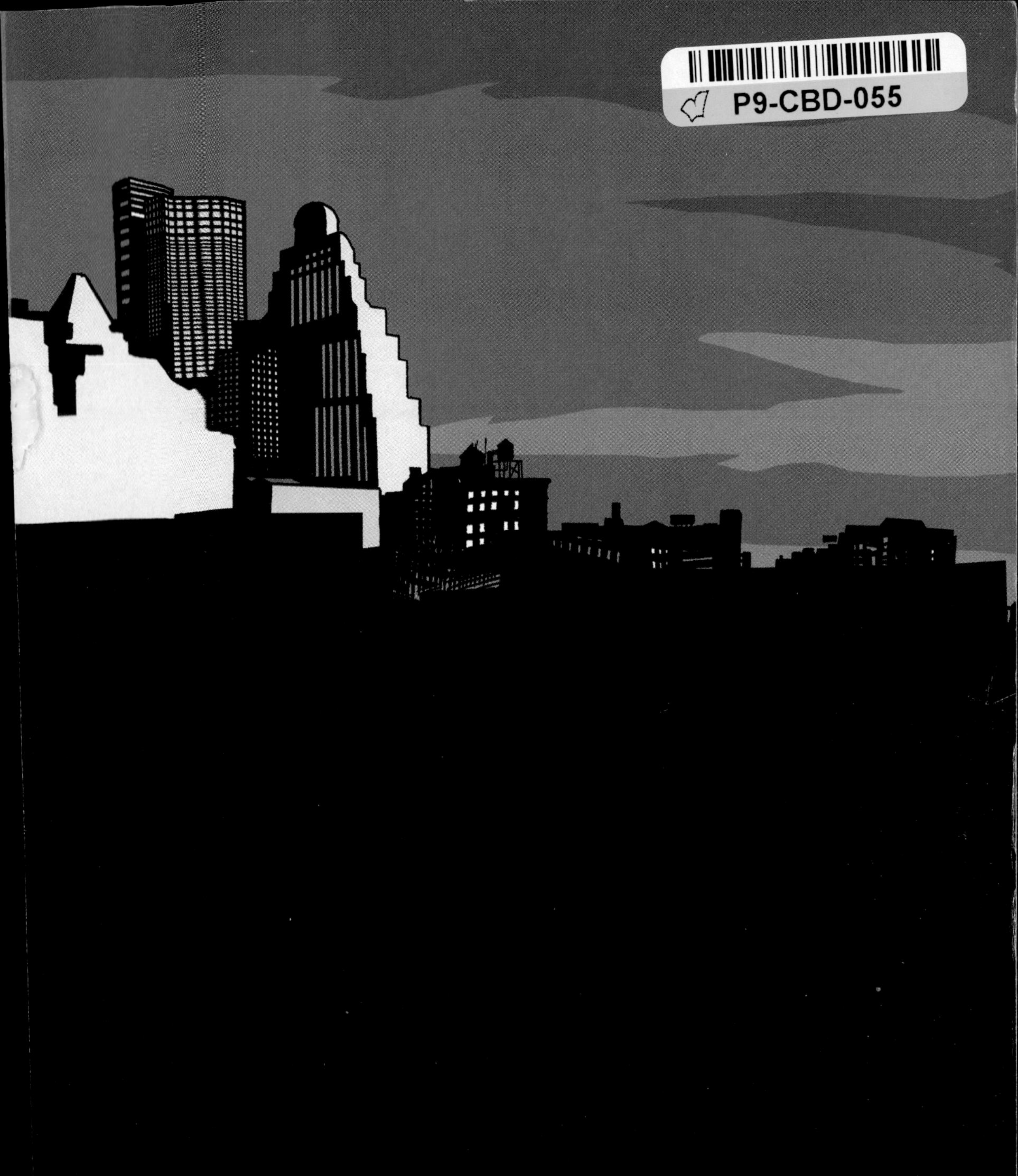

POW

CREATED AN
BRIAN MICHAEL BEND

COLOR ART
PETER PENTAZIS

TYPOGRAPHY
KEN BRUZENAK

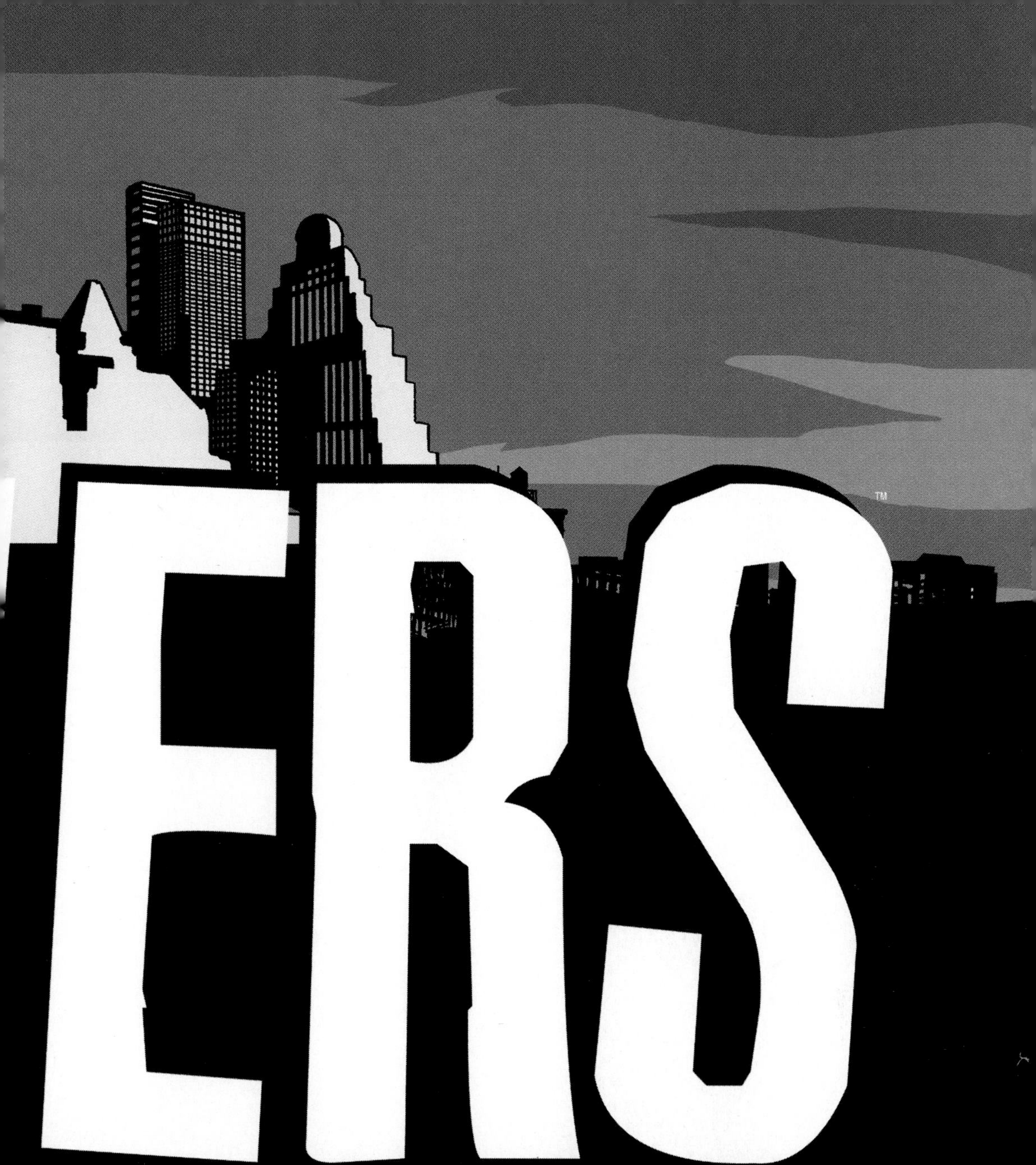

ERS™

RODUCED BY

AND MIKE AVON OEMING

EDITOR
KC MCCRORY

BUSINESS AFFAIRS
ALISA BENDIS

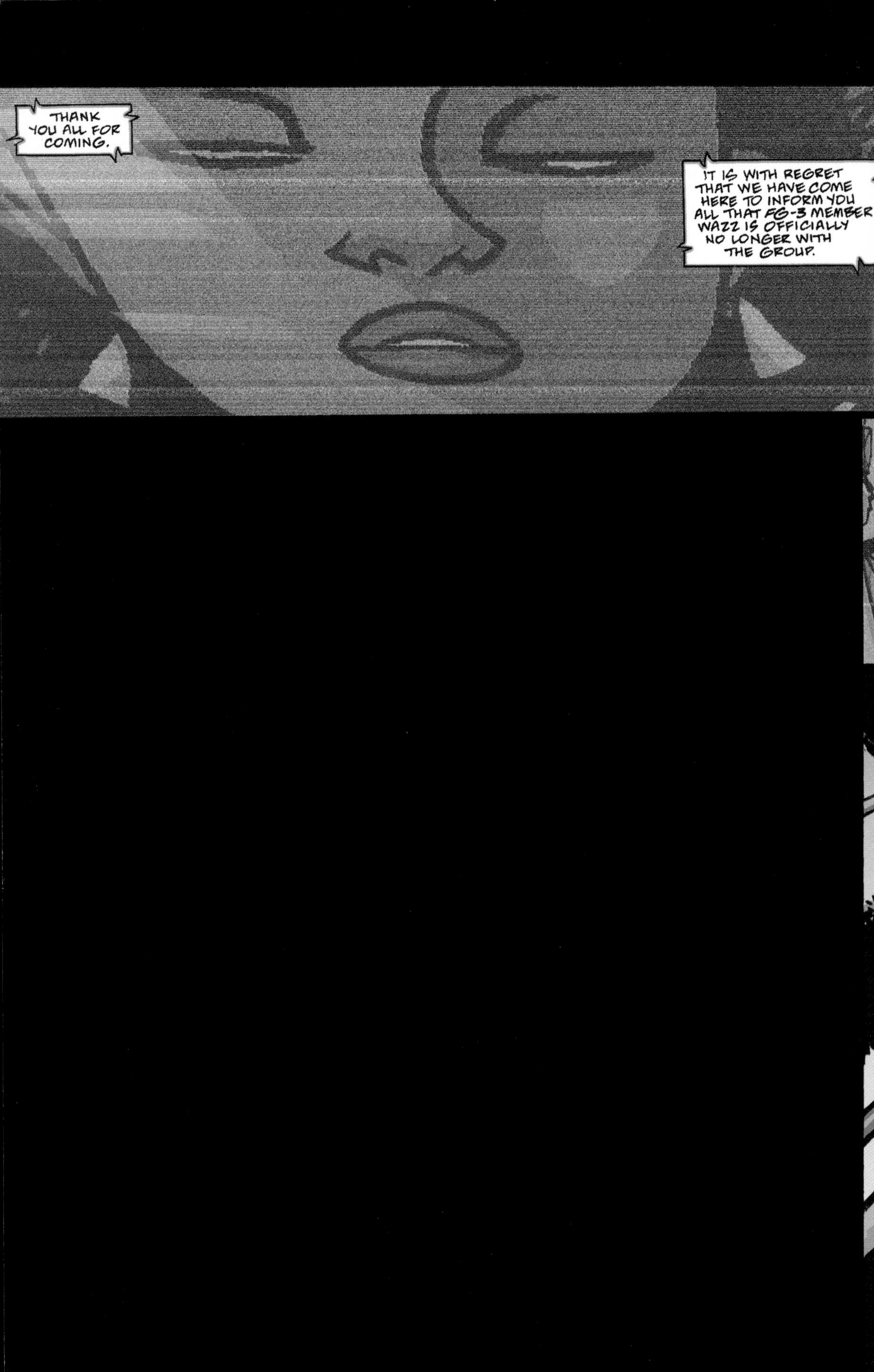
THANK YOU ALL FOR COMING.
IT IS WITH REGRET THAT WE HAVE COME HERE TO INFORM YOU ALL THAT FG-3 MEMBER WAZZ IS OFFICIALLY NO LONGER WITH THE GROUP.

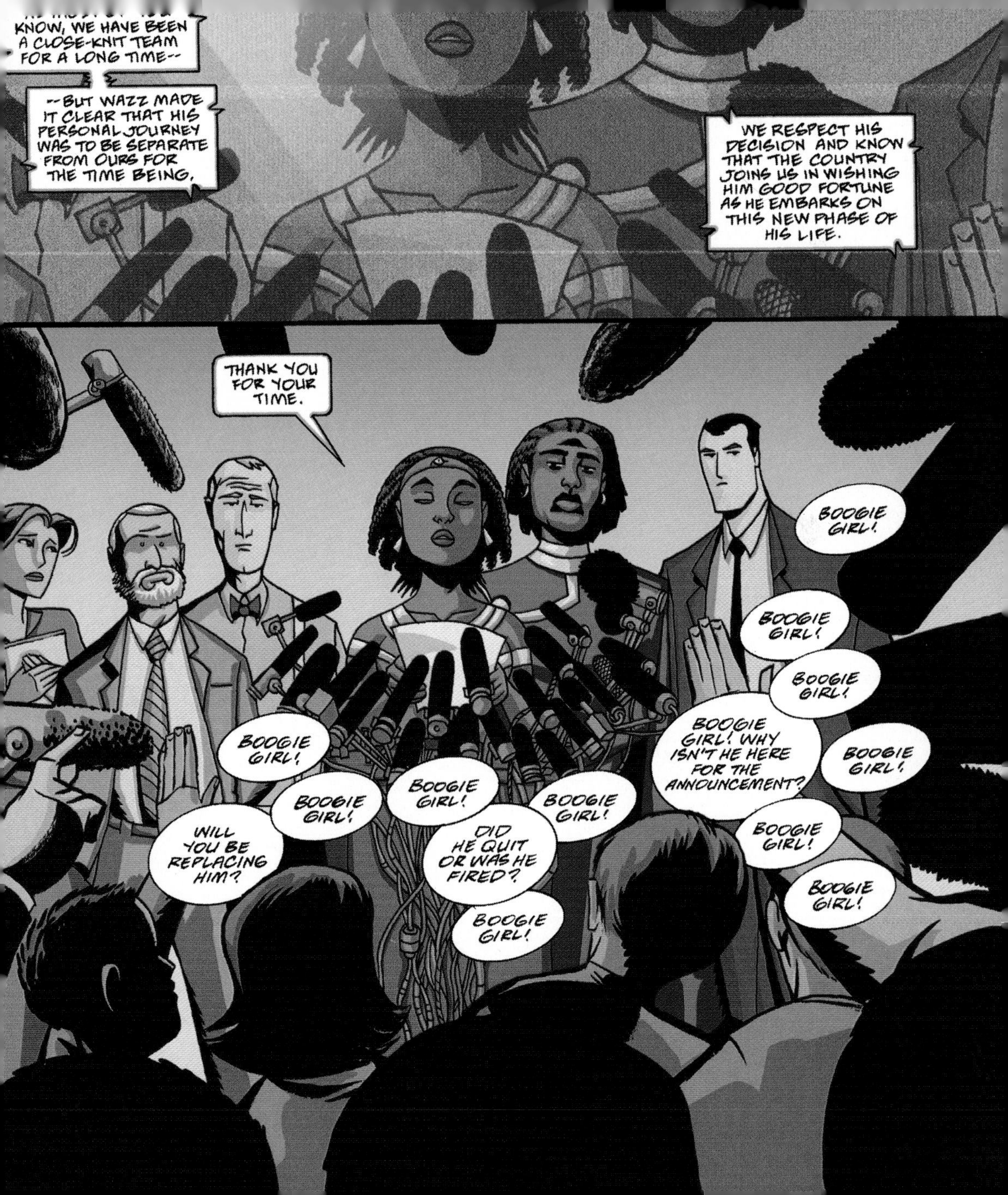

KNOW, WE HAVE BEEN A CLOSE-KNIT TEAM FOR A LONG TIME--
--BUT WAZZ MADE IT CLEAR THAT HIS PERSONAL JOURNEY WAS TO BE SEPARATE FROM OURS FOR THE TIME BEING.
WE RESPECT HIS DECISION AND KNOW THAT THE COUNTRY JOINS US IN WISHING HIM GOOD FORTUNE AS HE EMBARKS ON THIS NEW PHASE OF HIS LIFE.
THANK YOU FOR YOUR TIME.
BOOGIE GIRL!
BOOGIE GIRL!
BOOGIE GIRL!
BOOGIE GIRL! WHY ISN'T HE HERE FOR THE ANNOUNCEMENT?
BOOGIE GIRL!
BOOGIE GIRL!
BOOGIE GIRL!
BOOGIE GIRL!
BOOGIE GIRL!
WILL YOU BE REPLACING HIM?
DID HE QUIT OR WAS HE FIRED?
BOOGIE GIRL!
BOOGIE GIRL!
BOOGIE GIRL!

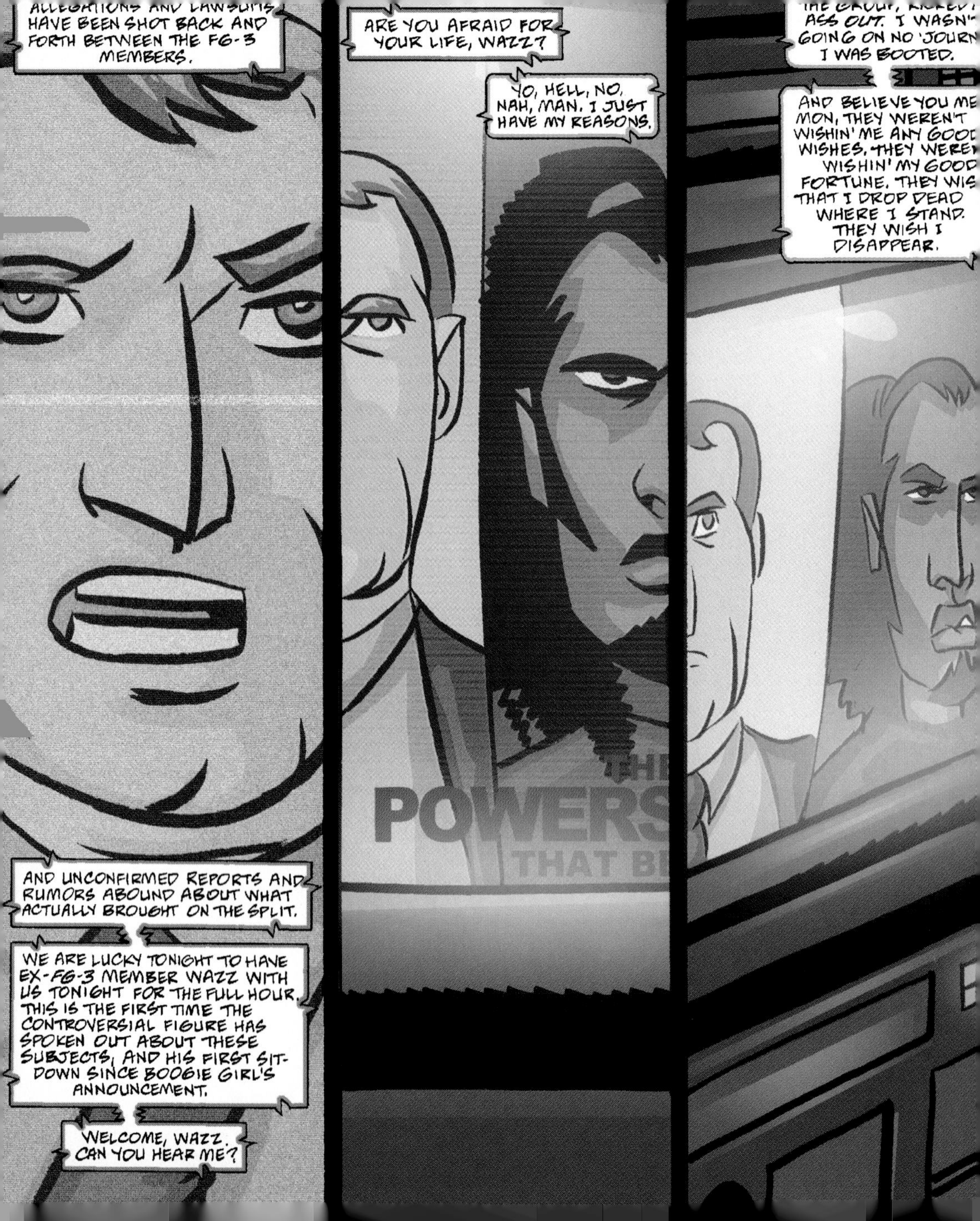
ALLEGATIONS AND LAWSUITS HAVE BEEN SHOT BACK AND FORTH BETWEEN THE FG-3 MEMBERS.
AND UNCONFIRMED REPORTS AND RUMORS ABOUND ABOUT WHAT ACTUALLY BROUGHT ON THE SPLIT.
WE ARE LUCKY TONIGHT TO HAVE EX-FG-3 MEMBER WAZZ WITH US TONIGHT FOR THE FULL HOUR. THIS IS THE FIRST TIME THE CONTROVERSIAL FIGURE HAS SPOKEN OUT ABOUT THESE SUBJECTS, AND HIS FIRST SIT-DOWN SINCE BOOGIE GIRL'S ANNOUNCEMENT.
WELCOME, WAZZ. CAN YOU HEAR ME?
ARE YOU AFRAID FOR YOUR LIFE, WAZZ?
YO, HELL, NO, NAH, MAN. I JUST HAVE MY REASONS.
POWERS
ASS OUT. I WASN'
GOING ON NO 'JOURN
I WAS BOOTED.
AND BELIEVE YOU ME MON, THEY WEREN'T WISHIN' ME ANY GOOD WISHES. THEY WERE WISHIN' MY GOOD FORTUNE. THEY WIS THAT I DROP DEAD WHERE I STAND. THEY WISH I DISAPPEAR.

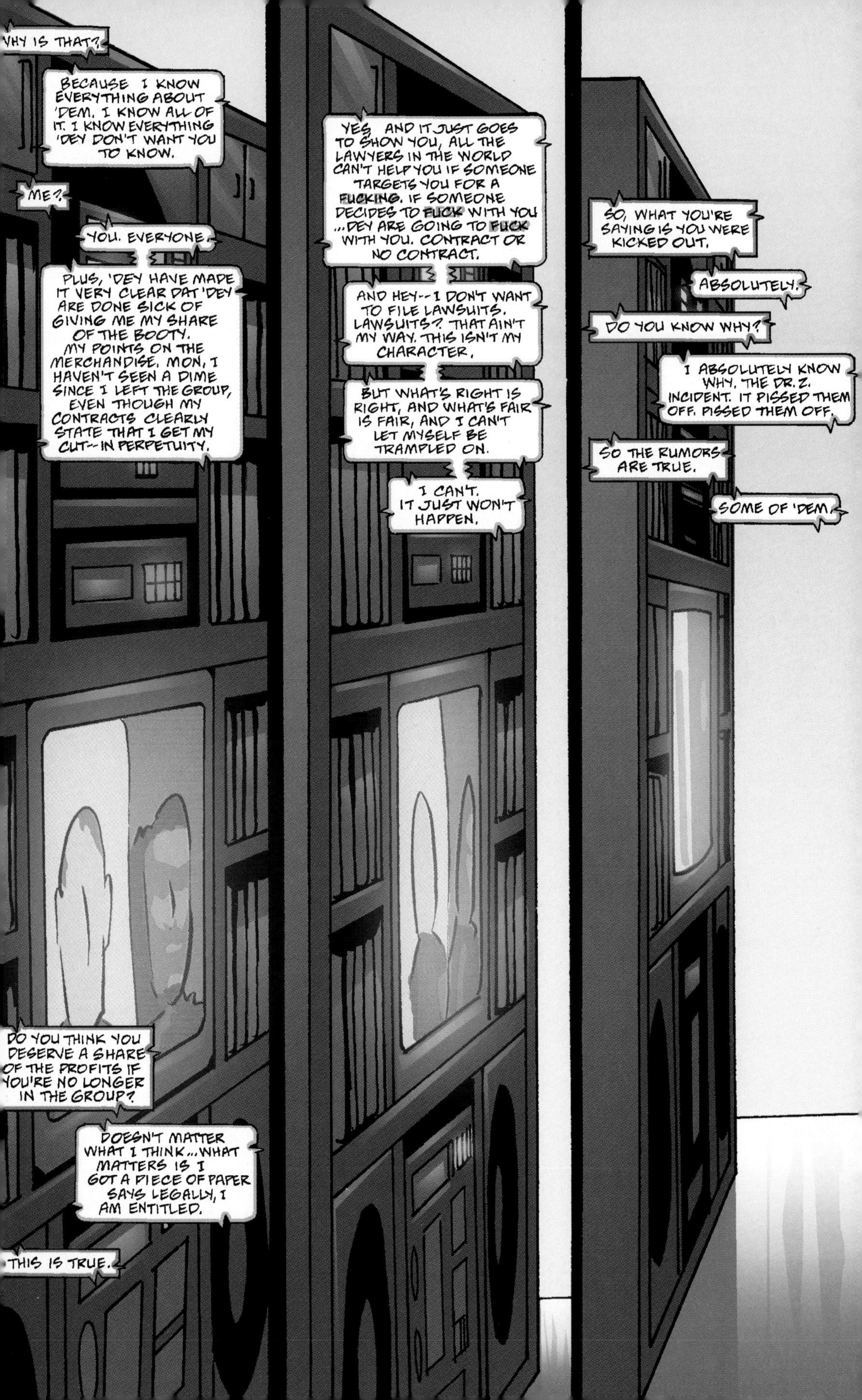
WHY IS THAT?
BECAUSE I KNOW EVERYTHING ABOUT 'DEM. I KNOW ALL OF IT. I KNOW EVERYTHING 'DEY DON'T WANT YOU TO KNOW.
ME?
YOU. EVERYONE.
PLUS, 'DEY HAVE MADE IT VERY CLEAR DAT 'DEY ARE DONE SICK OF GIVING ME MY SHARE OF THE BOOTY. MY POINTS ON THE MERCHANDISE, MON, I HAVEN'T SEEN A DIME SINCE I LEFT THE GROUP, EVEN THOUGH MY CONTRACTS CLEARLY STATE THAT I GET MY CUT-- IN PERPETUITY.
DO YOU THINK YOU DESERVE A SHARE OF THE PROFITS IF YOU'RE NO LONGER IN THE GROUP?
DOESN'T MATTER WHAT I THINK...WHAT MATTERS IS I GOT A PIECE OF PAPER SAYS LEGALLY, I AM ENTITLED.
THIS IS TRUE.
YES. AND IT JUST GOES TO SHOW YOU, ALL THE LAWYERS IN THE WORLD CAN'T HELP YOU IF SOMEONE TARGETS YOU FOR A FUCKING. IF SOMEONE DECIDES TO FUCK WITH YOU ...DEY ARE GOING TO FUCK WITH YOU. CONTRACT OR NO CONTRACT.
AND HEY-- I DON'T WANT TO FILE LAWSUITS. LAWSUITS? THAT AIN'T MY WAY. THIS ISN'T MY CHARACTER.
BUT WHAT'S RIGHT IS RIGHT, AND WHAT'S FAIR IS FAIR, AND I CAN'T LET MYSELF BE TRAMPLED ON.
I CAN'T. IT JUST WON'T HAPPEN.
SO, WHAT YOU'RE SAYING IS YOU WERE KICKED OUT.
ABSOLUTELY.
DO YOU KNOW WHY?
I ABSOLUTELY KNOW WHY. THE DR. Z. INCIDENT. IT PISSED THEM OFF. PISSED THEM OFF.
SO THE RUMORS ARE TRUE.
SOME OF 'DEM.

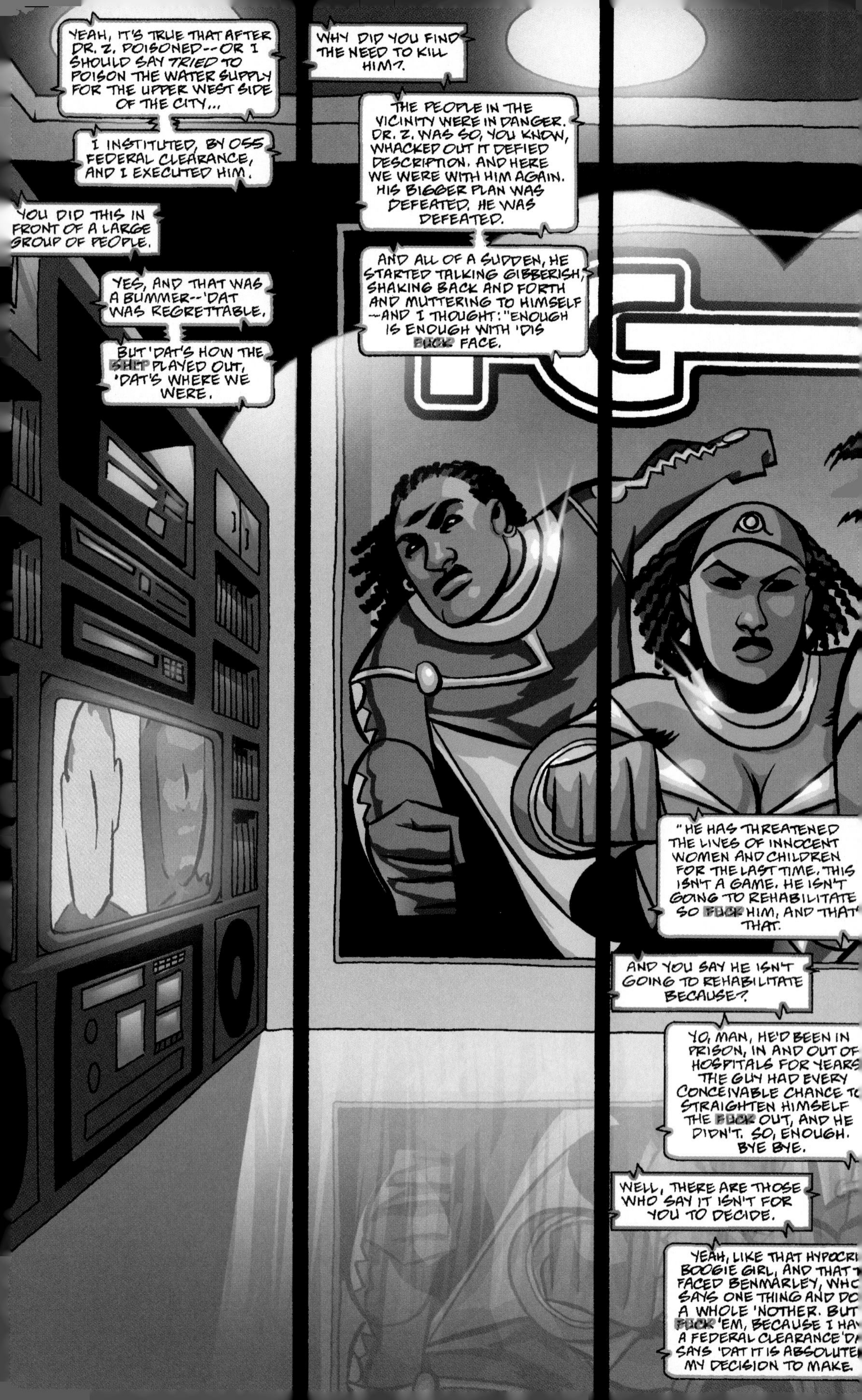
YEAH, IT'S TRUE THAT AFTER DR. Z. POISONED--OR I SHOULD SAY *TRIED* TO POISON THE WATER SUPPLY FOR THE UPPER WEST SIDE OF THE CITY...
I INSTITUTED, BY OSS FEDERAL CLEARANCE, AND I EXECUTED HIM.
YOU DID THIS IN FRONT OF A LARGE GROUP OF PEOPLE.
YES, AND THAT WAS A BUMMER--'DAT WAS REGRETTABLE.
BUT 'DAT'S HOW THE [redacted] PLAYED OUT, 'DAT'S WHERE WE WERE.
WHY DID YOU FIND THE NEED TO KILL HIM?
THE PEOPLE IN THE VICINITY WERE IN DANGER. DR. Z. WAS SO, YOU KNOW, WHACKED OUT IT DEFIED DESCRIPTION. AND HERE WE WERE WITH HIM AGAIN. HIS BIGGER PLAN WAS DEFEATED. HE WAS DEFEATED.
AND ALL OF A SUDDEN, HE STARTED TALKING GIBBERISH, SHAKING BACK AND FORTH AND MUTTERING TO HIMSELF --AND I THOUGHT: "ENOUGH IS ENOUGH WITH 'DIS [redacted] FACE.
"HE HAS THREATENED THE LIVES OF INNOCENT WOMEN AND CHILDREN FOR THE LAST TIME. THIS ISN'T A GAME. HE ISN'T GOING TO REHABILITATE SO [redacted] HIM, AND THAT' THAT.
AND YOU SAY HE ISN'T GOING TO REHABILITATE BECAUSE?
YO, MAN, HE'D BEEN IN PRISON, IN AND OUT OF HOSPITALS FOR YEARS THE GUY HAD EVERY CONCEIVABLE CHANCE TO STRAIGHTEN HIMSELF THE [redacted] OUT, AND HE DIDN'T. SO, ENOUGH. BYE BYE.
WELL, THERE ARE THOSE WHO SAY IT ISN'T FOR YOU TO DECIDE.
YEAH, LIKE THAT HYPOCRI BOOGIE GIRL, AND THAT FACED BENMARLEY, WHO SAYS ONE THING AND DO A WHOLE 'NOTHER. BUT [redacted] 'EM, BECAUSE I HA A FEDERAL CLEARANCE 'D SAYS 'DAT IT IS ABSOLUTE MY DECISION TO MAKE.

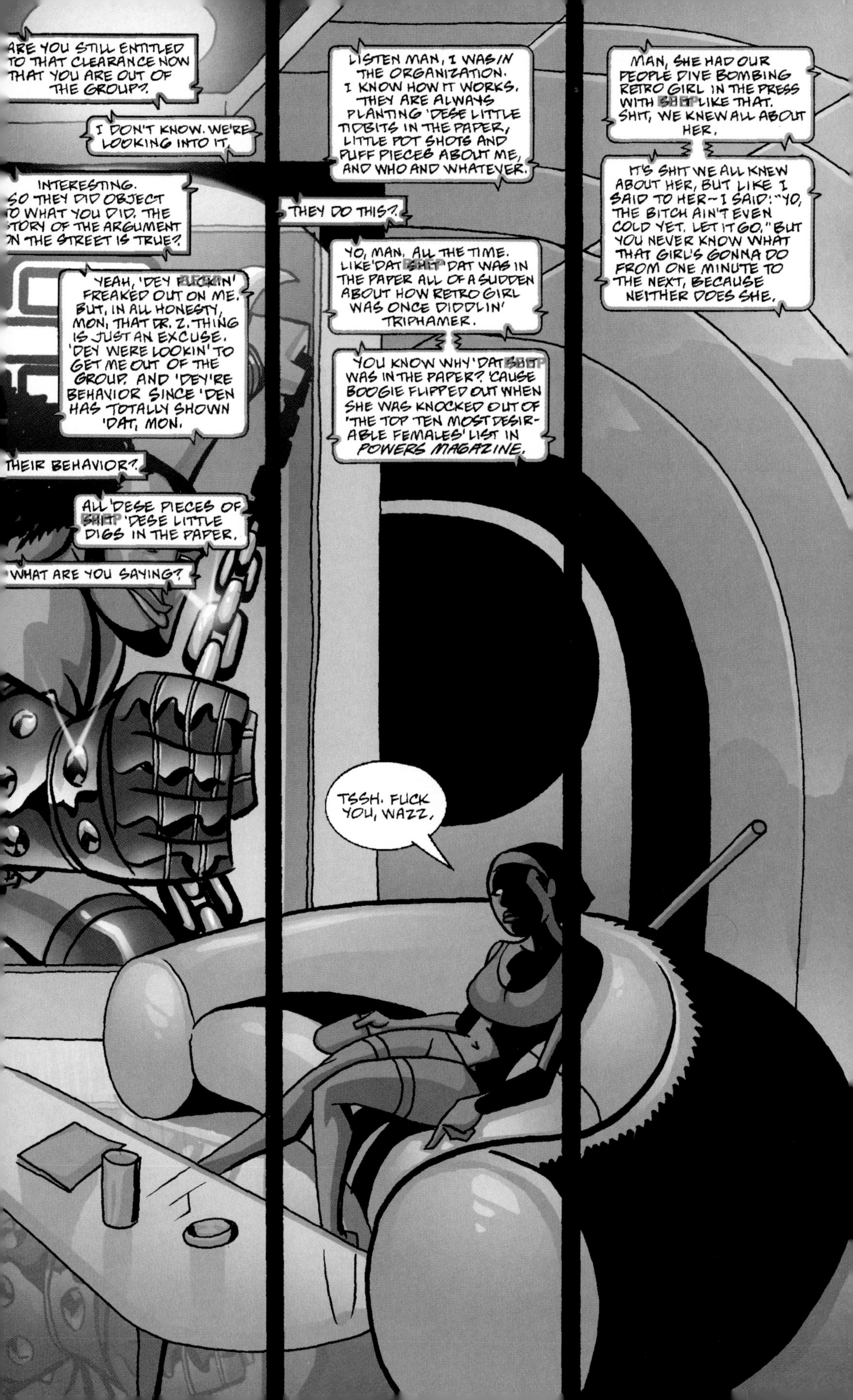

ARE YOU STILL ENTITLED TO THAT CLEARANCE NOW THAT YOU ARE OUT OF THE GROUP?
I DON'T KNOW. WE'RE LOOKING INTO IT.
INTERESTING. SO THEY DID OBJECT TO WHAT YOU DID. THE STORY OF THE ARGUMENT ON THE STREET IS TRUE?
YEAH, 'DEY FUCKIN' FREAKED OUT ON ME. BUT, IN ALL HONESTY, MON, THAT DR. Z. THING IS JUST AN EXCUSE. 'DEY WERE LOOKIN' TO GET ME OUT OF THE GROUP. AND 'DEY'RE BEHAVIOR SINCE 'DEN HAS TOTALLY SHOWN 'DAT, MON.
THEIR BEHAVIOR?
ALL 'DESE PIECES OF SHIT 'DESE LITTLE DIGS IN THE PAPER.
WHAT ARE YOU SAYING?
LISTEN MAN, I WAS IN THE ORGANIZATION. I KNOW HOW IT WORKS. THEY ARE ALWAYS PLANTING 'DESE LITTLE TIDBITS IN THE PAPER, LITTLE POT SHOTS AND PUFF PIECES ABOUT ME, AND WHO AND WHATEVER.
THEY DO THIS?
YO, MAN. ALL THE TIME. LIKE 'DAT SHIT 'DAT WAS IN THE PAPER ALL OF A SUDDEN ABOUT HOW RETRO GIRL WAS ONCE DIDDLIN' TRIPHAMER.
YOU KNOW WHY 'DAT SHIT WAS IN THE PAPER? 'CAUSE BOOGIE FLIPPED OUT WHEN SHE WAS KNOCKED OUT OF 'THE TOP TEN MOST DESIRABLE FEMALES' LIST IN POWERS MAGAZINE.
MAN, SHE HAD OUR PEOPLE DIVE BOMBING RETRO GIRL IN THE PRESS WITH SHIT LIKE THAT. SHIT, WE KNEW ALL ABOUT HER.
IT'S SHIT WE ALL KNEW ABOUT HER, BUT LIKE I SAID TO HER— I SAID: "YO, THE BITCH AIN'T EVEN COLD YET. LET IT GO." BUT YOU NEVER KNOW WHAT THAT GIRL'S GONNA DO FROM ONE MINUTE TO THE NEXT, BECAUSE NEITHER DOES SHE.
TSSH. FUCK YOU, WAZZ.

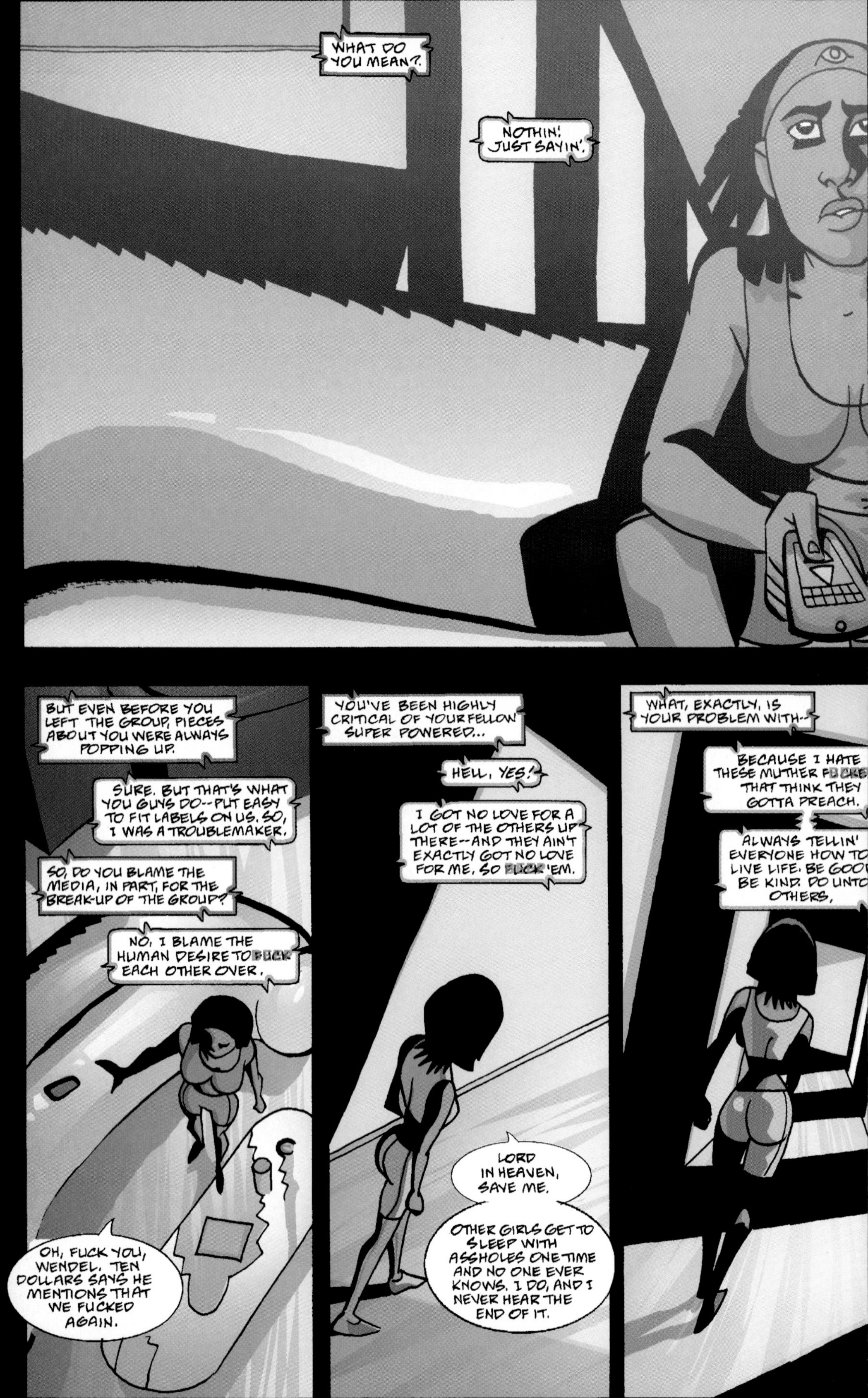
WHAT DO YOU MEAN?.
NOTHIN'. JUST SAYIN'.
BUT EVEN BEFORE YOU LEFT THE GROUP, PIECES ABOUT YOU WERE ALWAYS POPPING UP.
SURE. BUT THAT'S WHAT YOU GUYS DO--PUT EASY TO FIT LABELS ON US. SO, I WAS A TROUBLEMAKER.
SO, DO YOU BLAME THE MEDIA, IN PART, FOR THE BREAK-UP OF THE GROUP?
NO, I BLAME THE HUMAN DESIRE TO FUCK EACH OTHER OVER.
OH, FUCK YOU, WENDEL. TEN DOLLARS SAYS HE MENTIONS THAT WE FUCKED AGAIN.
YOU'VE BEEN HIGHLY CRITICAL OF YOUR FELLOW SUPER POWERED...
HELL, YES!
I GOT NO LOVE FOR A LOT OF THE OTHERS UP THERE--AND THEY AIN'T EXACTLY GOT NO LOVE FOR ME. SO FUCK 'EM.
LORD IN HEAVEN, SAVE ME.
OTHER GIRLS GET TO SLEEP WITH ASSHOLES ONE TIME AND NO ONE EVER KNOWS. I DO, AND I NEVER HEAR THE END OF IT.
WHAT, EXACTLY, IS YOUR PROBLEM WITH--
BECAUSE I HATE THESE MUTHER FUCKE THAT THINK THEY GOTTA PREACH.
ALWAYS TELLIN' EVERYONE HOW TO LIVE LIFE. BE GOOD BE KIND. DO UNTO OTHERS.

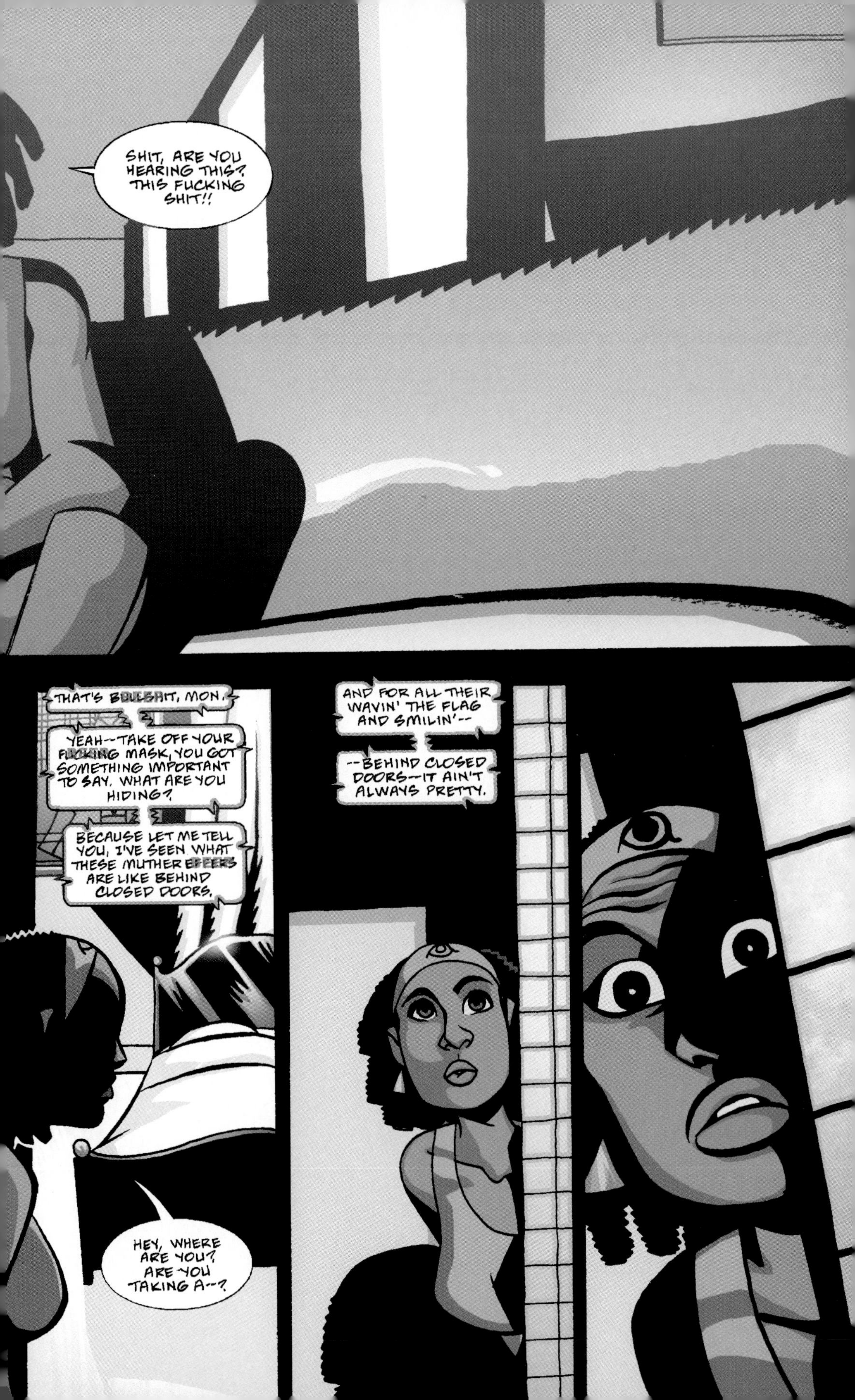
SHIT, ARE YOU HEARING THIS? THIS FUCKING SHIT!!
THAT'S BULLSHIT, MON.
YEAH--TAKE OFF YOUR FUCKING MASK, YOU GOT SOMETHING IMPORTANT TO SAY. WHAT ARE YOU HIDING?
BECAUSE LET ME TELL YOU, I'VE SEEN WHAT THESE MUTHER EFFERS ARE LIKE BEHIND CLOSED DOORS.
HEY, WHERE ARE YOU? ARE YOU TAKING A--?
AND FOR ALL THEIR WAVIN' THE FLAG AND SMILIN'--
--BEHIND CLOSED DOORS--IT AIN'T ALWAYS PRETTY.

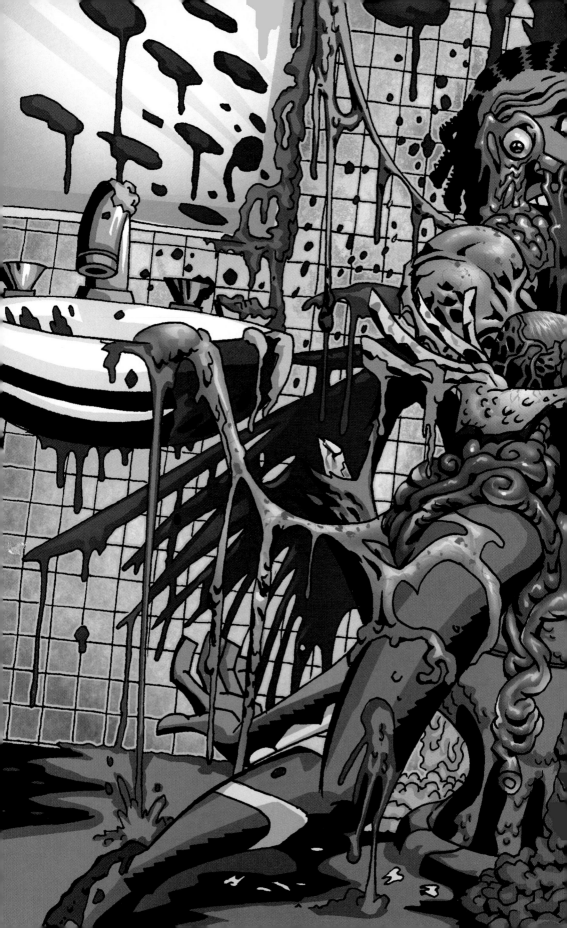

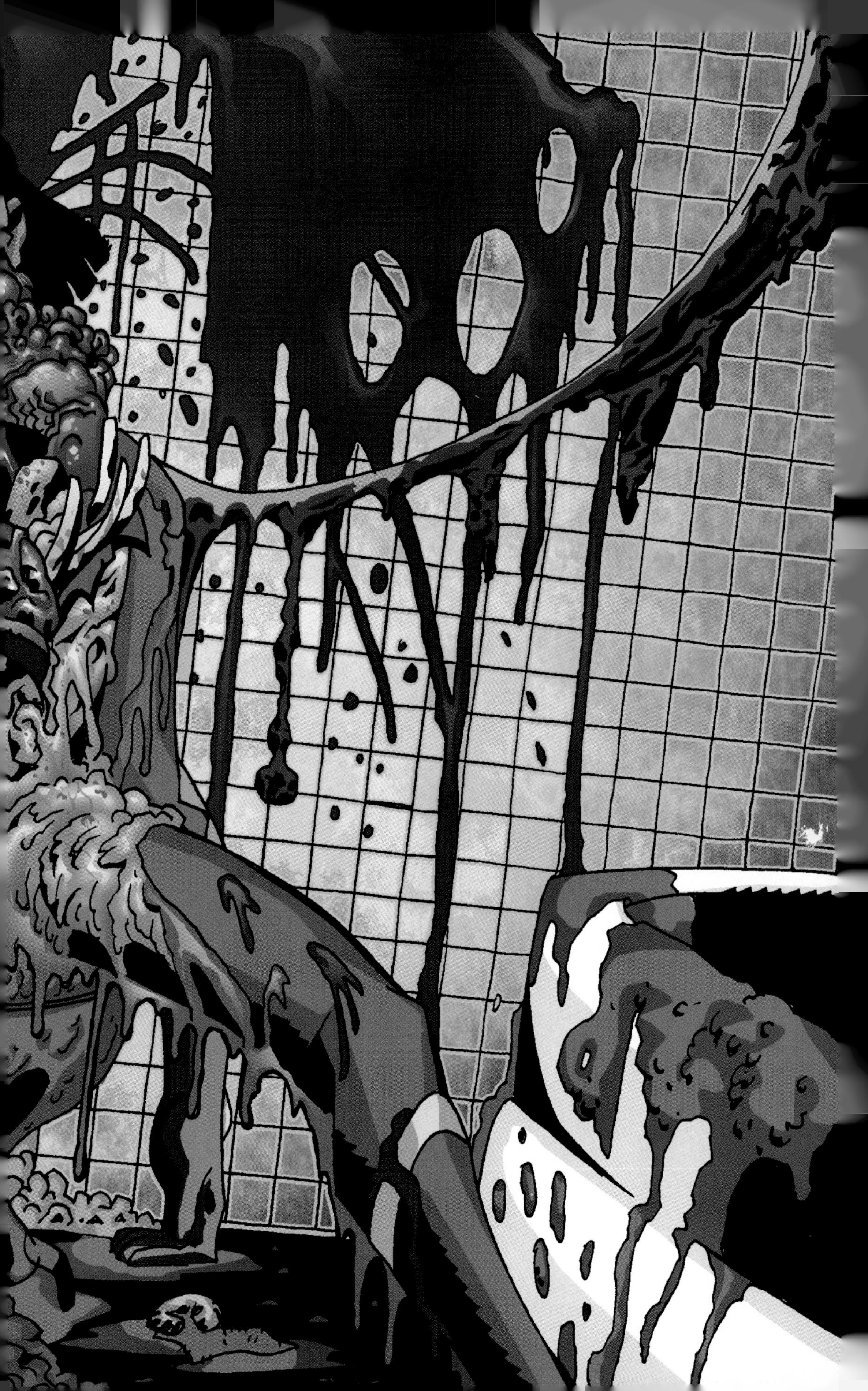

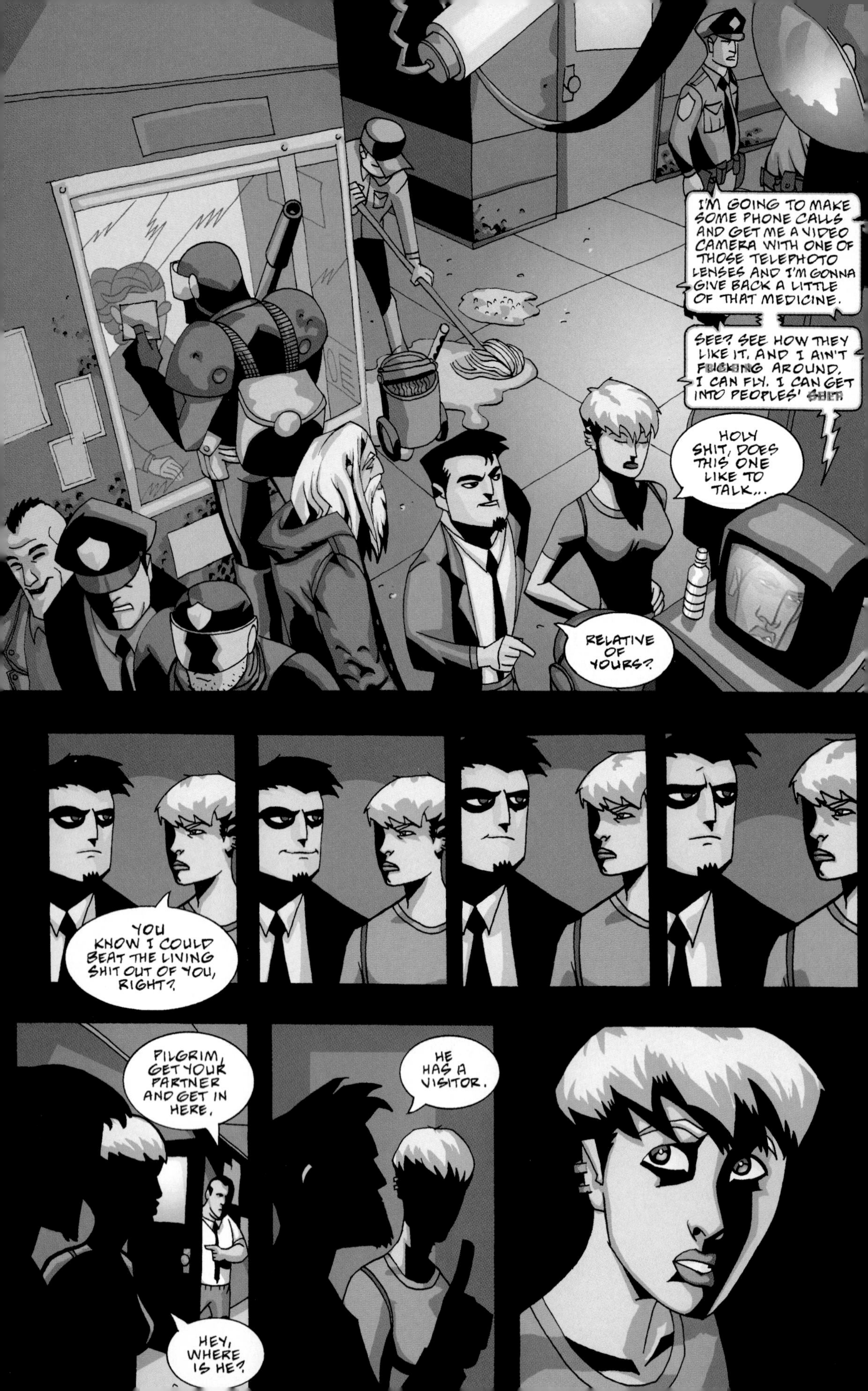
I'M GOING TO MAKE SOME PHONE CALLS AND GET ME A VIDEO CAMERA WITH ONE OF THOSE TELEPHOTO LENSES AND I'M GONNA GIVE BACK A LITTLE OF THAT MEDICINE.
SEE? SEE HOW THEY LIKE IT. AND I AIN'T FUCKING AROUND. I CAN FLY. I CAN GET INTO PEOPLES' SHIT.
HOLY SHIT, DOES THIS ONE LIKE TO TALK...
RELATIVE OF YOURS?
YOU KNOW I COULD BEAT THE LIVING SHIT OUT OF YOU, RIGHT?
PILGRIM, GET YOUR PARTNER AND GET IN HERE.
HEY, WHERE IS HE?
HE HAS A VISITOR.

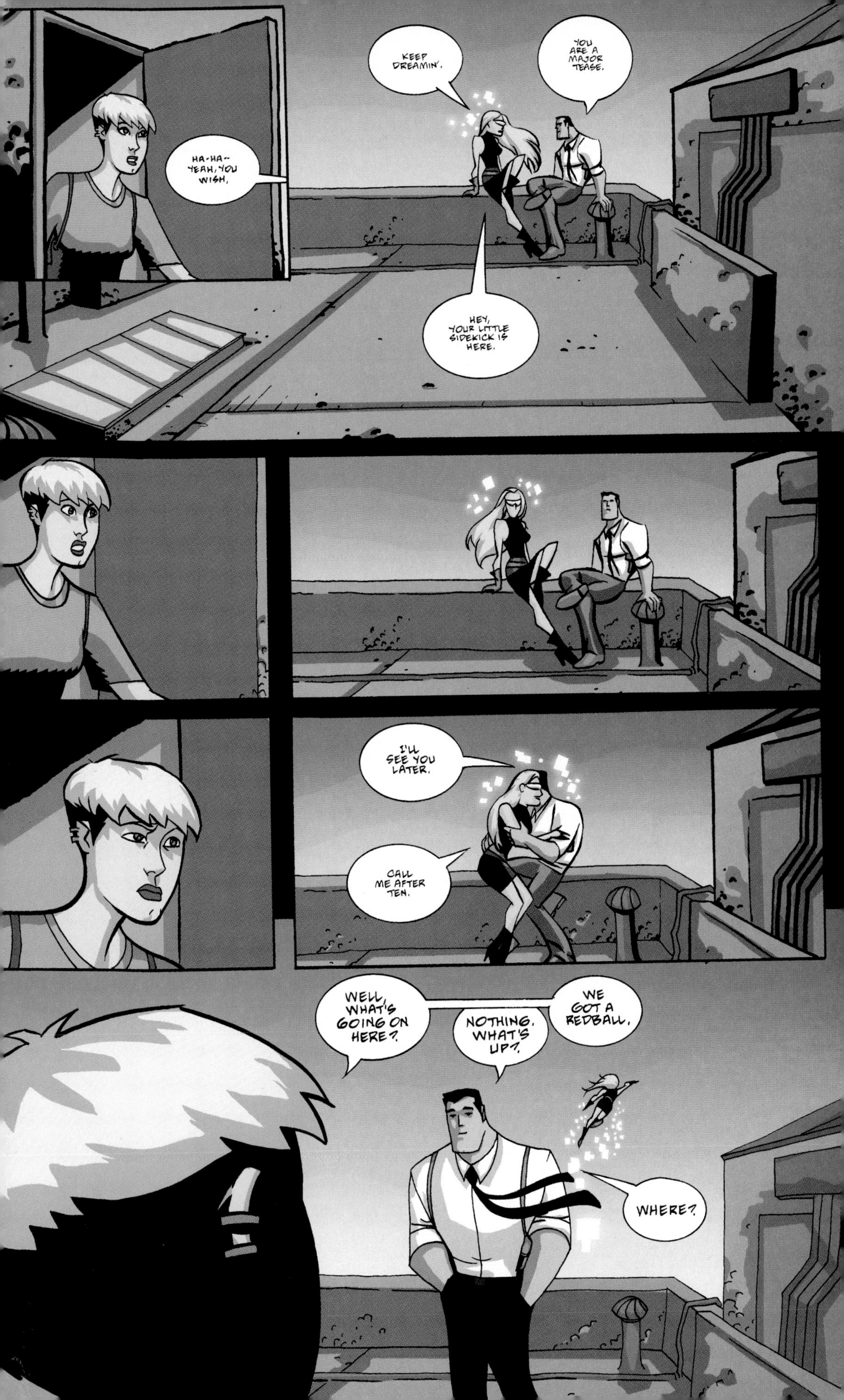
KEEP DREAMIN'.
YOU ARE A MAJOR TEASE.
HA-HA-- YEAH, YOU WISH.
HEY, YOUR LITTLE SIDEKICK IS HERE.
I'LL SEE YOU LATER.
CALL ME AFTER TEN.
WELL, WHAT'S GOING ON HERE?
NOTHING. WHAT'S UP?
WE GOT A REDBALL.
WHERE?

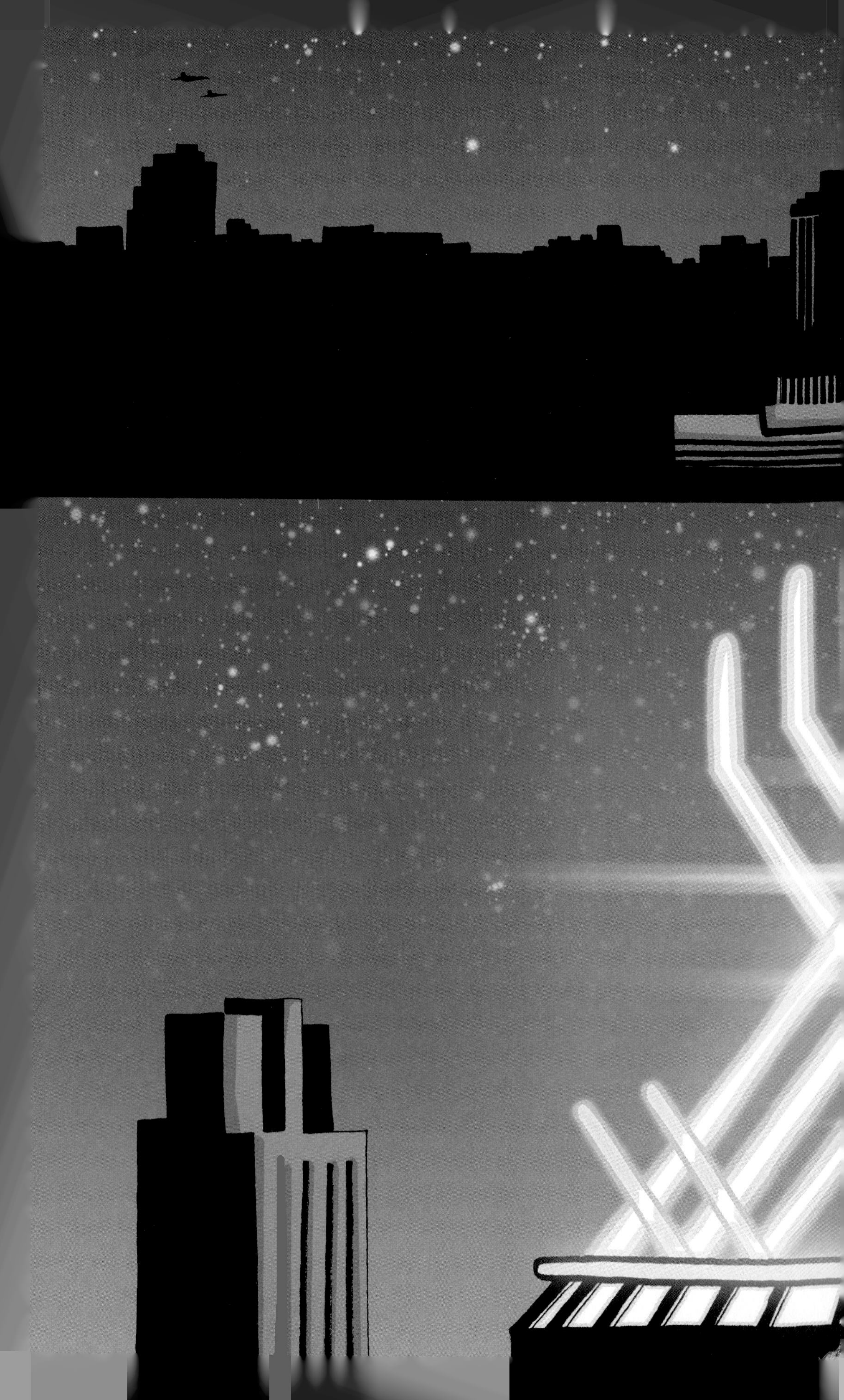

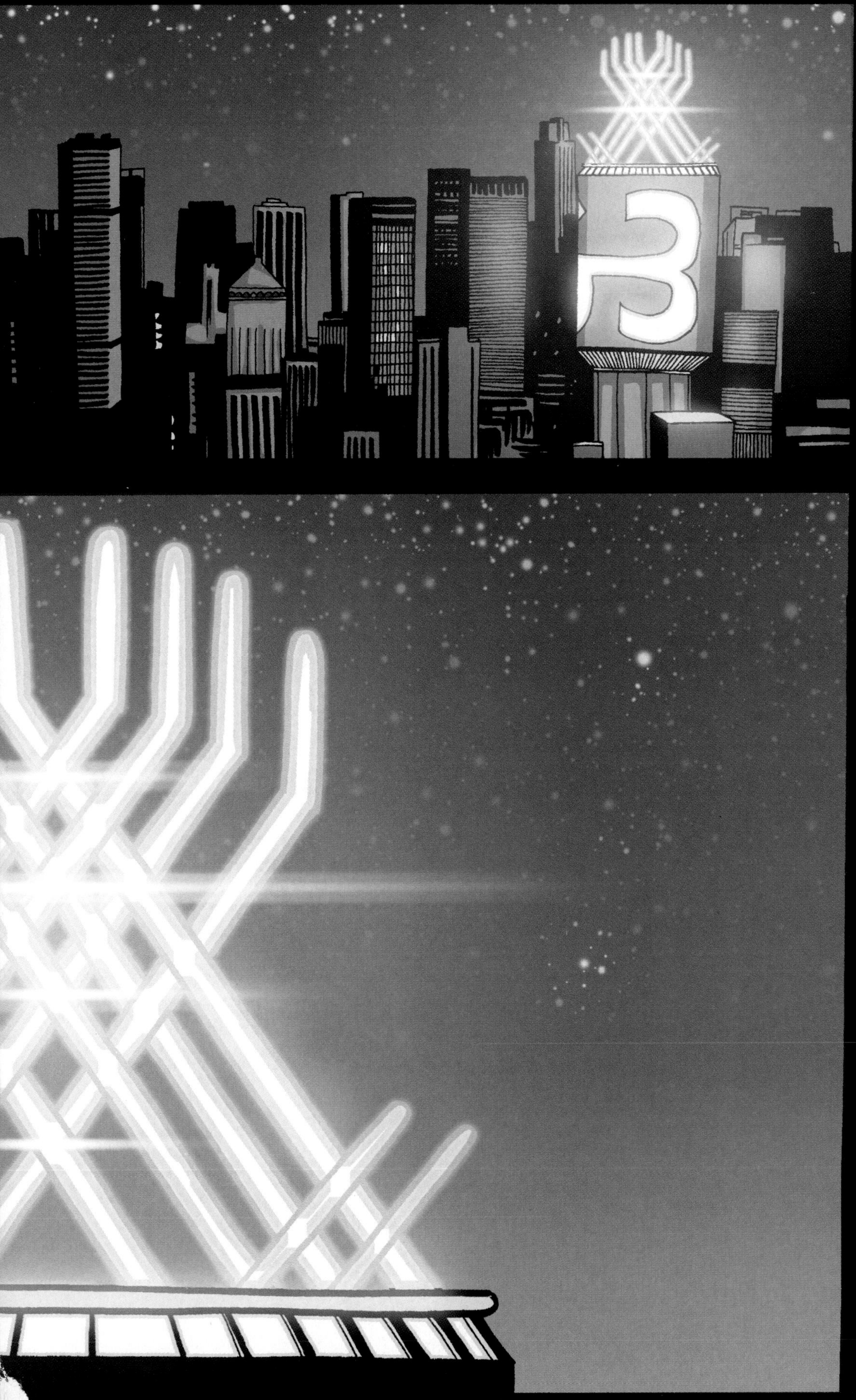
3

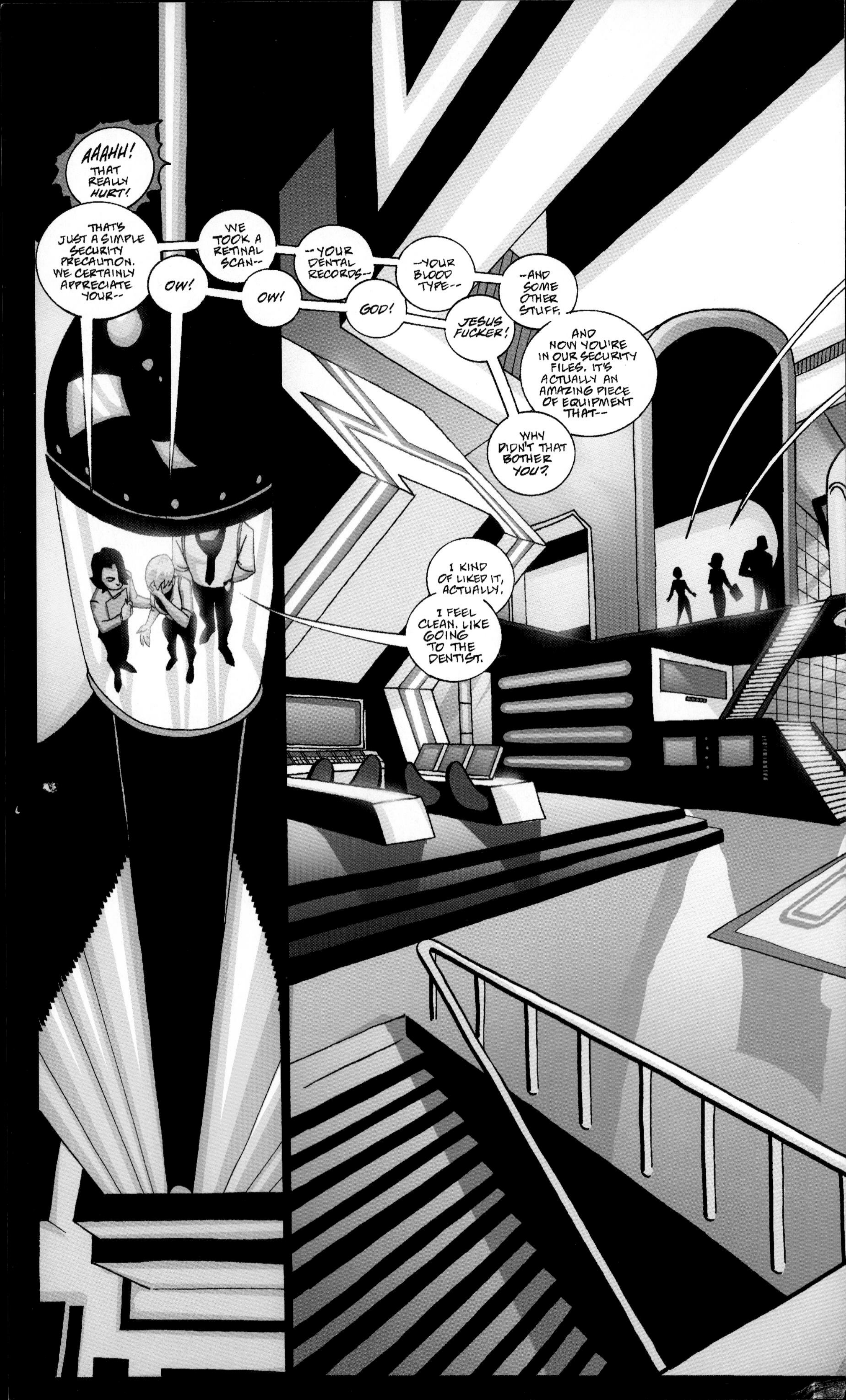
AAAHH! THAT REALLY HURT!
THAT'S JUST A SIMPLE SECURITY PRECAUTION. WE CERTAINLY APPRECIATE YOUR--
OW!
WE TOOK A RETINAL SCAN--
OW!
--YOUR DENTAL RECORDS--
GOD!
--YOUR BLOOD TYPE--
JESUS FUCKER!
--AND SOME OTHER STUFF.
AND NOW YOU'RE IN OUR SECURITY FILES. IT'S ACTUALLY AN AMAZING PIECE OF EQUIPMENT THAT--
WHY DIDN'T THAT BOTHER YOU?
I KIND OF LIKED IT, ACTUALLY.
I FEEL CLEAN. LIKE GOING TO THE DENTIST.

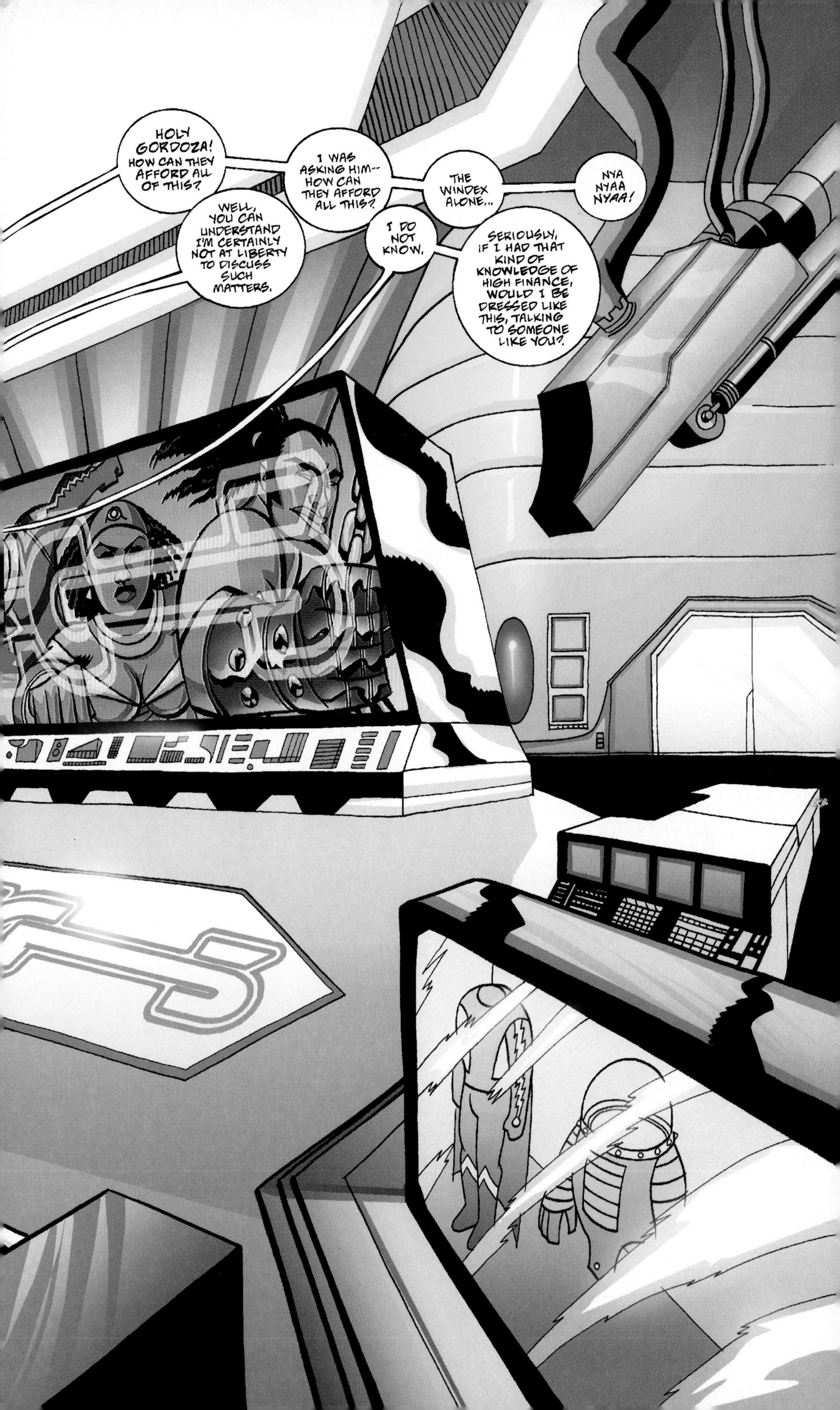
HOLY GORDOZA! HOW CAN THEY AFFORD ALL OF THIS?
WELL, YOU CAN UNDERSTAND I'M CERTAINLY NOT AT LIBERTY TO DISCUSS SUCH MATTERS.
I WAS ASKING HIM-- HOW CAN THEY AFFORD ALL THIS?
I DO NOT KNOW.
THE WINDEX ALONE...
SERIOUSLY, IF I HAD THAT KIND OF KNOWLEDGE OF HIGH FINANCE, WOULD I BE DRESSED LIKE THIS, TALKING TO SOMEONE LIKE YOU?
NYA NYA NYAA NYAA!

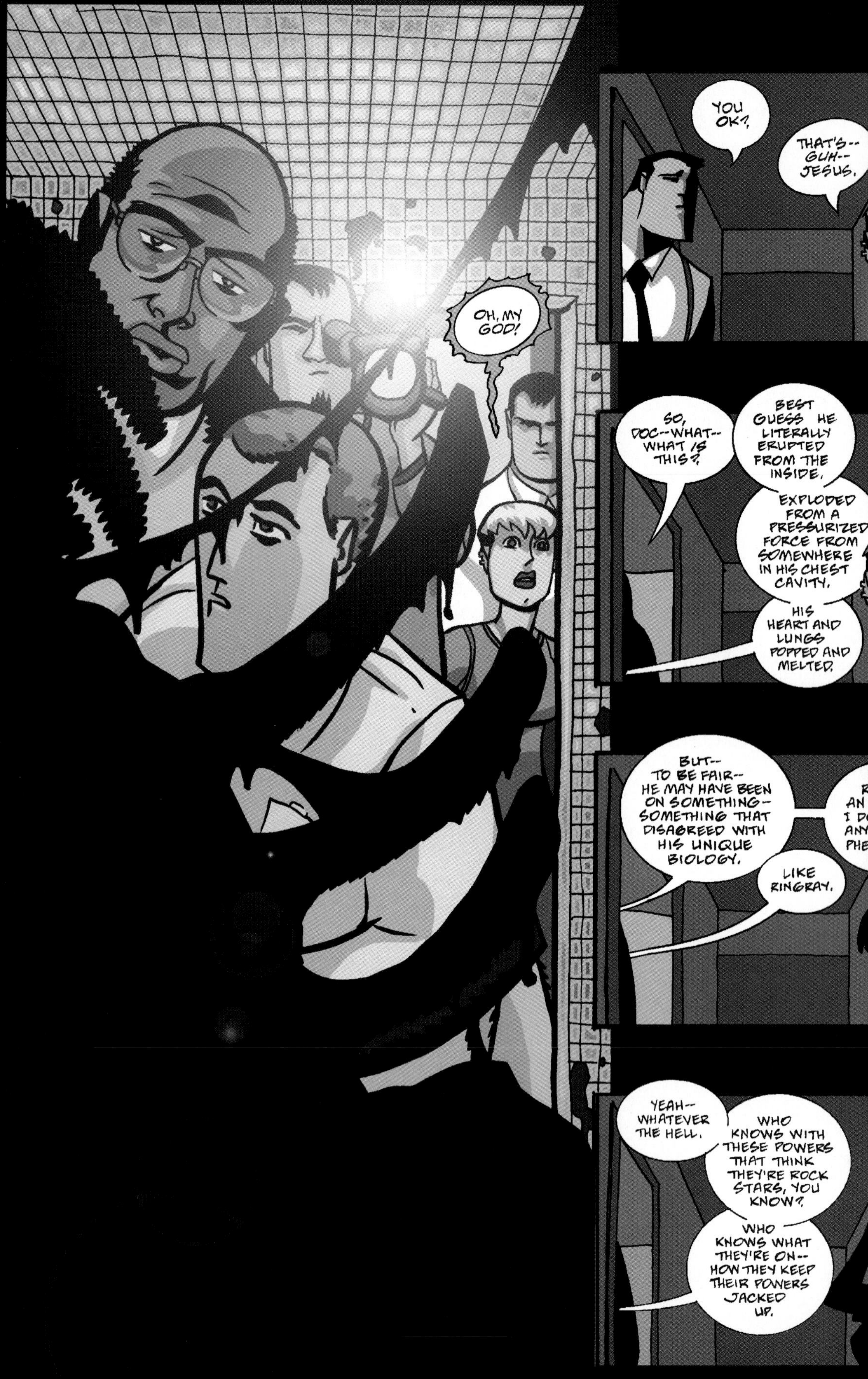
OH, MY GOD!
YOU OK?
THAT'S-- GUH-- JESUS.
SO, DOC--WHAT-- WHAT IS THIS?
BEST GUESS HE LITERALLY ERUPTED FROM THE INSIDE.
EXPLODED FROM A PRESSURIZED FORCE FROM SOMEWHERE IN HIS CHEST CAVITY.
HIS HEART AND LUNGS POPPED AND MELTED.
BUT-- TO BE FAIR-- HE MAY HAVE BEEN ON SOMETHING-- SOMETHING THAT DISAGREED WITH HIS UNIQUE BIOLOGY.
LIKE RINGRAY.
YEAH-- WHATEVER THE HELL.
WHO KNOWS WITH THESE POWERS THAT THINK THEY'RE ROCK STARS, YOU KNOW?
WHO KNOWS WHAT THEY'RE ON-- HOW THEY KEEP THEIR POWERS JACKED UP.

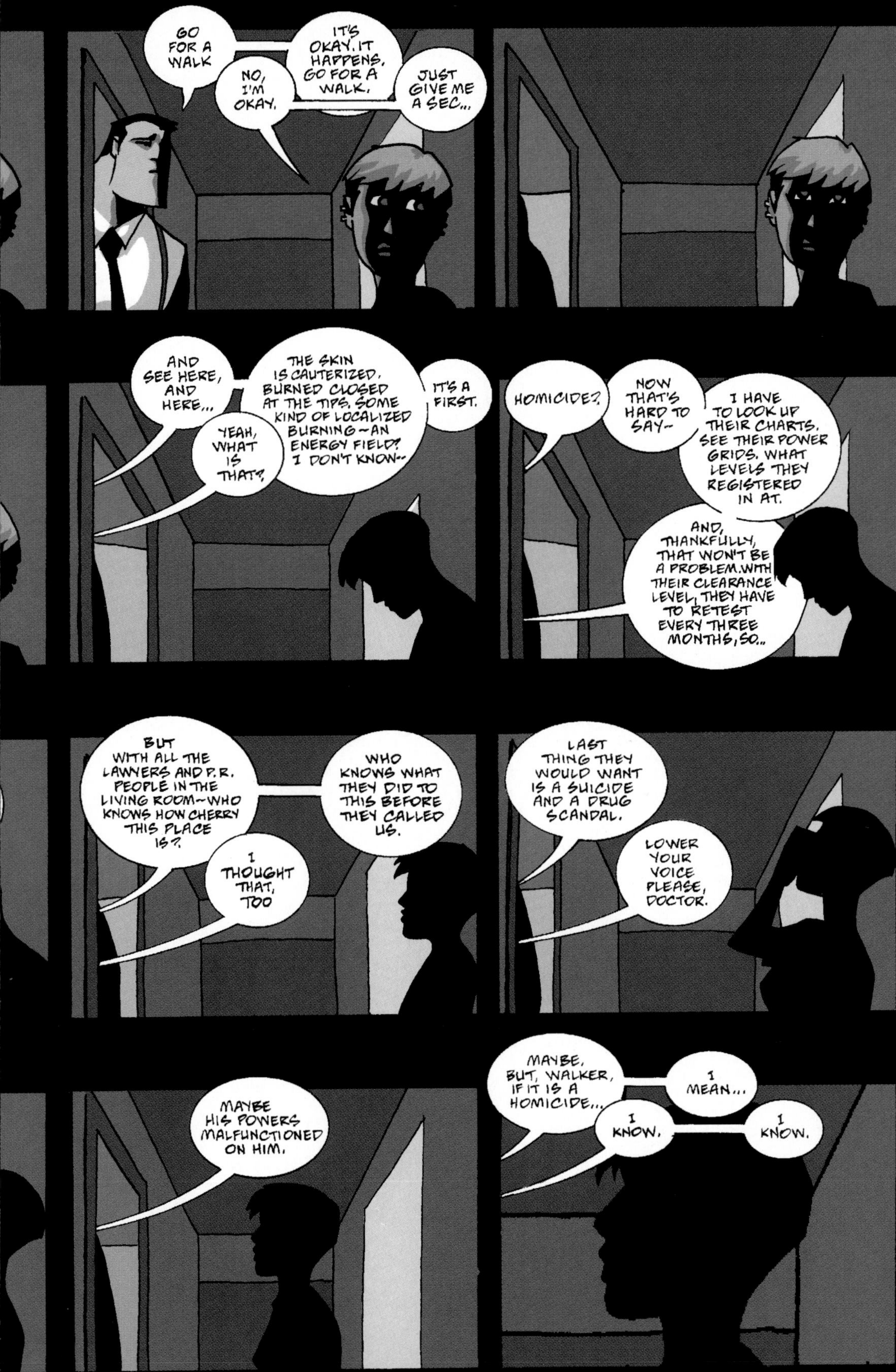
GO FOR A WALK
IT'S OKAY. IT HAPPENS, GO FOR A WALK.
NO, I'M OKAY.
JUST GIVE ME A SEC...
AND SEE HERE, AND HERE...
THE SKIN IS CAUTERIZED, BURNED CLOSED AT THE TIPS. SOME KIND OF LOCALIZED BURNING~AN ENERGY FIELD? I DON'T KNOW--
YEAH, WHAT IS THAT?
IT'S A FIRST.
HOMICIDE?
NOW THAT'S HARD TO SAY--
I HAVE TO LOOK UP THEIR CHARTS. SEE THEIR POWER GRIDS. WHAT LEVELS THEY REGISTERED IN AT.
AND, THANKFULLY, THAT WON'T BE A PROBLEM. WITH THEIR CLEARANCE LEVEL, THEY HAVE TO RETEST EVERY THREE MONTHS, SO...
BUT WITH ALL THE LAWYERS AND P.R. PEOPLE IN THE LIVING ROOM~WHO KNOWS HOW CHERRY THIS PLACE IS?
WHO KNOWS WHAT THEY DID TO THIS BEFORE THEY CALLED US.
I THOUGHT THAT, TOO
LAST THING THEY WOULD WANT IS A SUICIDE AND A DRUG SCANDAL.
LOWER YOUR VOICE PLEASE, DOCTOR.
MAYBE HIS POWERS MALFUNCTIONED ON HIM.
MAYBE, BUT, WALKER, IF IT IS A HOMICIDE...
I MEAN...
I KNOW.
I KNOW.

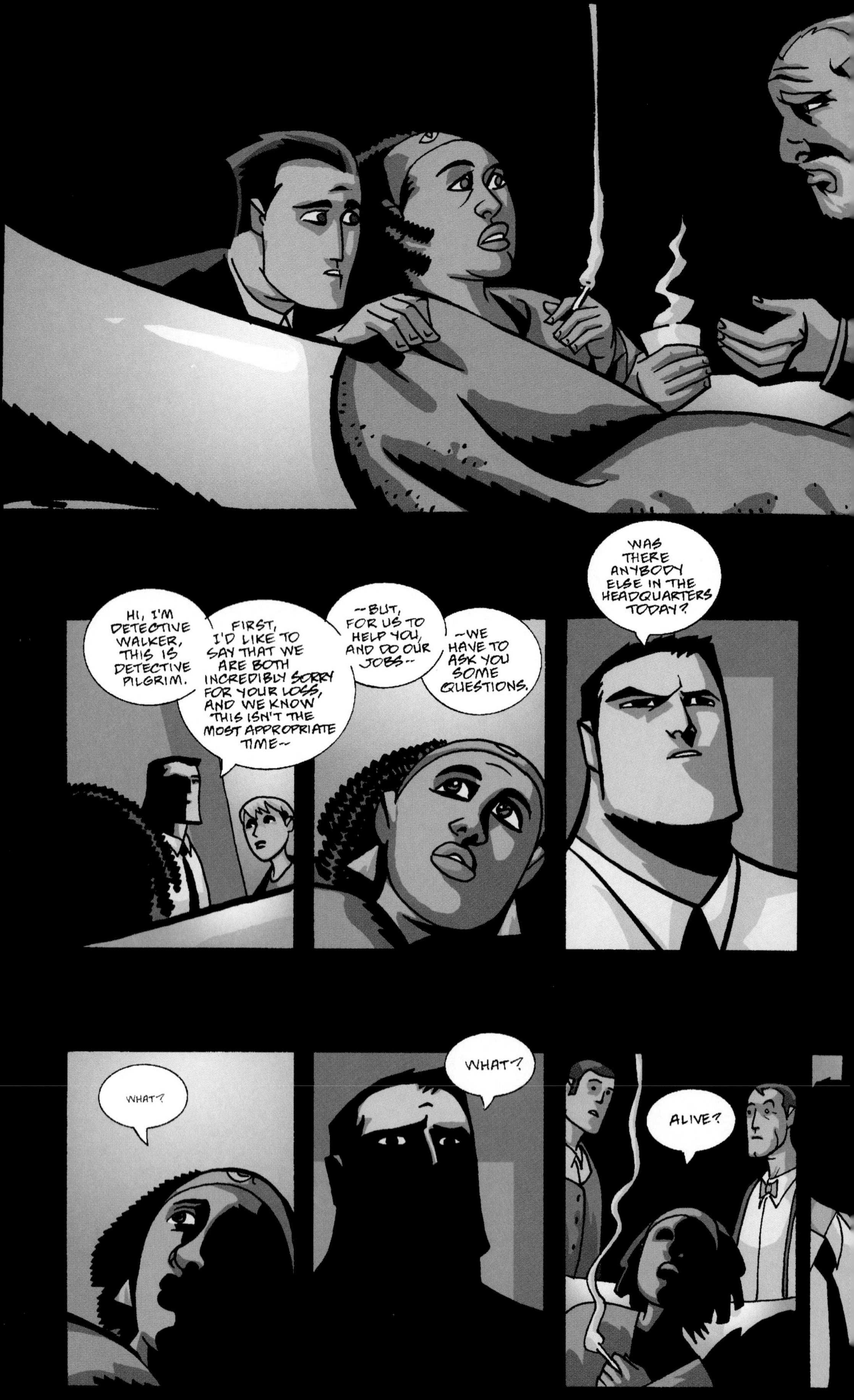

HI, I'M DETECTIVE WALKER, THIS IS DETECTIVE PILGRIM.
FIRST, I'D LIKE TO SAY THAT WE ARE BOTH INCREDIBLY SORRY FOR YOUR LOSS, AND WE KNOW THIS ISN'T THE MOST APPROPRIATE TIME--
--BUT, FOR US TO HELP YOU, AND DO OUR JOBS--
--WE HAVE TO ASK YOU SOME QUESTIONS.
WAS THERE ANYBODY ELSE IN THE HEADQUARTERS TODAY?
WHAT?
WHAT?
ALIVE?

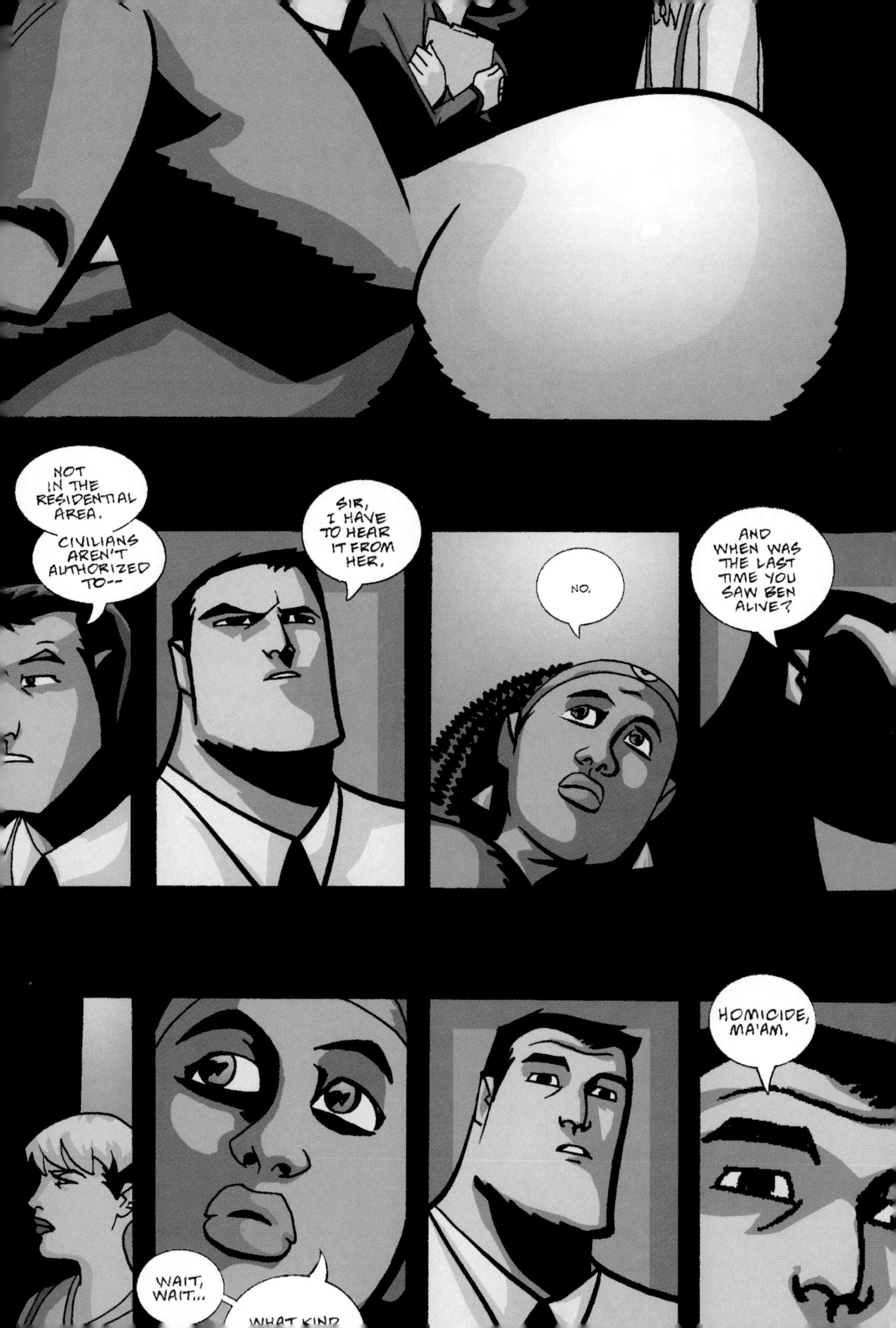
NOT IN THE RESIDENTIAL AREA.
CIVILIANS AREN'T AUTHORIZED TO--
SIR, I HAVE TO HEAR IT FROM HER.
NO.
AND WHEN WAS THE LAST TIME YOU SAW BEN ALIVE?
WAIT, WAIT...
WHAT KIND
HOMICIDE, MA'AM.

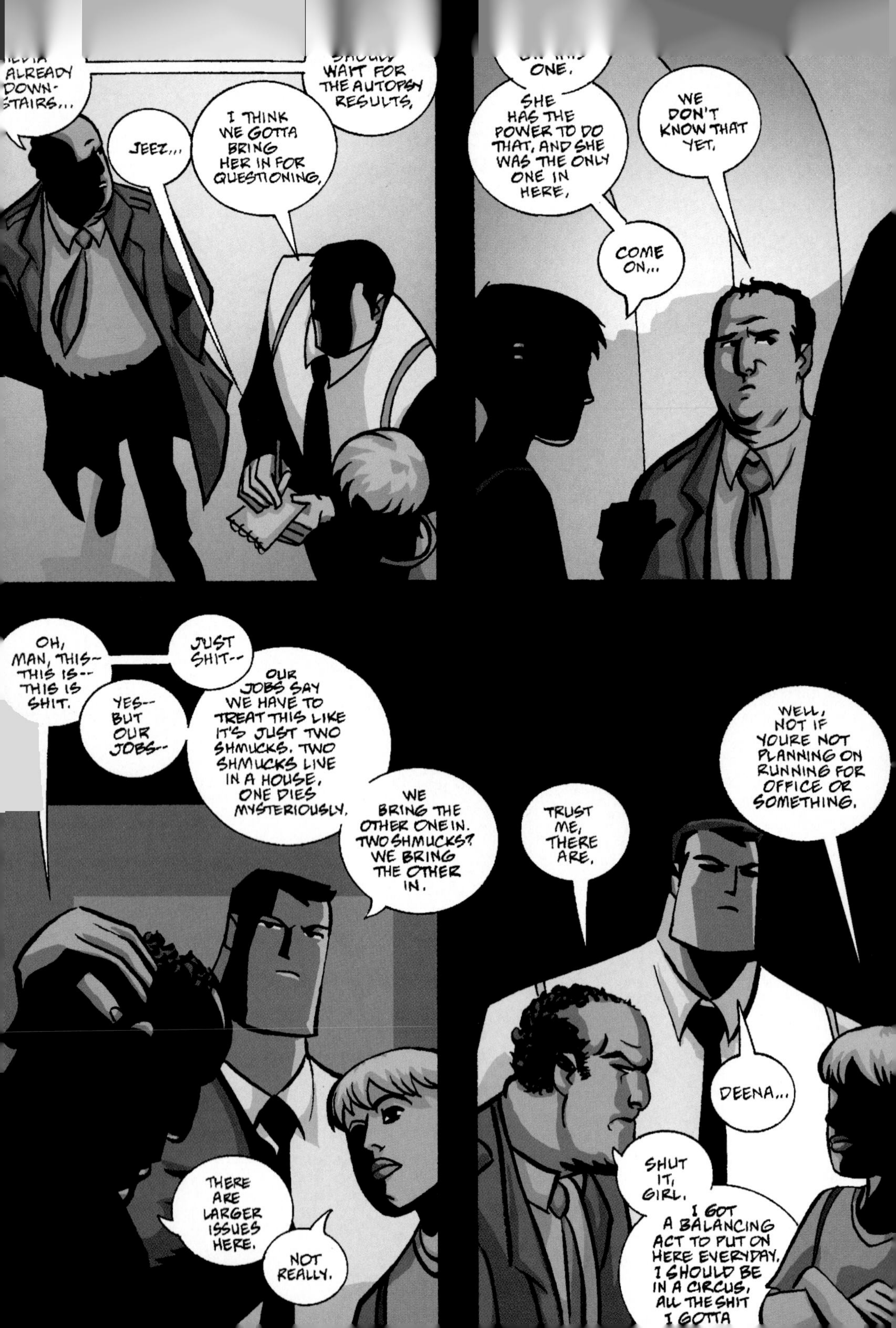

ALREADY DOWN- STAIRS...
WAIT FOR THE AUTOPSY RESULTS.
JEEZ...
I THINK WE GOTTA BRING HER IN FOR QUESTIONING.
ONE.
SHE HAS THE POWER TO DO THAT, AND SHE WAS THE ONLY ONE IN HERE.
WE DON'T KNOW THAT YET.
COME ON...
OH, MAN, THIS-- THIS IS-- THIS IS SHIT.
JUST SHIT--
YES-- BUT OUR JOBS--
OUR JOBS SAY WE HAVE TO TREAT THIS LIKE IT'S JUST TWO SHMUCKS. TWO SHMUCKS LIVE IN A HOUSE, ONE DIES MYSTERIOUSLY.
WE BRING THE OTHER ONE IN. TWO SHMUCKS? WE BRING THE OTHER IN.
THERE ARE LARGER ISSUES HERE.
NOT REALLY.
WELL, NOT IF YOURE NOT PLANNING ON RUNNING FOR OFFICE OR SOMETHING.
TRUST ME, THERE ARE.
DEENA...
SHUT IT, GIRL.
I GOT A BALANCING ACT TO PUT ON HERE EVERYDAY. I SHOULD BE IN A CIRCUS. ALL THE SHIT I GOTTA

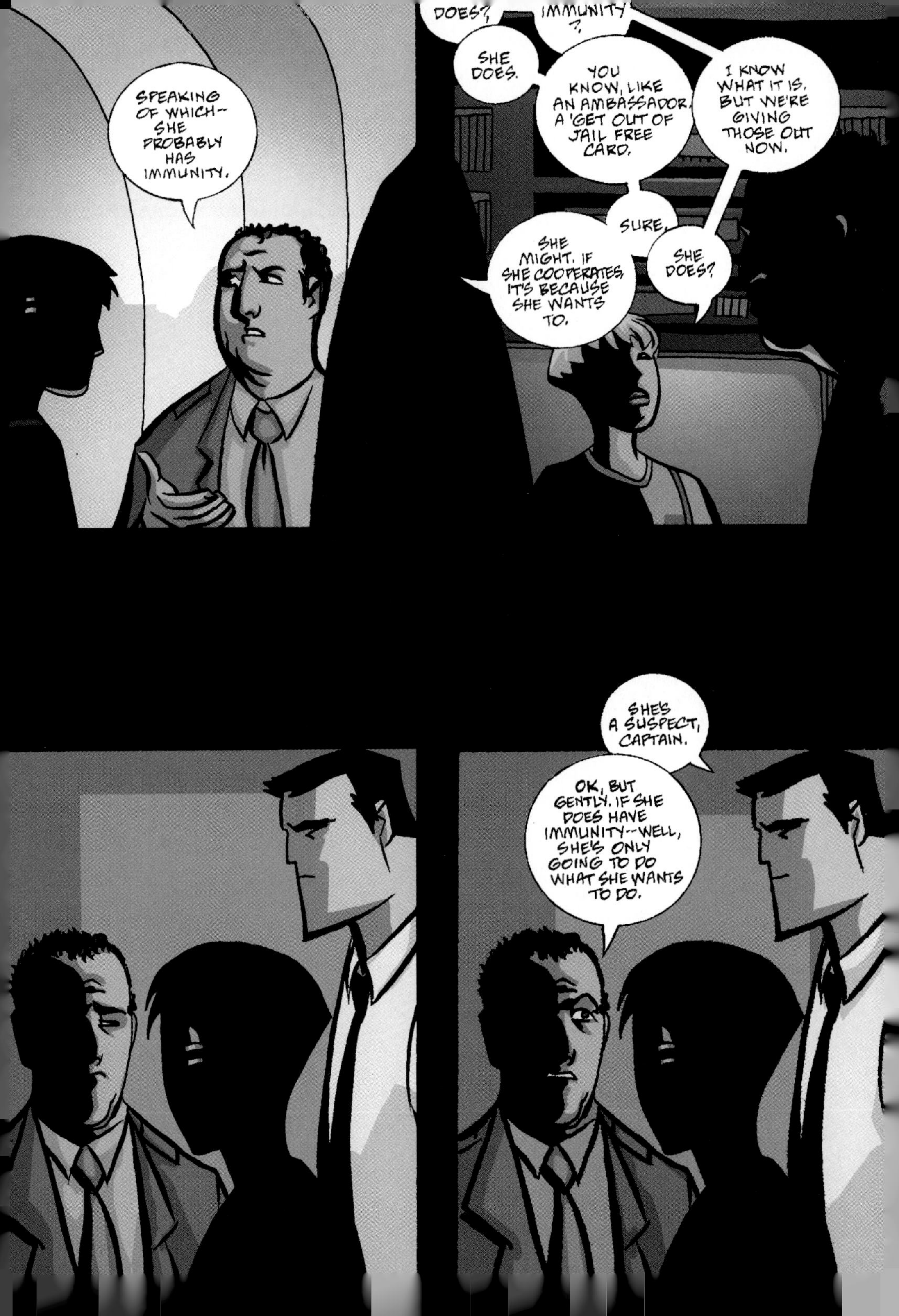
SPEAKING OF WHICH-- SHE PROBABLY HAS IMMUNITY.
DOES?
IMMUNITY?
SHE DOES.
YOU KNOW, LIKE AN AMBASSADOR. A 'GET OUT OF JAIL FREE CARD.
I KNOW WHAT IT IS. BUT WE'RE GIVING THOSE OUT NOW.
SURE.
SHE MIGHT. IF SHE COOPERATES, IT'S BECAUSE SHE WANTS TO.
SHE DOES?
SHE'S A SUSPECT, CAPTAIN.
OK, BUT GENTLY. IF SHE DOES HAVE IMMUNITY--WELL, SHE'S ONLY GOING TO DO WHAT SHE WANTS TO DO.

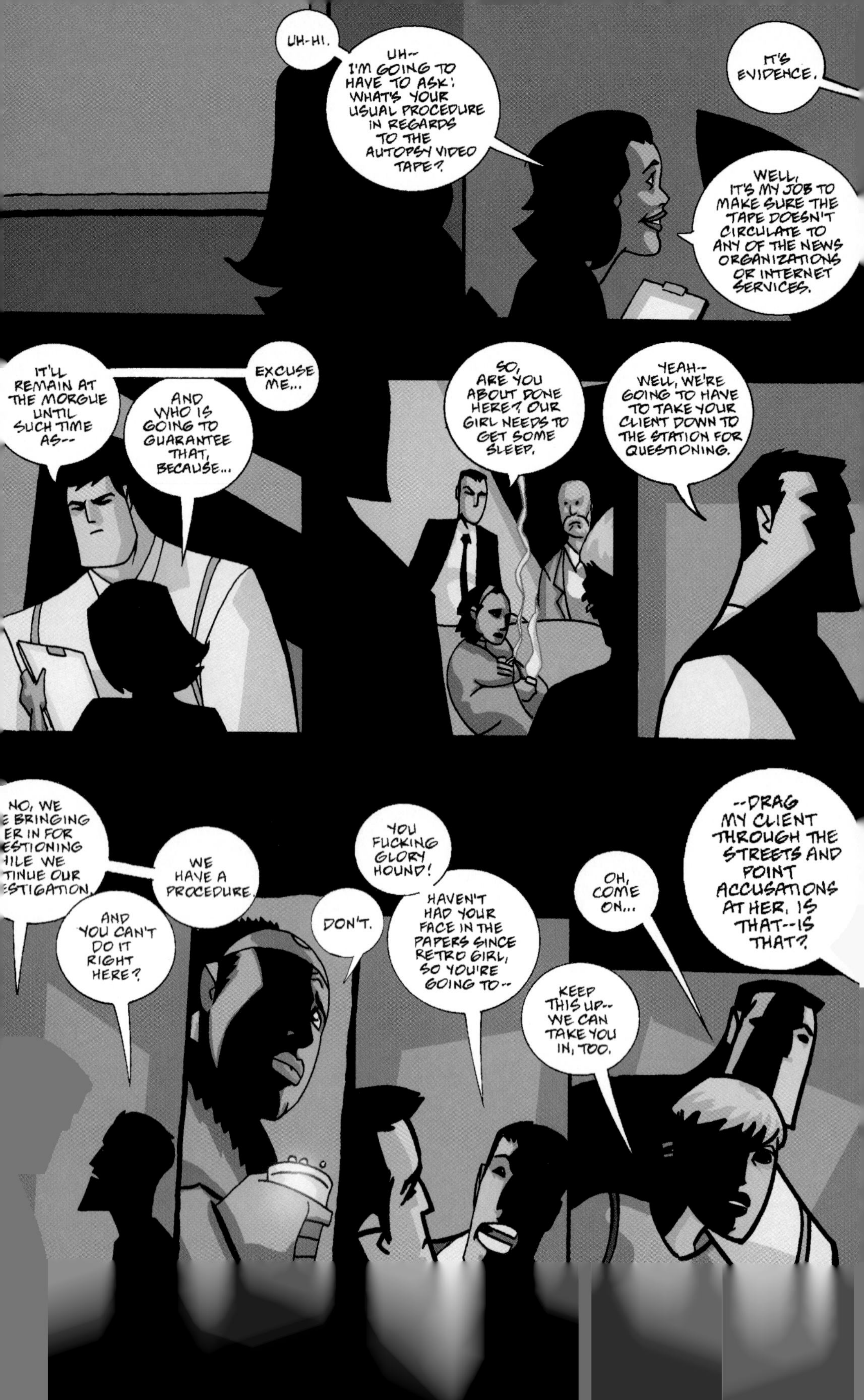
UH-HI.
UH-- I'M GOING TO HAVE TO ASK: WHAT'S YOUR USUAL PROCEDURE IN REGARDS TO THE AUTOPSY VIDEO TAPE?
IT'S EVIDENCE.
WELL, IT'S MY JOB TO MAKE SURE THE TAPE DOESN'T CIRCULATE TO ANY OF THE NEWS ORGANIZATIONS OR INTERNET SERVICES.
IT'LL REMAIN AT THE MORGUE UNTIL SUCH TIME AS--
EXCUSE ME...
AND WHO IS GOING TO GUARANTEE THAT, BECAUSE...
SO, ARE YOU ABOUT DONE HERE? OUR GIRL NEEDS TO GET SOME SLEEP.
YEAH-- WELL, WE'RE GOING TO HAVE TO TAKE YOUR CLIENT DOWN TO THE STATION FOR QUESTIONING.
NO, WE E BRINGING ER IN FOR ESTIONING HILE WE TINUE OUR ESTIGATION.
WE HAVE A PROCEDURE.
AND YOU CAN'T DO IT RIGHT HERE?
DON'T.
YOU FUCKING GLORY HOUND!
HAVEN'T HAD YOUR FACE IN THE PAPERS SINCE RETRO GIRL, SO YOU'RE GOING TO--
OH, COME ON...
KEEP THIS UP-- WE CAN TAKE YOU IN, TOO.
--DRAG MY CLIENT THROUGH THE STREETS AND POINT ACCUSATIONS AT HER. IS THAT--IS THAT?

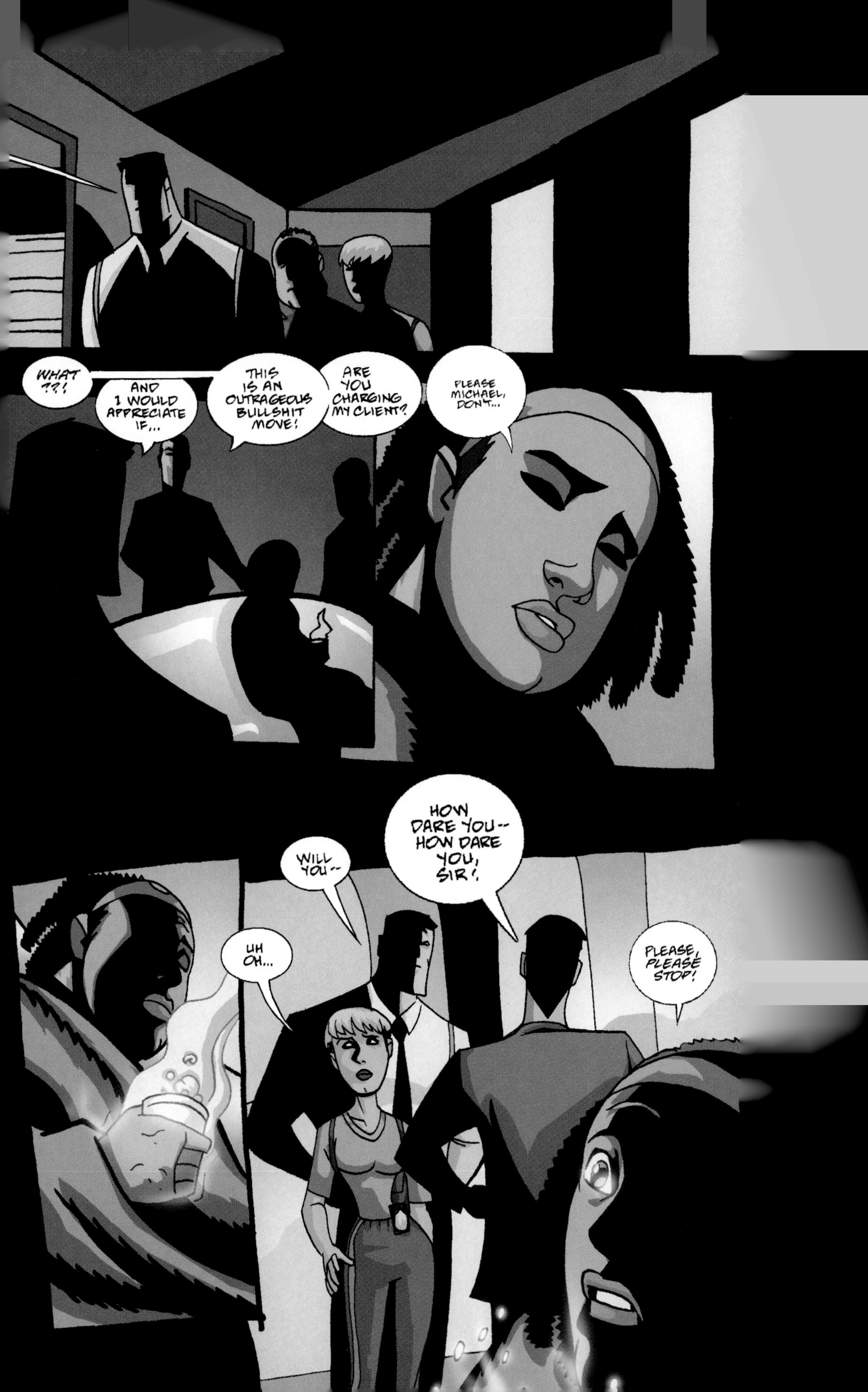
WHAT ???!
AND I WOULD APPRECIATE IF...
THIS IS AN OUTRAGEOUS BULLSHIT MOVE!
ARE YOU CHARGING MY CLIENT?
PLEASE MICHAEL, DON'T...
WILL YOU--
HOW DARE YOU-- HOW DARE YOU, SIR!
UH OH...
PLEASE, PLEASE STOP!

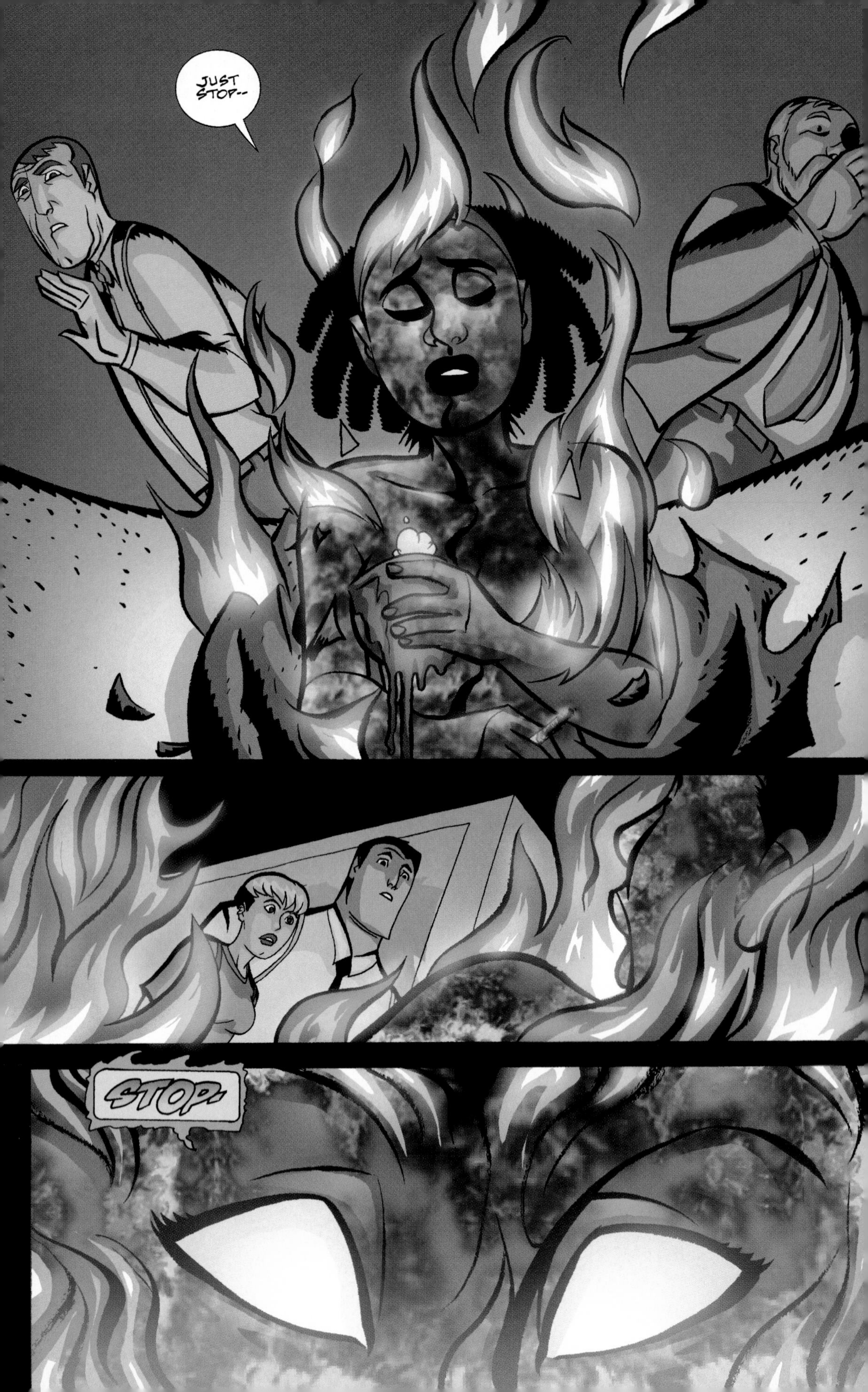
JUST STOP--
STOP-

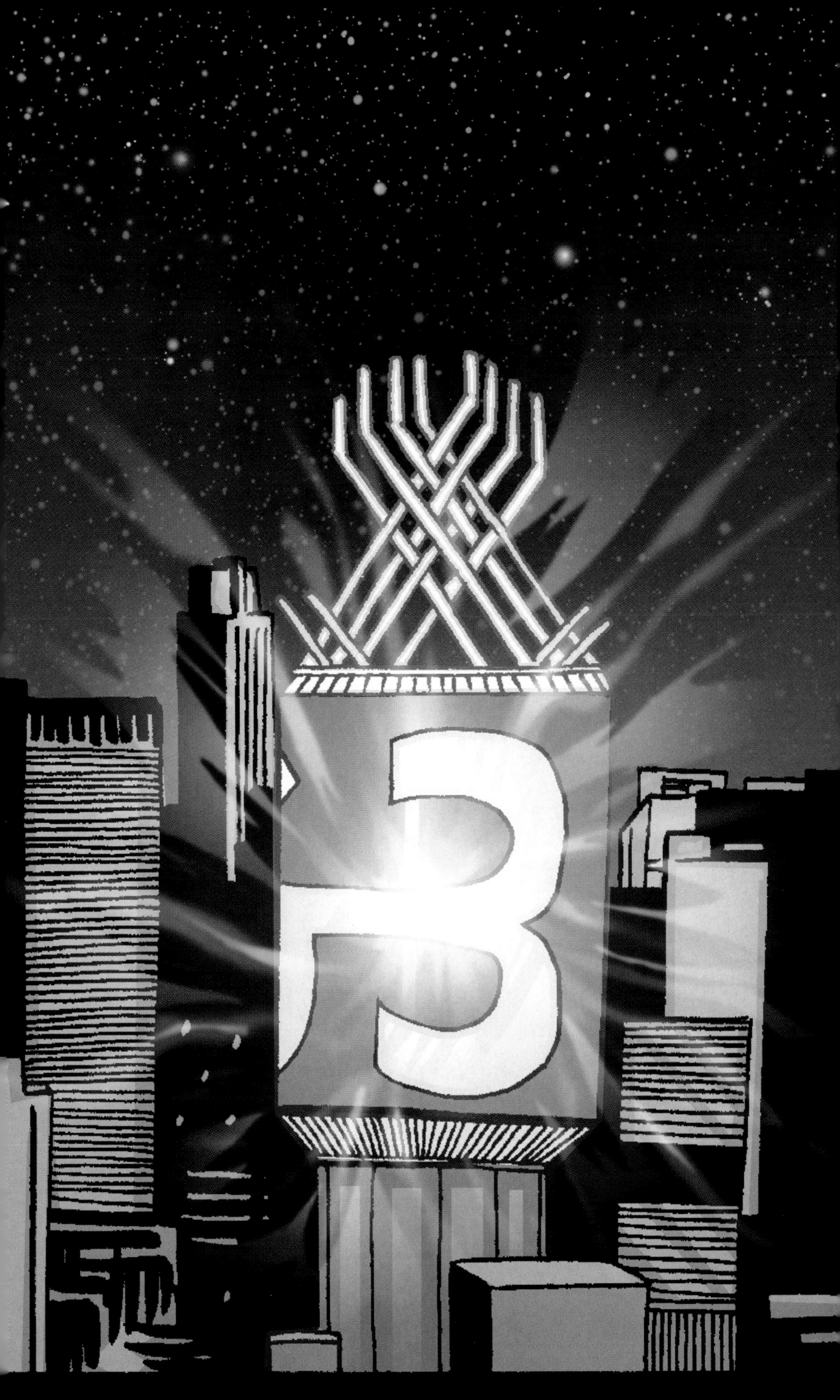

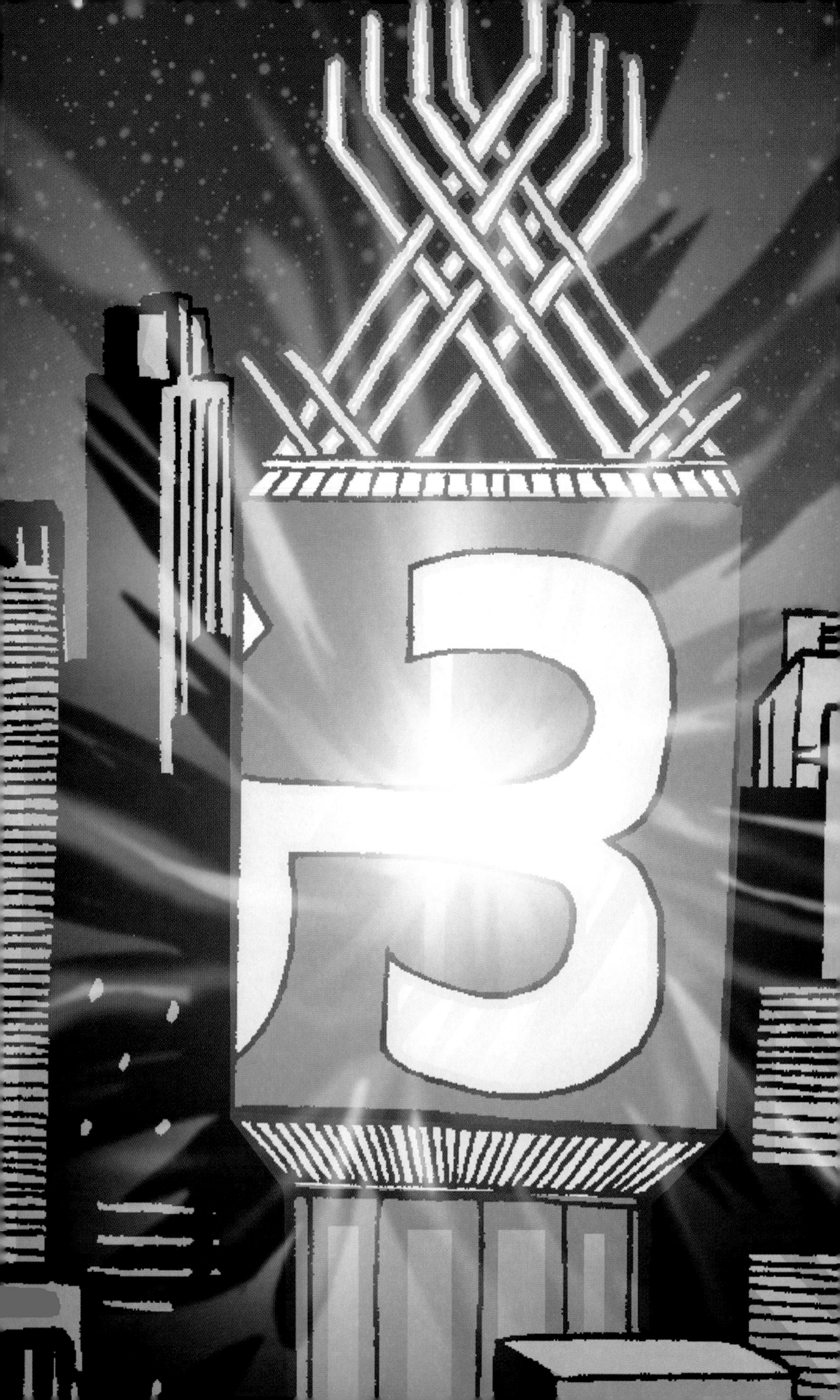

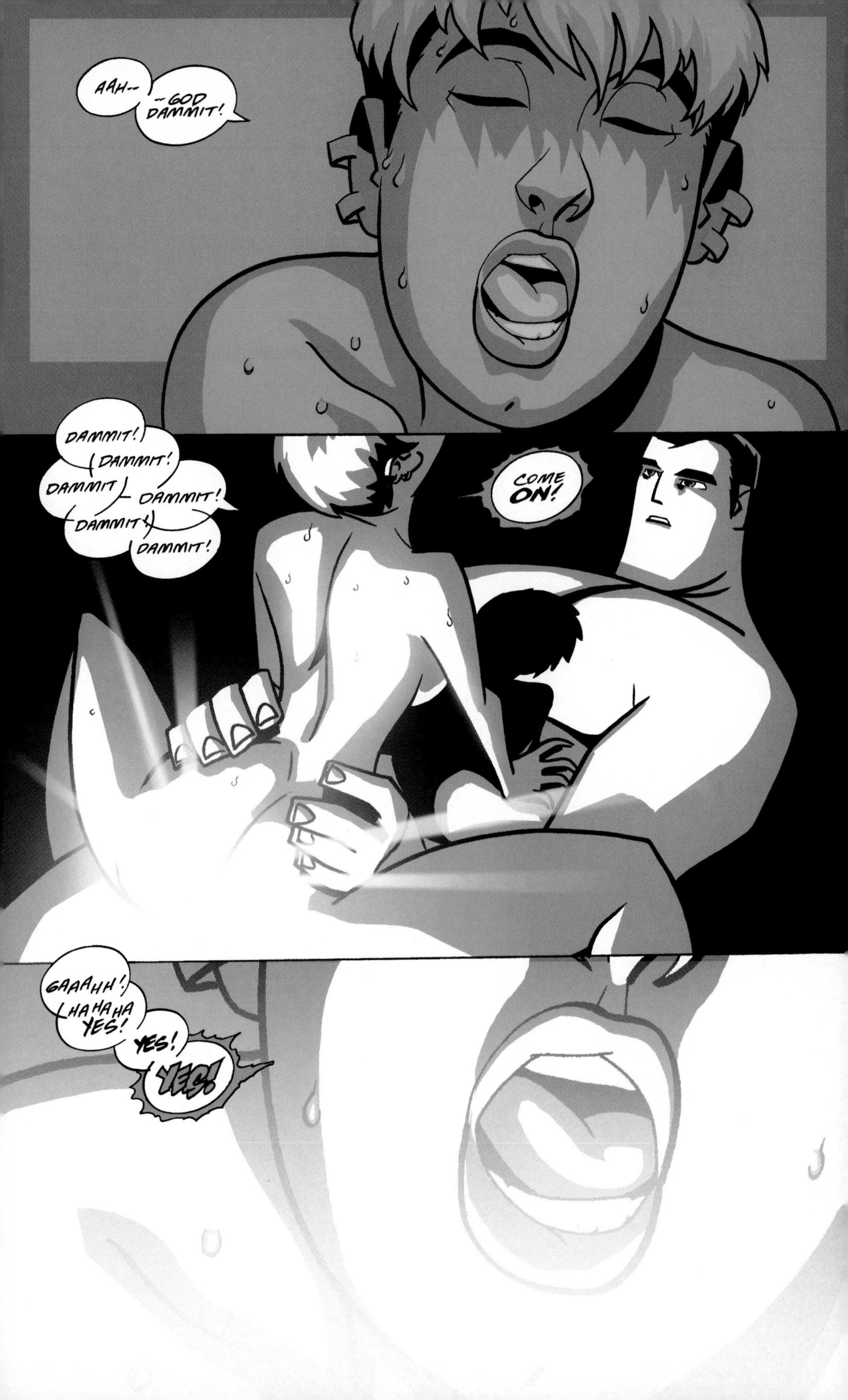
AAH--
--GOD DAMMIT!
DAMMIT!
DAMMIT!
DAMMIT
DAMMIT!
DAMMIT!
DAMMIT!
COME ON!
GAAAHH!
HAHAHA YES!
YES!
YES!

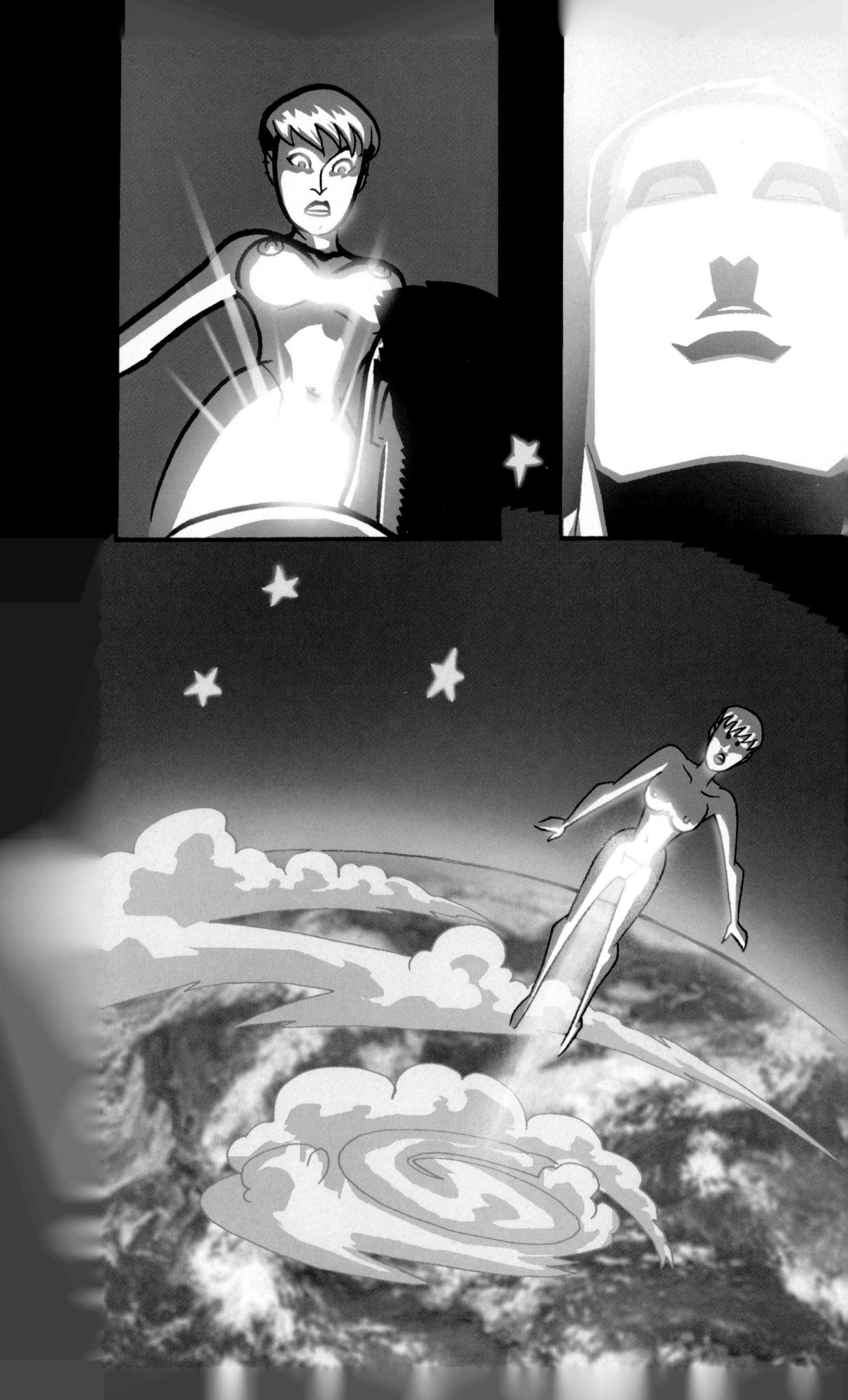

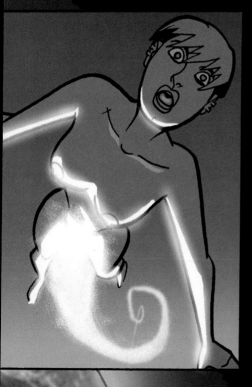

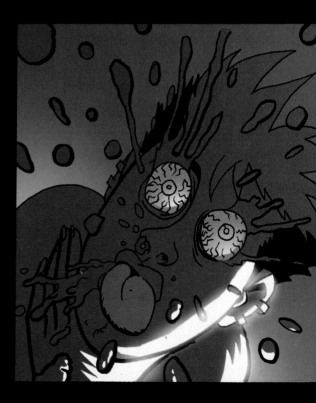

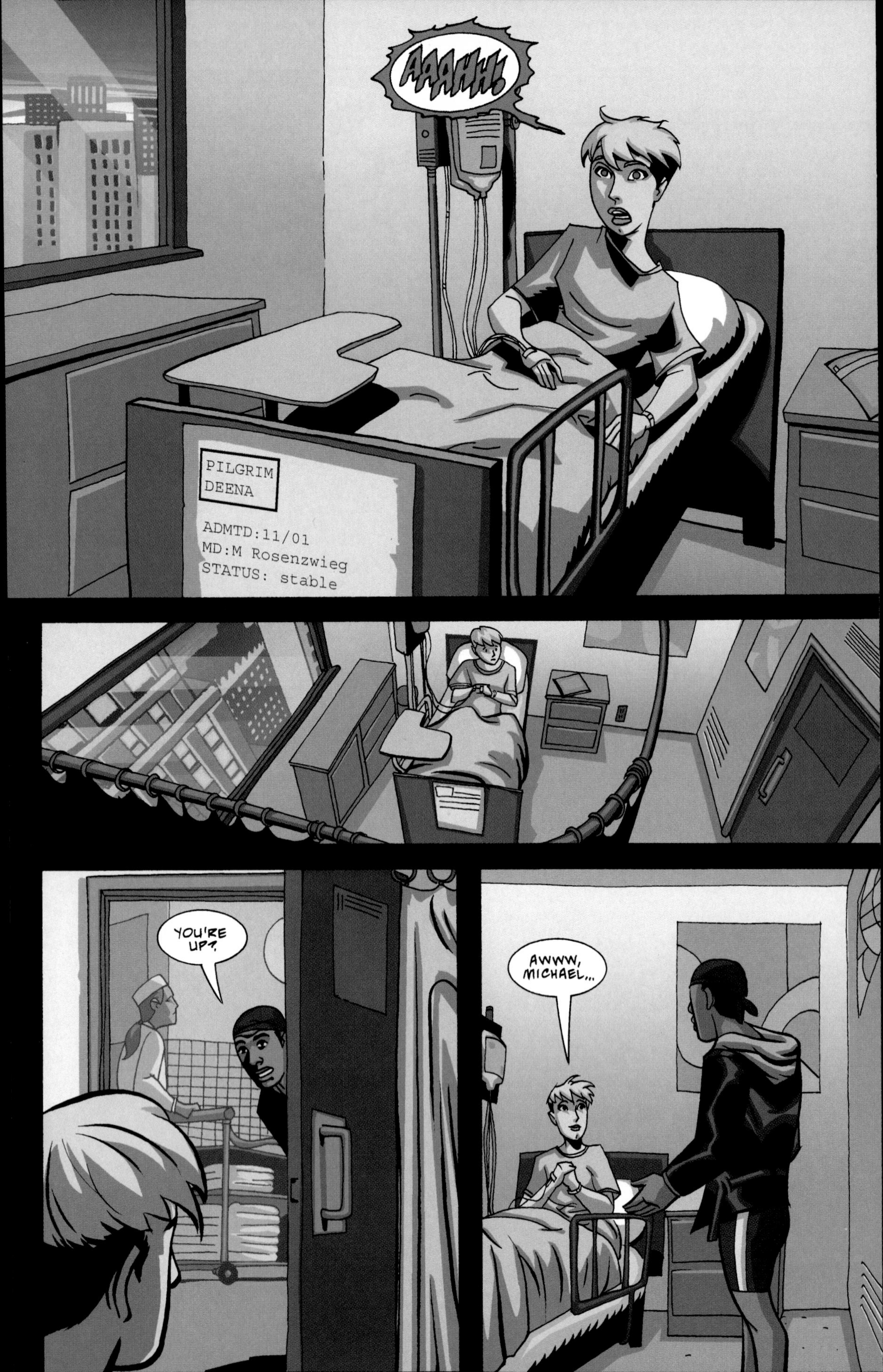
AAAHH!
PILGRIM
DEENA
ADMTD:11/01
MD:M Rosenzweig
STATUS: stable
YOU'RE UP?
AWWW, MICHAEL...

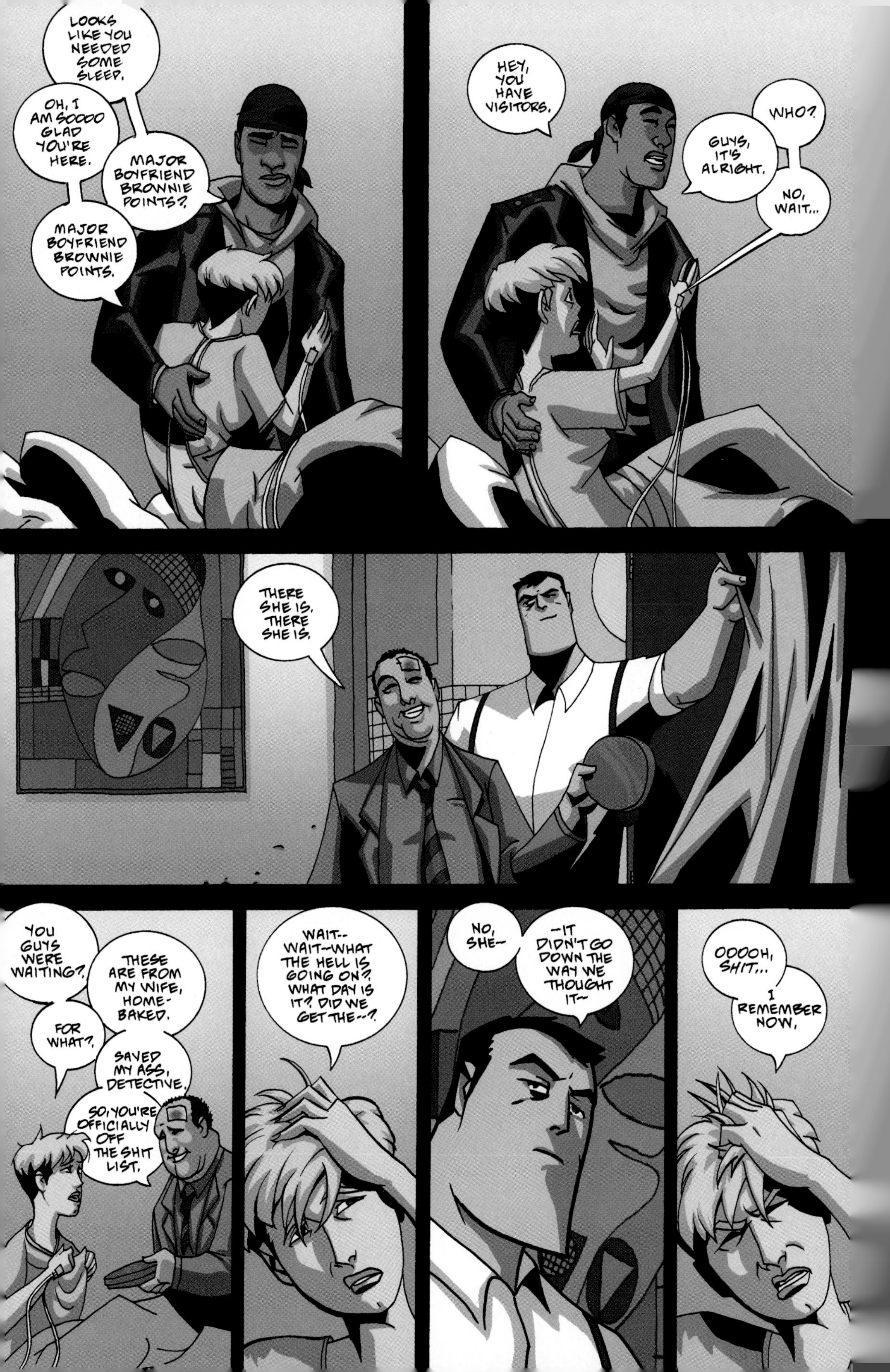
LOOKS LIKE YOU NEEDED SOME SLEEP.
OH, I AM SOOOO GLAD YOU'RE HERE.
MAJOR BOYFRIEND BROWNIE POINTS?
MAJOR BOYFRIEND BROWNIE POINTS.
HEY, YOU HAVE VISITORS.
WHO?
GUYS, IT'S ALRIGHT.
NO, WAIT...
THERE SHE IS. THERE SHE IS.
YOU GUYS WERE WAITING?
THESE ARE FROM MY WIFE, HOME-BAKED.
FOR WHAT?
SAVED MY ASS, DETECTIVE.
SO, YOU'RE OFFICIALLY OFF THE SHIT LIST.
WAIT-- WAIT--WHAT THE HELL IS GOING ON? WHAT DAY IS IT? DID WE GET THE--?
NO, SHE-
-IT DIDN'T GO DOWN THE WAY WE THOUGHT IT-
OOOOH, SHIT...
I REMEMBER NOW.

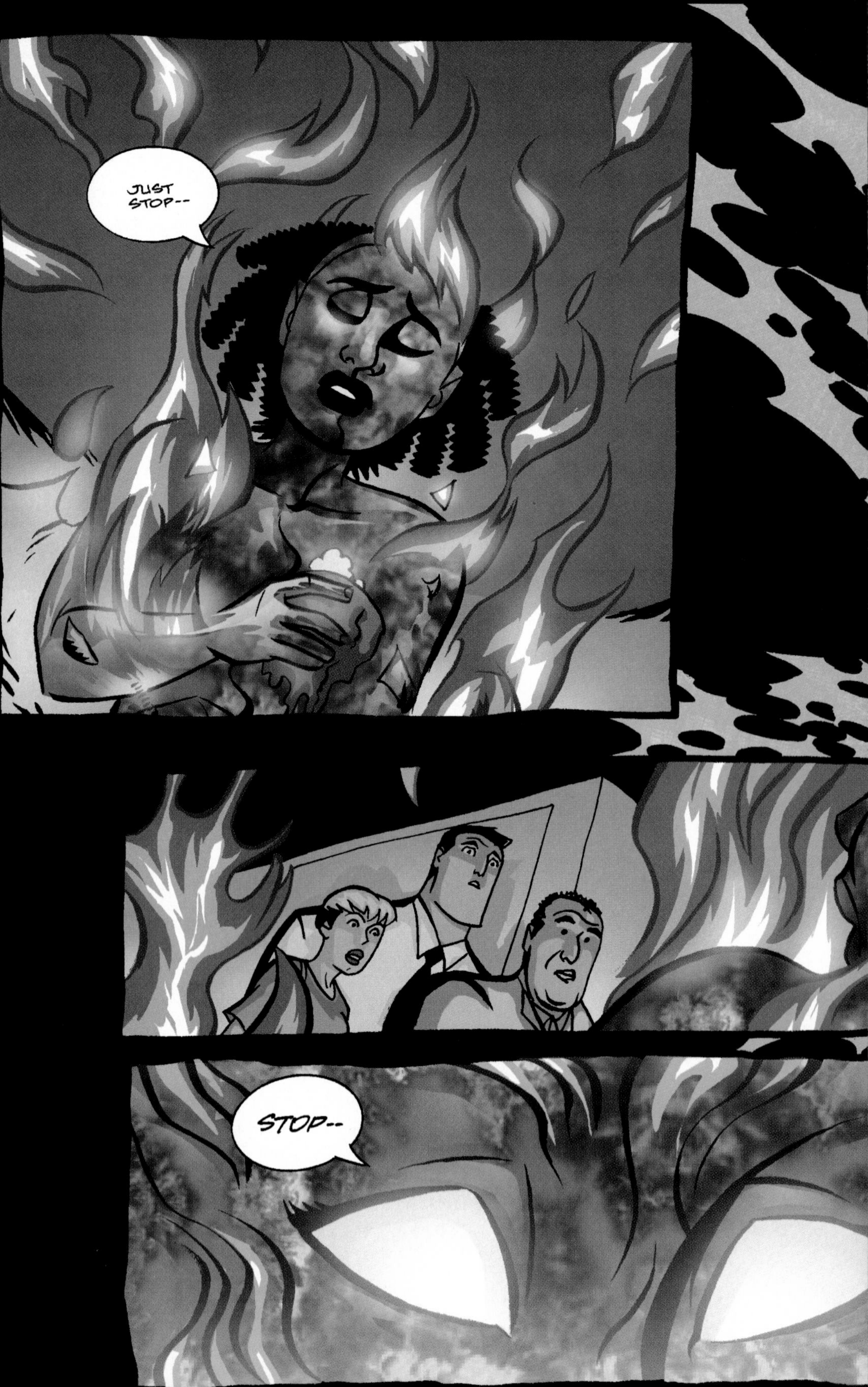
JUST STOP--
STOP--

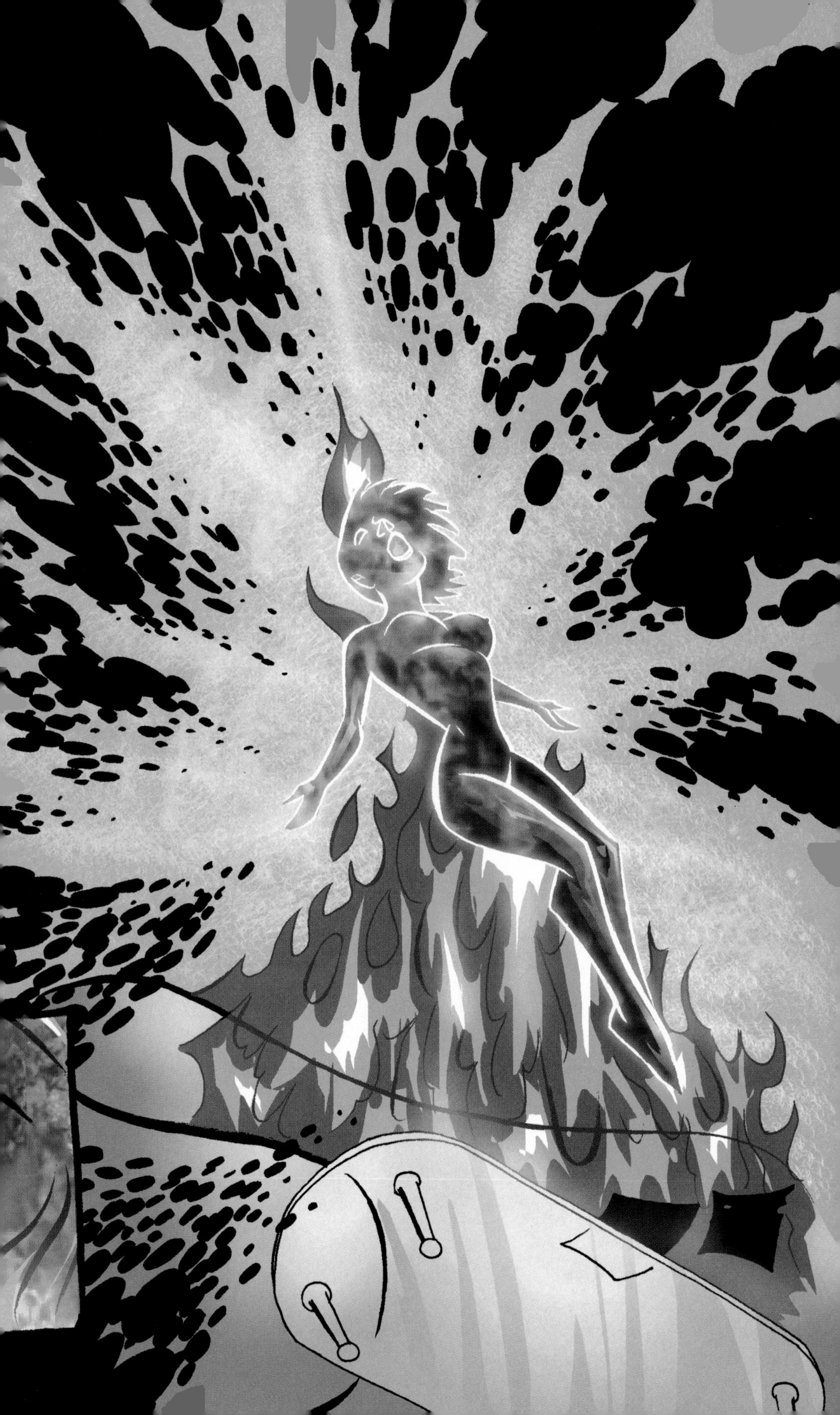

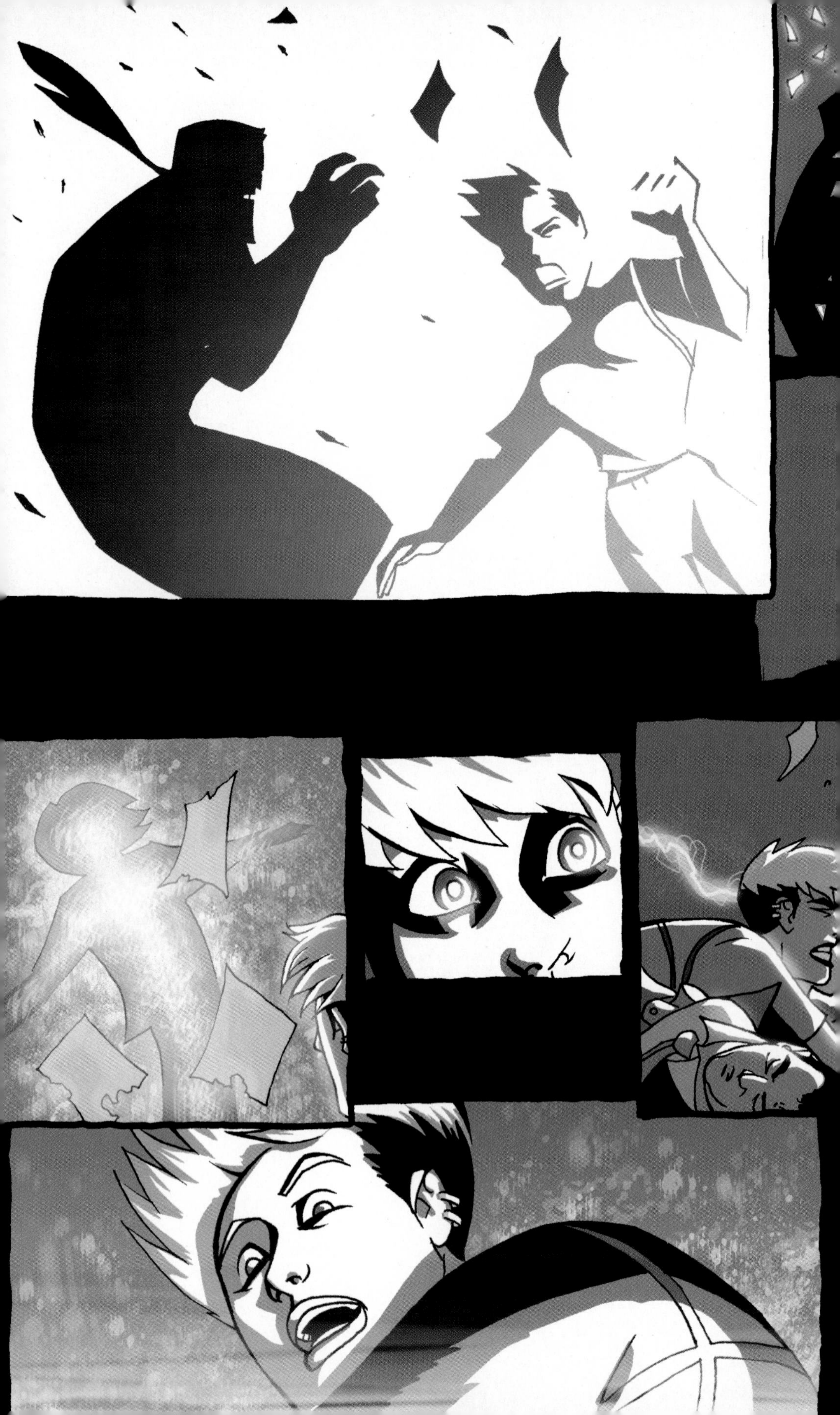

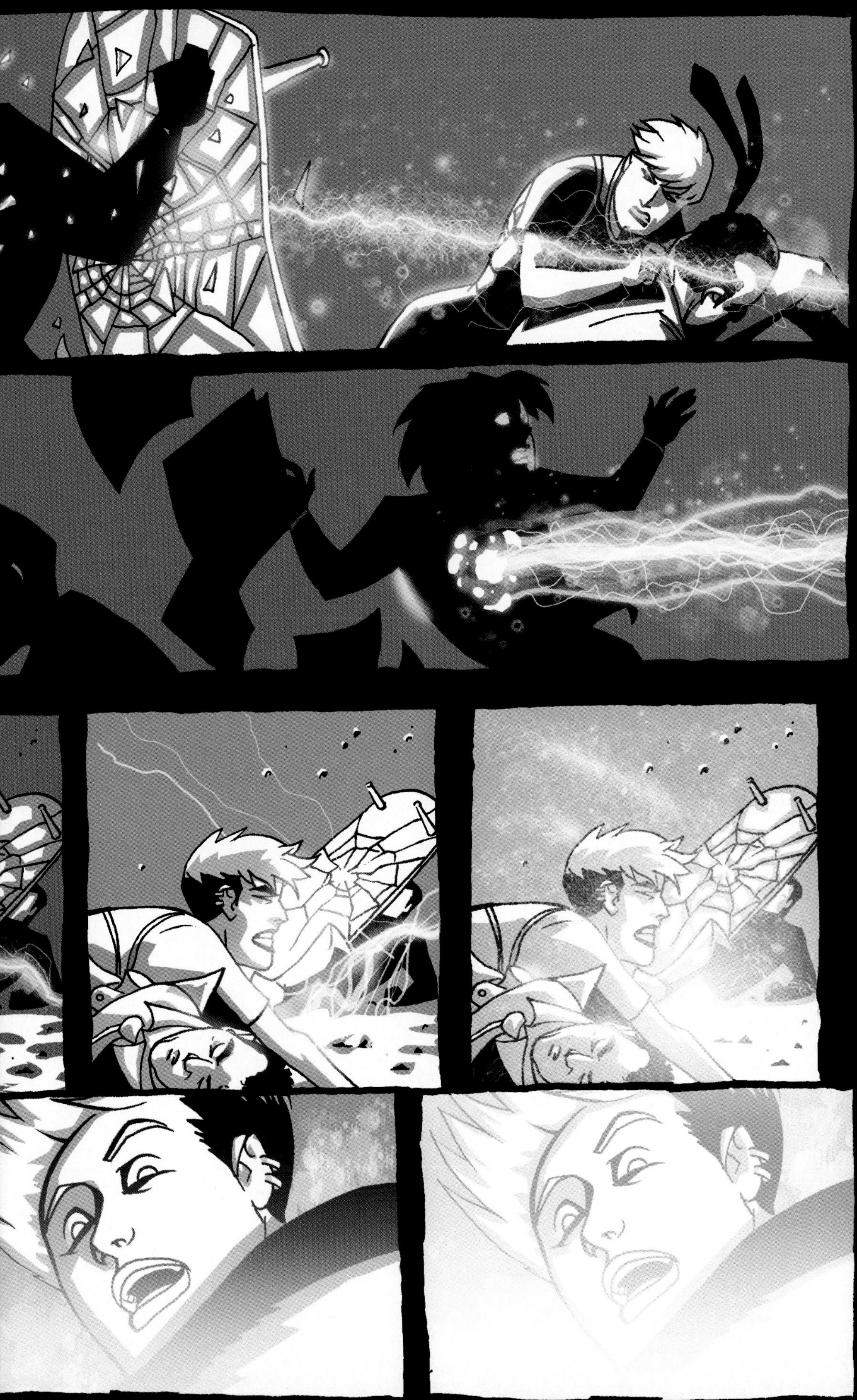

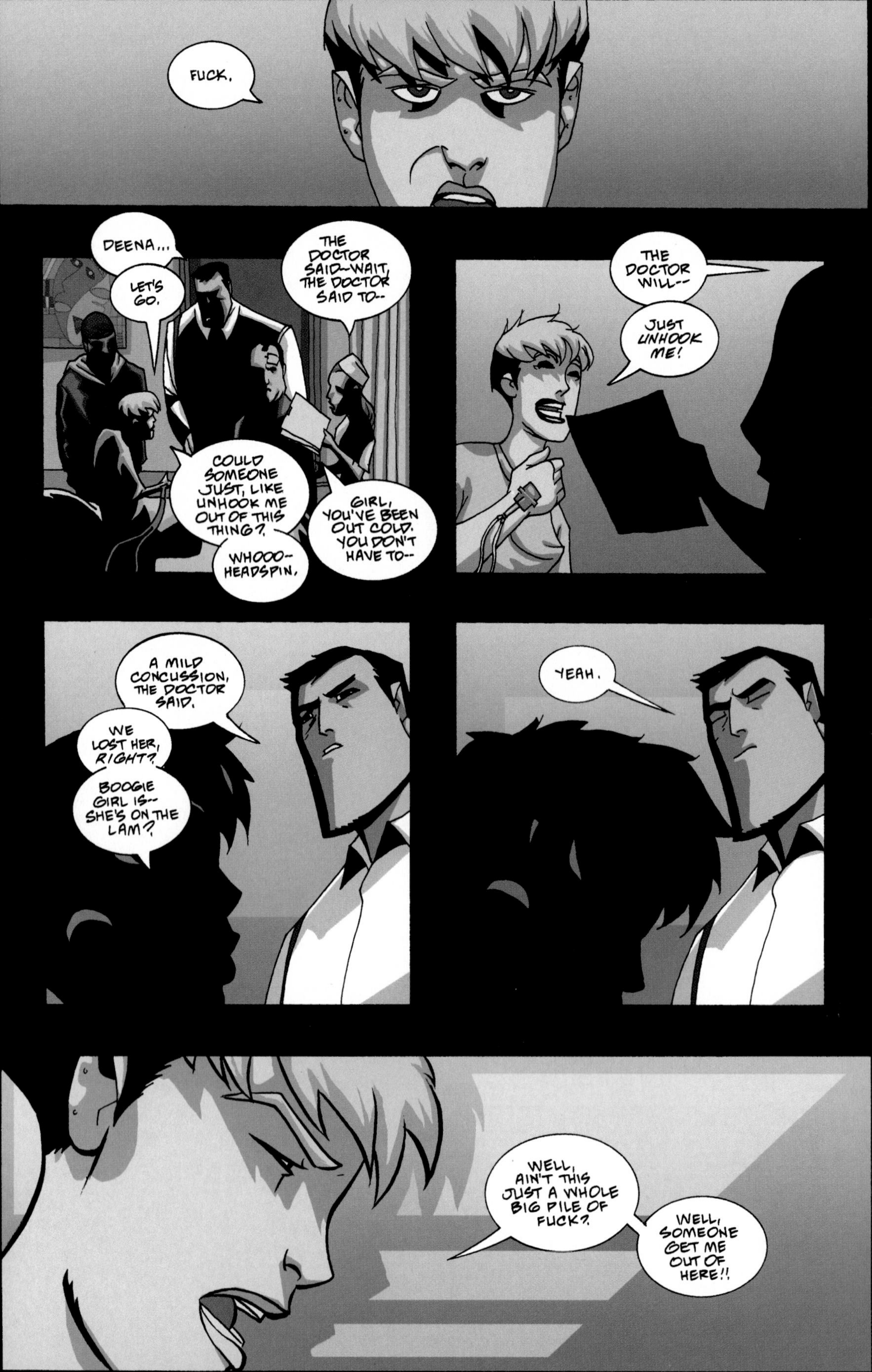
FUCK.
DEENA...
LET'S GO.
THE DOCTOR SAID--WAIT, THE DOCTOR SAID TO--
COULD SOMEONE JUST, LIKE UNHOOK ME OUT OF THIS THING?
WHOOO-- HEADSPIN.
GIRL, YOU'VE BEEN OUT COLD. YOU DON'T HAVE TO--
THE DOCTOR WILL--
JUST UNHOOK ME!
A MILD CONCUSSION, THE DOCTOR SAID.
WE LOST HER, RIGHT?
BOOGIE GIRL IS-- SHE'S ON THE LAM?
YEAH.
WELL, AIN'T THIS JUST A WHOLE BIG PILE OF FUCK?
WELL, SOMEONE GET ME OUT OF HERE!!

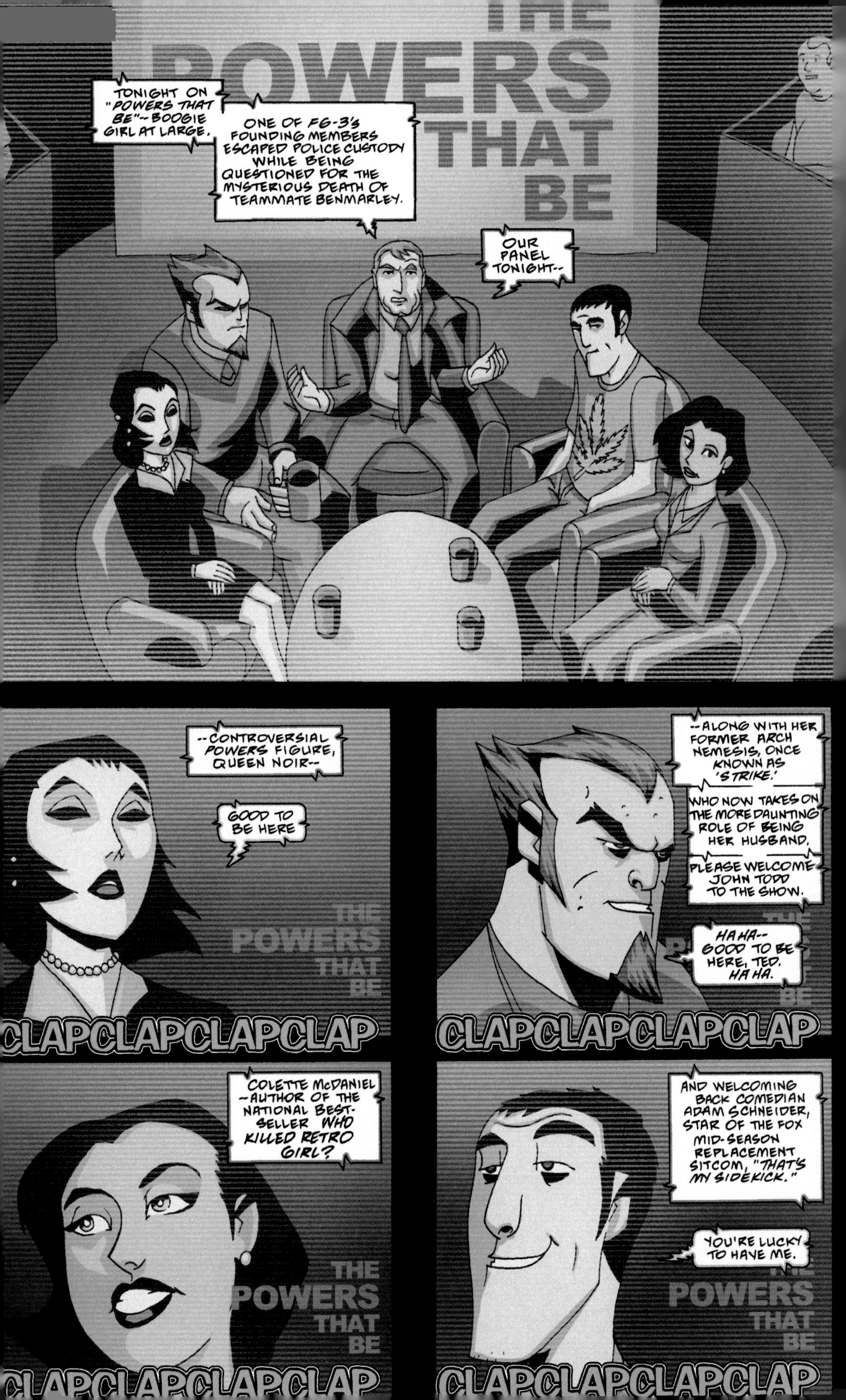
THE POWERS THAT BE
TONIGHT ON "POWERS THAT BE"-- BOOGIE GIRL AT LARGE.
ONE OF FG-3's FOUNDING MEMBERS ESCAPED POLICE CUSTODY WHILE BEING QUESTIONED FOR THE MYSTERIOUS DEATH OF TEAMMATE BENMARLEY.
OUR PANEL TONIGHT--
--CONTROVERSIAL POWERS FIGURE, QUEEN NOIR--
GOOD TO BE HERE
THE POWERS THAT BE
CLAPCLAPCLAPCLAP
--ALONG WITH HER FORMER ARCH NEMESIS, ONCE KNOWN AS 'STRIKE.'
WHO NOW TAKES ON THE MORE DAUNTING ROLE OF BEING HER HUSBAND,
PLEASE WELCOME JOHN TODD TO THE SHOW.
HA HA-- GOOD TO BE HERE, TED. HA HA.
CLAPCLAPCLAPCLAP
COLETTE McDANIEL --AUTHOR OF THE NATIONAL BEST-SELLER WHO KILLED RETRO GIRL?
THE POWERS THAT BE
CLAPCLAPCLAPCLAP
AND WELCOMING BACK COMEDIAN ADAM SCHNEIDER, STAR OF THE FOX MID-SEASON REPLACEMENT SITCOM, "THAT'S MY SIDEKICK."
YOU'RE LUCKY TO HAVE ME.
POWERS THAT BE
CLAPCLAPCLAPCLAP

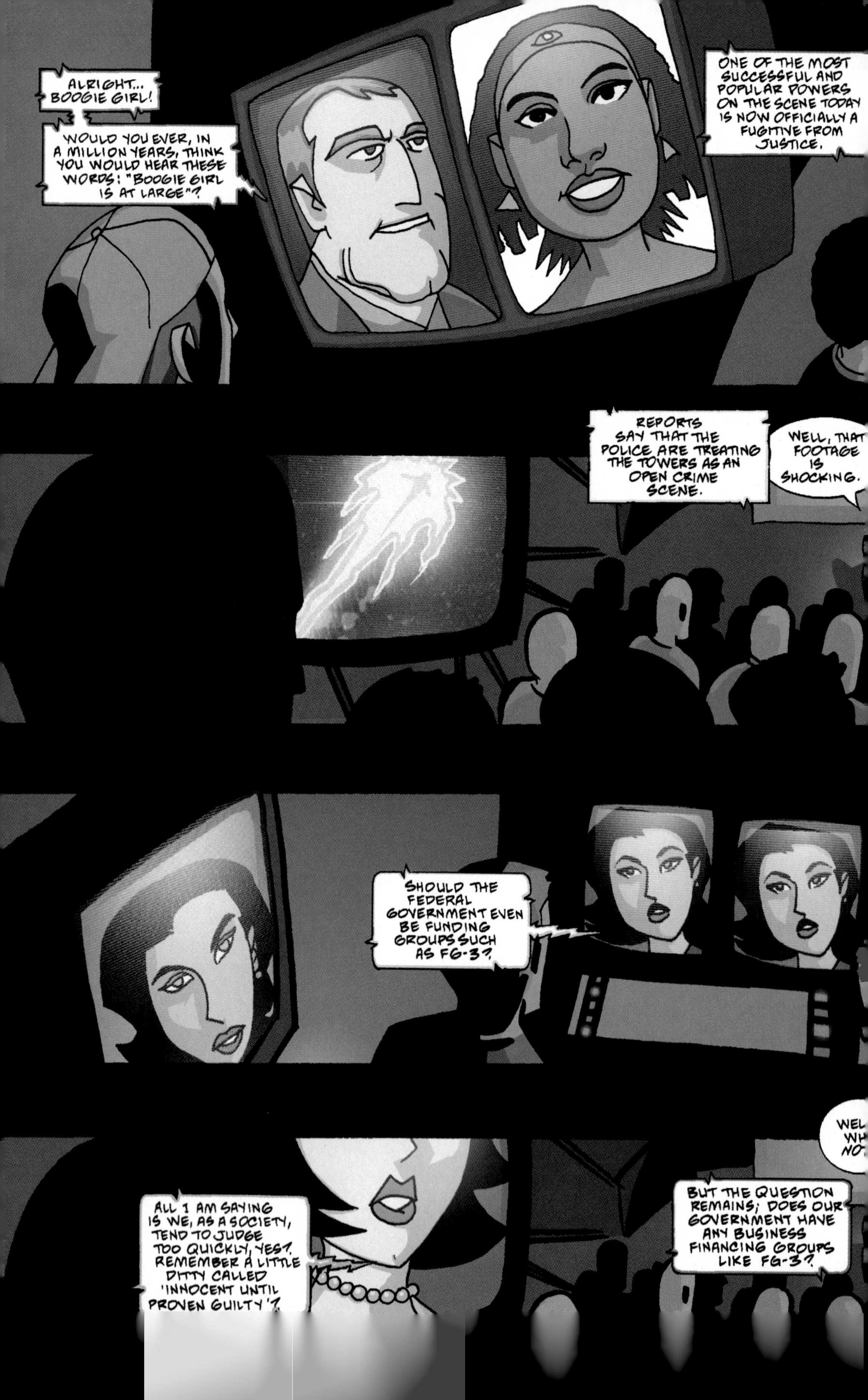
ALRIGHT... BOOGIE GIRL!
WOULD YOU EVER, IN A MILLION YEARS, THINK YOU WOULD HEAR THESE WORDS: "BOOGIE GIRL IS AT LARGE"?
ONE OF THE MOST SUCCESSFUL AND POPULAR POWERS ON THE SCENE TODAY IS NOW OFFICIALLY A FUGITIVE FROM JUSTICE.
REPORTS SAY THAT THE POLICE ARE TREATING THE TOWERS AS AN OPEN CRIME SCENE.
WELL, THAT FOOTAGE IS SHOCKING.
SHOULD THE FEDERAL GOVERNMENT EVEN BE FUNDING GROUPS SUCH AS FG-3?
ALL I AM SAYING IS WE, AS A SOCIETY, TEND TO JUDGE TOO QUICKLY, YES? REMEMBER A LITTLE DITTY CALLED 'INNOCENT UNTIL PROVEN GUILTY'?
BUT THE QUESTION REMAINS; DOES OUR GOVERNMENT HAVE ANY BUSINESS FINANCING GROUPS LIKE FG-3?

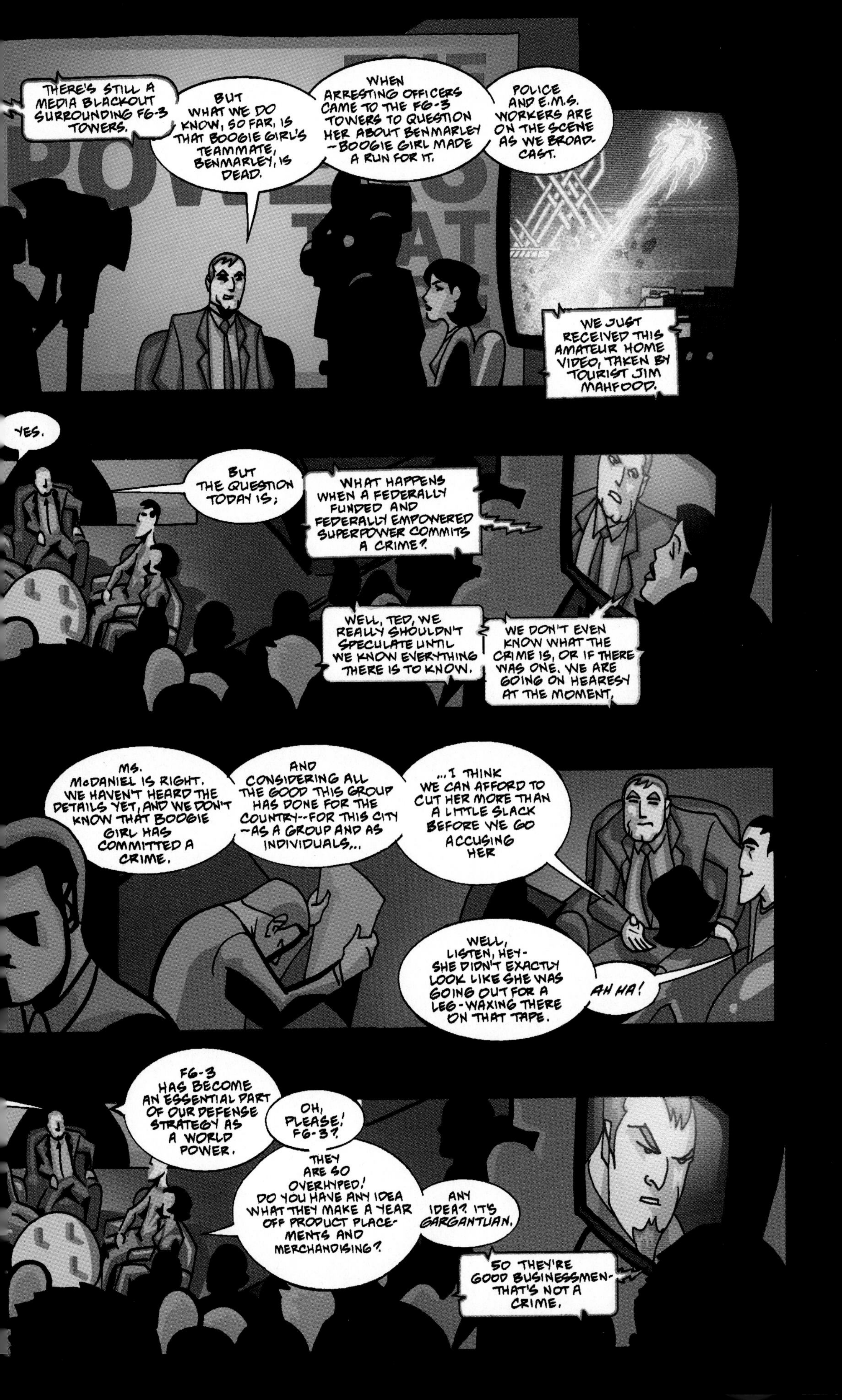

THERE'S STILL A MEDIA BLACKOUT SURROUNDING FG-3 TOWERS.
BUT WHAT WE DO KNOW, SO FAR, IS THAT BOOGIE GIRL'S TEAMMATE, BENMARLEY, IS DEAD.
WHEN ARRESTING OFFICERS CAME TO THE FG-3 TOWERS TO QUESTION HER ABOUT BENMARLEY --BOOGIE GIRL MADE A RUN FOR IT.
POLICE AND E.M.S. WORKERS ARE ON THE SCENE AS WE BROADCAST.
WE JUST RECEIVED THIS AMATEUR HOME VIDEO, TAKEN BY TOURIST JIM MAHFOOD.
YES.
BUT THE QUESTION TODAY IS;
WHAT HAPPENS WHEN A FEDERALLY FUNDED AND FEDERALLY EMPOWERED SUPERPOWER COMMITS A CRIME?
WELL, TED, WE REALLY SHOULDN'T SPECULATE UNTIL WE KNOW EVERYTHING THERE IS TO KNOW.
WE DON'T EVEN KNOW WHAT THE CRIME IS, OR IF THERE WAS ONE. WE ARE GOING ON HEARESY AT THE MOMENT.
MS. McDANIEL IS RIGHT. WE HAVEN'T HEARD THE DETAILS YET, AND WE DON'T KNOW THAT BOOGIE GIRL HAS COMMITTED A CRIME.
AND CONSIDERING ALL THE GOOD THIS GROUP HAS DONE FOR THE COUNTRY--FOR THIS CITY --AS A GROUP AND AS INDIVIDUALS...
...I THINK WE CAN AFFORD TO CUT HER MORE THAN A LITTLE SLACK BEFORE WE GO ACCUSING HER
WELL, LISTEN, HEY- SHE DIDN'T EXACTLY LOOK LIKE SHE WAS GOING OUT FOR A LEG-WAXING THERE ON THAT TAPE.
AH HA!
FG-3 HAS BECOME AN ESSENTIAL PART OF OUR DEFENSE STRATEGY AS A WORLD POWER.
OH, PLEASE! FG-3?
THEY ARE SO OVERHYPED! DO YOU HAVE ANY IDEA WHAT THEY MAKE A YEAR OFF PRODUCT PLACEMENTS AND MERCHANDISING?
ANY IDEA? IT'S GARGANTUAN.
SO THEY'RE GOOD BUSINESSMEN- THAT'S NOT A CRIME.

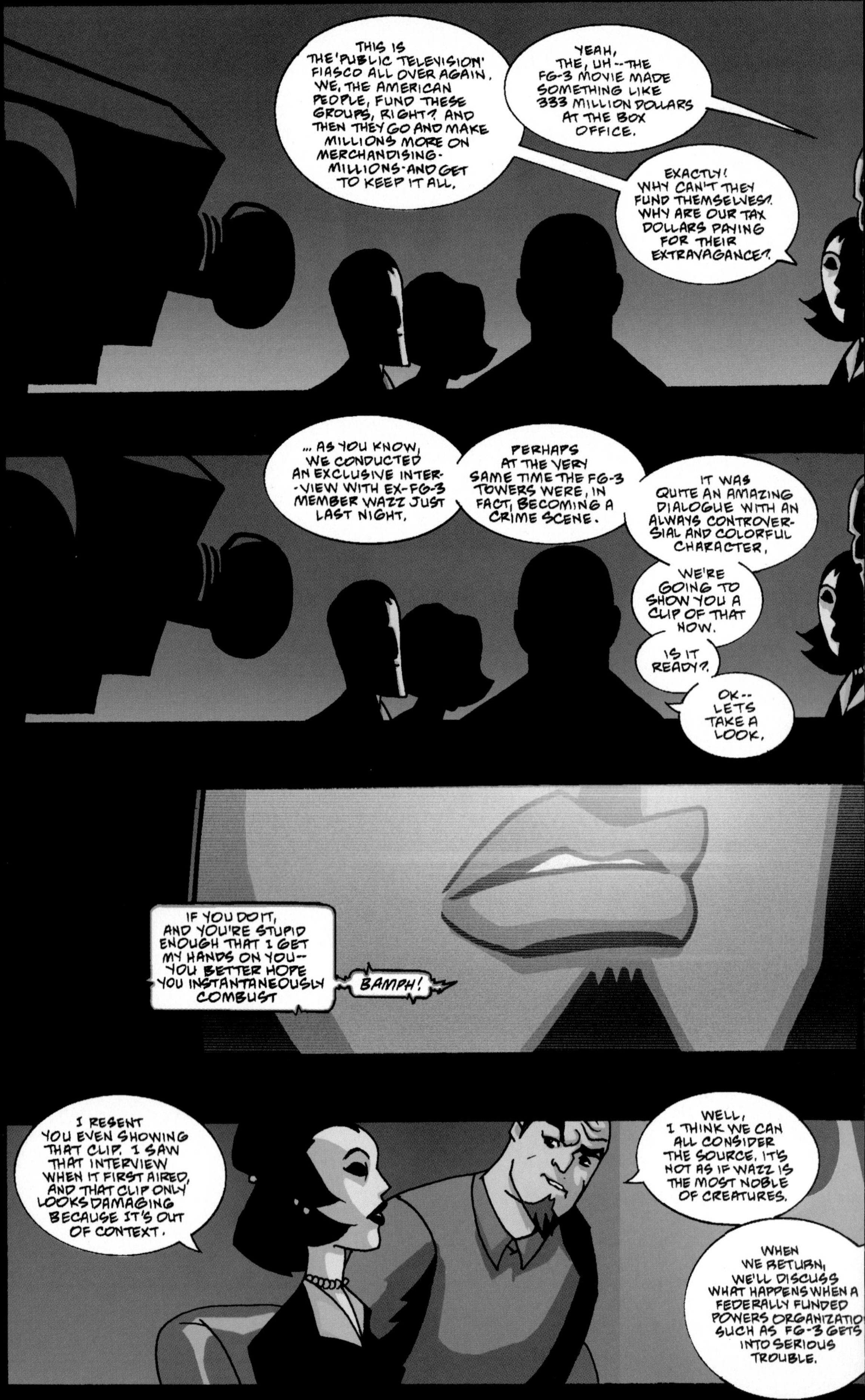
THIS IS THE 'PUBLIC TELEVISION' FIASCO ALL OVER AGAIN. WE, THE AMERICAN PEOPLE, FUND THESE GROUPS, RIGHT? AND THEN THEY GO AND MAKE MILLIONS MORE ON MERCHANDISING- MILLIONS- AND GET TO KEEP IT ALL.
YEAH, THE, UH -- THE FG-3 MOVIE MADE SOMETHING LIKE 333 MILLION DOLLARS AT THE BOX OFFICE.
EXACTLY! WHY CAN'T THEY FUND THEMSELVES?! WHY ARE OUR TAX DOLLARS PAYING FOR THEIR EXTRAVAGANCE?!
... AS YOU KNOW, WE CONDUCTED AN EXCLUSIVE INTER--VIEW WITH EX-FG-3 MEMBER WAZZ JUST LAST NIGHT.
PERHAPS AT THE VERY SAME TIME THE FG-3 TOWERS WERE, IN FACT, BECOMING A CRIME SCENE.
IT WAS QUITE AN AMAZING DIALOGUE WITH AN ALWAYS CONTROVER-SIAL AND COLORFUL CHARACTER.
WE'RE GOING TO SHOW YOU A CLIP OF THAT NOW.
IS IT READY?!
OK-- LETS TAKE A LOOK.
IF YOU DO IT, AND YOU'RE STUPID ENOUGH THAT I GET MY HANDS ON YOU-- YOU BETTER HOPE YOU INSTANTANEOUSLY COMBUST
BAMPH!
I RESENT YOU EVEN SHOWING THAT CLIP. I SAW THAT INTERVIEW WHEN IT FIRST AIRED, AND THAT CLIP ONLY LOOKS DAMAGING BECAUSE IT'S OUT OF CONTEXT.
WELL, I THINK WE CAN ALL CONSIDER THE SOURCE. IT'S NOT AS IF WAZZ IS THE MOST NOBLE OF CREATURES.
WHEN WE RETURN, WE'LL DISCUSS WHAT HAPPENS WHEN A FEDERALLY FUNDED POWERS ORGANIZATIO SUCH AS FG-3 GETS INTO SERIOUS TROUBLE.

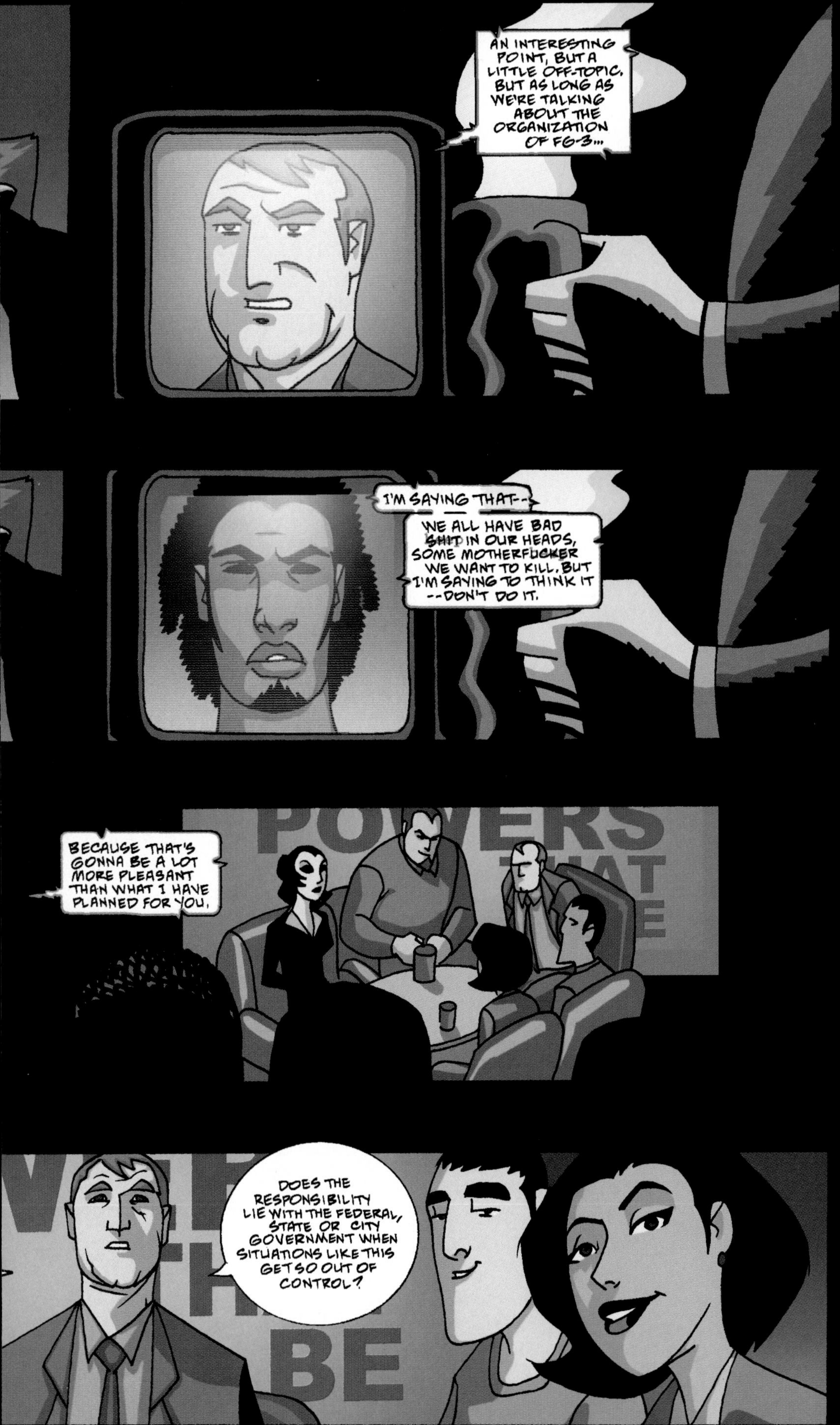
AN INTERESTING POINT, BUT A LITTLE OFF-TOPIC. BUT AS LONG AS WE'RE TALKING ABOUT THE ORGANIZATION OF FG-3...
I'M SAYING THAT--
WE ALL HAVE BAD SHIT IN OUR HEADS, SOME MOTHERFUCKER WE WANT TO KILL. BUT I'M SAYING TO THINK IT --DON'T DO IT.
POWERS
BECAUSE THAT'S GONNA BE A LOT MORE PLEASANT THAN WHAT I HAVE PLANNED FOR YOU.
DOES THE RESPONSIBILITY LIE WITH THE FEDERAL, STATE OR CITY GOVERNMENT WHEN SITUATIONS LIKE THIS GET SO OUT OF CONTROL?
BE

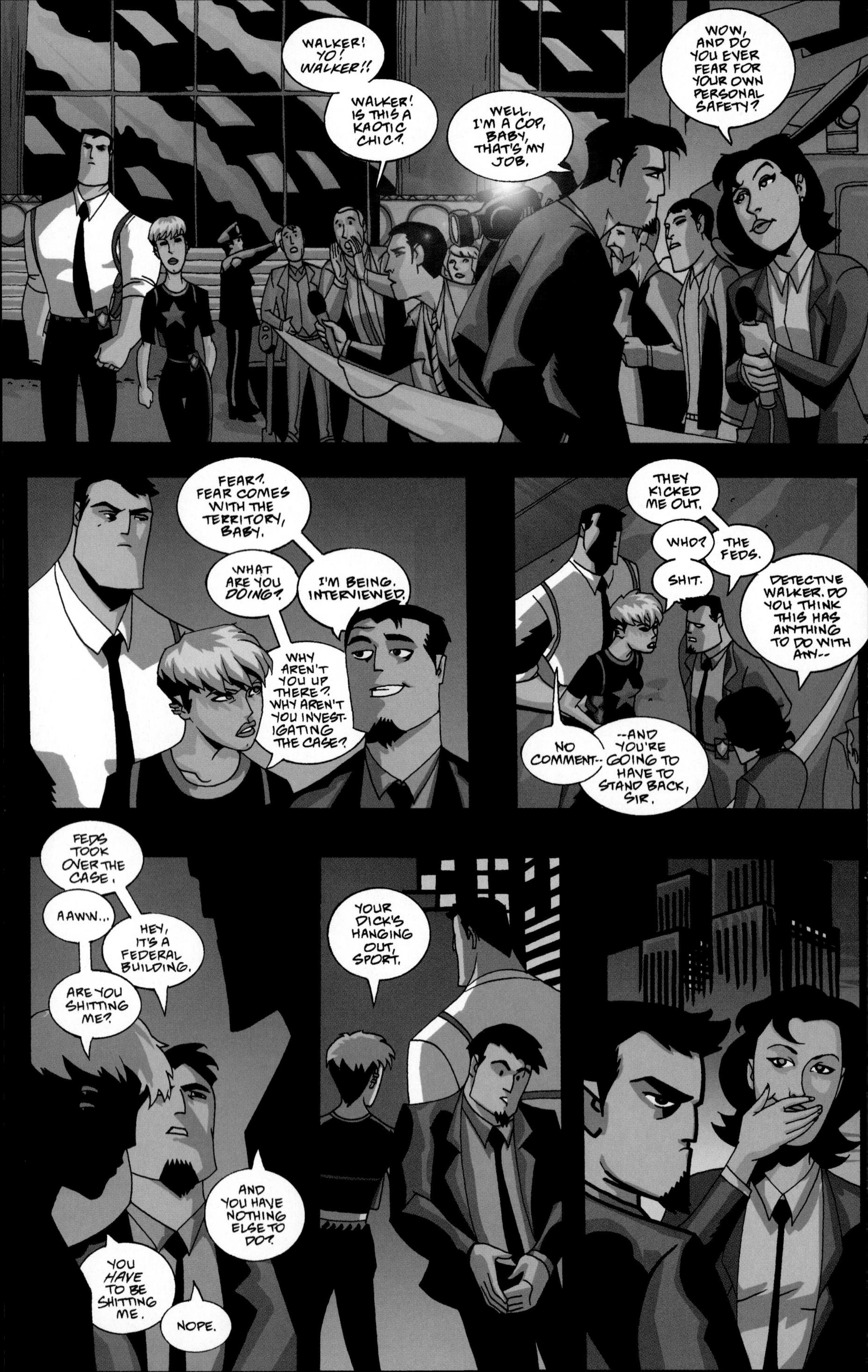
WALKER! YO! WALKER!!
WALKER! IS THIS A KAOTIC CHIC?
WELL, I'M A COP, BABY, THAT'S MY JOB.
WOW, AND DO YOU EVER FEAR FOR YOUR OWN PERSONAL SAFETY?
FEAR? FEAR COMES WITH THE TERRITORY, BABY.
WHAT ARE YOU *DOING*?
I'M BEING. INTERVIEWED.
WHY AREN'T YOU UP THERE? WHY AREN'T YOU INVESTIGATING THE CASE?
THEY KICKED ME OUT.
WHO?
THE FEDS.
SHIT.
DETECTIVE WALKER, DO YOU THINK THIS HAS ANYTHING TO DO WITH ANY--
NO COMMENT--
--AND YOU'RE GOING TO HAVE TO STAND BACK, SIR.
FEDS TOOK OVER THE CASE.
AAWW...
HEY, IT'S A FEDERAL BUILDING.
ARE YOU SHITTING ME?
AND YOU HAVE NOTHING ELSE TO DO?
YOU *HAVE* TO BE SHITTING ME.
NOPE.
YOUR DICK'S HANGING OUT, SPORT.

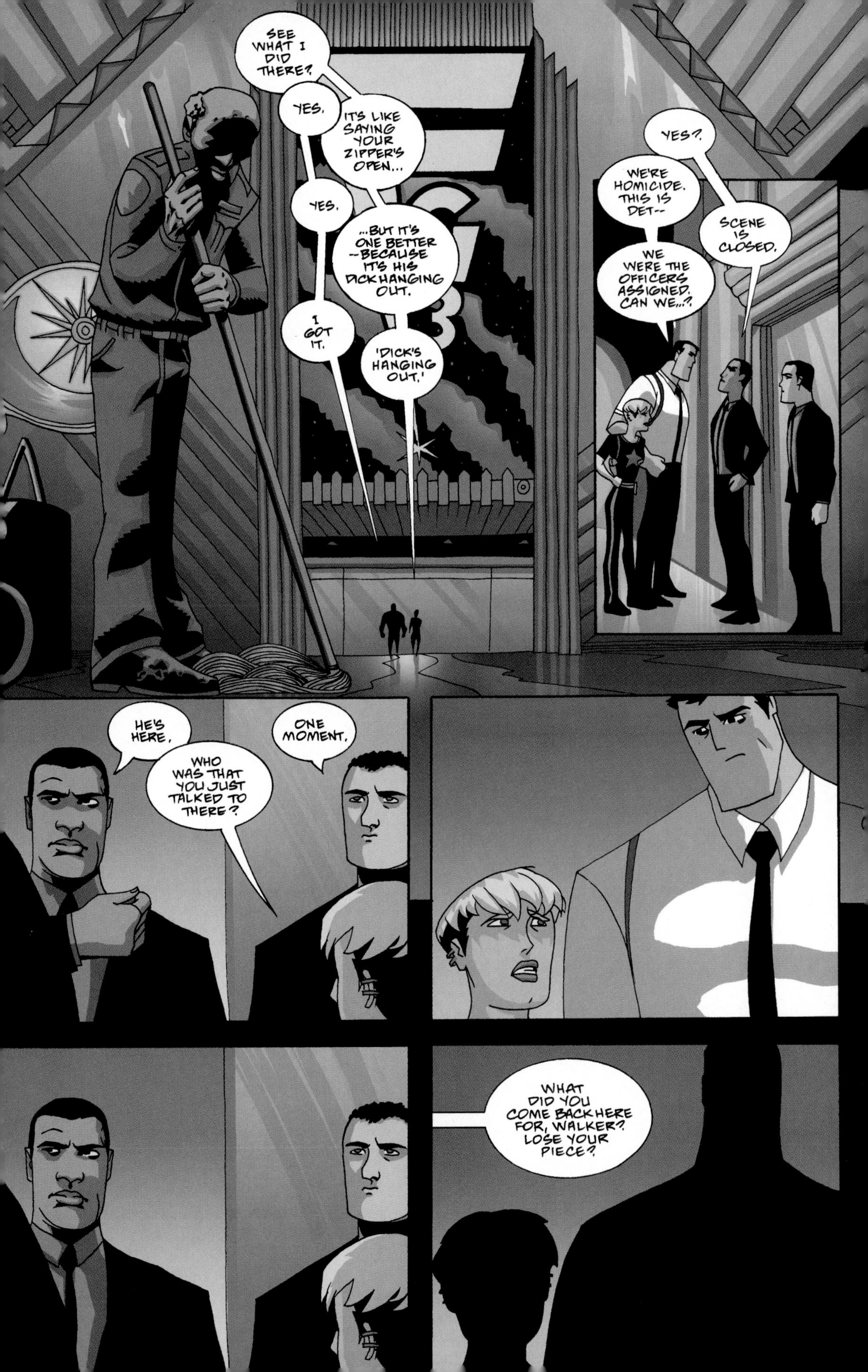
SEE WHAT I DID THERE?
YES.
IT'S LIKE SAYING YOUR ZIPPER'S OPEN...
YES.
...BUT IT'S ONE BETTER --BECAUSE IT'S HIS DICK HANGING OUT.
I GOT IT.
'DICK'S HANGING OUT.'
YES?
WE'RE HOMICIDE. THIS IS DET--
SCENE IS CLOSED.
WE WERE THE OFFICERS ASSIGNED. CAN WE...?
HE'S HERE.
ONE MOMENT.
WHO WAS THAT YOU JUST TALKED TO THERE?
WHAT DID YOU COME BACK HERE FOR, WALKER? LOSE YOUR PIECE?

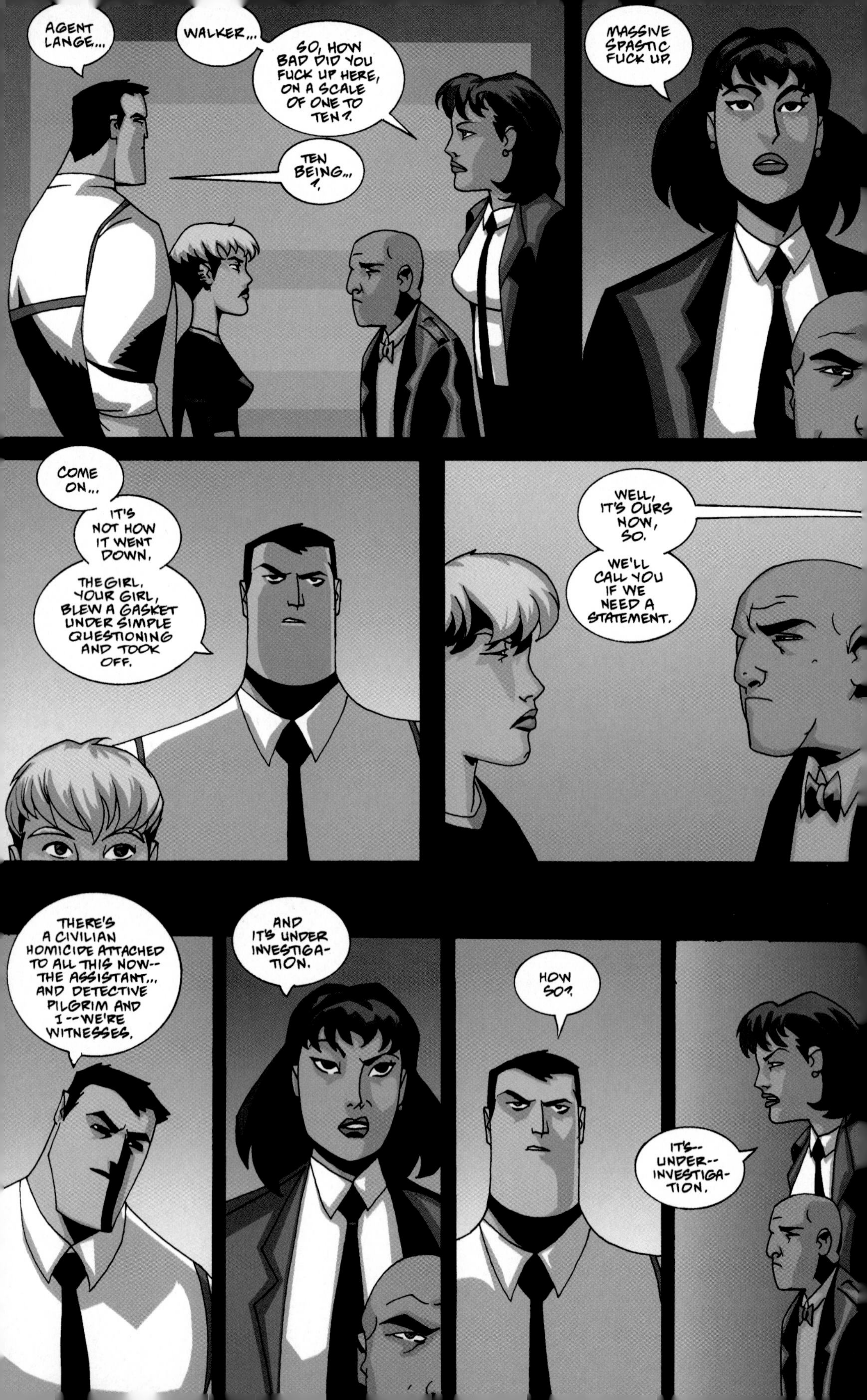
AGENT LANGE...
WALKER...
SO, HOW BAD DID YOU FUCK UP HERE, ON A SCALE OF ONE TO TEN?.
TEN BEING...?.
MASSIVE SPASTIC FUCK UP.
COME ON...
IT'S NOT HOW IT WENT DOWN.
THE GIRL, YOUR GIRL, BLEW A GASKET UNDER SIMPLE QUESTIONING AND TOOK OFF.
WELL, IT'S OURS NOW, SO.
WE'LL CALL YOU IF WE NEED A STATEMENT.
THERE'S A CIVILIAN HOMICIDE ATTACHED TO ALL THIS NOW-- THE ASSISTANT... AND DETECTIVE PILGRIM AND I--WE'RE WITNESSES.
AND IT'S UNDER INVESTIGATION.
HOW SO?
IT'S-- UNDER-- INVESTIGATION.

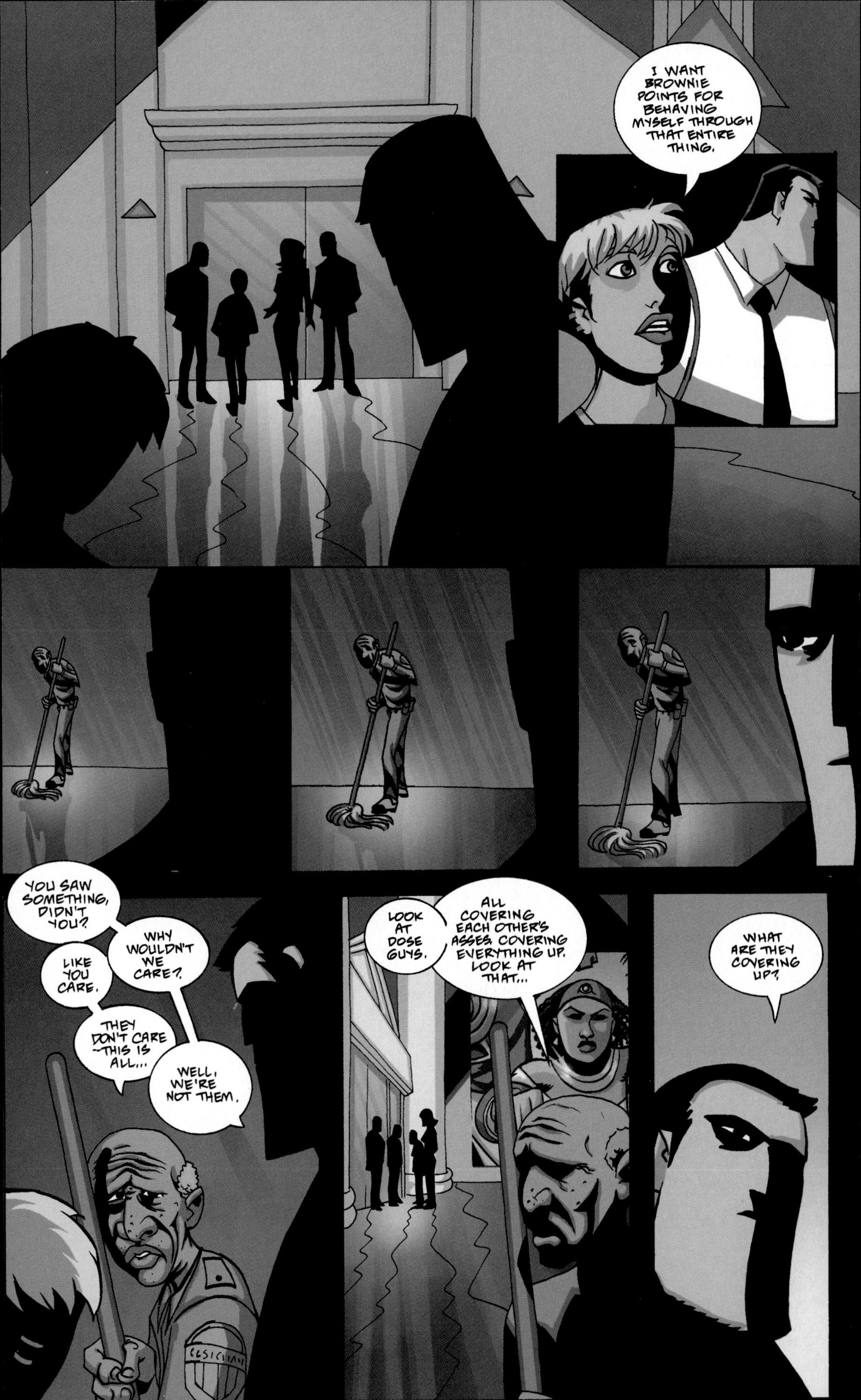
I WANT BROWNIE POINTS FOR BEHAVING MYSELF THROUGH THAT ENTIRE THING.
YOU SAW SOMETHING, DIDN'T YOU?
WHY WOULDN'T WE CARE?
LIKE YOU CARE.
THEY DON'T CARE --THIS IS ALL...
WELL, WE'RE NOT THEM.
LOOK AT DOSE GUYS.
ALL COVERING EACH OTHER'S ASSES, COVERING EVERYTHING UP. LOOK AT THAT...
WHAT ARE THEY COVERING UP?

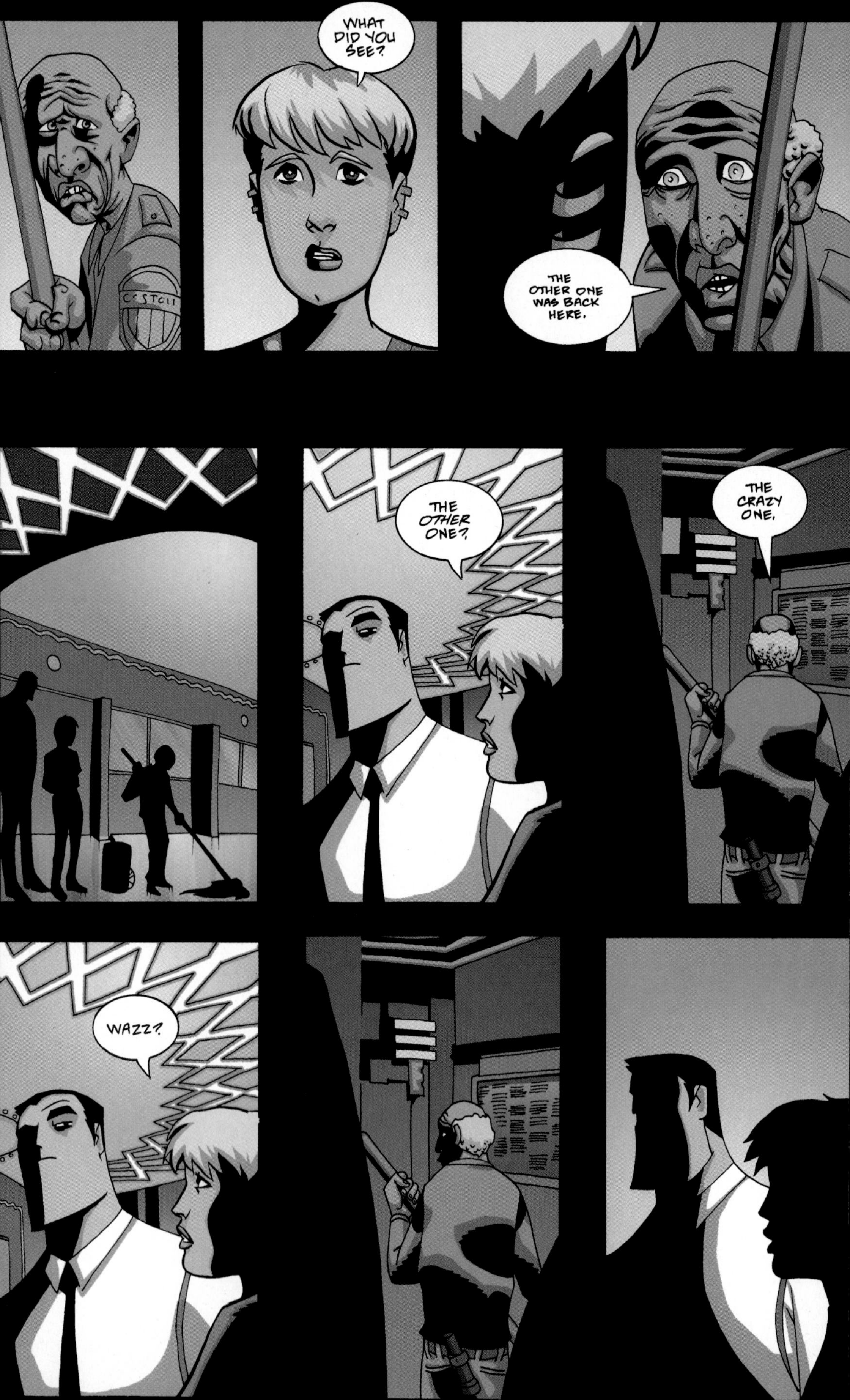
WHAT DID YOU SEE?
THE OTHER ONE WAS BACK HERE.
THE OTHER ONE?
THE CRAZY ONE.
WAZZ?

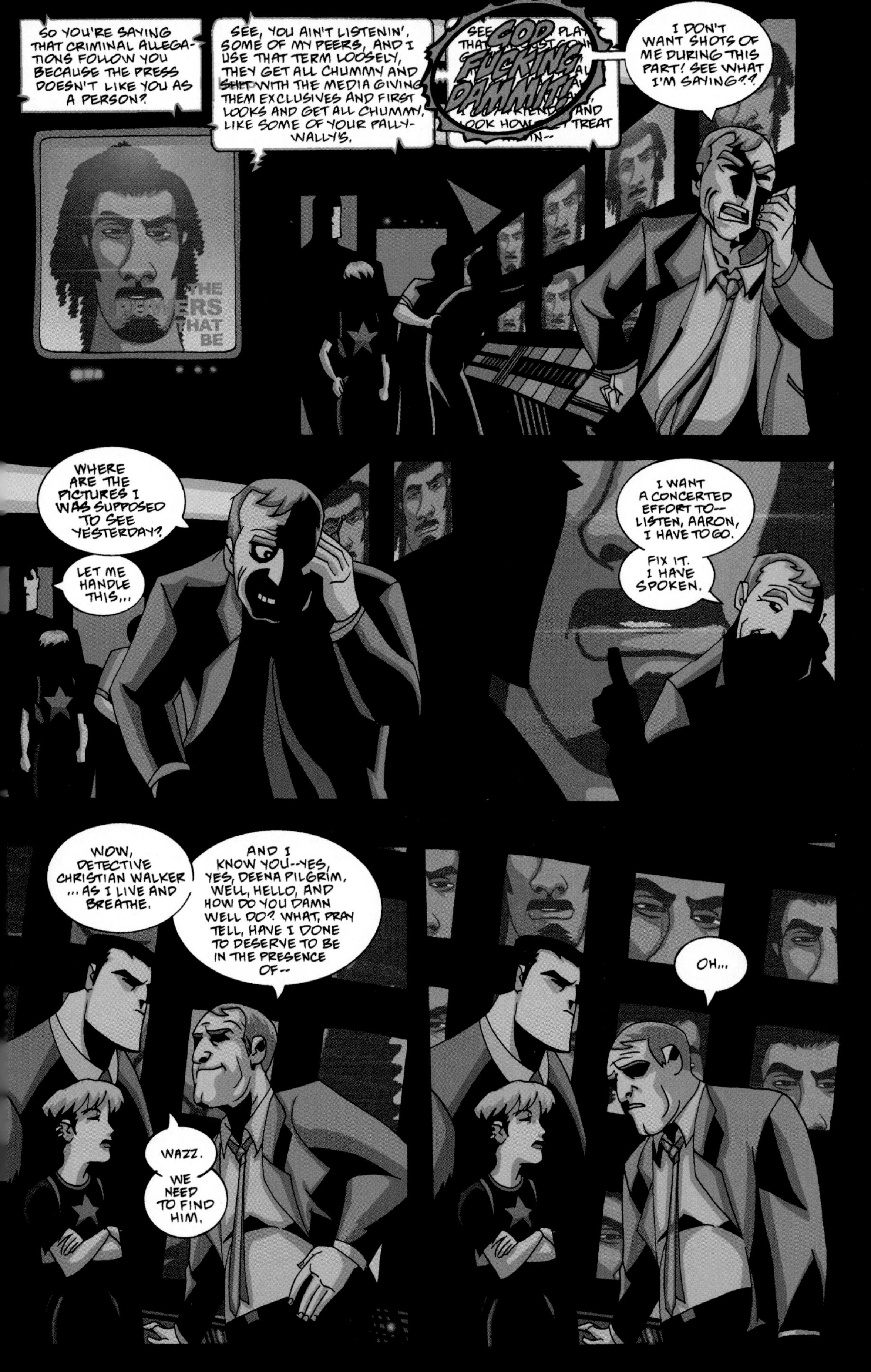

SO YOU'RE SAYING THAT CRIMINAL ALLEGATIONS FOLLOW YOU BECAUSE THE PRESS DOESN'T LIKE YOU AS A PERSON?
SEE, YOU AIN'T LISTENIN'. SOME OF MY PEERS, AND I USE THAT TERM LOOSELY, THEY GET ALL CHUMMY AND SHIT WITH THE MEDIA GIVING THEM EXCLUSIVES AND FIRST LOOKS AND GET ALL CHUMMY, LIKE SOME OF YOUR PALLY-WALLY'S.
GOD FUCKING DAMMIT!
I DON'T WANT SHOTS OF ME DURING THIS PART! SEE WHAT I'M SAYING??
THE POWERS THAT BE
WHERE ARE THE PICTURES I WAS SUPPOSED TO SEE YESTERDAY?
LET ME HANDLE THIS...
I WANT A CONCERTED EFFORT TO-- LISTEN, AARON, I HAVE TO GO.
FIX IT. I HAVE SPOKEN.
WOW, DETECTIVE CHRISTIAN WALKER ...AS I LIVE AND BREATHE.
AND I KNOW YOU--YES, YES, DEENA PILGRIM. WELL, HELLO, AND HOW DO YOU DAMN WELL DO? WHAT, PRAY TELL, HAVE I DONE TO DESERVE TO BE IN THE PRESENCE OF--
WAZZ.
WE NEED TO FIND HIM.
OH...

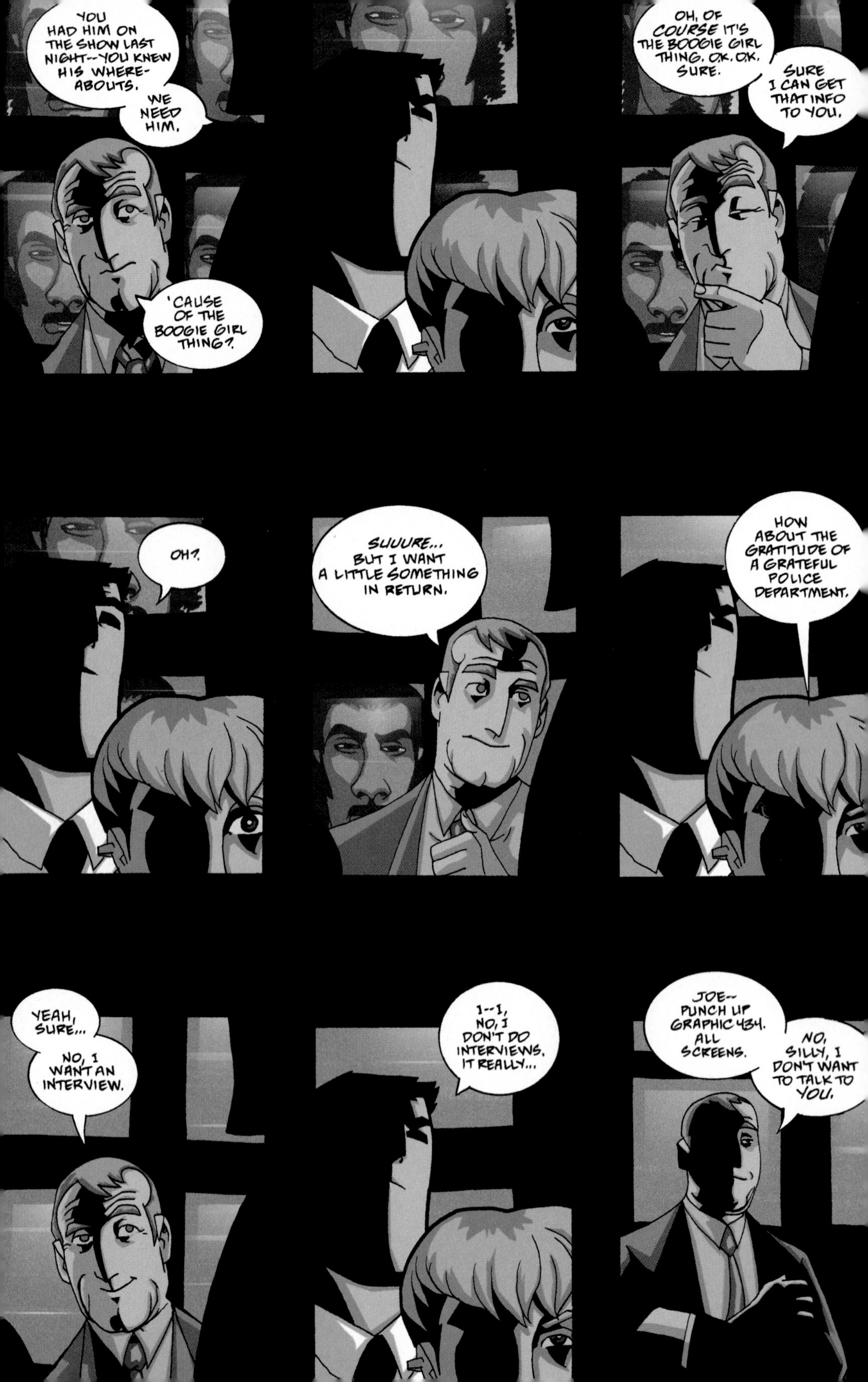
YOU HAD HIM ON THE SHOW LAST NIGHT--YOU KNEW HIS WHERE-ABOUTS.
WE NEED HIM.
'CAUSE OF THE BOOGIE GIRL THING?
OH, OF COURSE IT'S THE BOOGIE GIRL THING. O.K. O.K. SURE.
SURE I CAN GET THAT INFO TO YOU.
OH?
SUUURE... BUT I WANT A LITTLE SOMETHING IN RETURN.
HOW ABOUT THE GRATITUDE OF A GRATEFUL POLICE DEPARTMENT.
YEAH, SURE...
NO, I WANT AN INTERVIEW.
I--I, NO, I DON'T DO INTERVIEWS. IT REALLY...
JOE-- PUNCH UP GRAPHIC 434. ALL SCREENS.
NO, SILLY, I DON'T WANT TO TALK TO YOU.

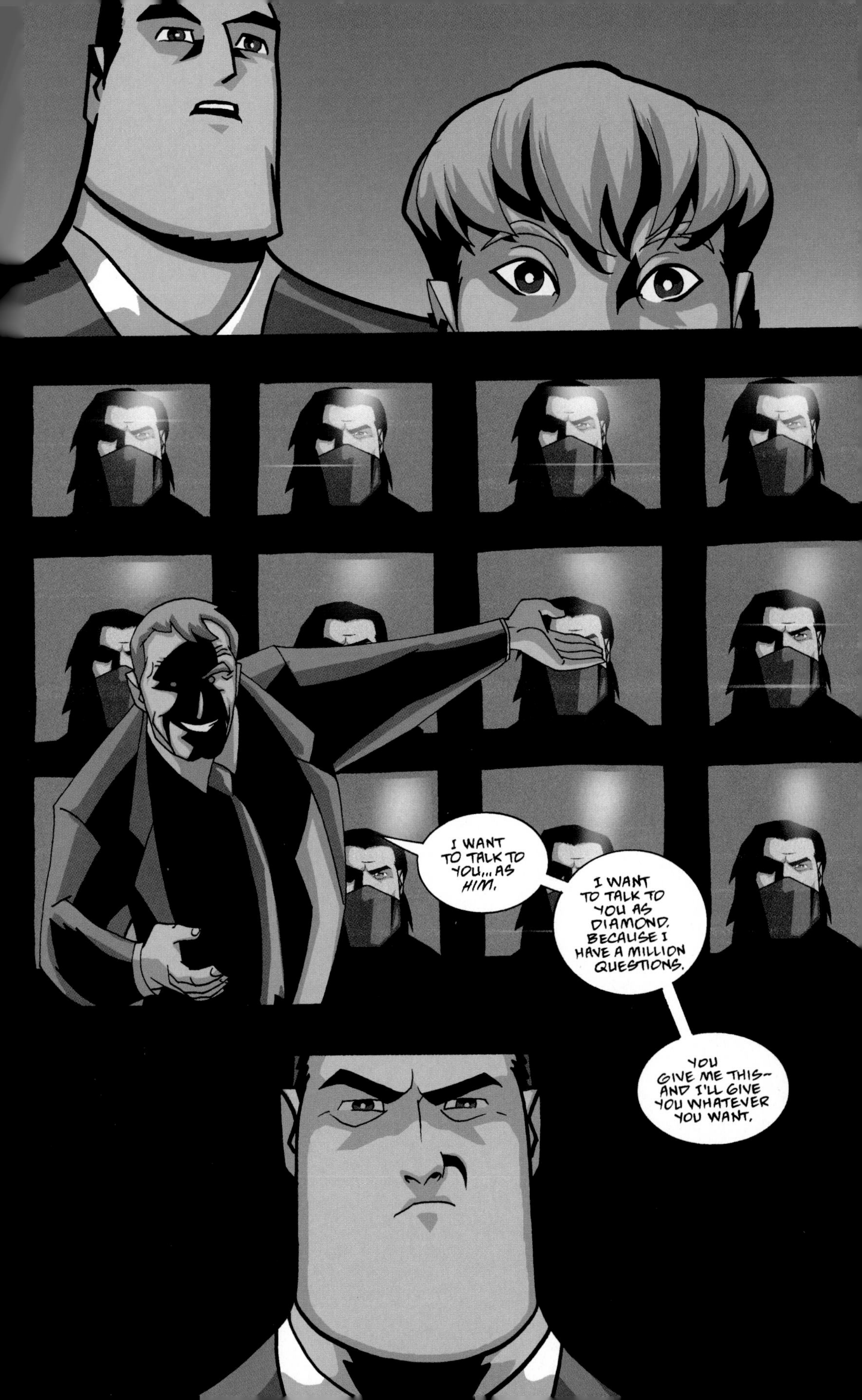
I WANT TO TALK TO YOU,,, AS HIM.
I WANT TO TALK TO YOU AS DIAMOND. BECAUSE I HAVE A MILLION QUESTIONS.
YOU GIVE ME THIS-- AND I'LL GIVE YOU WHATEVER YOU WANT.

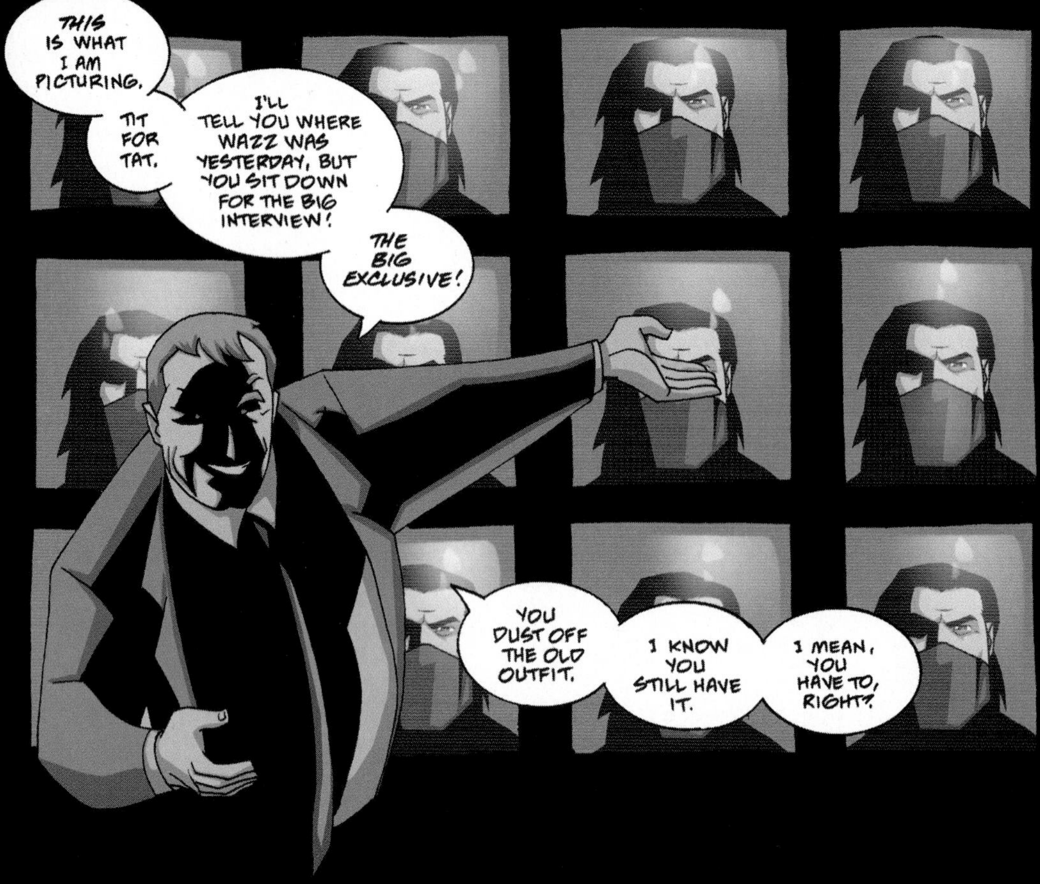
THIS IS WHAT I AM PICTURING.
TIT FOR TAT.
I'LL TELL YOU WHERE WAZZ WAS YESTERDAY, BUT YOU SIT DOWN FOR THE BIG INTERVIEW!
THE BIG EXCLUSIVE!
YOU DUST OFF THE OLD OUTFIT.
I KNOW YOU STILL HAVE IT.
I MEAN, YOU HAVE TO, RIGHT?

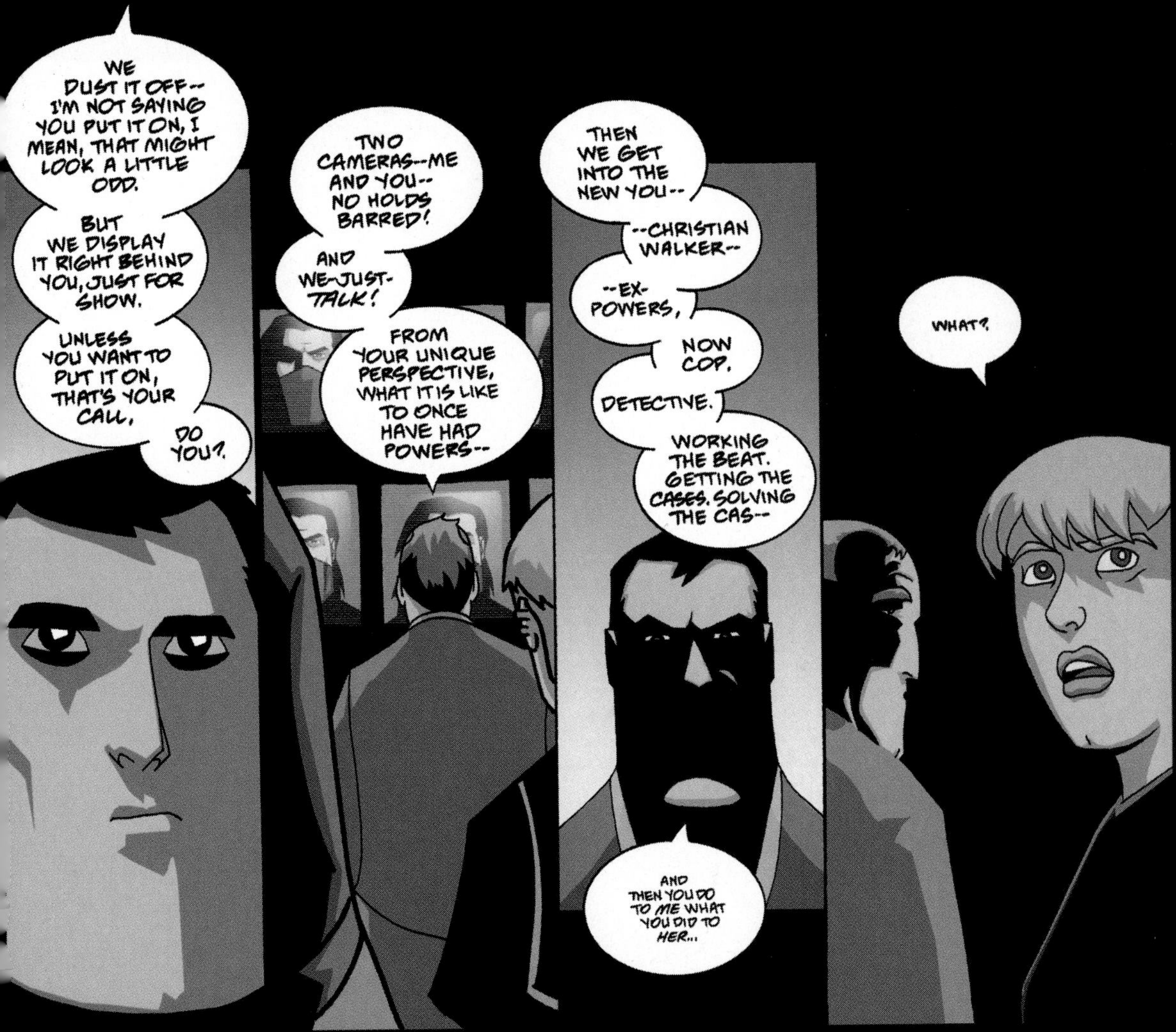
WE DUST IT OFF-- I'M NOT SAYING YOU PUT IT ON, I MEAN, THAT MIGHT LOOK A LITTLE ODD.
BUT WE DISPLAY IT RIGHT BEHIND YOU, JUST FOR SHOW.
UNLESS YOU WANT TO PUT IT ON, THAT'S YOUR CALL.
DO YOU?
TWO CAMERAS--ME AND YOU-- NO HOLDS BARRED!
AND WE--JUST--TALK!
FROM YOUR UNIQUE PERSPECTIVE, WHAT IT IS LIKE TO ONCE HAVE HAD POWERS--
THEN WE GET INTO THE NEW YOU--
--CHRISTIAN WALKER--
--EX-POWERS,
NOW COP.
DETECTIVE.
WORKING THE BEAT. GETTING THE CASES. SOLVING THE CAS--
AND THEN YOU DO TO ME WHAT YOU DID TO HER...
WHAT?

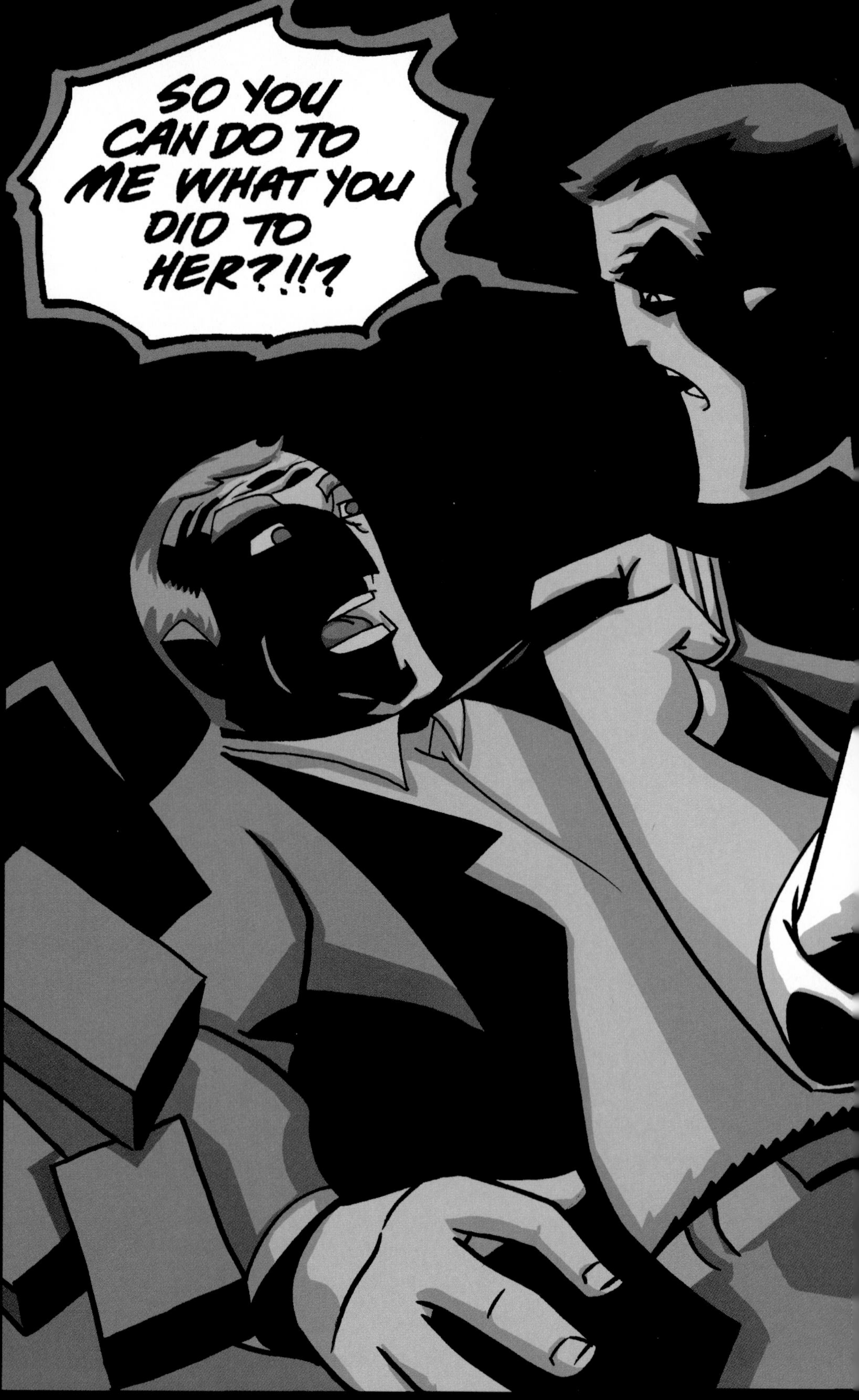
SO YOU CAN DO TO ME WHAT YOU DID TO HER?!!?

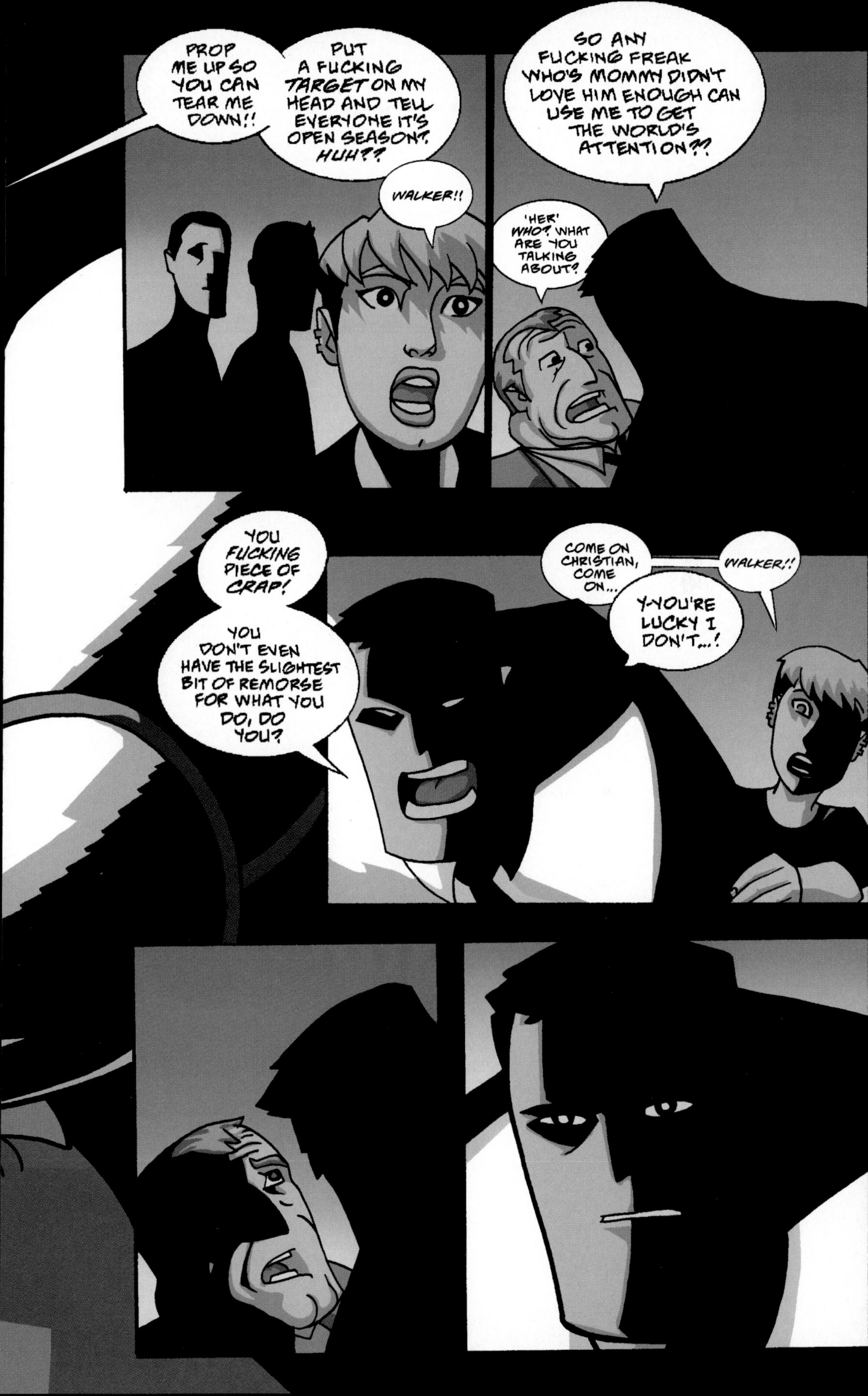
PROP ME UP SO YOU CAN TEAR ME DOWN!!
PUT A FUCKING TARGET ON MY HEAD AND TELL EVERYONE IT'S OPEN SEASON? HUH??
WALKER!!
SO ANY FUCKING FREAK WHO'S MOMMY DIDN'T LOVE HIM ENOUGH CAN USE ME TO GET THE WORLD'S ATTENTION??
'HER' WHO? WHAT ARE YOU TALKING ABOUT?
YOU FUCKING PIECE OF CRAP!
YOU DON'T EVEN HAVE THE SLIGHTEST BIT OF REMORSE FOR WHAT YOU DO, DO YOU?
COME ON CHRISTIAN, COME ON...
WALKER!!
Y-YOU'RE LUCKY I DON'T...!

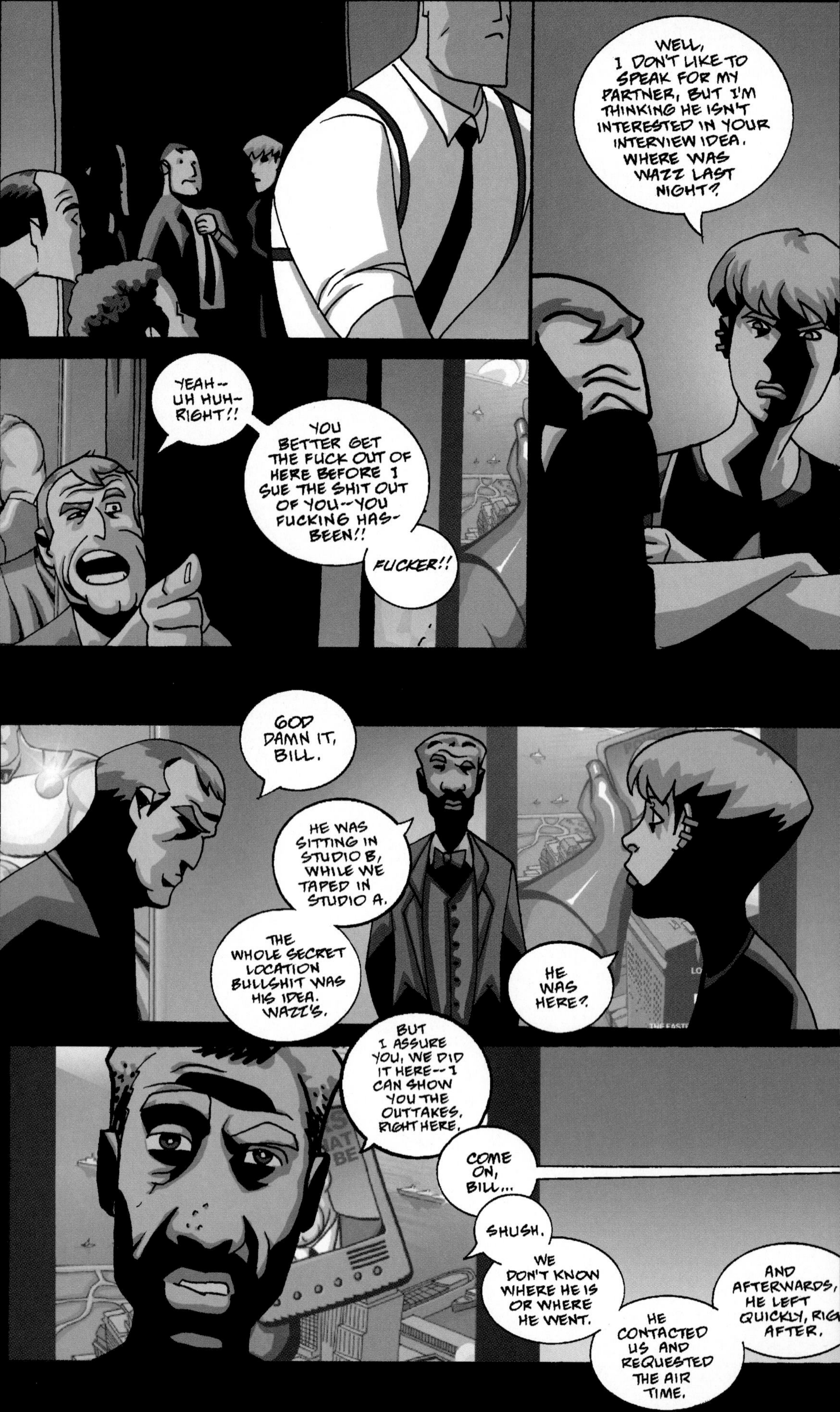
WELL, I DON'T LIKE TO SPEAK FOR MY PARTNER, BUT I'M THINKING HE ISN'T INTERESTED IN YOUR INTERVIEW IDEA. WHERE WAS WAZZ LAST NIGHT?
YEAH-- UH HUH- RIGHT!!
YOU BETTER GET THE FUCK OUT OF HERE BEFORE I SUE THE SHIT OUT OF YOU--YOU FUCKING HAS-BEEN!!
FUCKER!!
GOD DAMN IT, BILL.
HE WAS SITTING IN STUDIO B, WHILE WE TAPED IN STUDIO A.
THE WHOLE SECRET LOCATION BULLSHIT WAS HIS IDEA. WAZZ'S.
HE WAS HERE?
BUT I ASSURE YOU, WE DID IT HERE-- I CAN SHOW YOU THE OUTTAKES, RIGHT HERE.
COME ON, BILL...
SHUSH.
WE DON'T KNOW WHERE HE IS OR WHERE HE WENT.
HE CONTACTED US AND REQUESTED THE AIR TIME.
AND AFTERWARDS, HE LEFT QUICKLY, RIG AFTER.

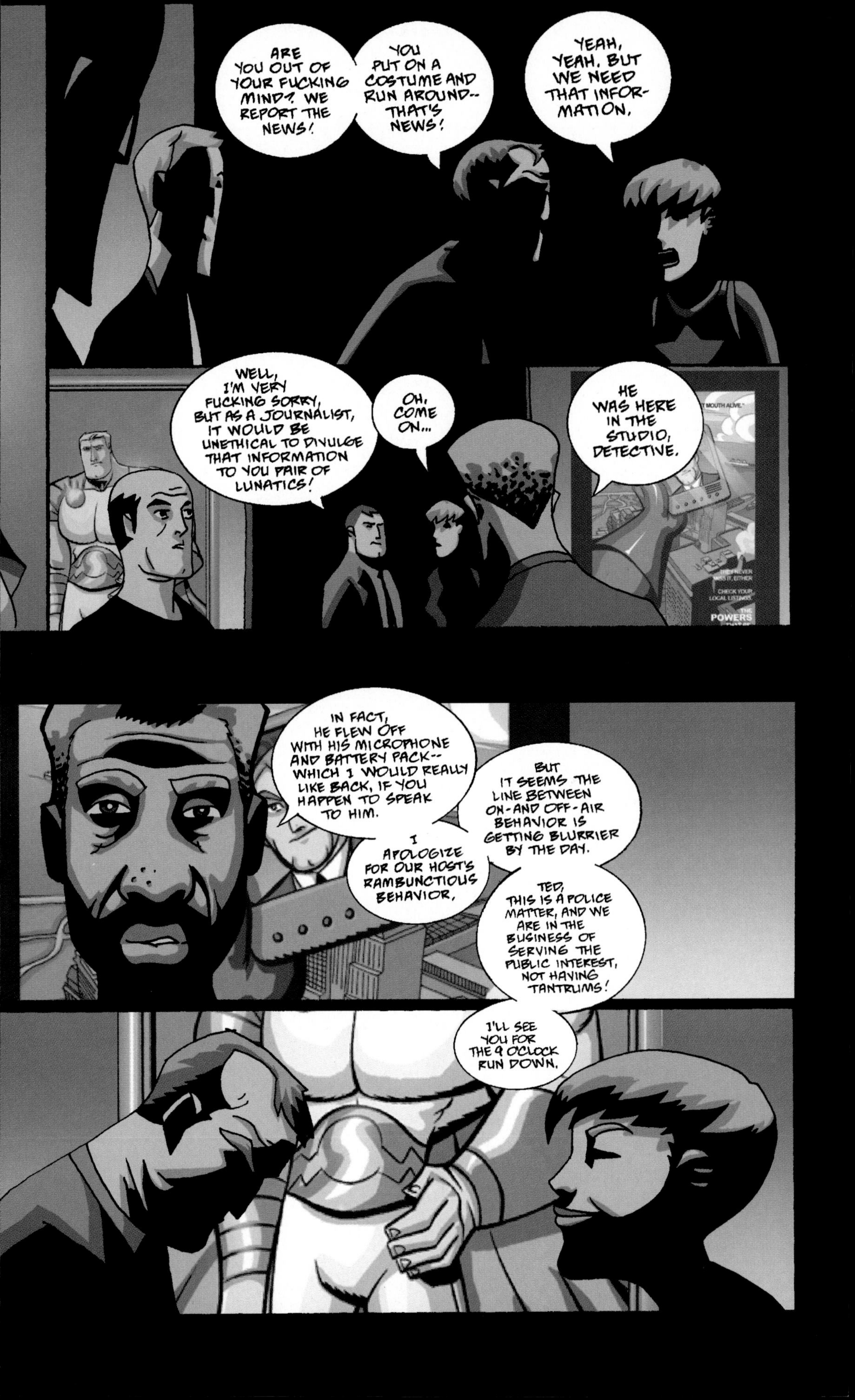
ARE YOU OUT OF YOUR FUCKING MIND? WE REPORT THE NEWS!
YOU PUT ON A COSTUME AND RUN AROUND-- THAT'S NEWS!
YEAH, YEAH, BUT WE NEED THAT INFORMATION.
WELL, I'M VERY FUCKING SORRY, BUT AS A JOURNALIST, IT WOULD BE UNETHICAL TO DIVULGE THAT INFORMATION TO YOU PAIR OF LUNATICS!
OH, COME ON...
HE WAS HERE IN THE STUDIO, DETECTIVE.
THE POWERS
IN FACT, HE FLEW OFF WITH HIS MICROPHONE AND BATTERY PACK-- WHICH I WOULD REALLY LIKE BACK, IF YOU HAPPEN TO SPEAK TO HIM.
I APOLOGIZE FOR OUR HOST'S RAMBUNCTIOUS BEHAVIOR.
BUT IT SEEMS THE LINE BETWEEN ON- AND OFF-AIR BEHAVIOR IS GETTING BLURRIER BY THE DAY.
TED, THIS IS A POLICE MATTER, AND WE ARE IN THE BUSINESS OF SERVING THE PUBLIC INTEREST, NOT HAVING TANTRUMS!
I'LL SEE YOU FOR THE 9 O'CLOCK RUN DOWN.

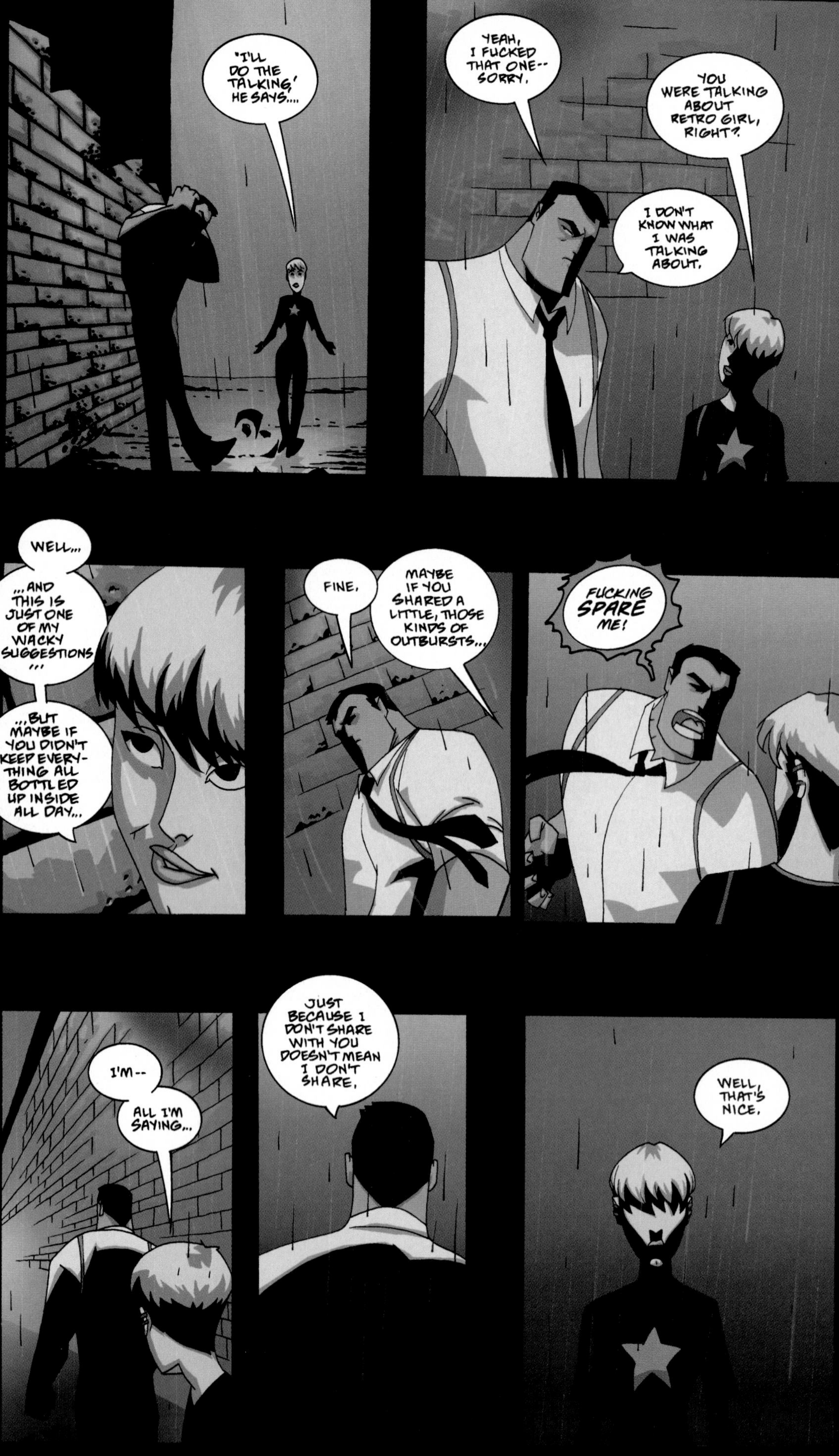
"I'LL DO THE TALKING,' HE SAYS....
YEAH, I FUCKED THAT ONE-- SORRY.
YOU WERE TALKING ABOUT RETRO GIRL, RIGHT?
I DON'T KNOW WHAT I WAS TALKING ABOUT.
WELL...
...AND THIS IS JUST ONE OF MY WACKY SUGGESTIONS...
...BUT MAYBE IF YOU DIDN'T KEEP EVERY-THING ALL BOTTLED UP INSIDE ALL DAY...
FINE.
MAYBE IF YOU SHARED A LITTLE, THOSE KINDS OF OUTBURSTS...
FUCKING SPARE ME!
I'M--
ALL I'M SAYING...
JUST BECAUSE I DON'T SHARE WITH YOU DOESN'T MEAN I DON'T SHARE.
WELL, THAT'S NICE.

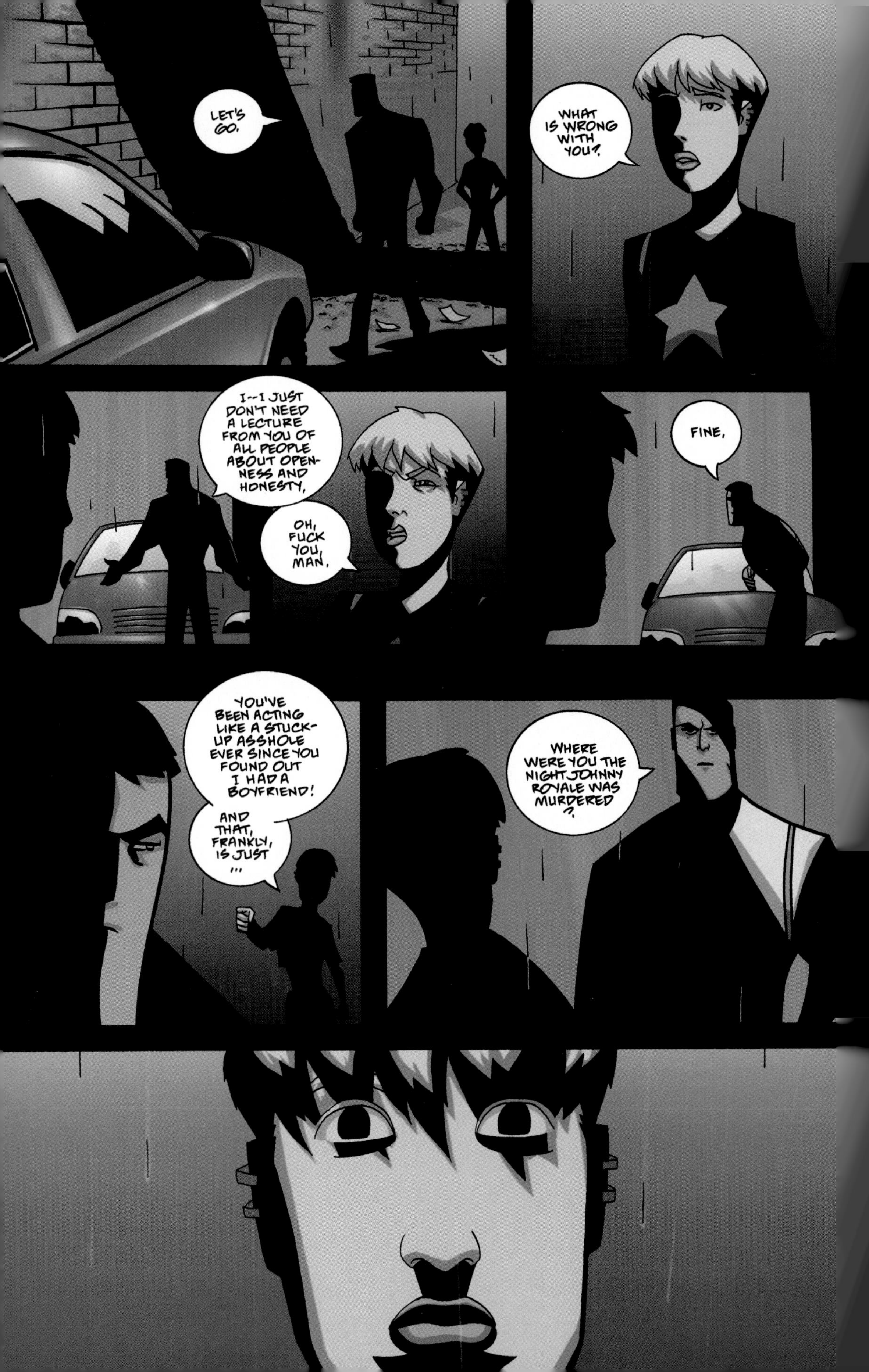
LET'S GO.
WHAT IS WRONG WITH YOU?
I--I JUST DON'T NEED A LECTURE FROM YOU OF ALL PEOPLE ABOUT OPENNESS AND HONESTY.
OH, FUCK YOU, MAN.
FINE.
YOU'VE BEEN ACTING LIKE A STUCK-UP ASSHOLE EVER SINCE YOU FOUND OUT I HAD A BOYFRIEND!
AND THAT, FRANKLY, IS JUST ...
WHERE WERE YOU THE NIGHT JOHNNY ROYALE WAS MURDERED?

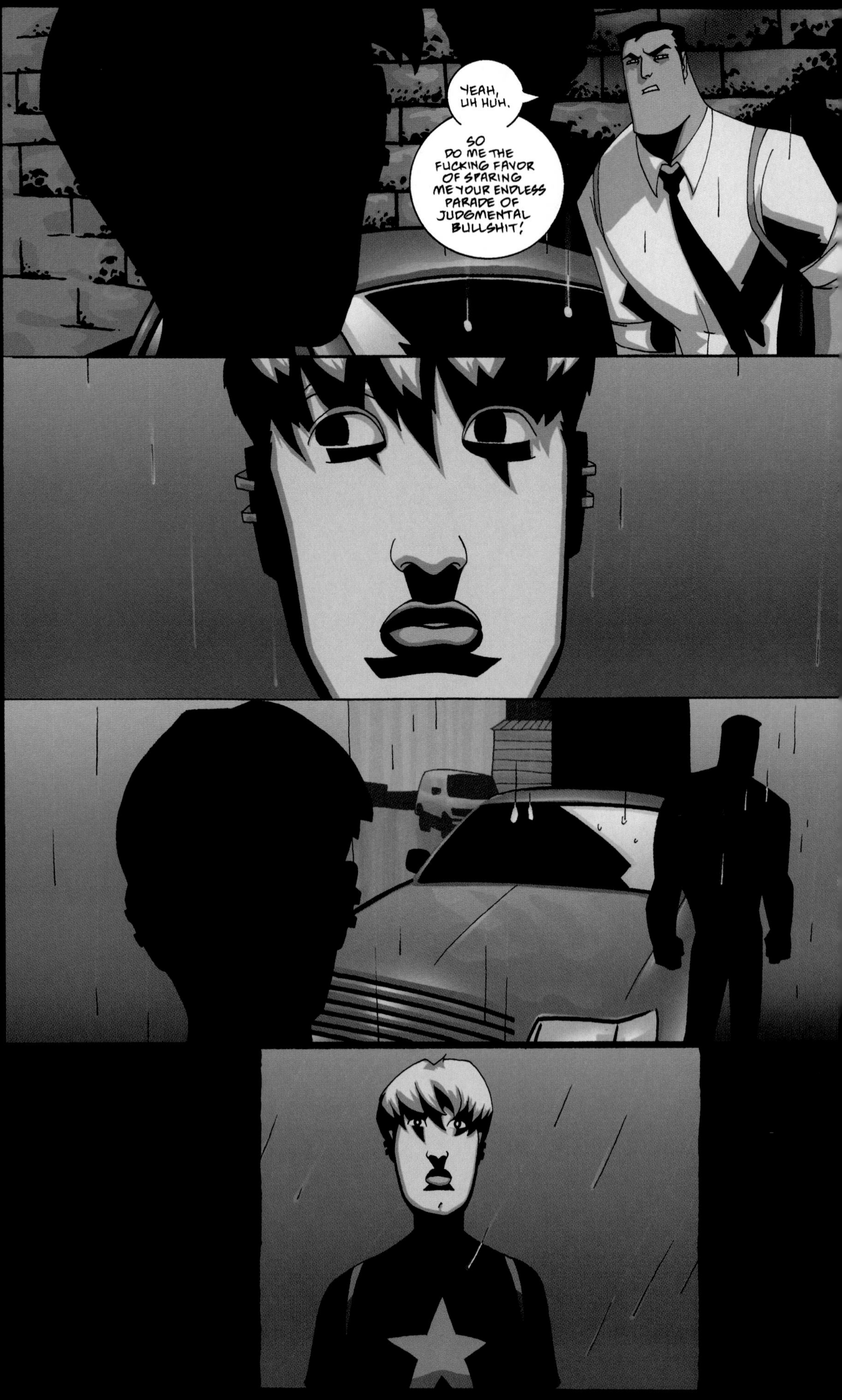
YEAH, UH HUH.
SO DO ME THE FUCKING FAVOR OF SPARING ME YOUR ENDLESS PARADE OF JUDGMENTAL BULLSHIT!

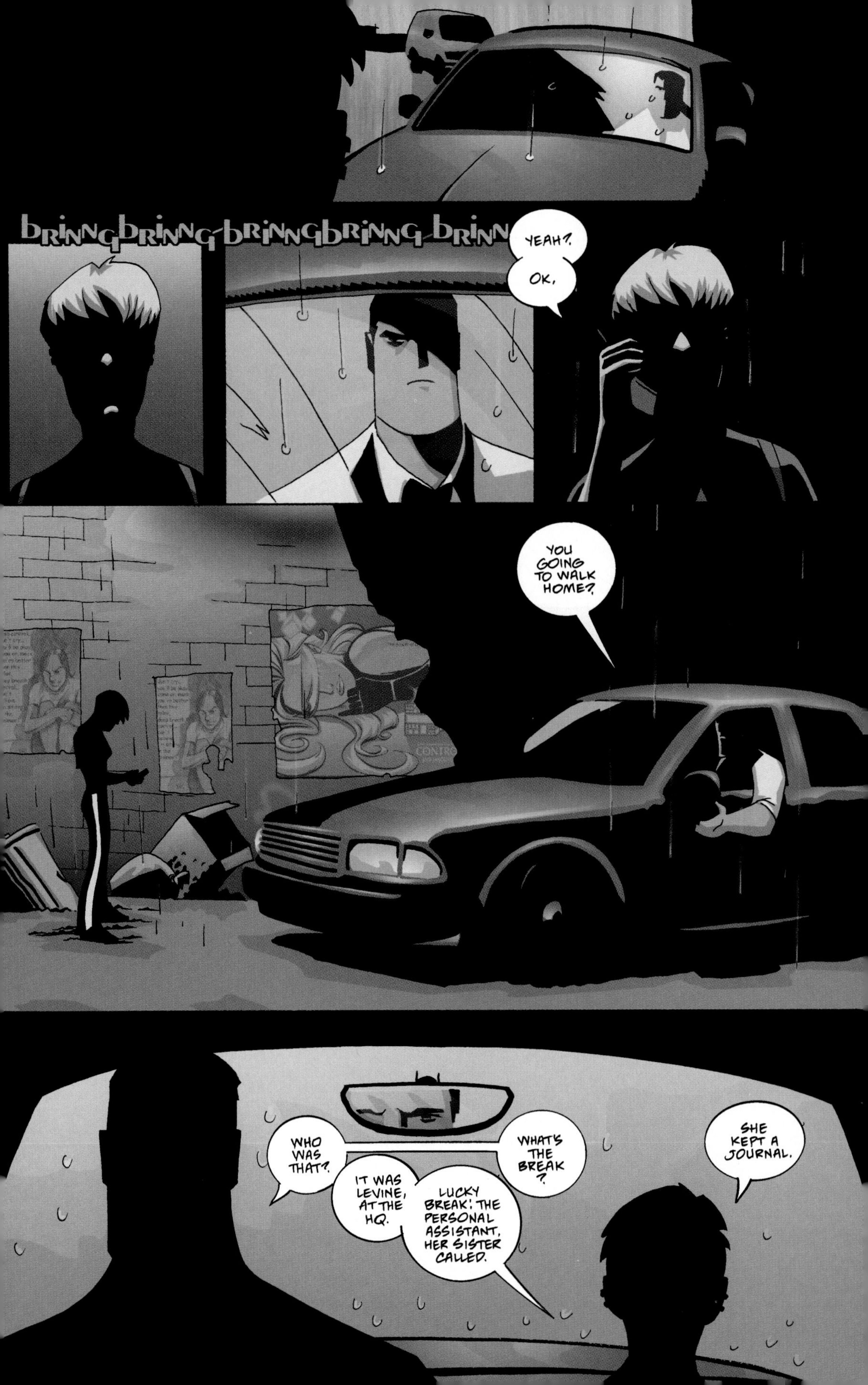
bRiNNGbRiNNG bRiNNGbRiNNG bRiNN
YEAH?
OK.
YOU GOING TO WALK HOME?
WHO WAS THAT?
IT WAS LEVINE, AT THE HQ.
WHAT'S THE BREAK?
LUCKY BREAK: THE PERSONAL ASSISTANT, HER SISTER CALLED.
SHE KEPT A JOURNAL.

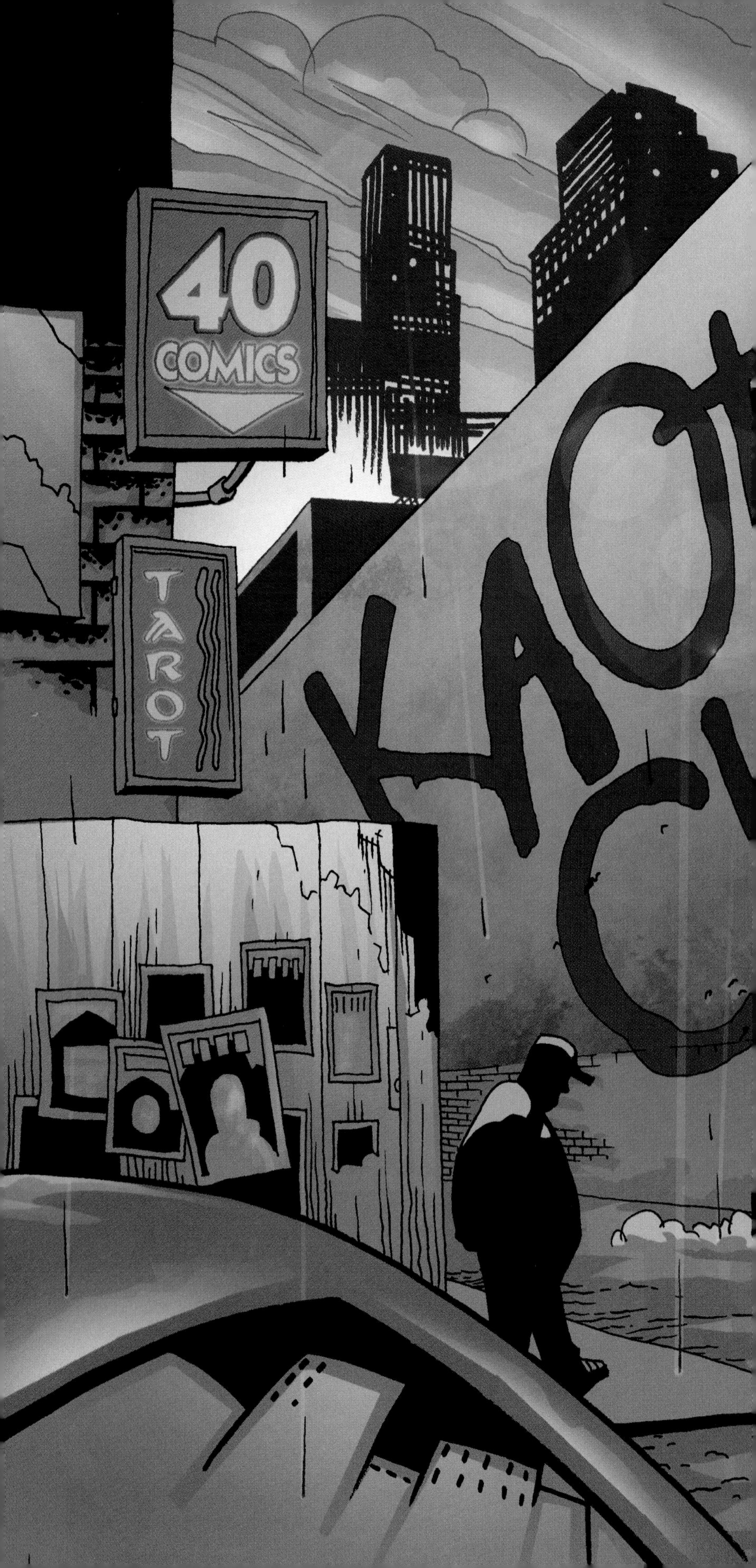
40
COMICS
TAROT

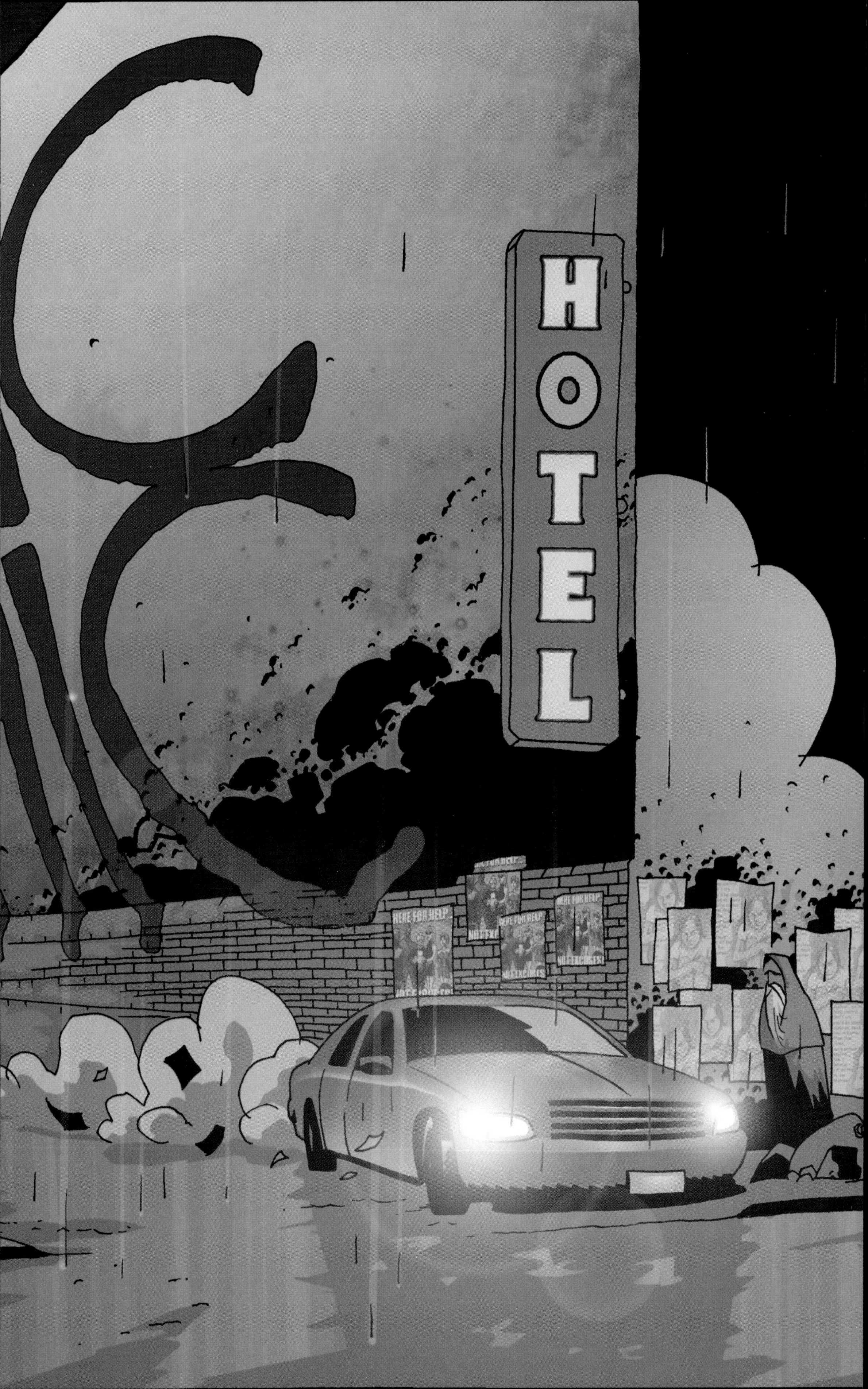
HOTEL

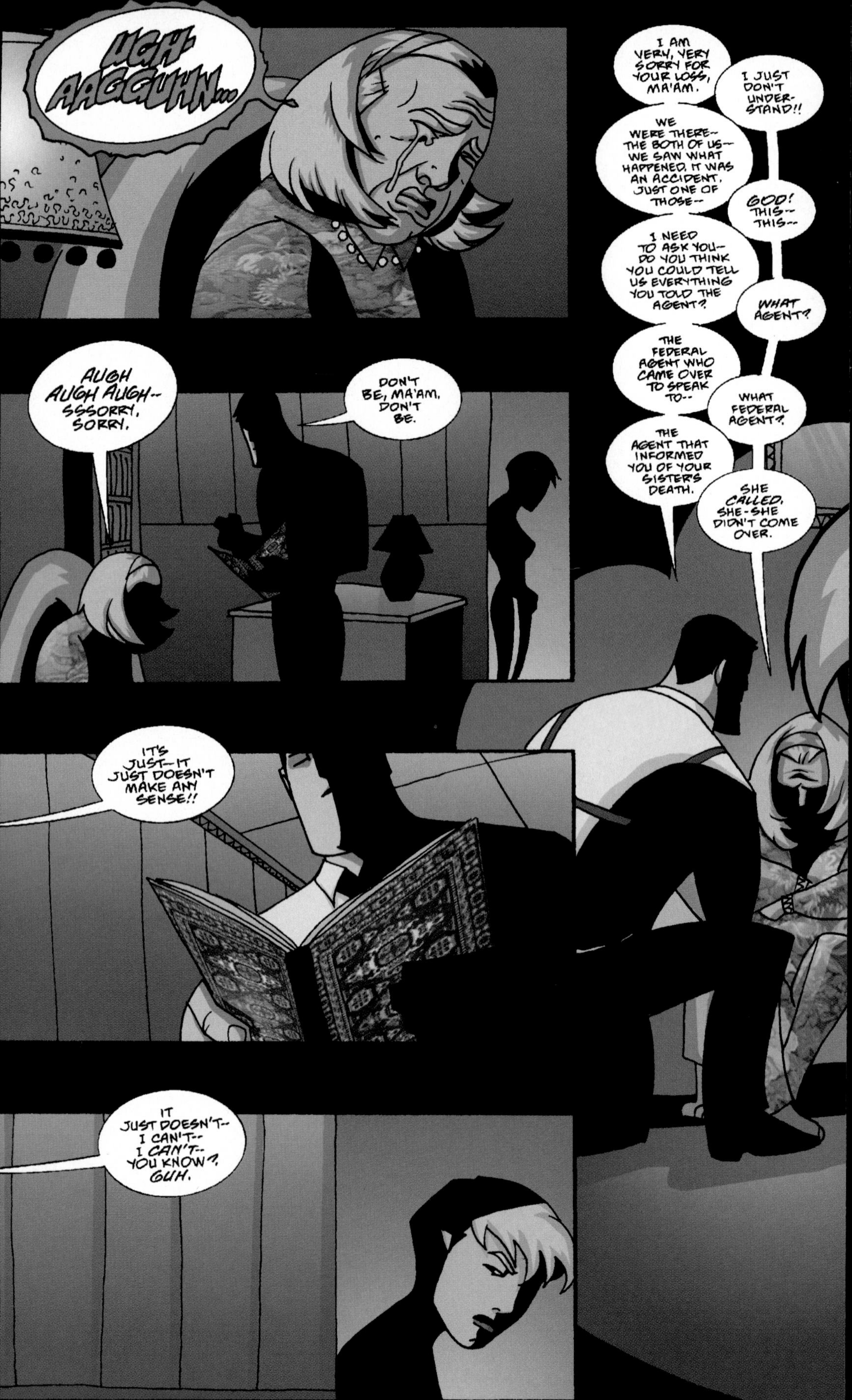
UGH-AAGGUHN...
AUGH AUGH AUGH-- SSSORRY, SORRY.
DON'T BE, MA'AM, DON'T BE.
IT'S JUST--IT JUST DOESN'T MAKE ANY SENSE!!
IT JUST DOESN'T-- I CAN'T-- I CAN'T-- YOU KNOW? GUH.
I AM VERY, VERY SORRY FOR YOUR LOSS, MA'AM.
I JUST DON'T UNDER-STAND!!
WE WERE THERE-- THE BOTH OF US-- WE SAW WHAT HAPPENED. IT WAS AN ACCIDENT. JUST ONE OF THOSE--
GOD! THIS-- THIS--
I NEED TO ASK YOU-- DO YOU THINK YOU COULD TELL US EVERYTHING YOU TOLD THE AGENT?
WHAT AGENT?
THE FEDERAL AGENT WHO CAME OVER TO SPEAK TO--
WHAT FEDERAL AGENT?
THE AGENT THAT INFORMED YOU OF YOUR SISTER'S DEATH.
SHE CALLED. SHE-SHE DIDN'T COME OVER.

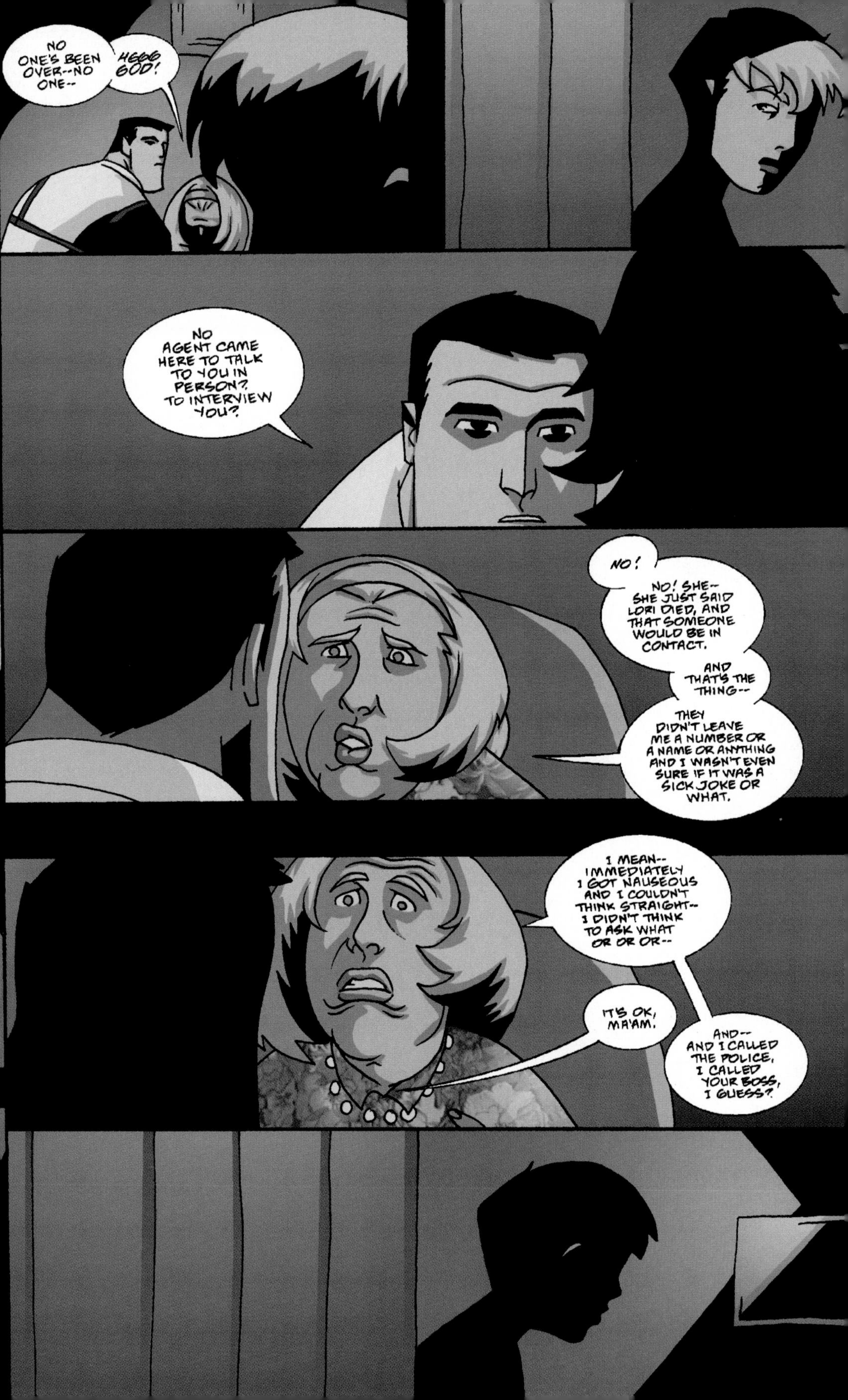
NO ONE'S BEEN OVER--NO ONE--
UGGG GOD!
NO AGENT CAME HERE TO TALK TO YOU IN PERSON? TO INTERVIEW YOU?
NO!
NO! SHE-- SHE JUST SAID LORI DIED, AND THAT SOMEONE WOULD BE IN CONTACT.
AND THAT'S THE THING--
THEY DIDN'T LEAVE ME A NUMBER OR A NAME OR ANYTHING AND I WASN'T EVEN SURE IF IT WAS A SICK JOKE OR WHAT.
I MEAN-- IMMEDIATELY I GOT NAUSEOUS AND I COULDN'T THINK STRAIGHT-- I DIDN'T THINK TO ASK WHAT OR OR OR--
IT'S OK, MA'AM.
AND-- AND I CALLED THE POLICE, I CALLED YOUR BOSS, I GUESS?

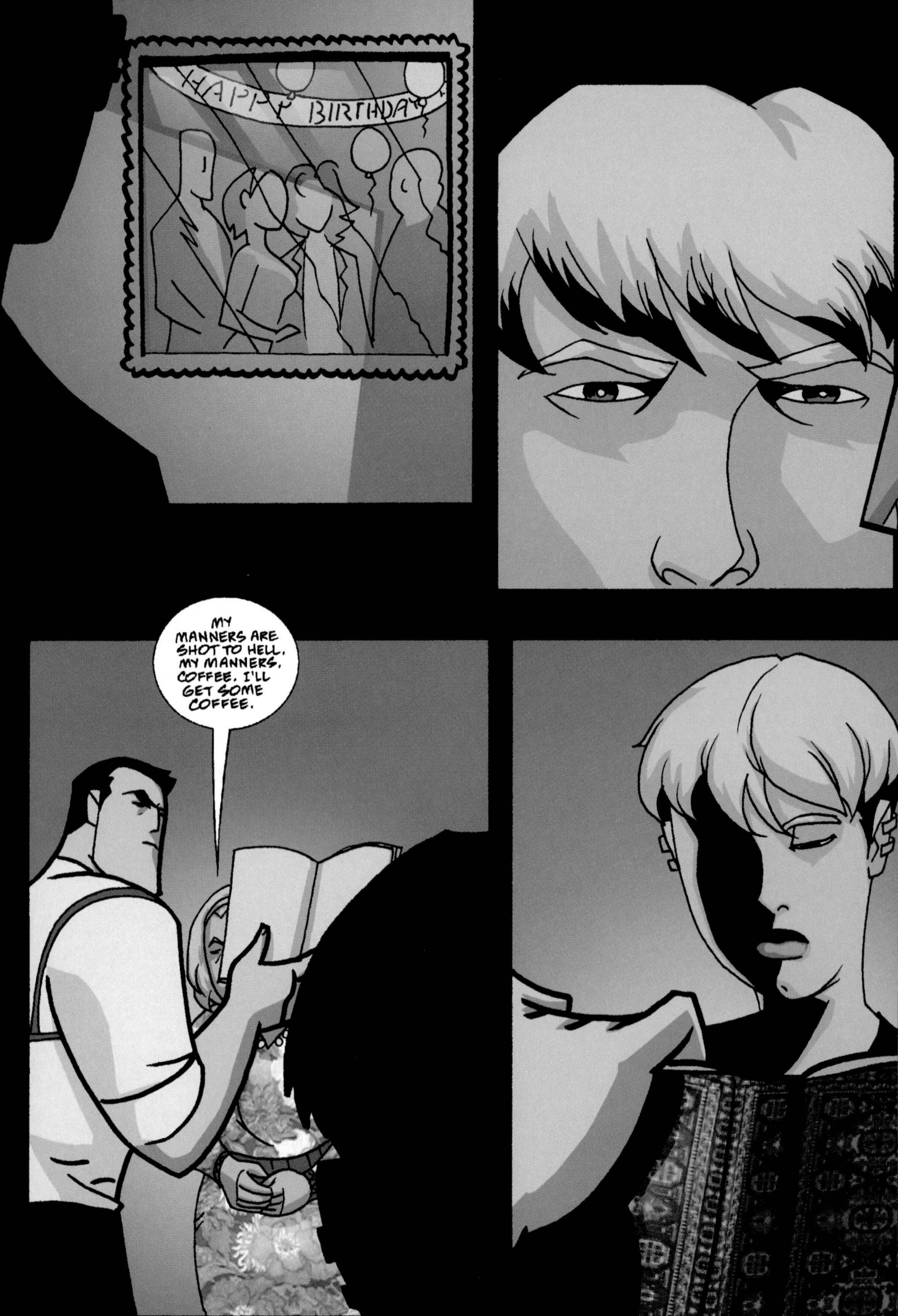
HAPPY BIRTHDAY
MY MANNERS ARE SHOT TO HELL. MY MANNERS. COFFEE. I'LL GET SOME COFFEE.

COFFEE! COFFEE! I SHOULD HAVE GOTTEN YOU SOME COFFEE!

THAT'S OK, MA'AM,

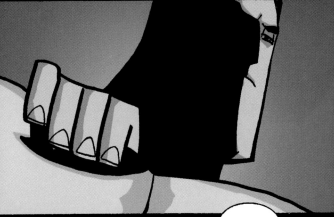

WHAT A FUCKER,

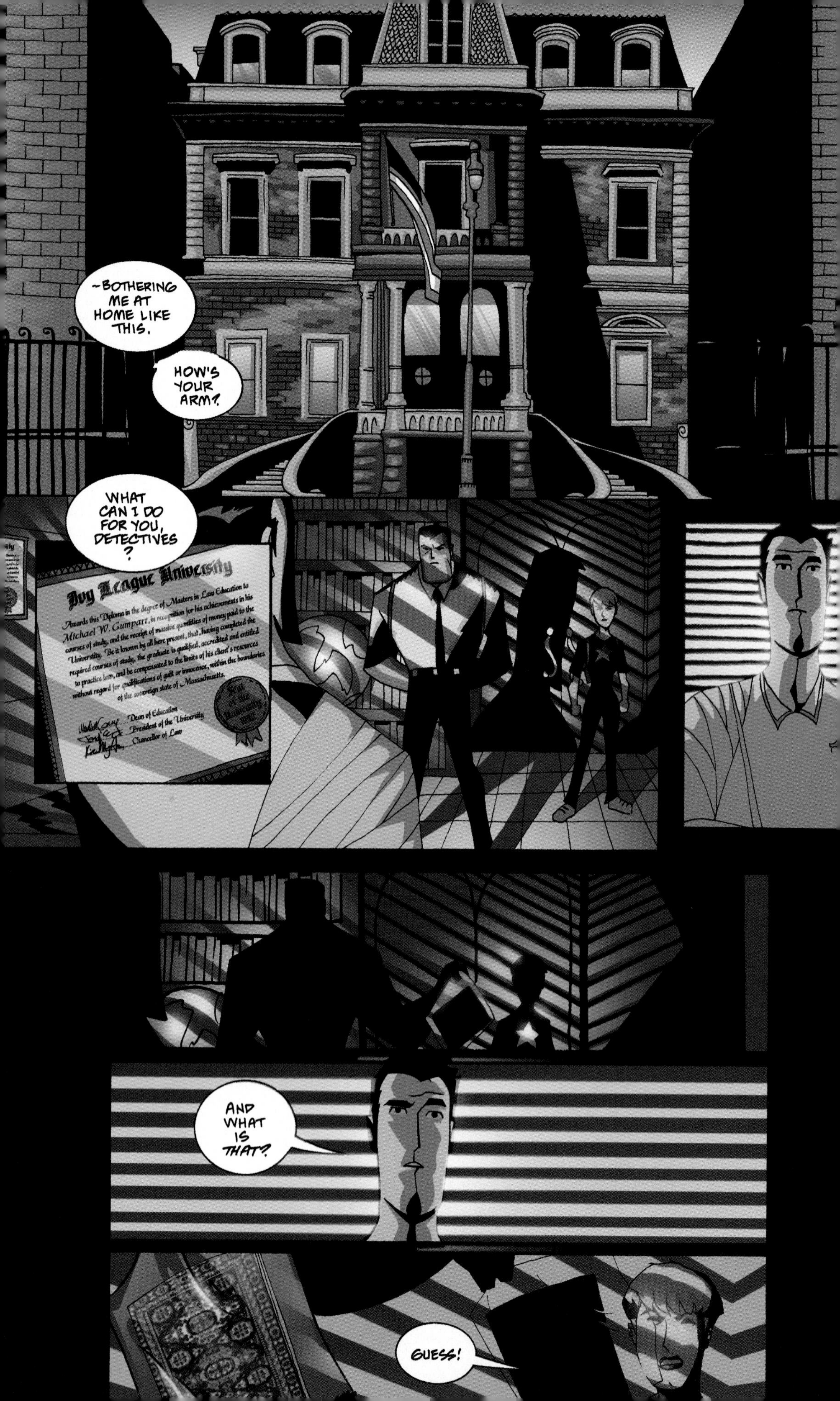
~BOTHERING ME AT HOME LIKE THIS.
HOW'S YOUR ARM?
WHAT CAN I DO FOR YOU, DETECTIVES?
Ivy League University
Awards this Diploma in the degree of Masters in Law Education to Michael W. Gumpart, in recognition for his achievements in his courses of study, and the receipt of massive quantities of money paid to the University. Be it known by all here present, that, having completed the required courses of study, the graduate is qualified, accredited and entitled to practice law, and be compensated to the limits of his client's resources without regard for qualifications of guilt or innocence, within the boundaries of the sovereign state of Massachusetts.
Seal of the University
Dean of Education
President of the University
Chancellor of Law
AND WHAT IS *THAT*?
GUESS!

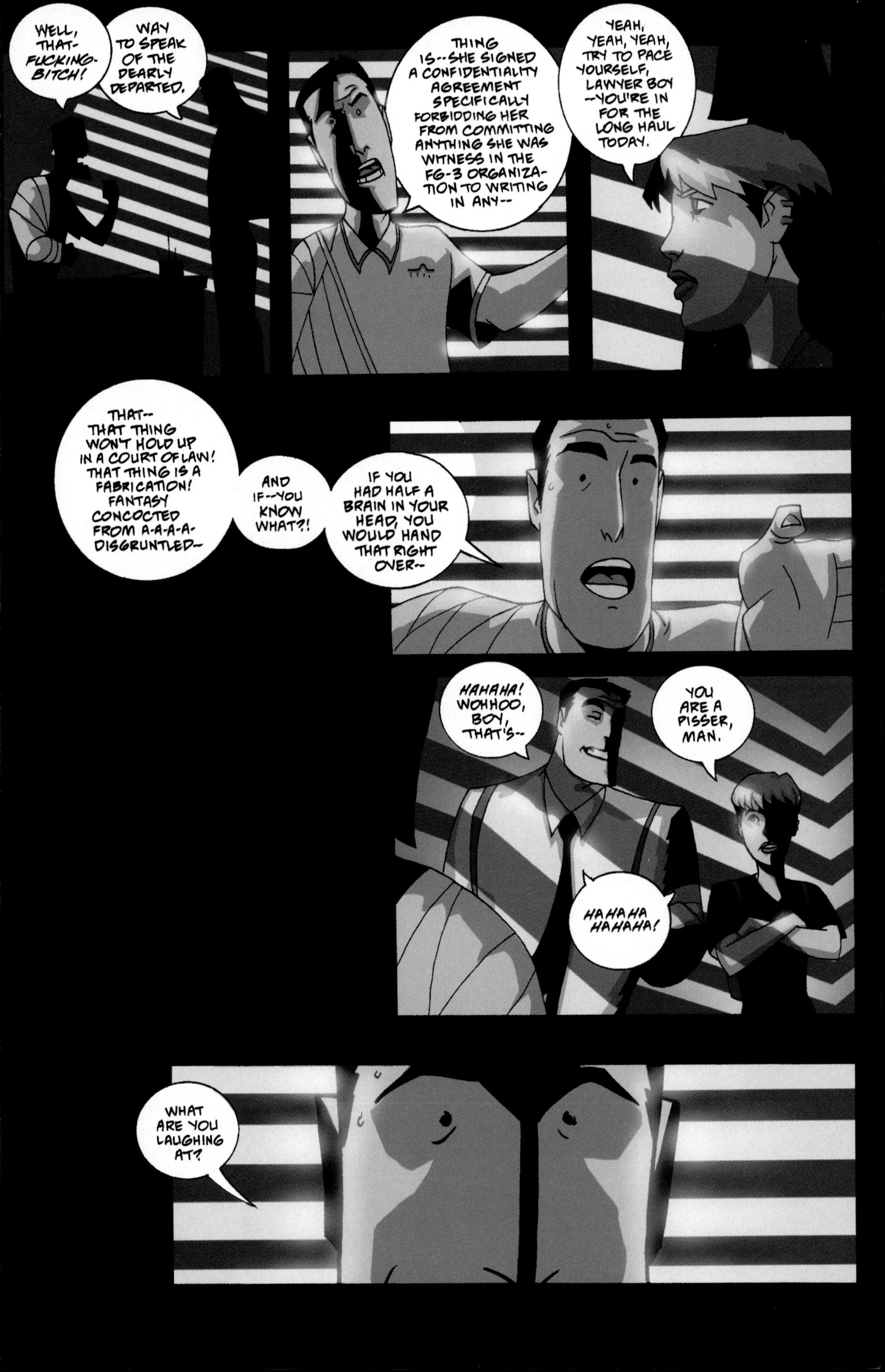
WELL, THAT-FUCKING-BITCH!
WAY TO SPEAK OF THE DEARLY DEPARTED.
THING IS--SHE SIGNED A CONFIDENTIALITY AGREEMENT SPECIFICALLY FORBIDDING HER FROM COMMITTING ANYTHING SHE WAS WITNESS IN THE FG-3 ORGANIZATION TO WRITING IN ANY--
YEAH, YEAH, YEAH, TRY TO PACE YOURSELF, LAWYER BOY --YOU'RE IN FOR THE LONG HAUL TODAY.
THAT--THAT THING WON'T HOLD UP IN A COURT OF LAW! THAT THING IS A FABRICATION! FANTASY CONCOCTED FROM A-A-A-A-DISGRUNTLED--
AND IF--YOU KNOW WHAT?!
IF YOU HAD HALF A BRAIN IN YOUR HEAD, YOU WOULD HAND THAT RIGHT OVER--
HAHAHA! WOHHOO, BOY, THAT'S--
YOU ARE A PISSER, MAN.
HAHAHA HAHAHA!
WHAT ARE YOU LAUGHING AT?

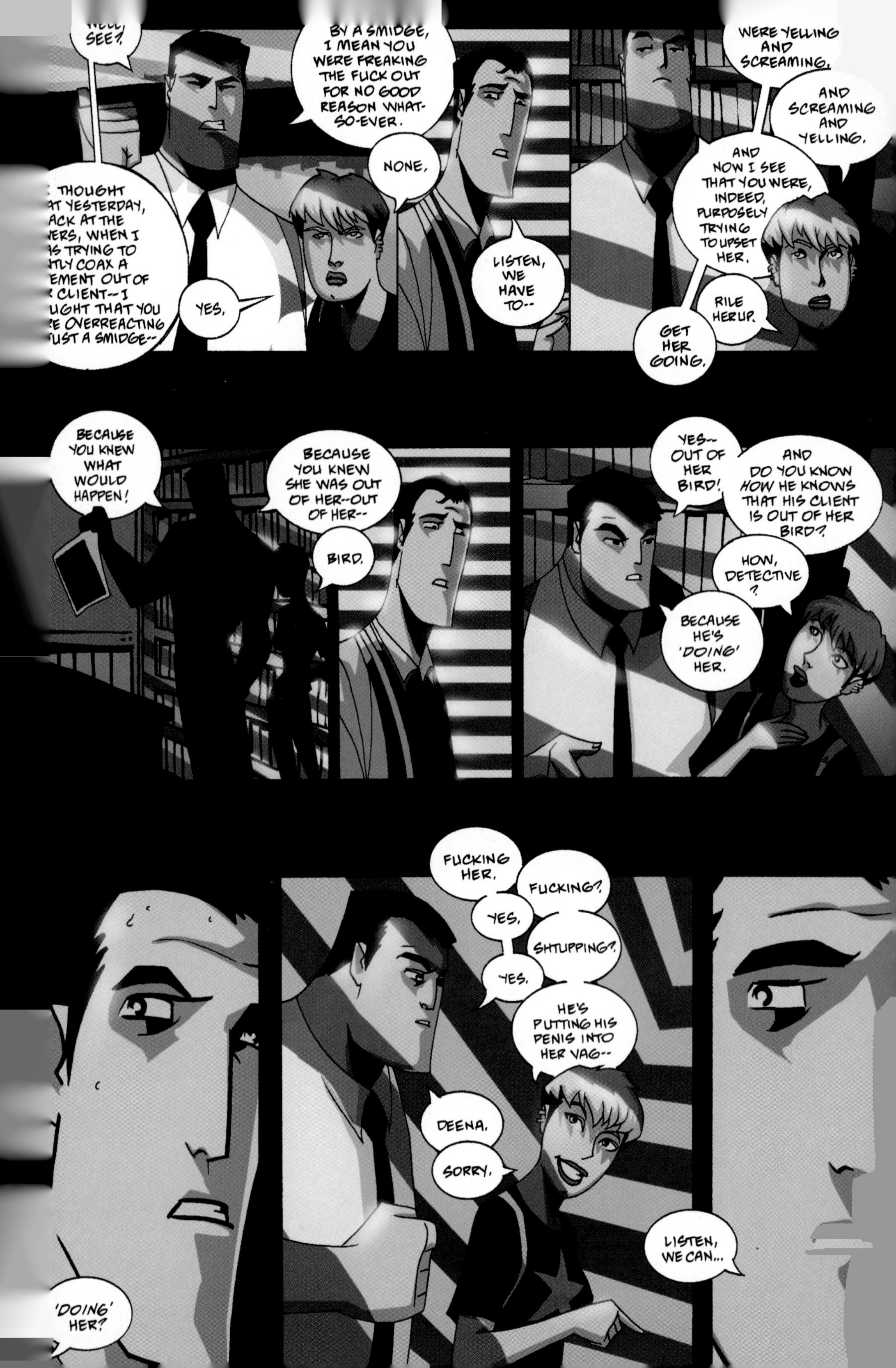
E THOUGHT AT YESTERDAY, ACK AT THE VERS, WHEN I S TRYING TO NTLY COAX A EMENT OUT OF R CLIENT--I UGHT THAT YOU E OVERREACTING JUST A SMIDGE--
YES.
SEE?
BY A SMIDGE, I MEAN YOU WERE FREAKING THE FUCK OUT FOR NO GOOD REASON WHAT-SO-EVER.
NONE.
LISTEN, WE HAVE TO--
WERE YELLING AND SCREAMING.
AND SCREAMING AND YELLING.
AND NOW I SEE THAT YOU WERE, INDEED, PURPOSELY TRYING TO UPSET HER.
RILE HER UP.
GET HER GOING.
BECAUSE YOU KNEW WHAT WOULD HAPPEN!
BECAUSE YOU KNEW SHE WAS OUT OF HER--OUT OF HER--
BIRD.
YES-- OUT OF HER BIRD!
AND DO YOU KNOW HOW HE KNOWS THAT HIS CLIENT IS OUT OF HER BIRD?
HOW, DETECTIVE?
BECAUSE HE'S 'DOING' HER.
'DOING' HER?
FUCKING HER.
FUCKING?
YES.
SHTUPPING?
YES.
HE'S PUTTING HIS PENIS INTO HER VAG--
DEENA.
SORRY.
LISTEN, WE CAN...

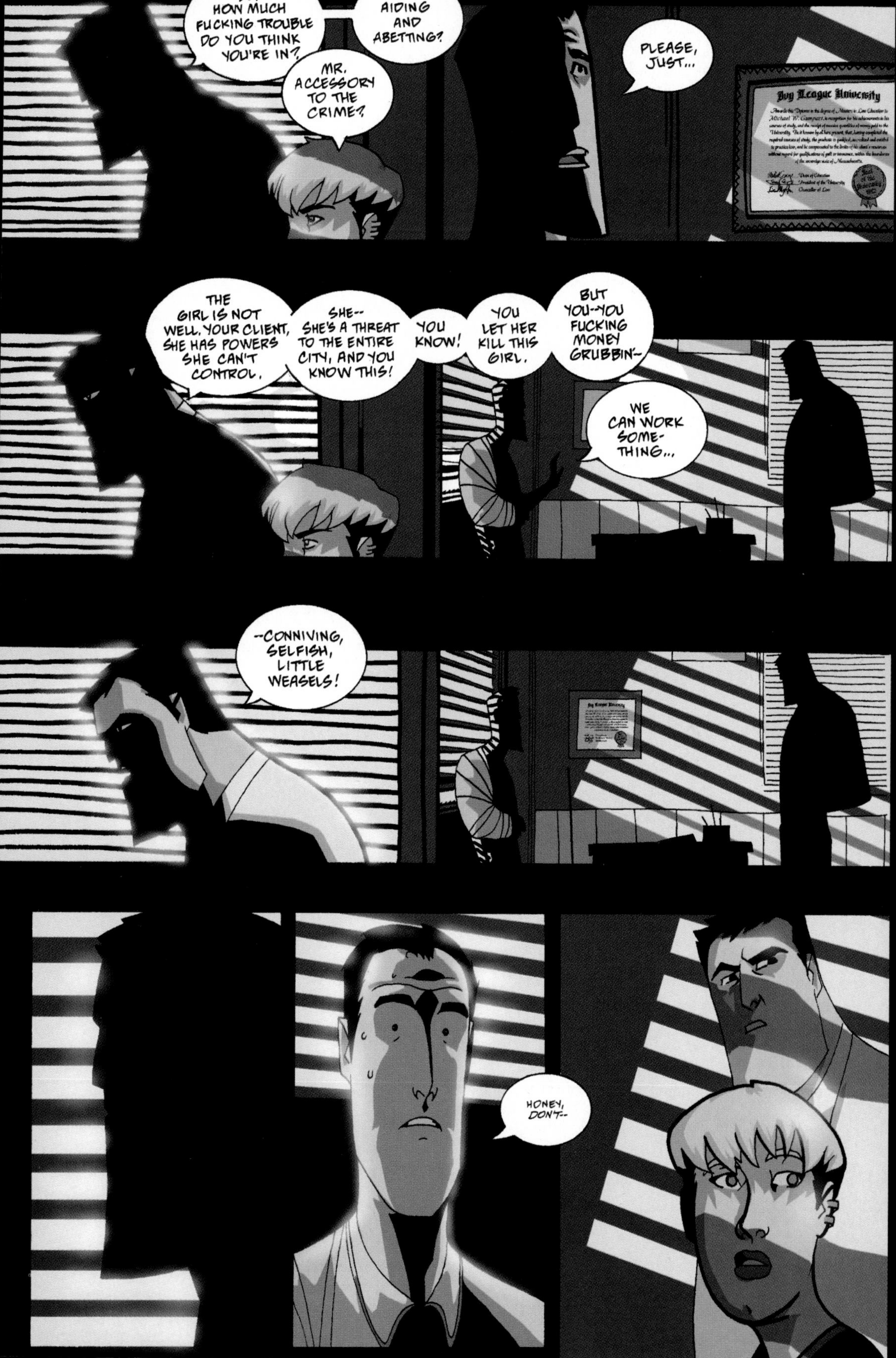
SO, HOW MUCH FUCKING TROUBLE DO YOU THINK YOU'RE IN?
MR. AIDING AND ABETTING?
MR. ACCESSORY TO THE CRIME?
PLEASE, JUST...
Ivy League University
THE GIRL IS NOT WELL. YOUR CLIENT, SHE HAS POWERS SHE CAN'T CONTROL.
SHE-- SHE'S A THREAT TO THE ENTIRE CITY, AND YOU KNOW THIS!
YOU KNOW!
YOU LET HER KILL THIS GIRL.
BUT YOU--YOU FUCKING MONEY GRUBBIN'--
WE CAN WORK SOME-THING...
--CONNIVING, SELFISH, LITTLE WEASELS!
HONEY, DON'T--

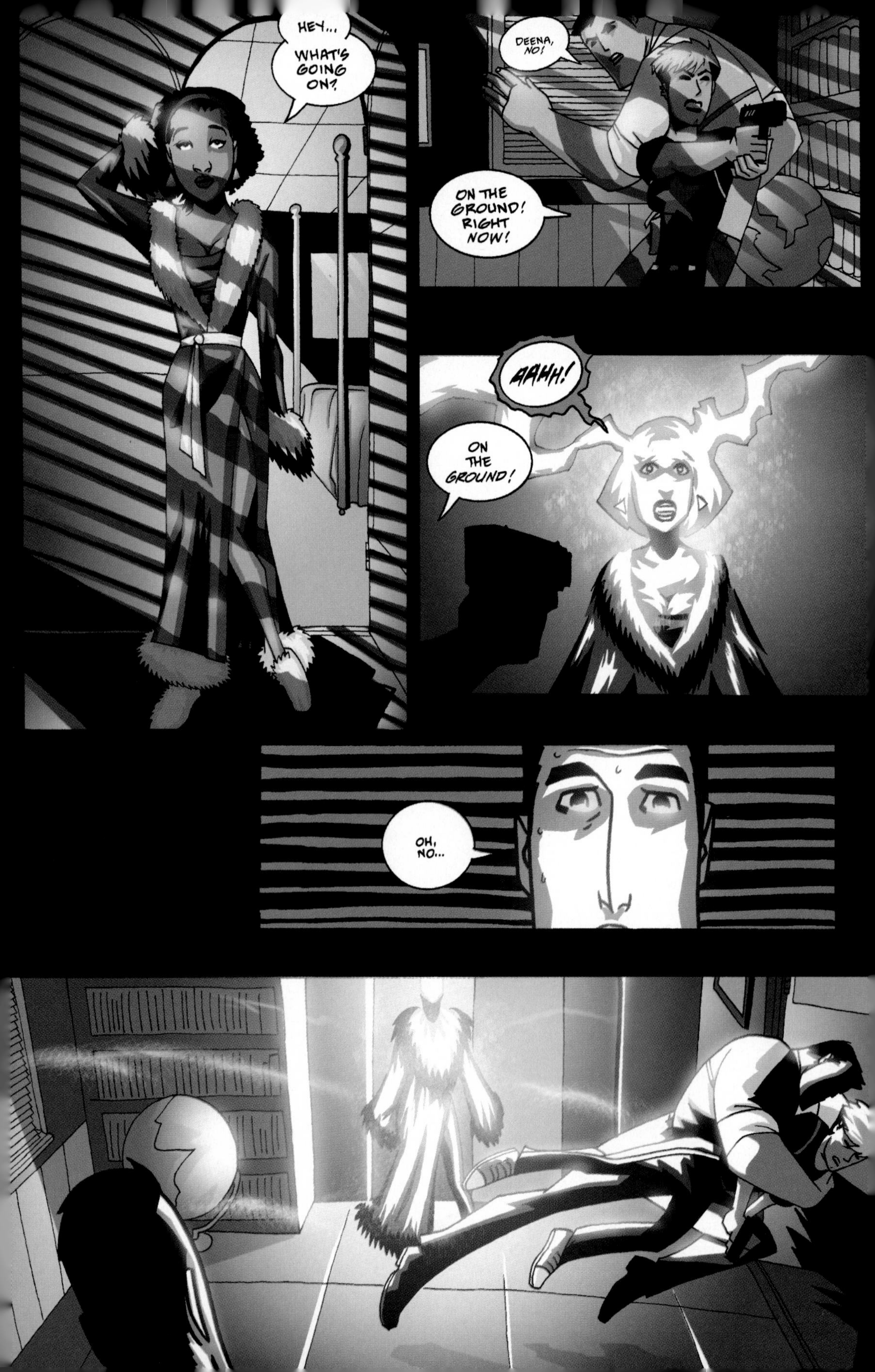
HEY... WHAT'S GOING ON?
DEENA, NO!
ON THE GROUND! RIGHT NOW!
AAHH!
ON THE GROUND!
OH, NO...

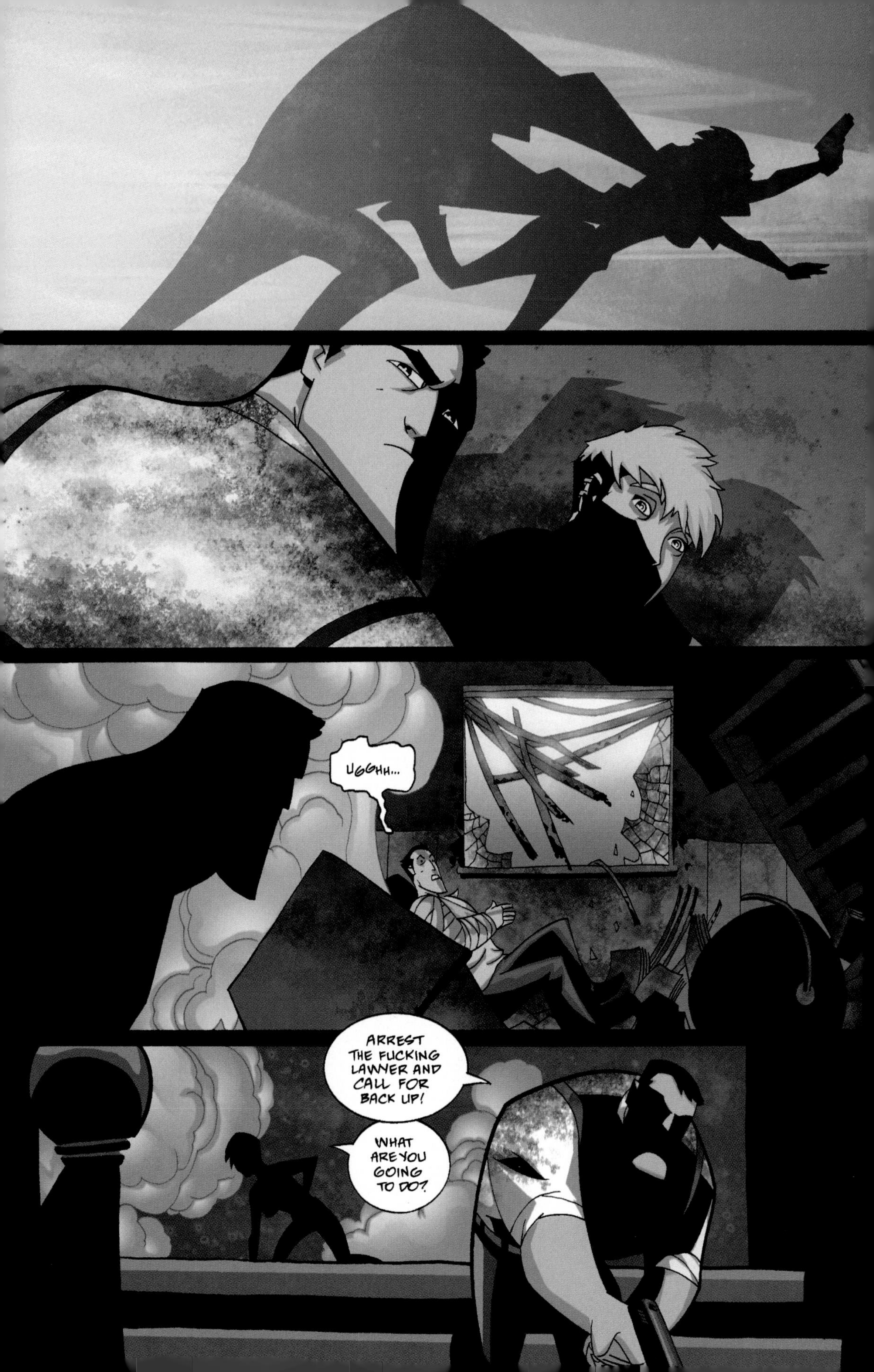
UGGHH...
ARREST THE FUCKING LAWYER AND CALL FOR BACK UP!
WHAT ARE YOU GOING TO DO?

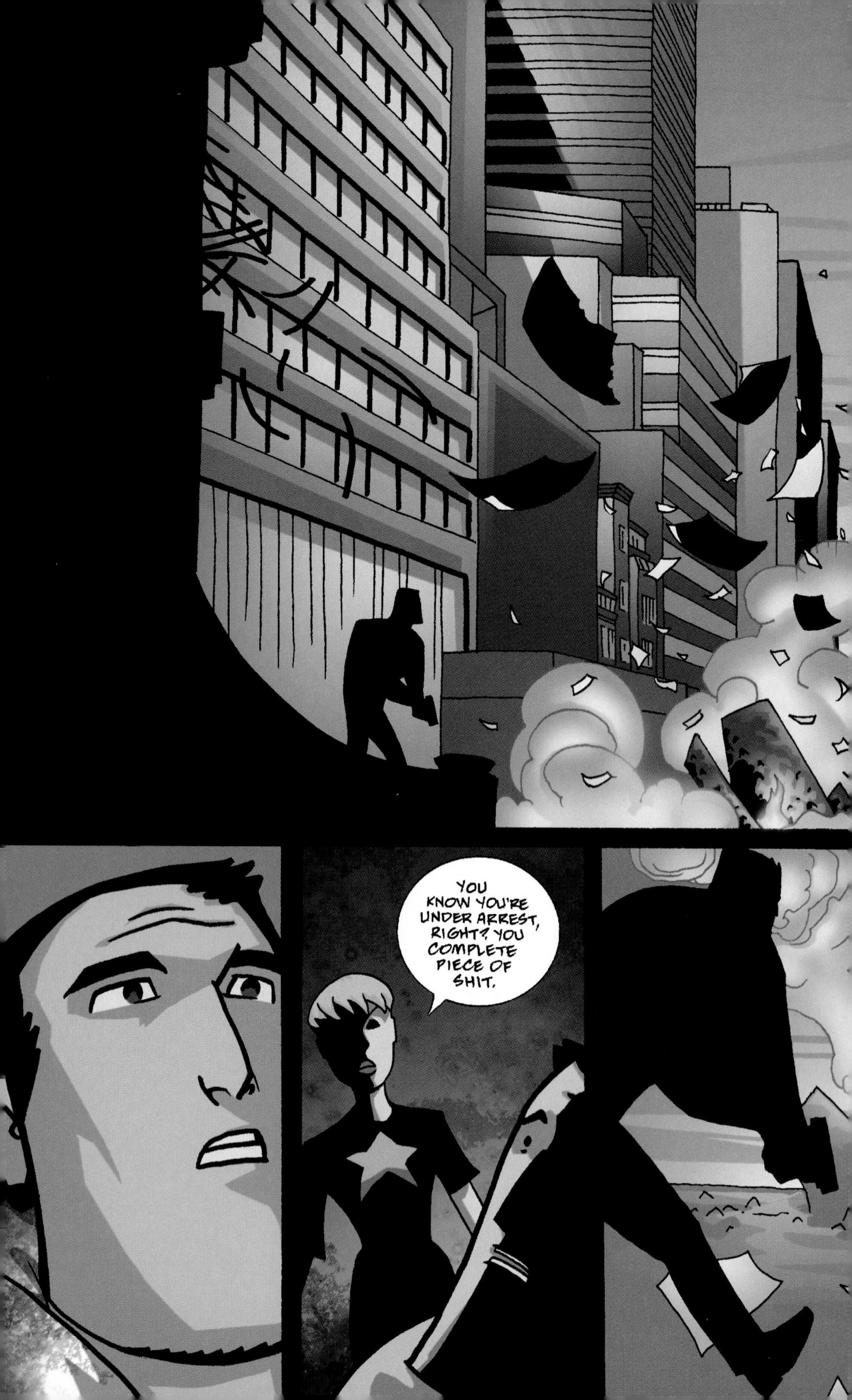
YOU KNOW YOU'RE UNDER ARREST, RIGHT? YOU COMPLETE PIECE OF SHIT.

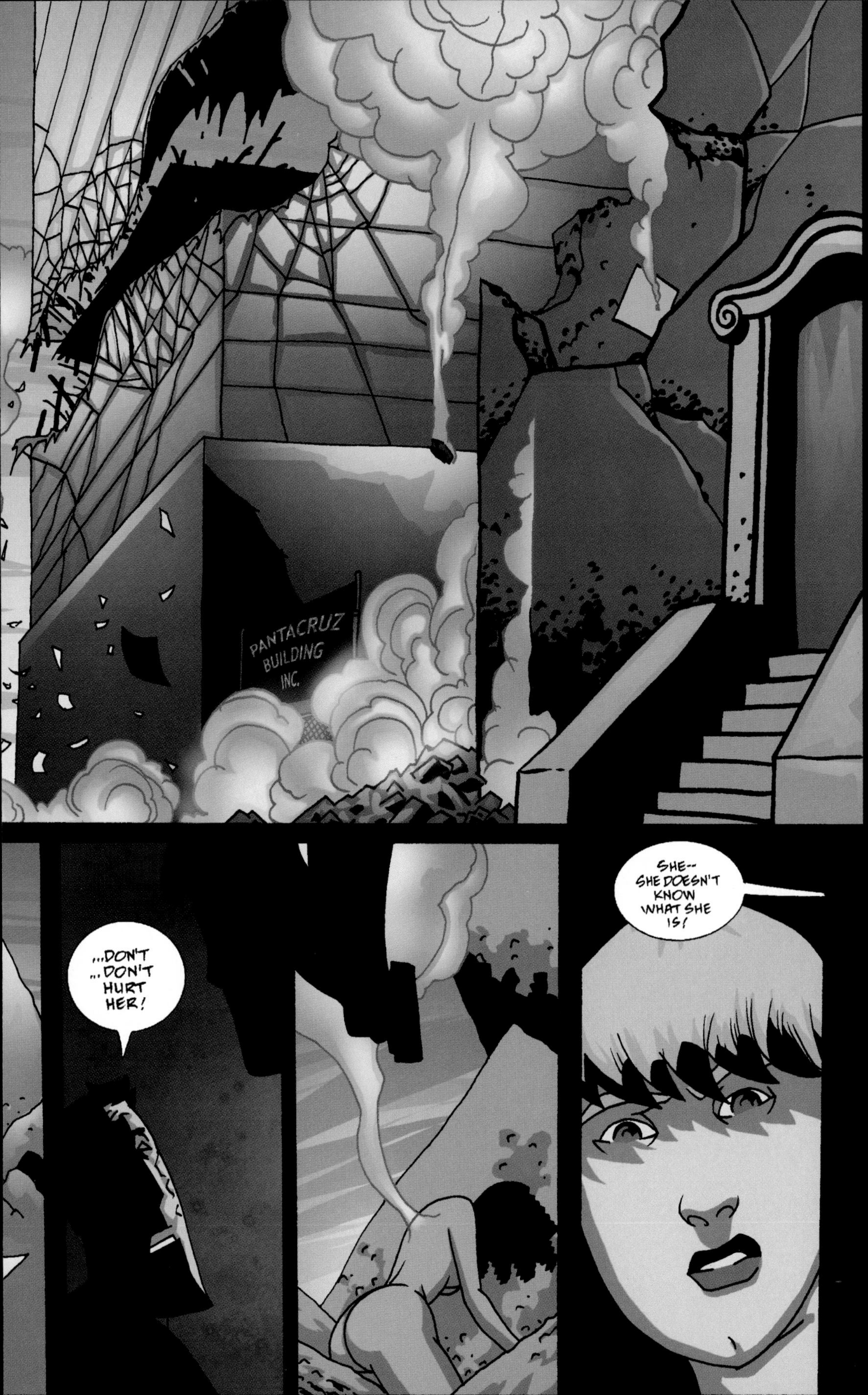

PANTACRUZ BUILDING INC.
...DON'T ...DON'T HURT HER!
SHE-- SHE DOESN'T KNOW WHAT SHE IS!

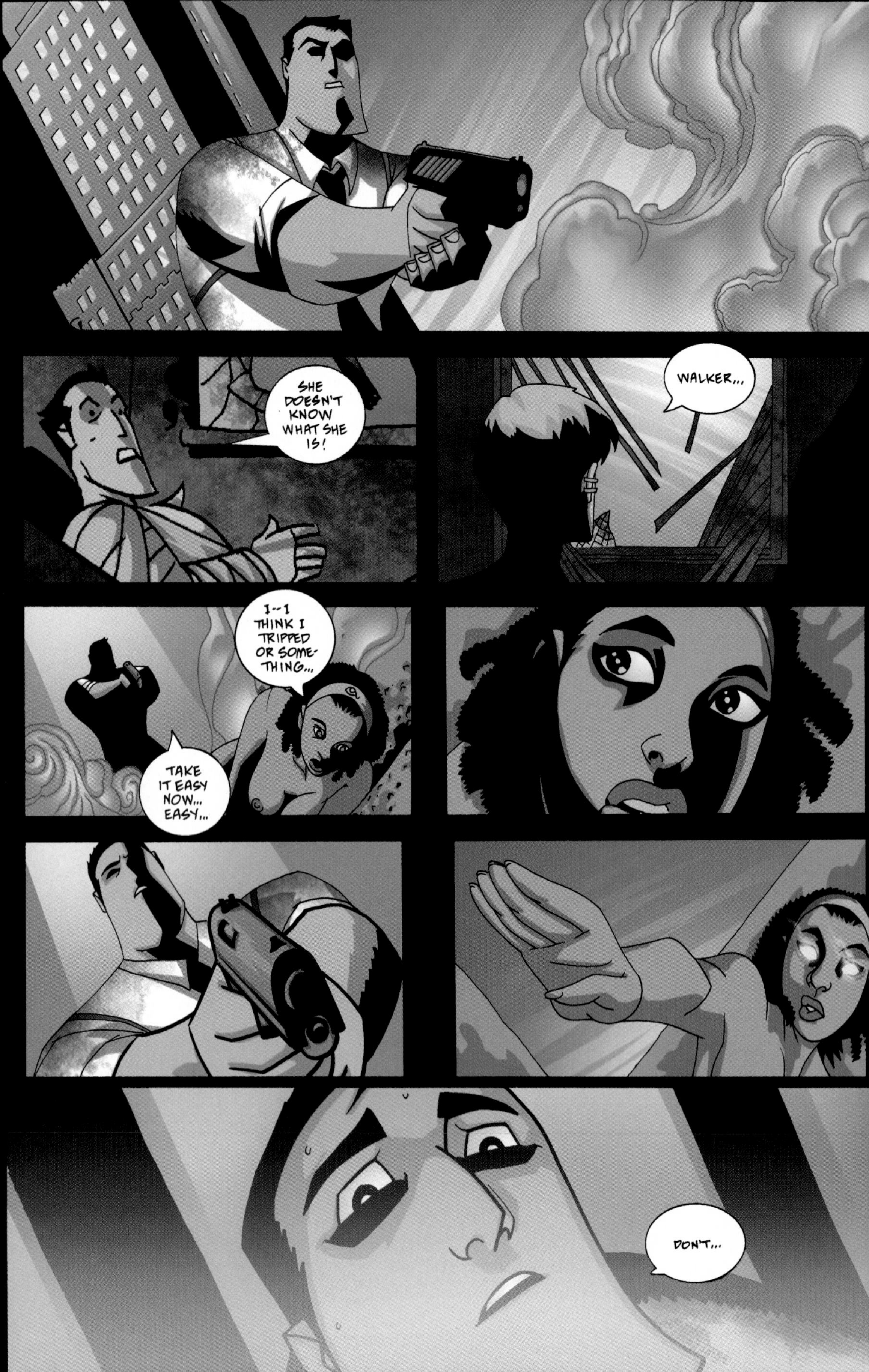
SHE DOESN'T KNOW WHAT SHE IS!
WALKER...
I--I THINK I TRIPPED OR SOMETHING...
TAKE IT EASY NOW... EASY...
DON'T...

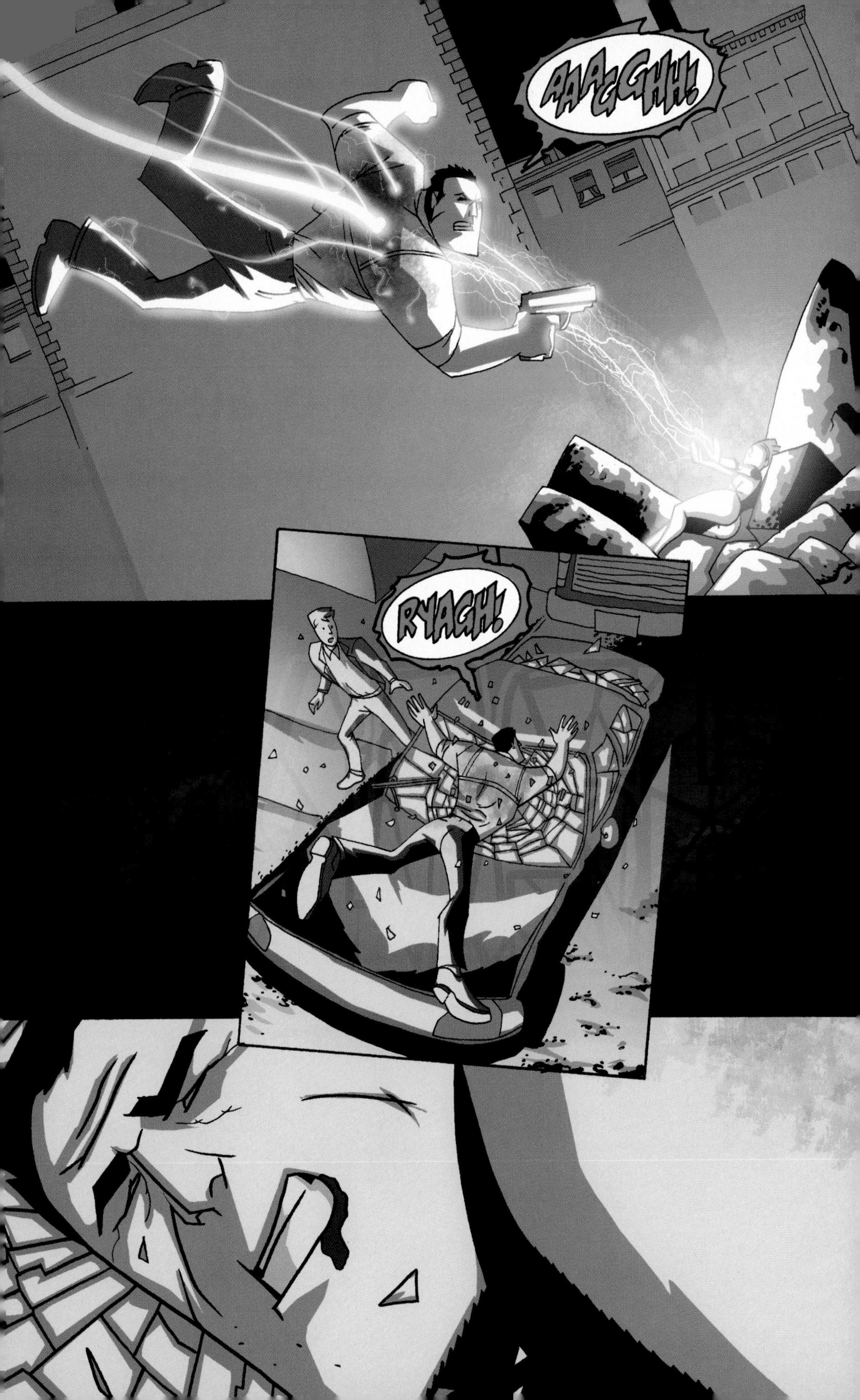
AAAGGHH!
RYAGH!

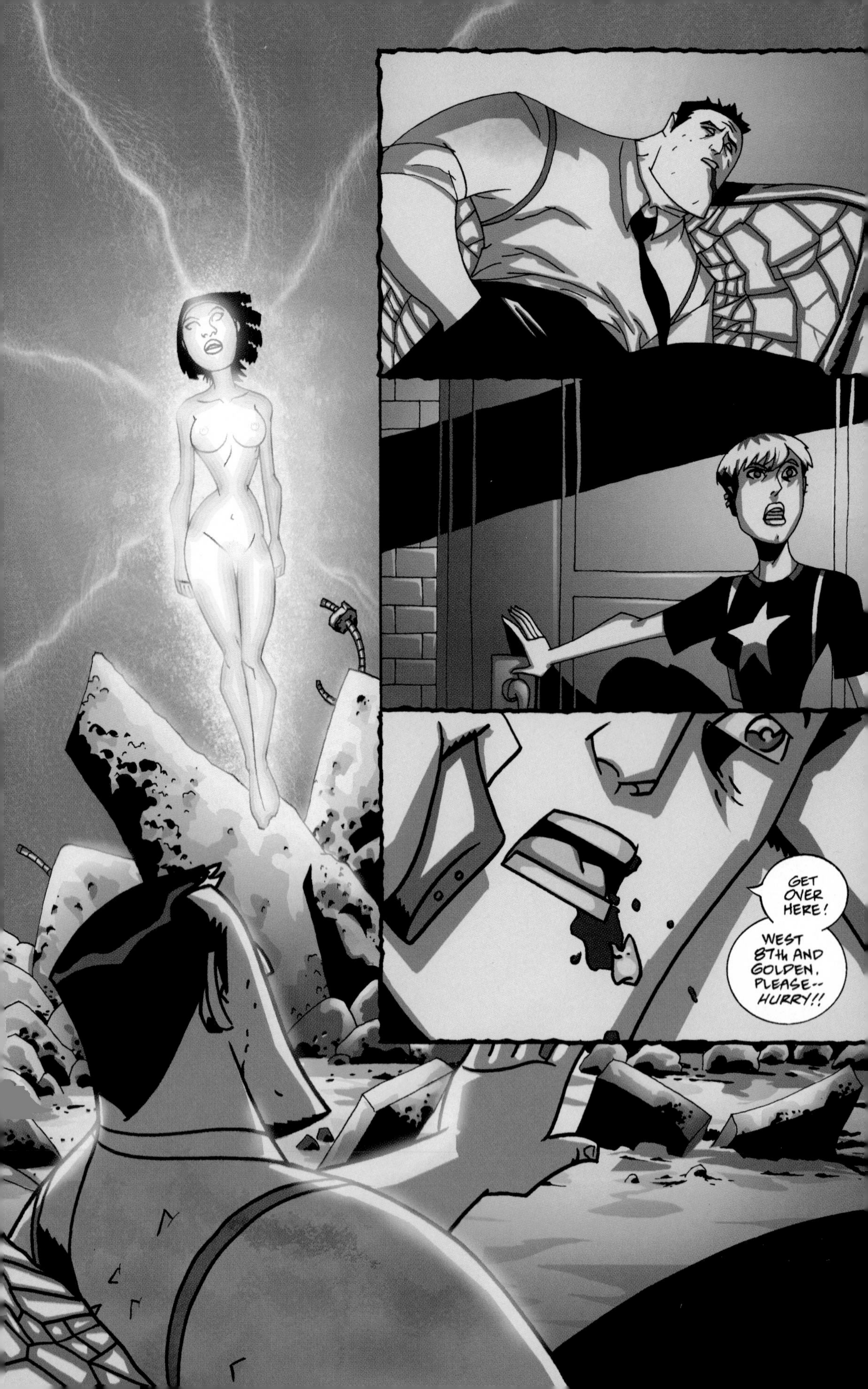
GET OVER HERE!
WEST 8Th AND GOLDEN, PLEASE-- HURRY!!

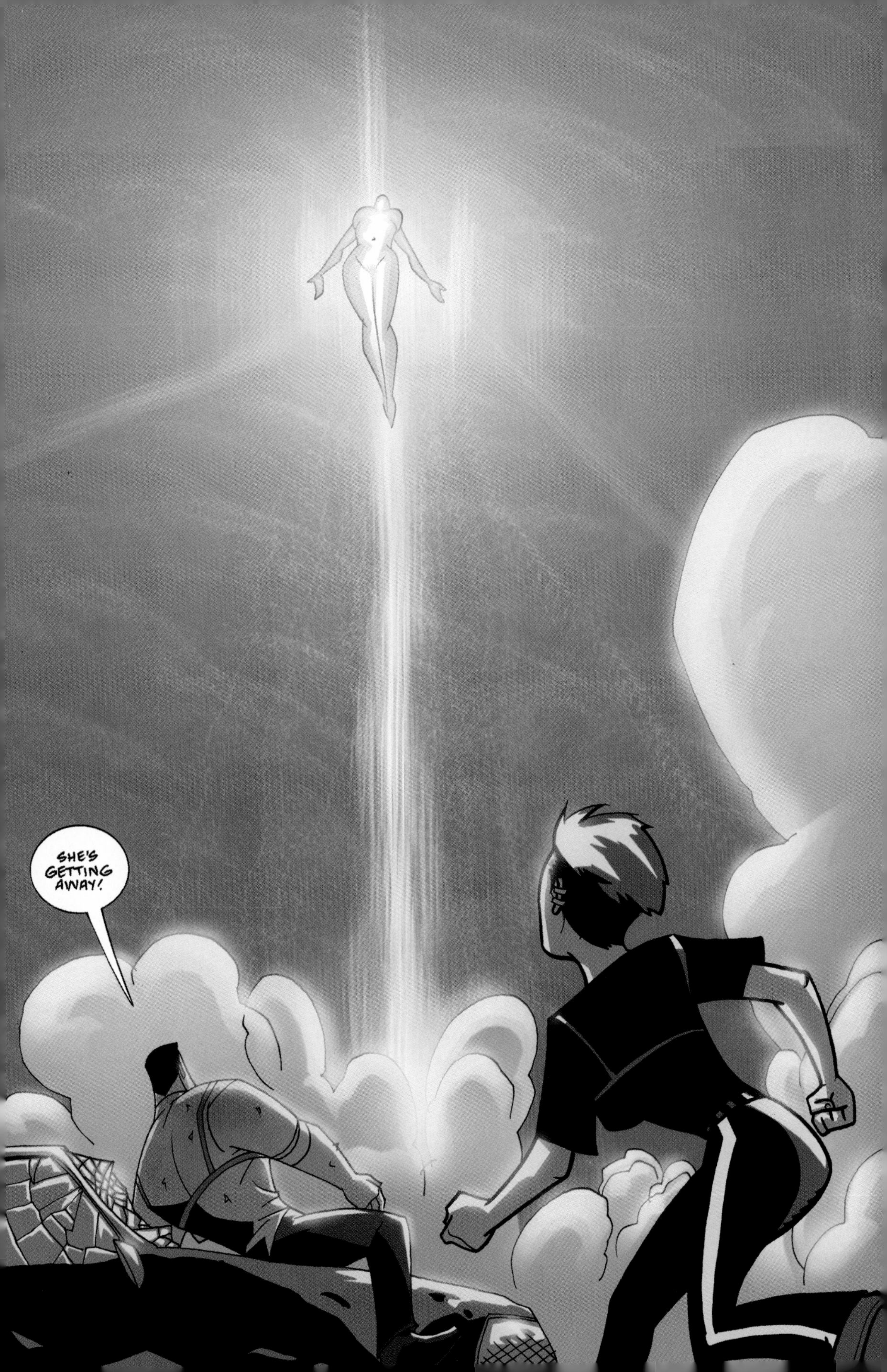
SHE'S GETTING AWAY!

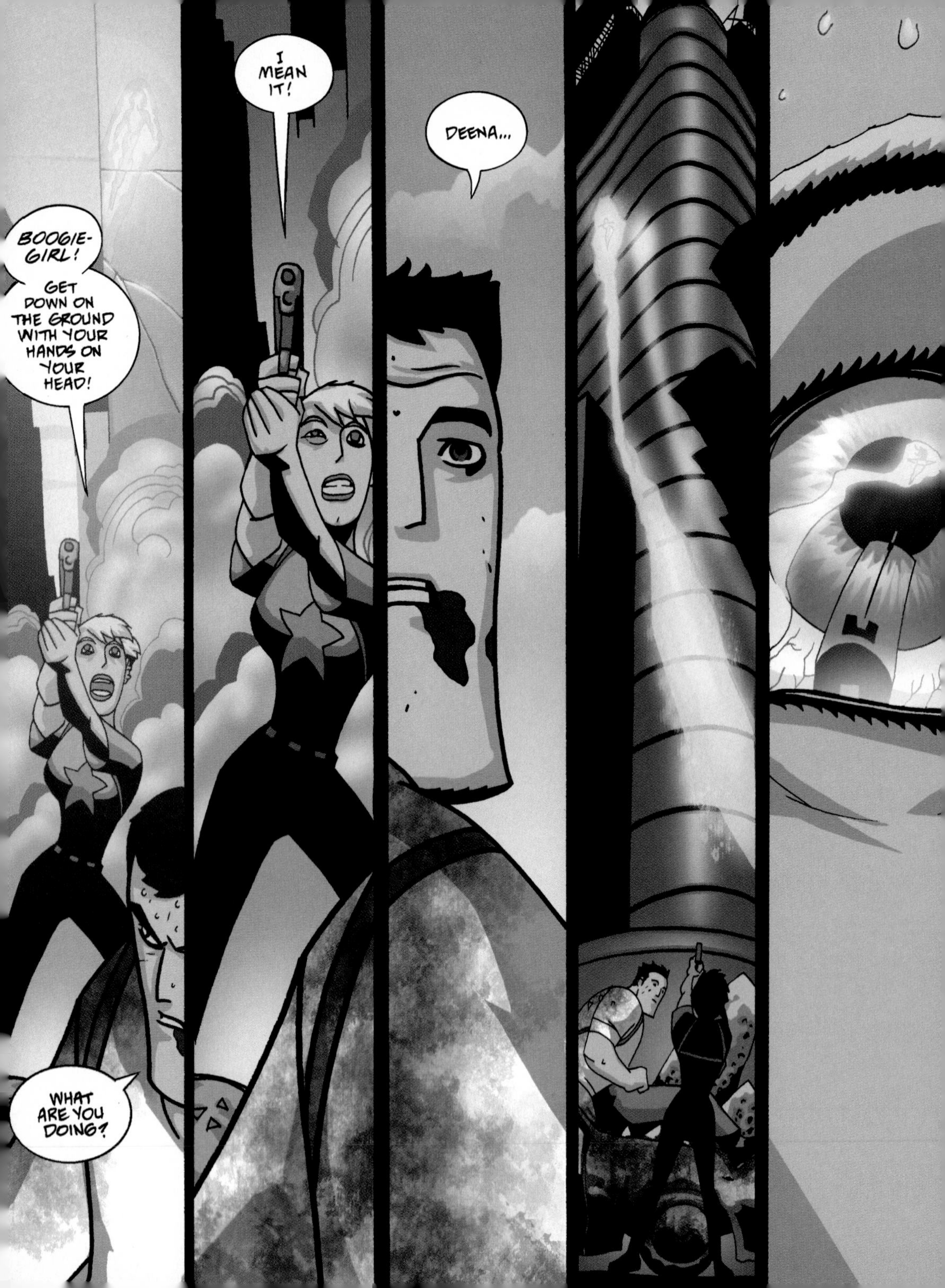
BOOGIE-GIRL!
GET DOWN ON THE GROUND WITH YOUR HANDS ON YOUR HEAD!
WHAT ARE YOU DOING?
I MEAN IT!
DEENA...

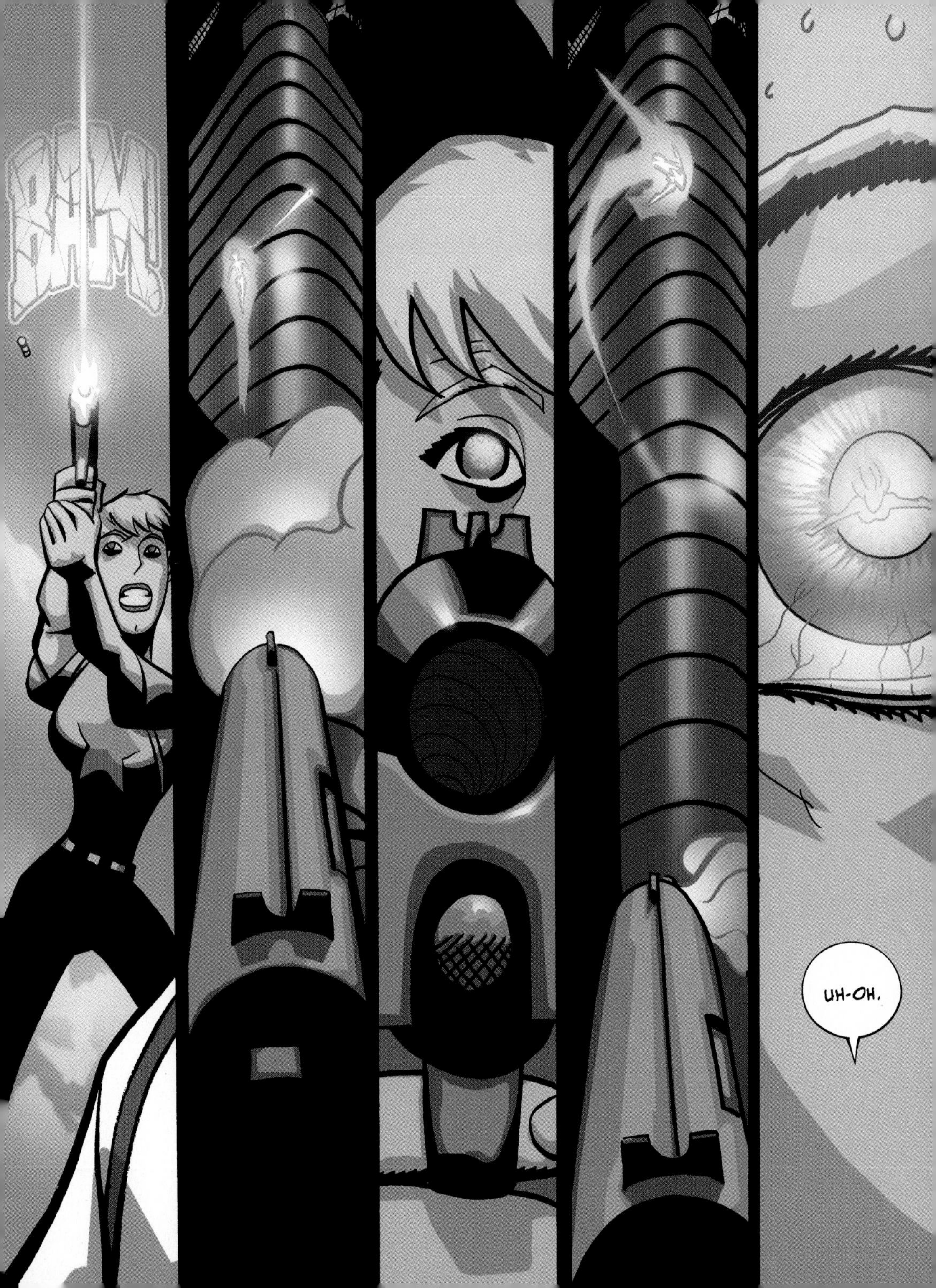
BAM!
UH-OH.

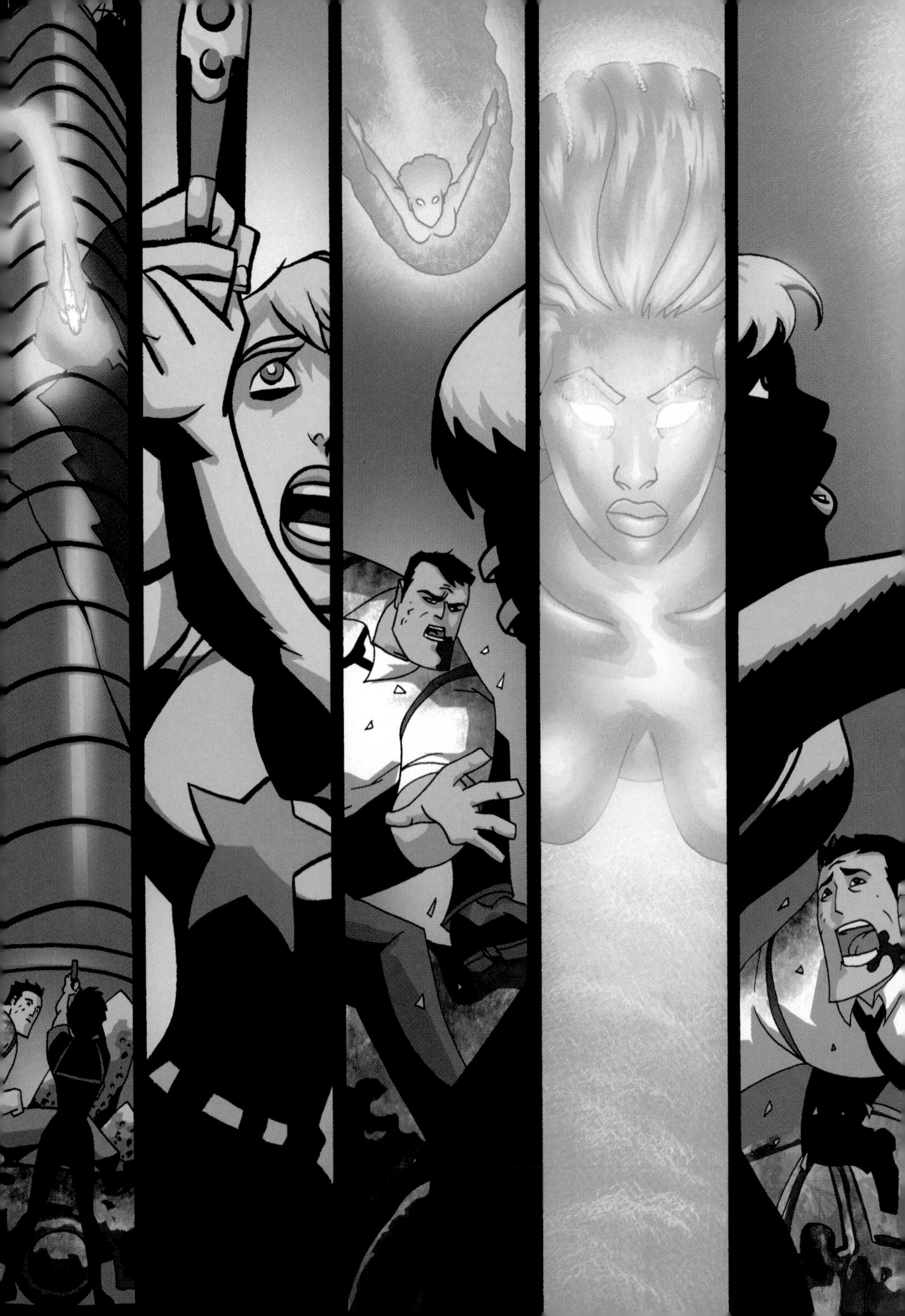

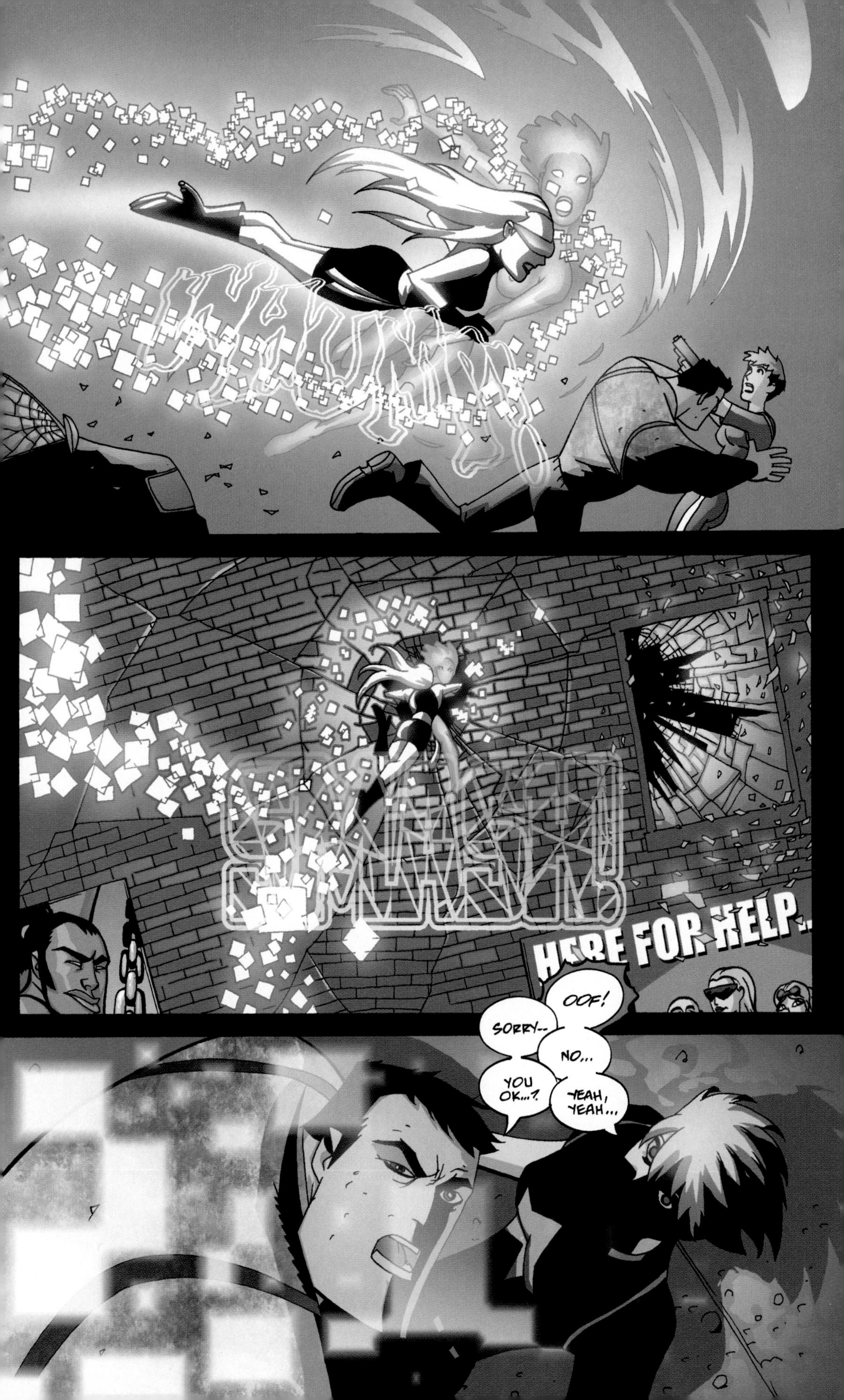
SMASH!
HERE FOR HELP..
OOF!
SORRY--
NO...
YOU OK...?
YEAH, YEAH...

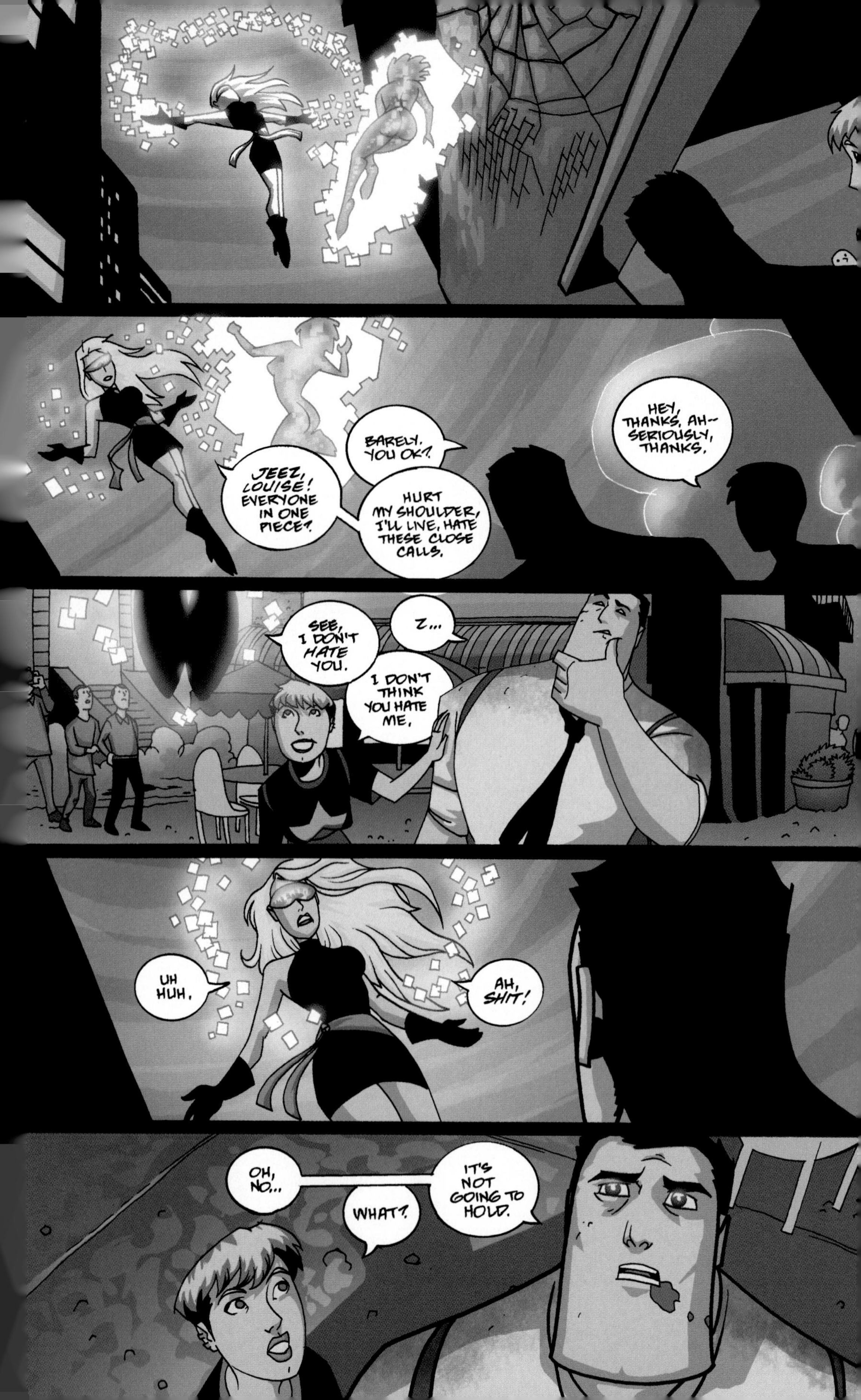

JEEZ, LOUISE! EVERYONE IN ONE PIECE?
BARELY. YOU OK?
HURT MY SHOULDER, I'LL LIVE, HATE THESE CLOSE CALLS.
HEY, THANKS, AH-- SERIOUSLY, THANKS.
SEE, I DON'T HATE YOU.
Z...
I DON'T THINK YOU HATE ME.
UH HUH.
AH, SHIT!
OH, NO...
WHAT?
IT'S NOT GOING TO HOLD.

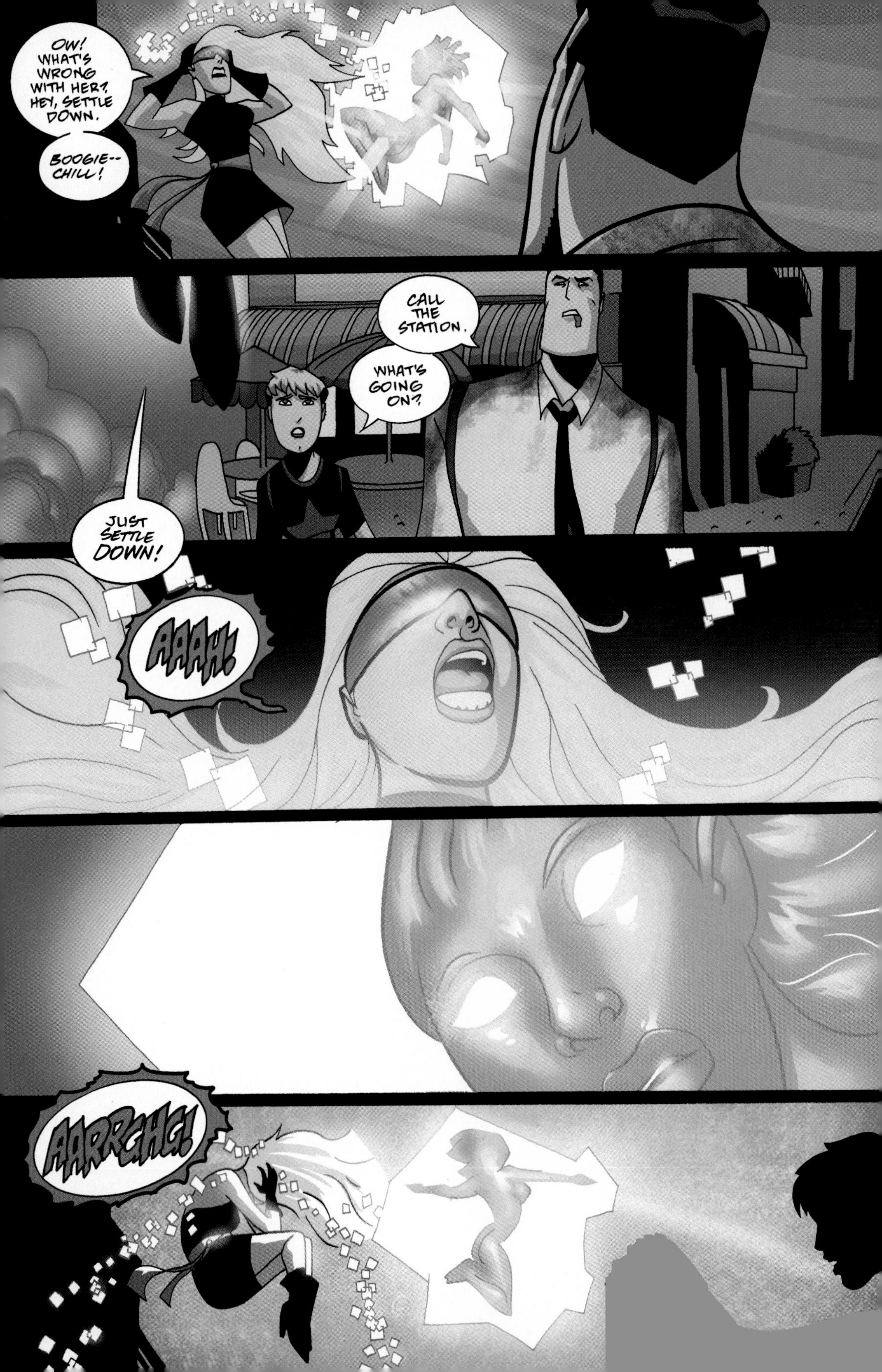
OW! WHAT'S WRONG WITH HER? HEY, SETTLE DOWN.
BOOGIE--CHILL!
CALL THE STATION.
WHAT'S GOING ON?
JUST SETTLE DOWN!
AAAH!
AARRGHG!

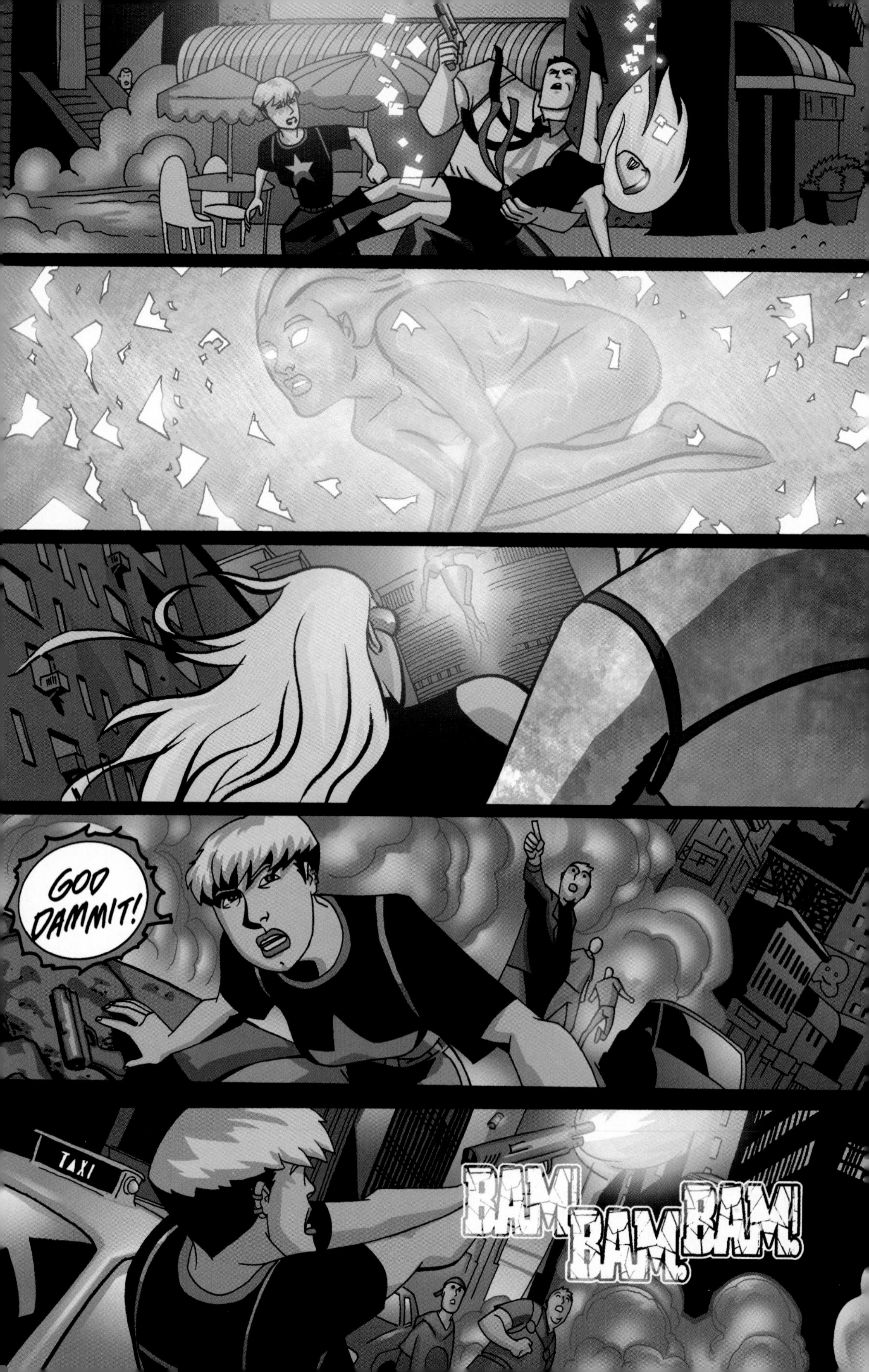
GOD DAMMIT!
TAXI
BAM! BAM! BAM!

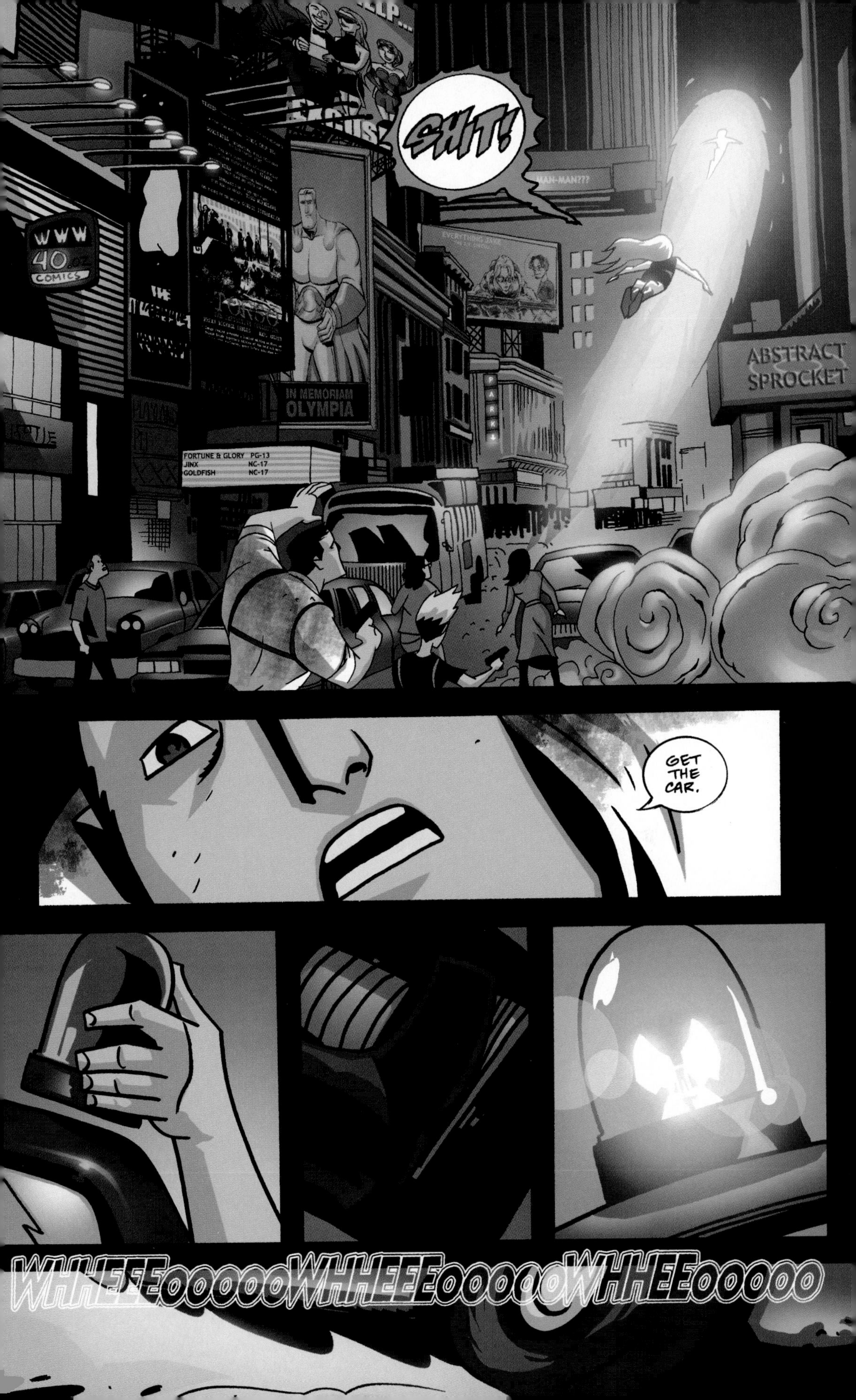
WWW
40.oz
COMICS
IN MEMORIAM
OLYMPIA
FORTUNE & GLORY PG-13
JINX NC-17
GOLDFISH NC-17
PARK
ABSTRACT
SPROCKET
SHIT!
MAN-MAN???
GET THE CAR.
WHHEEEooooooWHHEEEooooooWHHEEooooo

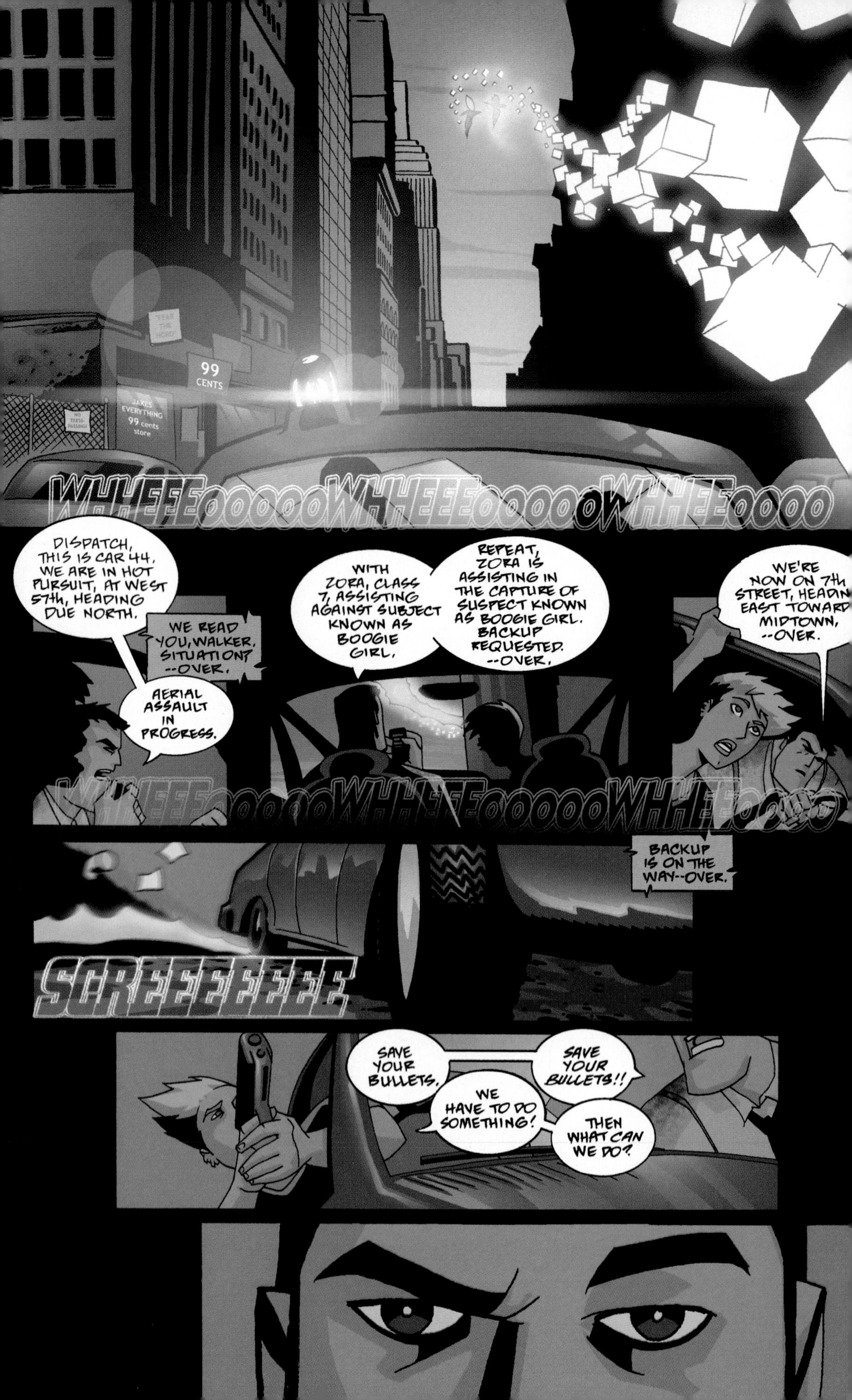
99 CENTS
JAXES EVERYTHING 99 cents store
WHHEEEOOOOOOWHHEEEOOOOOOWHHEEOOOO
DISPATCH, THIS IS CAR 44, WE ARE IN HOT PURSUIT, AT WEST 57th, HEADING DUE NORTH.
WE READ YOU, WALKER. SITUATION? --OVER.
AERIAL ASSAULT IN PROGRESS.
WITH ZORA, CLASS 7, ASSISTING AGAINST SUBJECT KNOWN AS BOOGIE GIRL.
REPEAT, ZORA IS ASSISTING IN THE CAPTURE OF SUSPECT KNOWN AS BOOGIE GIRL. BACKUP REQUESTED. --OVER.
WE'RE NOW ON 7th STREET, HEADIN EAST TOWARD MIDTOWN, --OVER.
WHHEEEOOOOOWHHEEEOOOOOWHHEEOOOO
BACKUP IS ON THE WAY--OVER.
SCREEEEEEEE
SAVE YOUR BULLETS.
SAVE YOUR BULLETS!!
WE HAVE TO DO SOMETHING!
THEN WHAT CAN WE DO?

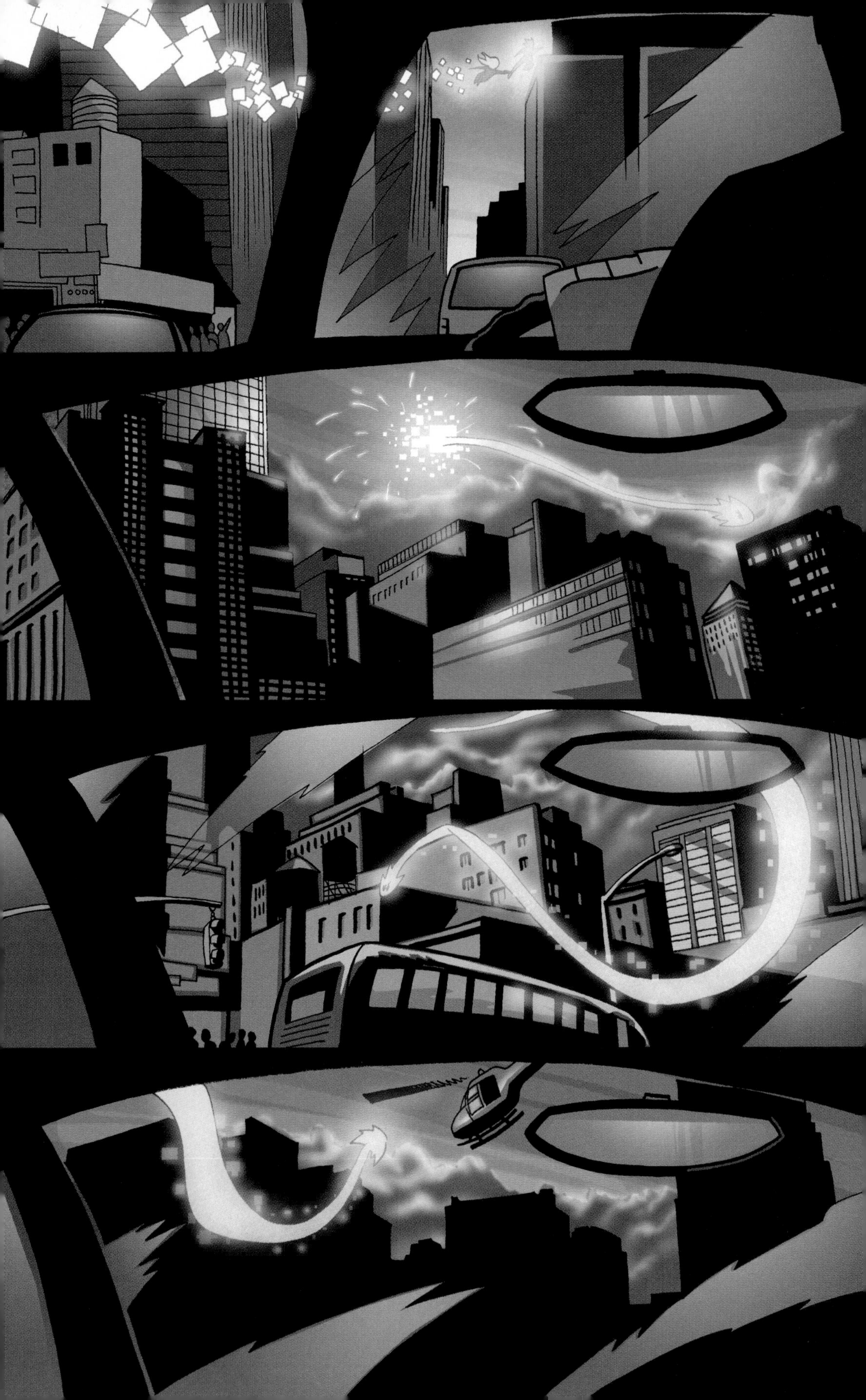

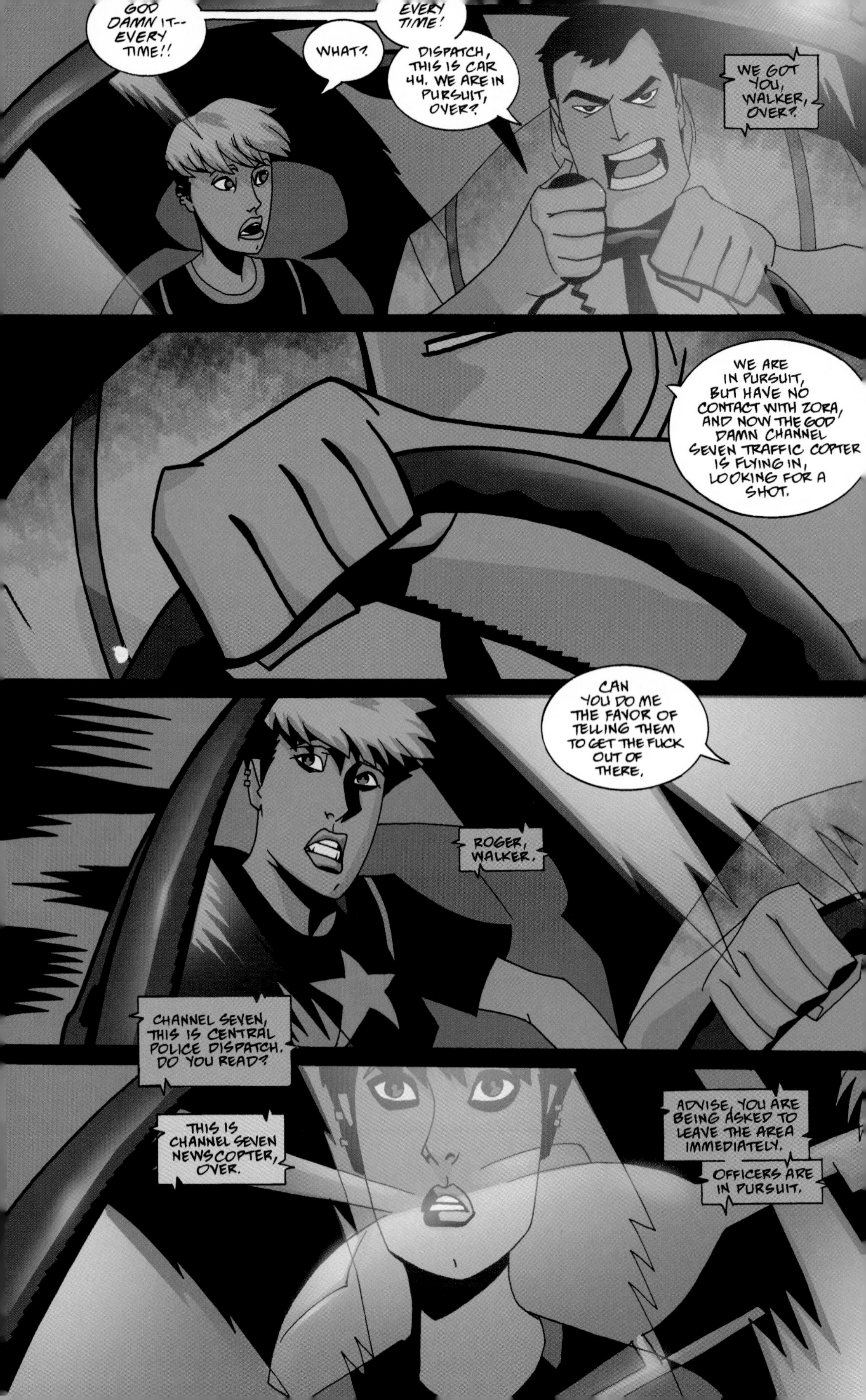
GOD DAMN IT-- EVERY TIME!!
EVERY TIME!
WHAT?
DISPATCH, THIS IS CAR 44. WE ARE IN PURSUIT, OVER?
WE GOT YOU, WALKER, OVER?
WE ARE IN PURSUIT, BUT HAVE NO CONTACT WITH ZORA, AND NOW THE GOD DAMN CHANNEL SEVEN TRAFFIC COPTER IS FLYING IN, LOOKING FOR A SHOT.
CAN YOU DO ME THE FAVOR OF TELLING THEM TO GET THE FUCK OUT OF THERE.
ROGER, WALKER.
CHANNEL SEVEN, THIS IS CENTRAL POLICE DISPATCH. DO YOU READ?
THIS IS CHANNEL SEVEN NEWSCOPTER, OVER.
ADVISE, YOU ARE BEING ASKED TO LEAVE THE AREA IMMEDIATELY.
OFFICERS ARE IN PURSUIT.

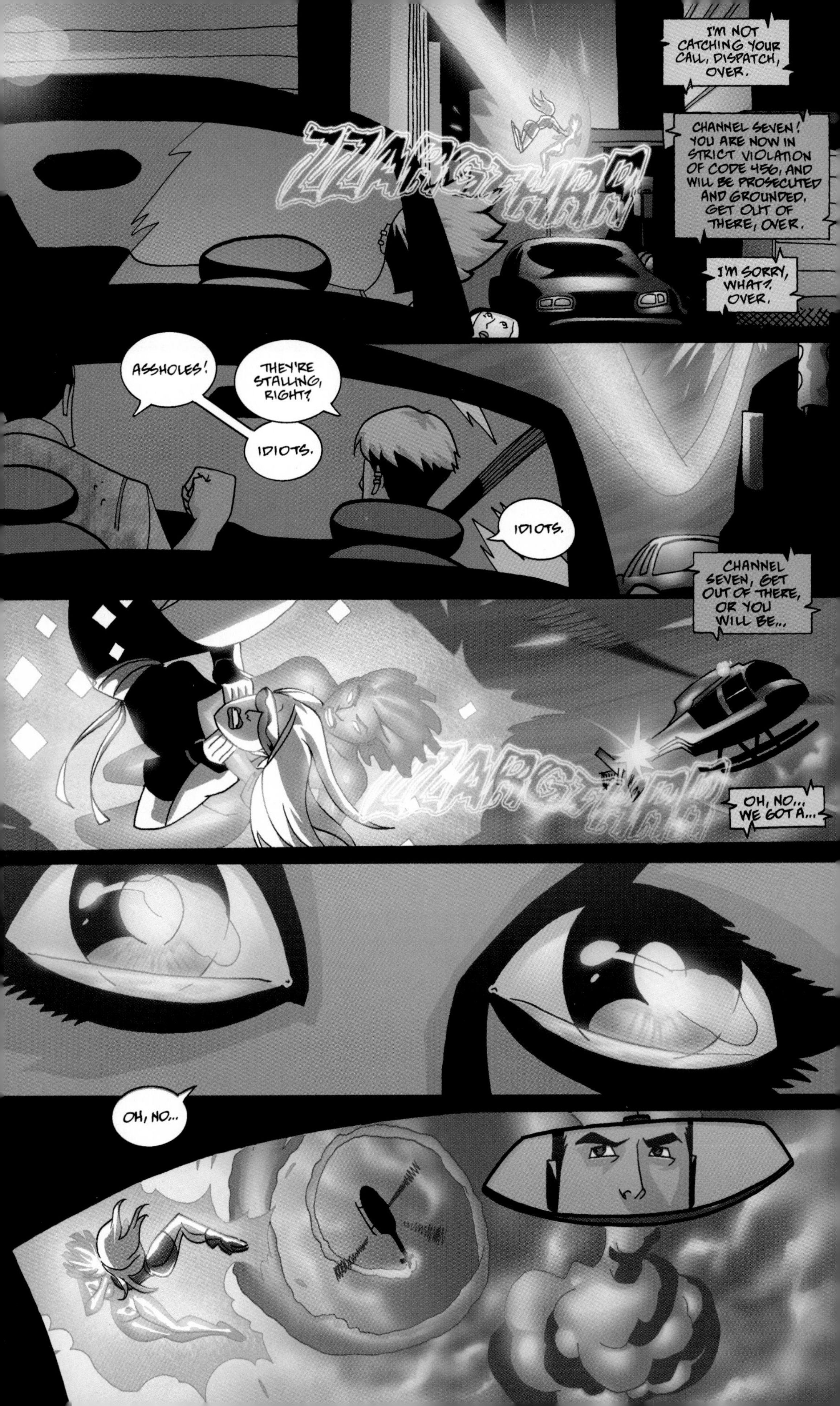
I'M NOT CATCHING YOUR CALL, DISPATCH, OVER.
CHANNEL SEVEN! YOU ARE NOW IN STRICT VIOLATION OF CODE 456, AND WILL BE PROSECUTED AND GROUNDED. GET OUT OF THERE, OVER.
I'M SORRY, WHAT?. OVER.
ASSHOLES!
THEY'RE STALLING, RIGHT?
IDIOTS.
IDIOTS.
CHANNEL SEVEN, GET OUT OF THERE, OR YOU WILL BE...
OH, NO... WE GOT A...
OH, NO...

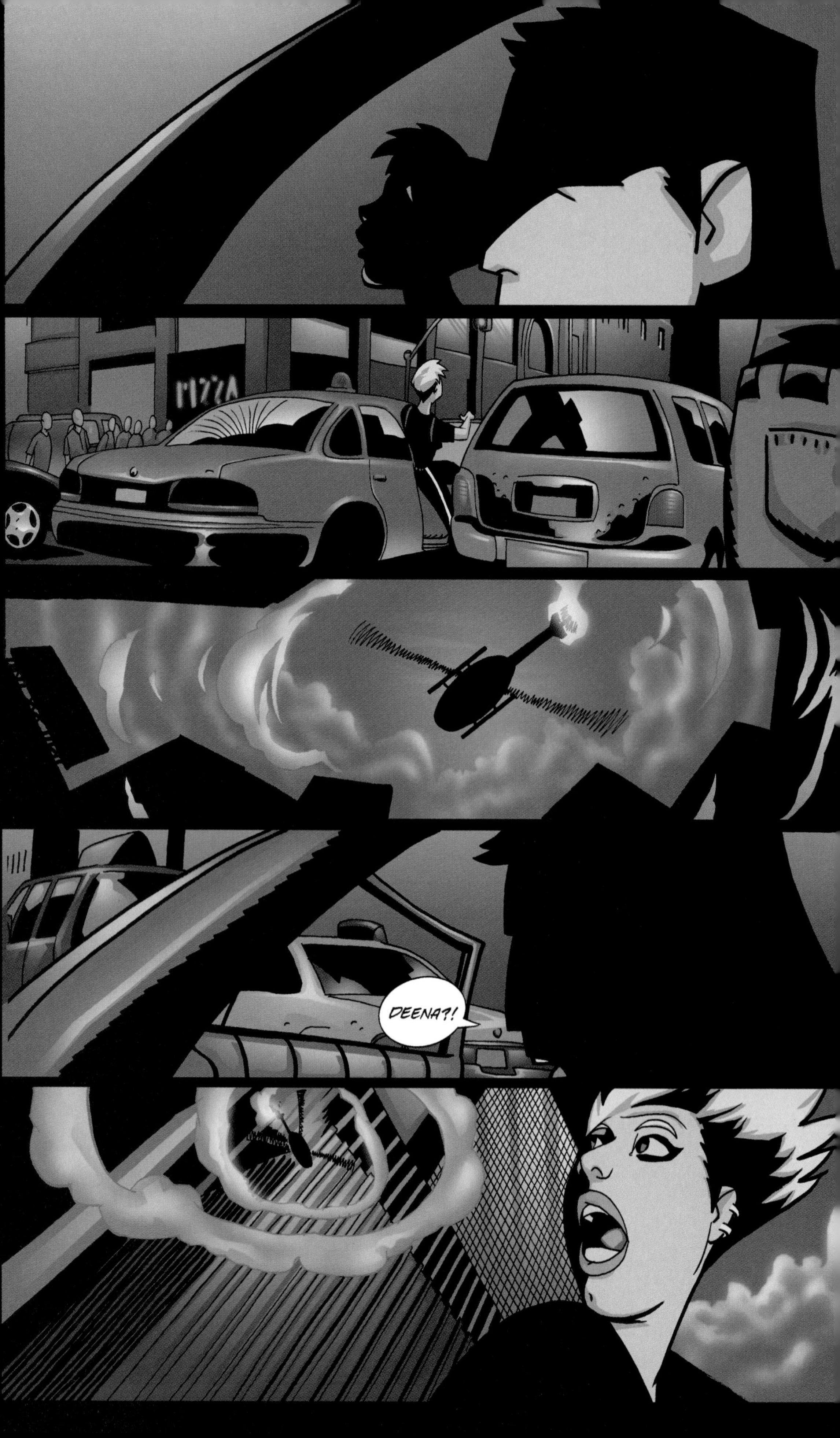
PIZZA
DEENA?!

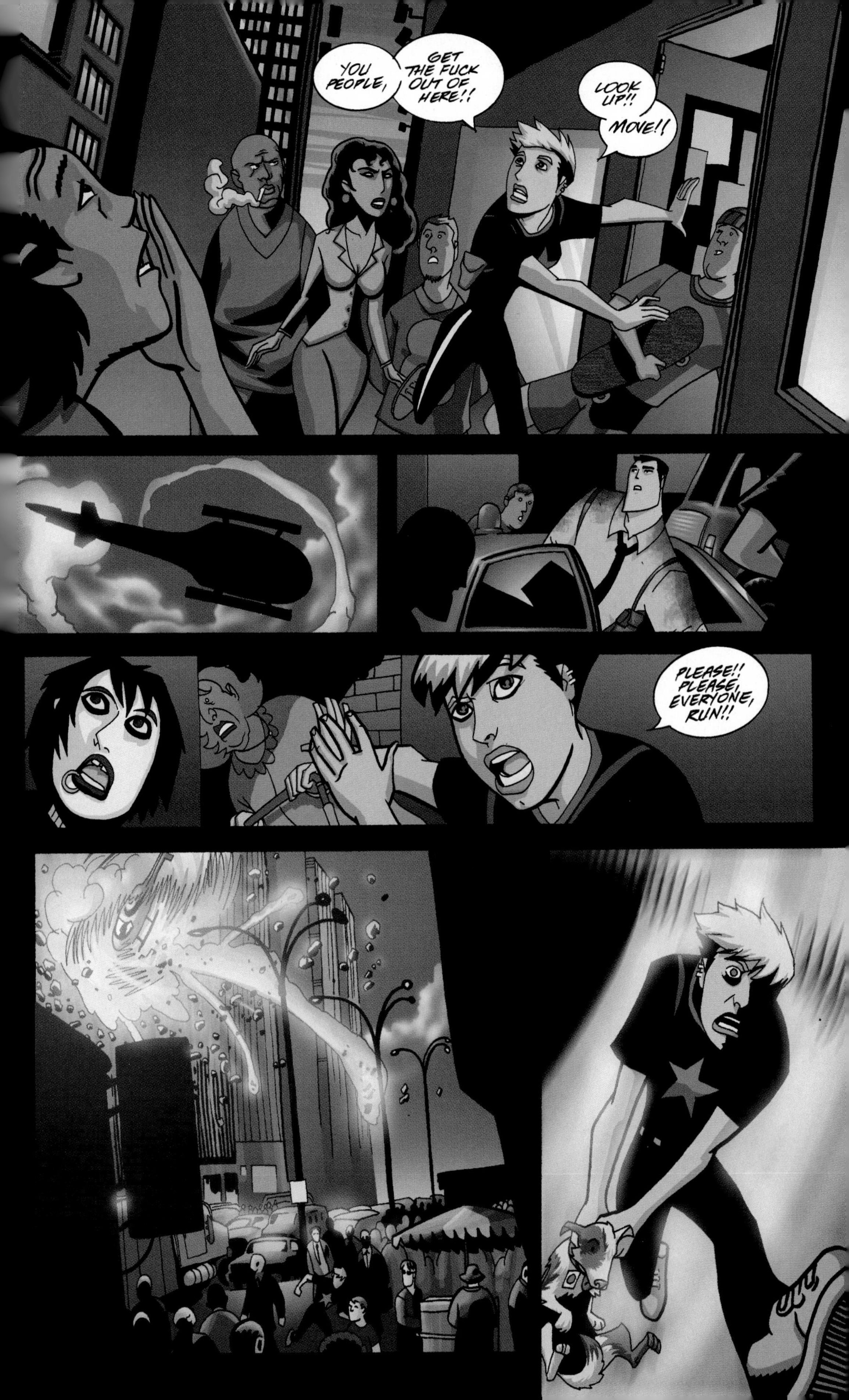
YOU PEOPLE,
GET THE FUCK OUT OF HERE!!
LOOK UP!!
MOVE!!
PLEASE!! PLEASE, EVERYONE, RUN!!

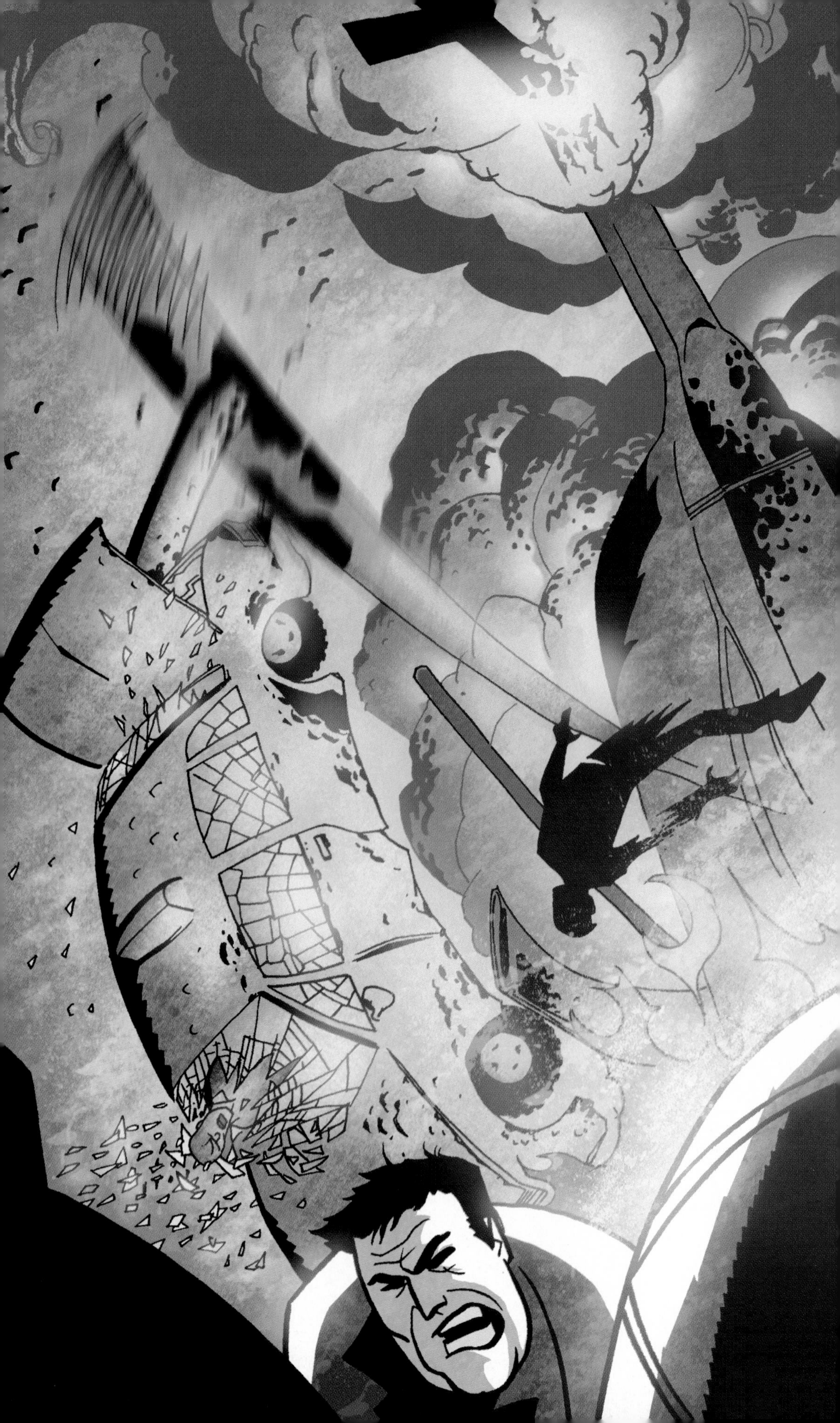

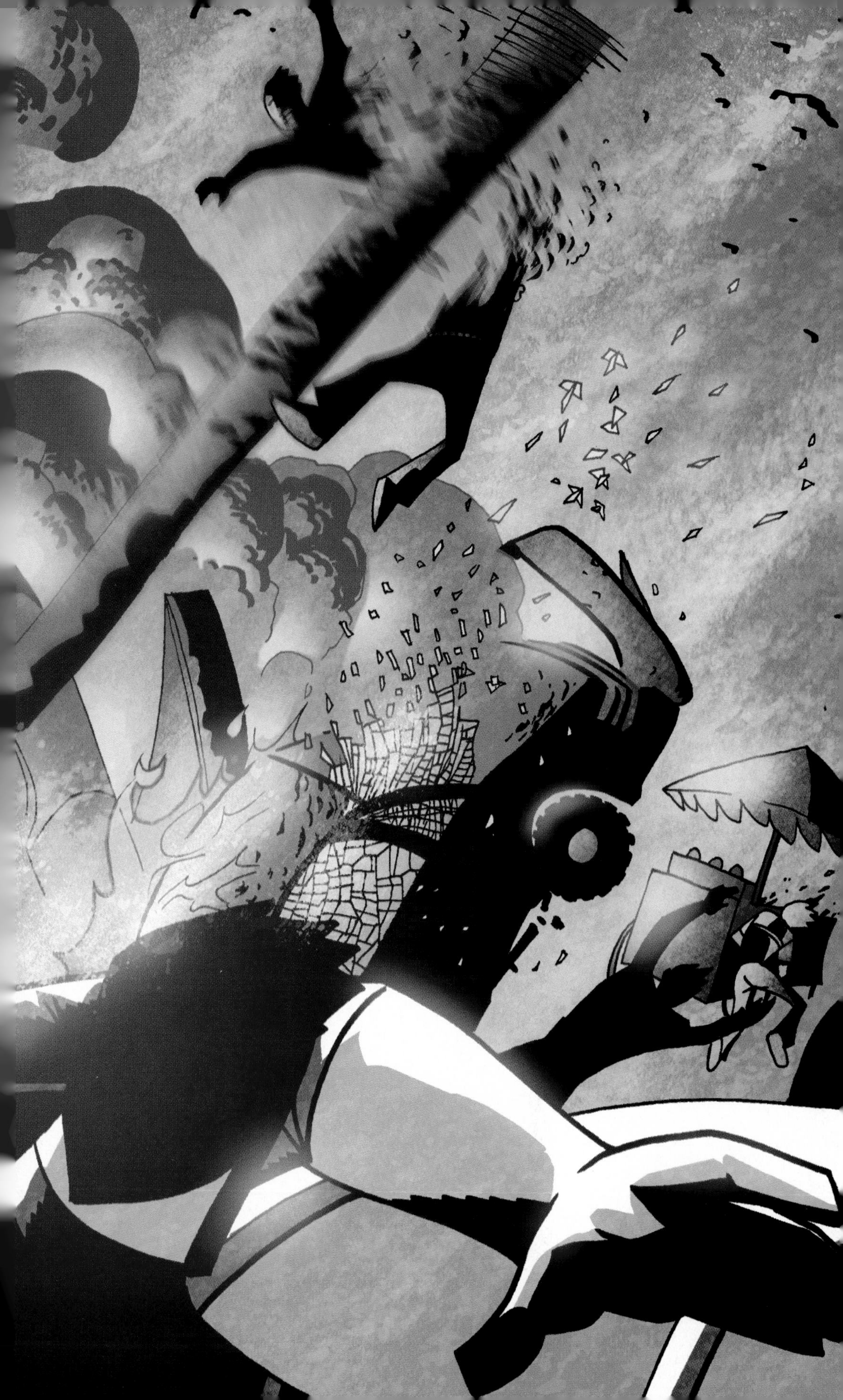

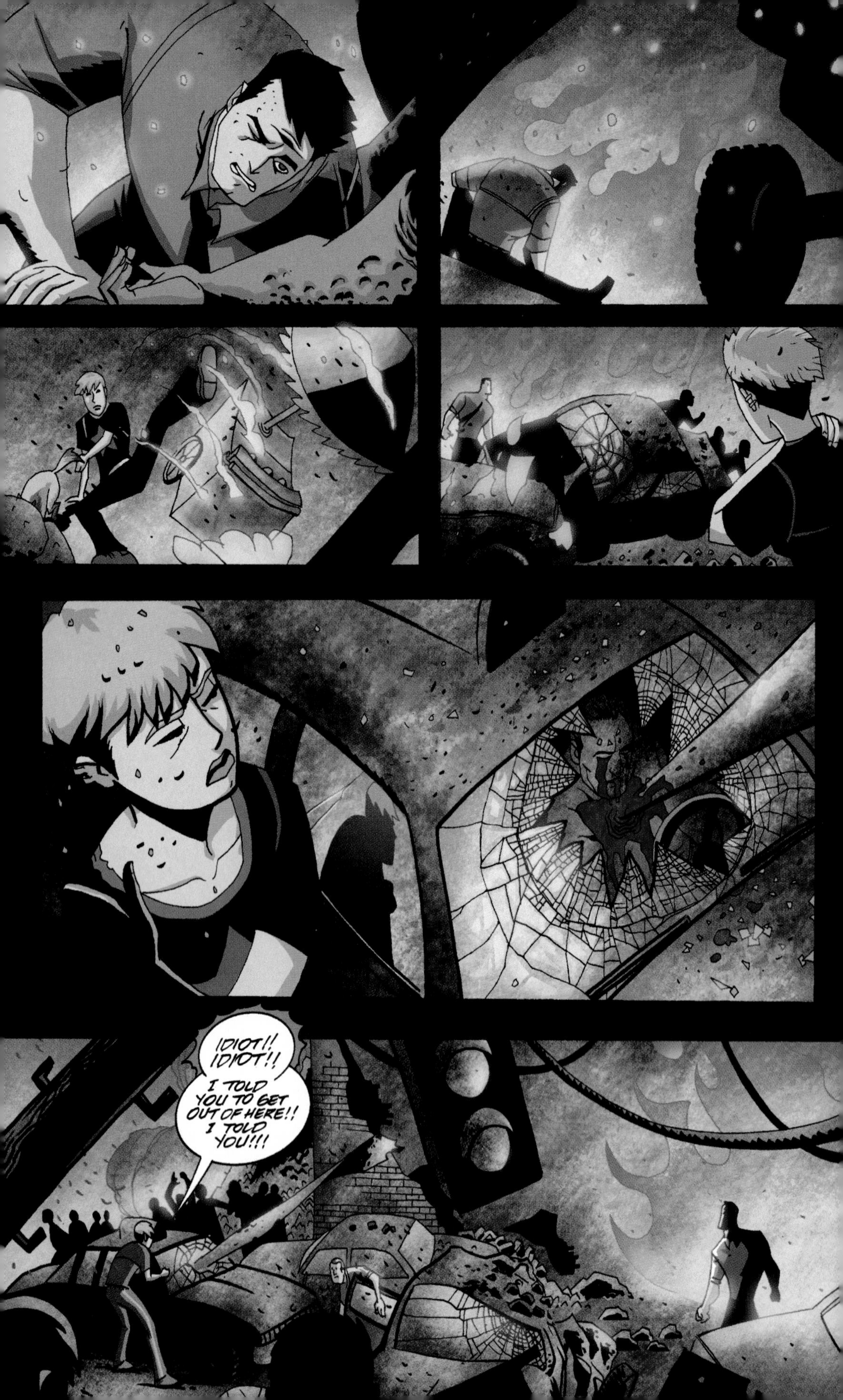
IDIOT!! IDIOT!! I TOLD YOU TO GET OUT OF HERE!! I TOLD YOU!!!

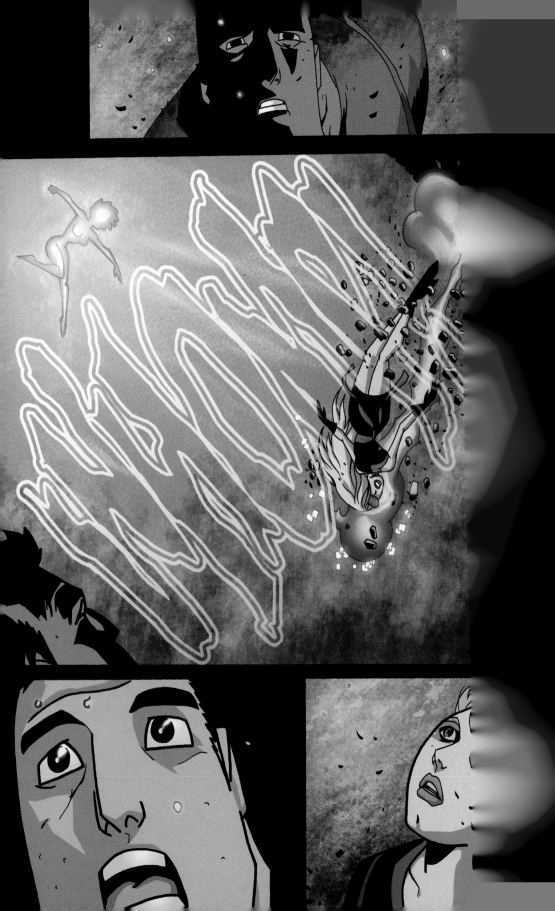

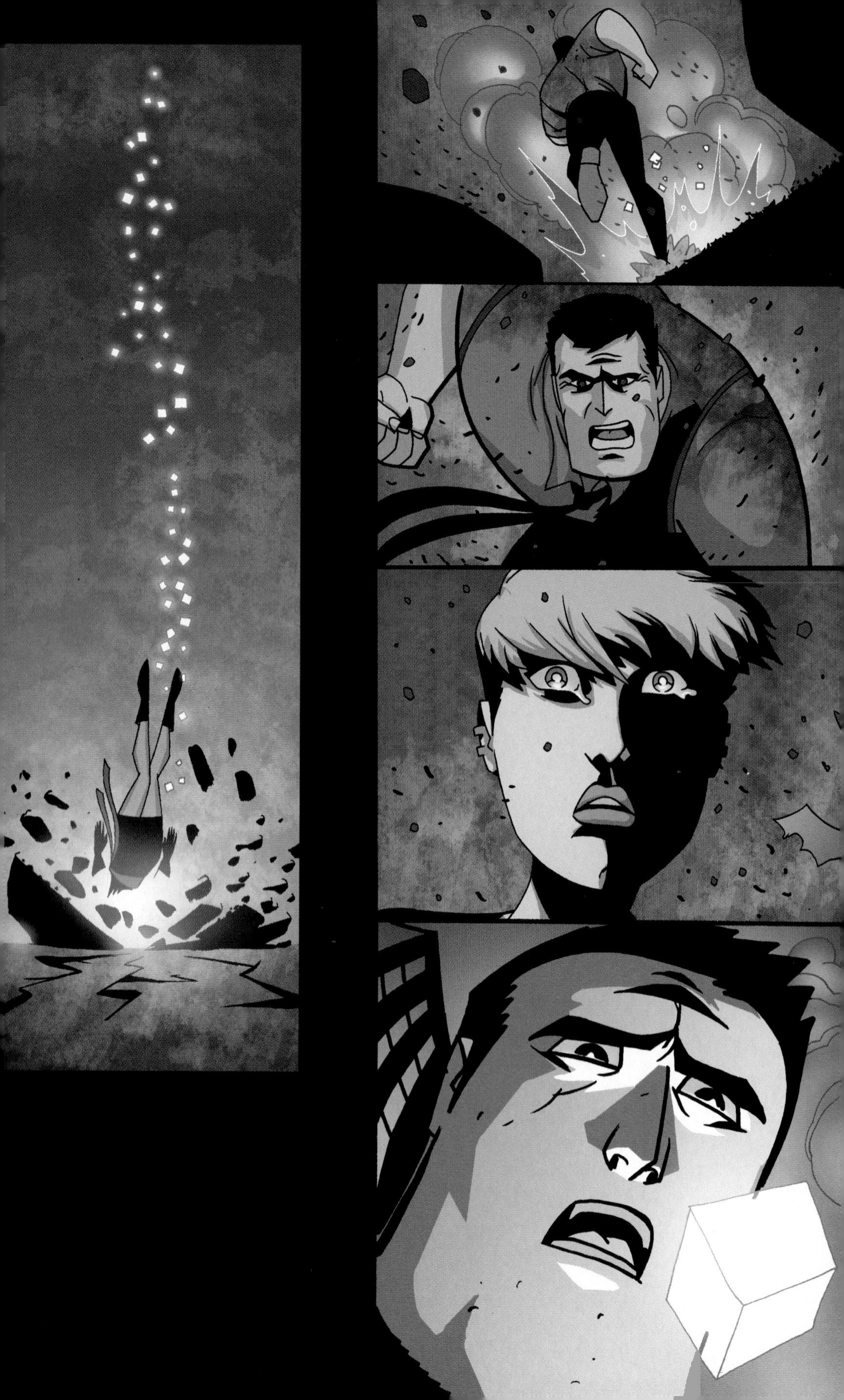

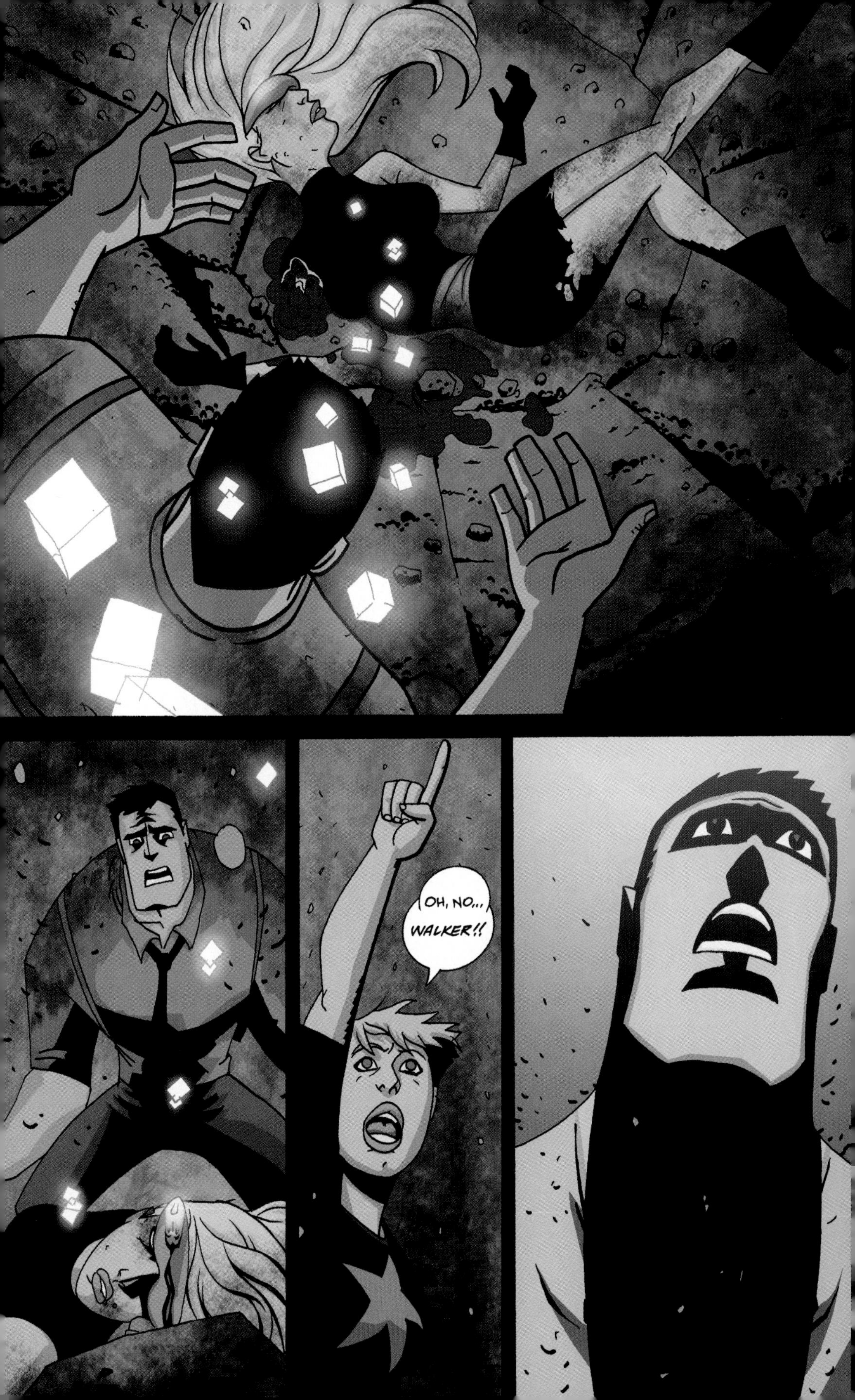
OH, NO...
WALKER!!

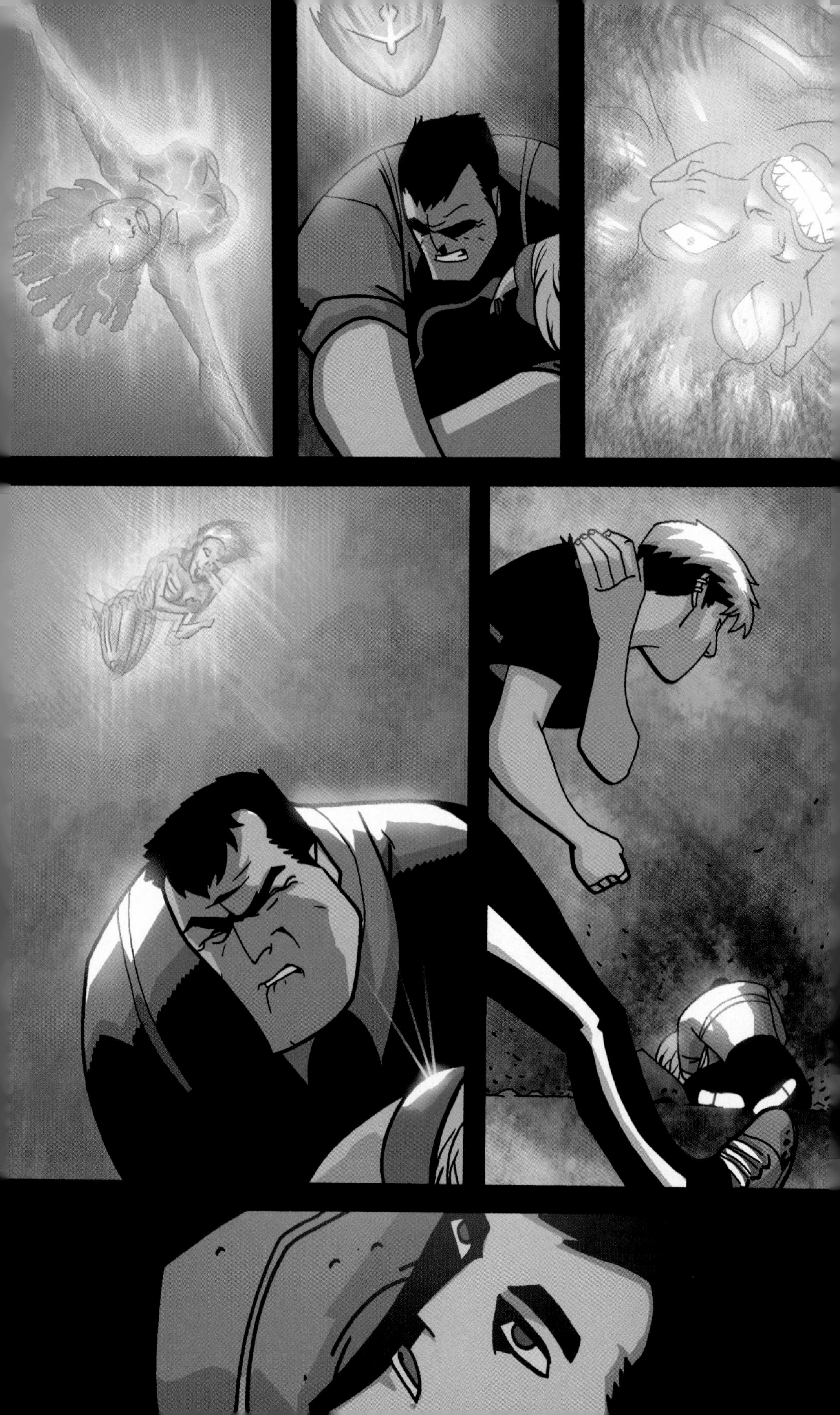

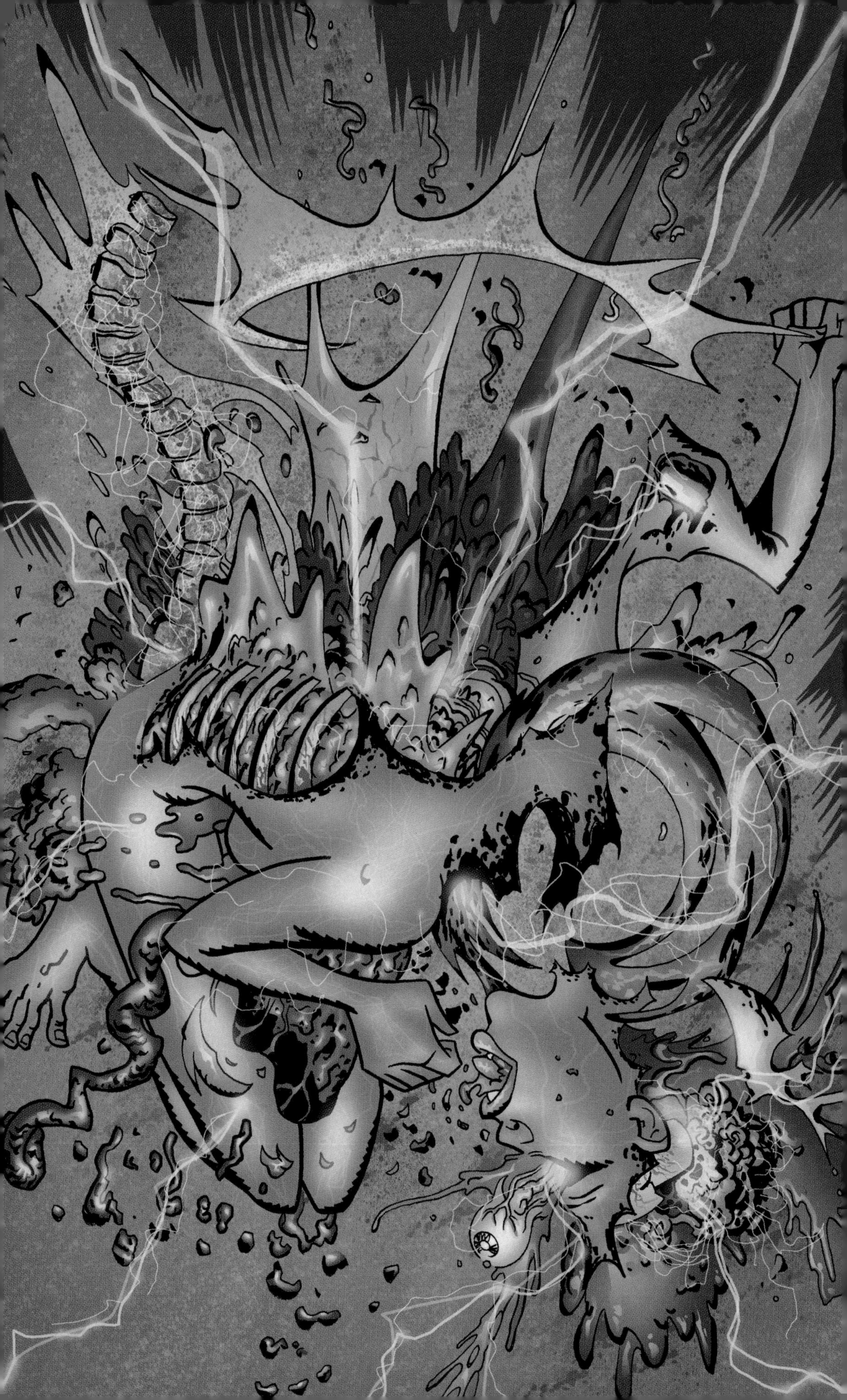

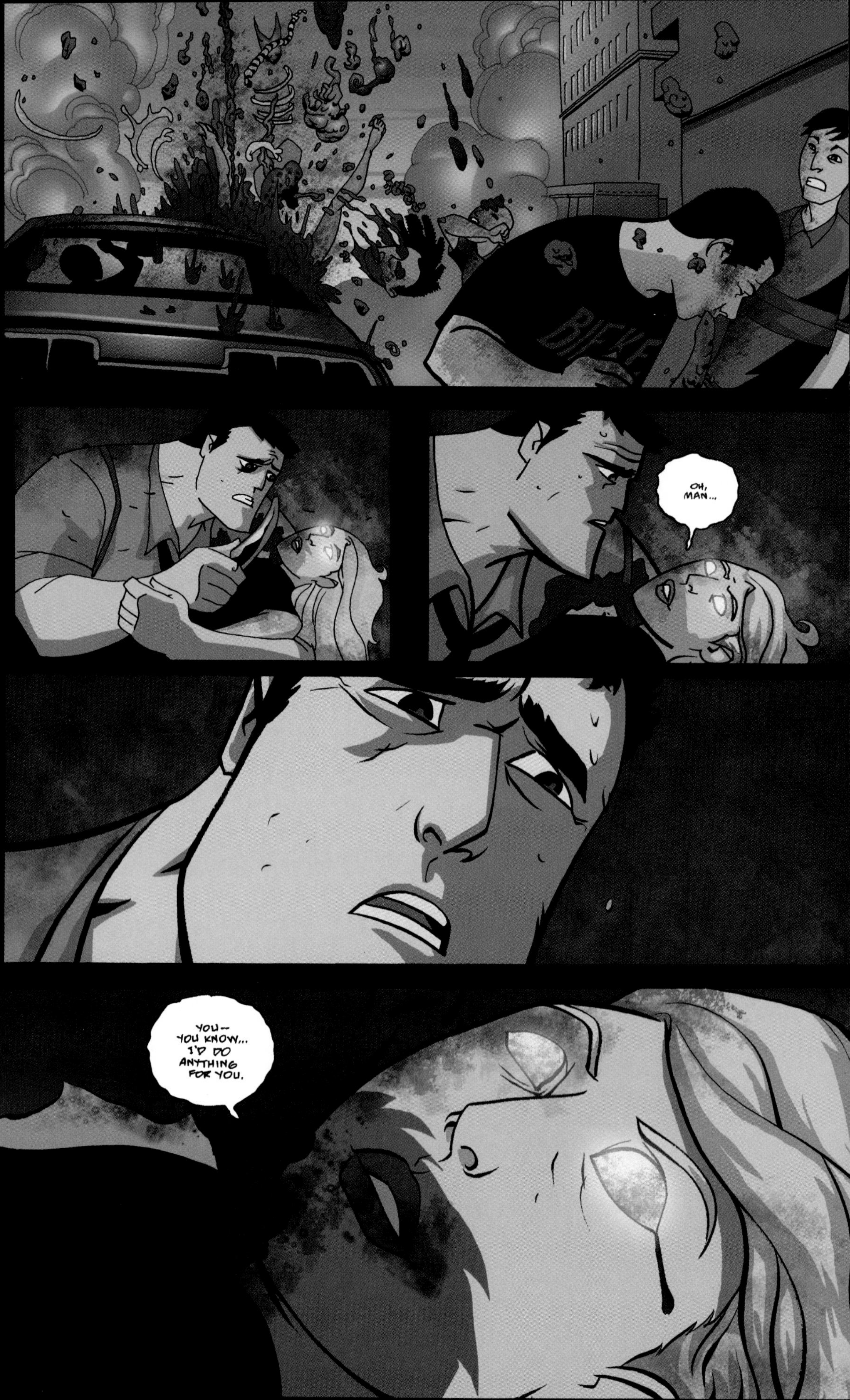
OH, MAN...
YOU-- YOU KNOW... I'D DO ANYTHING FOR YOU.

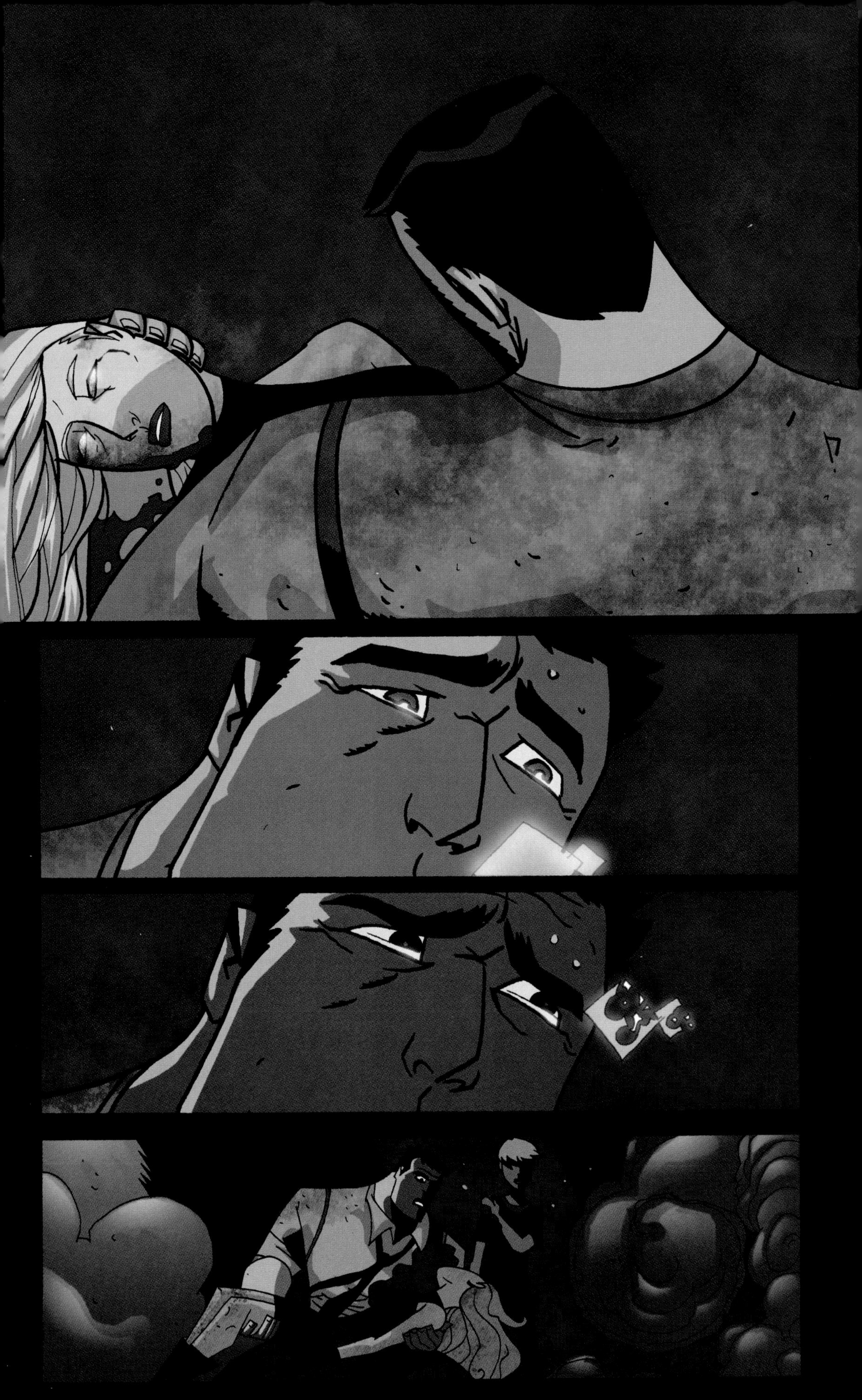

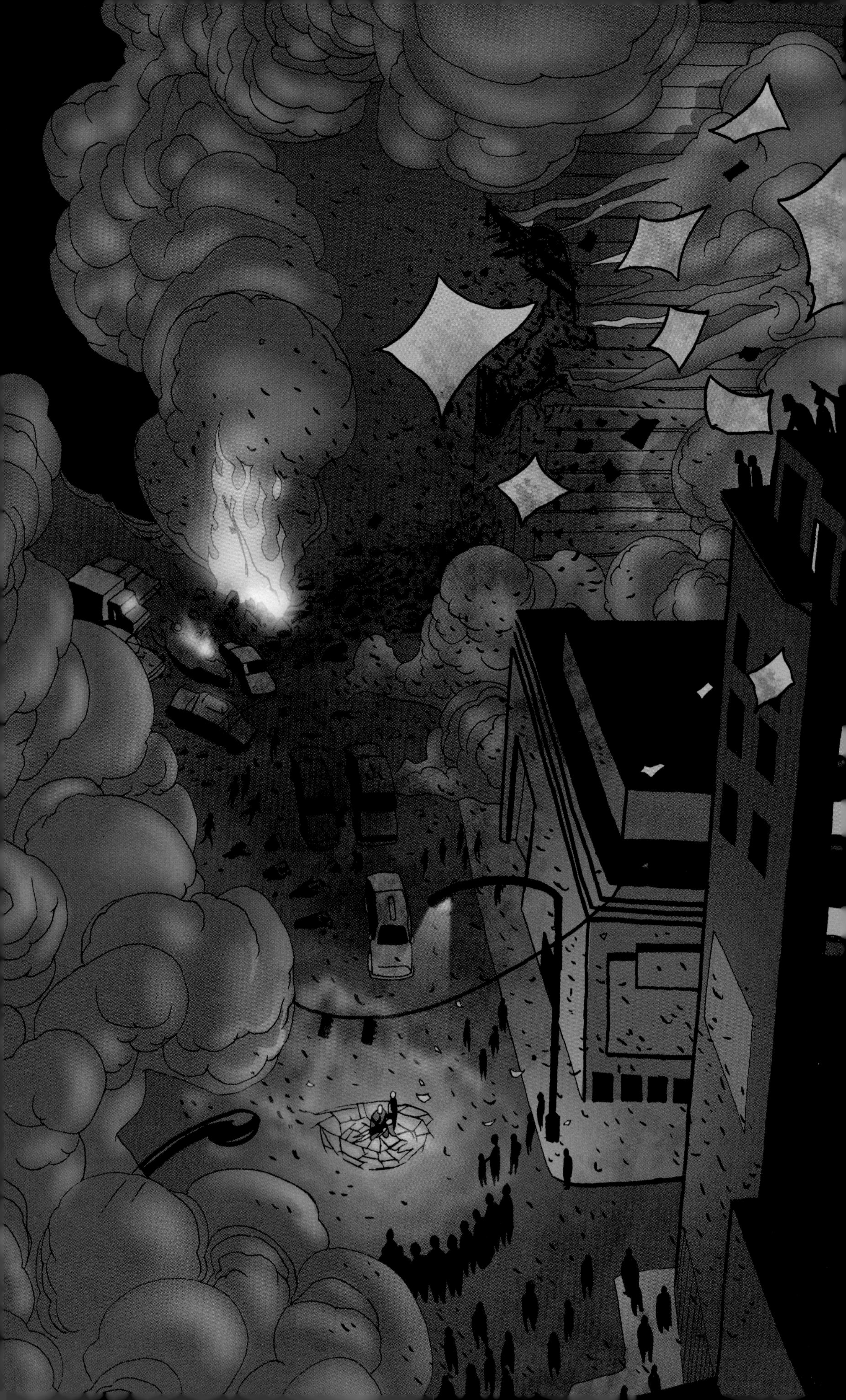

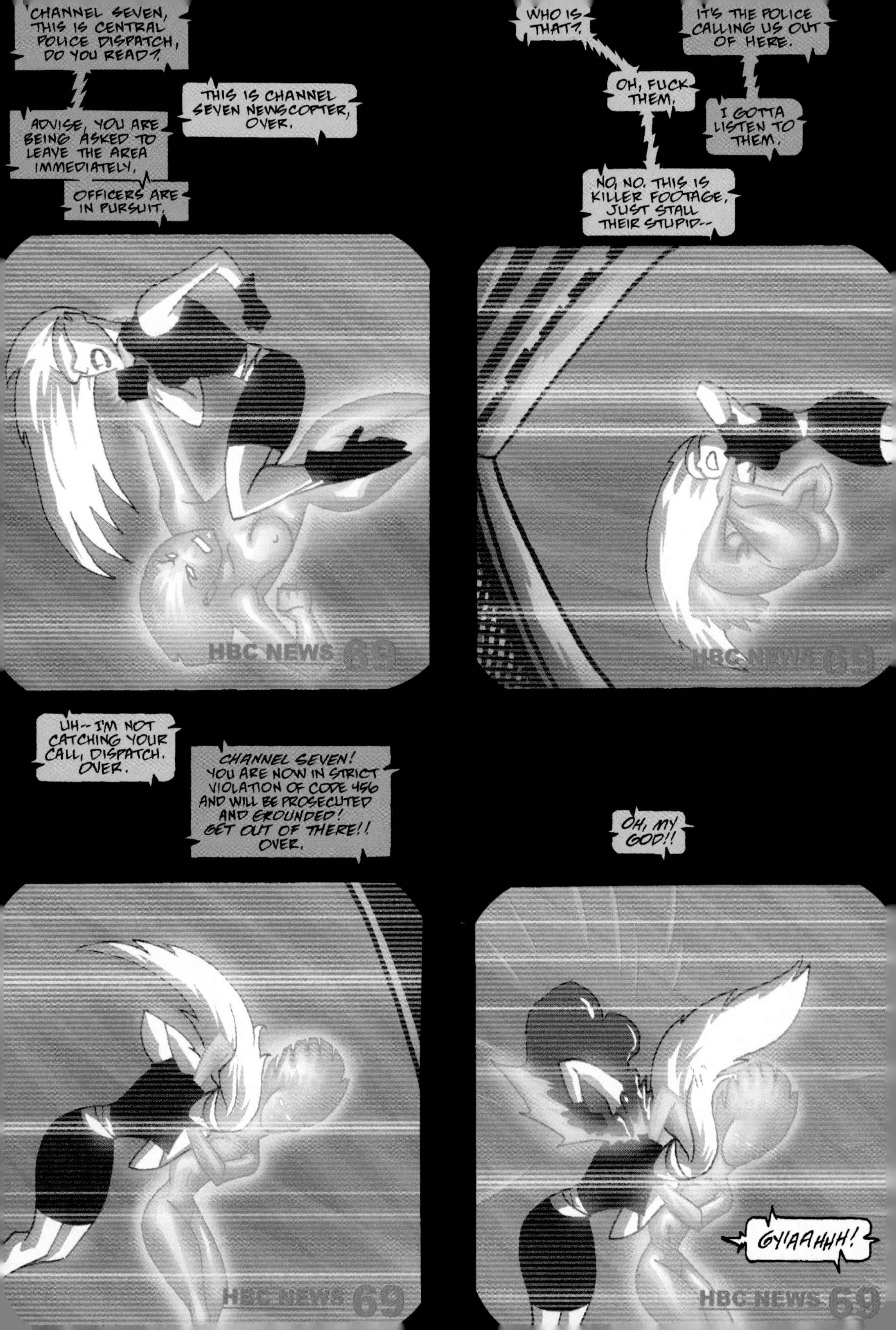
CHANNEL SEVEN, THIS IS CENTRAL POLICE DISPATCH, DO YOU READ?
THIS IS CHANNEL SEVEN NEWSCOPTER, OVER.
ADVISE, YOU ARE BEING ASKED TO LEAVE THE AREA IMMEDIATELY.
OFFICERS ARE IN PURSUIT.
HBC NEWS 69
WHO IS THAT?
IT'S THE POLICE CALLING US OUT OF HERE.
OH, FUCK THEM.
I GOTTA LISTEN TO THEM.
NO, NO. THIS IS KILLER FOOTAGE. JUST STALL THEIR STUPID--
HBC NEWS 69
UH--I'M NOT CATCHING YOUR CALL, DISPATCH. OVER.
CHANNEL SEVEN! YOU ARE NOW IN STRICT VIOLATION OF CODE 456 AND WILL BE PROSECUTED AND GROUNDED! GET OUT OF THERE!! OVER.
HBC NEWS 69
OH, MY GOD!!
GYAAHHH!
HBC NEWS 69

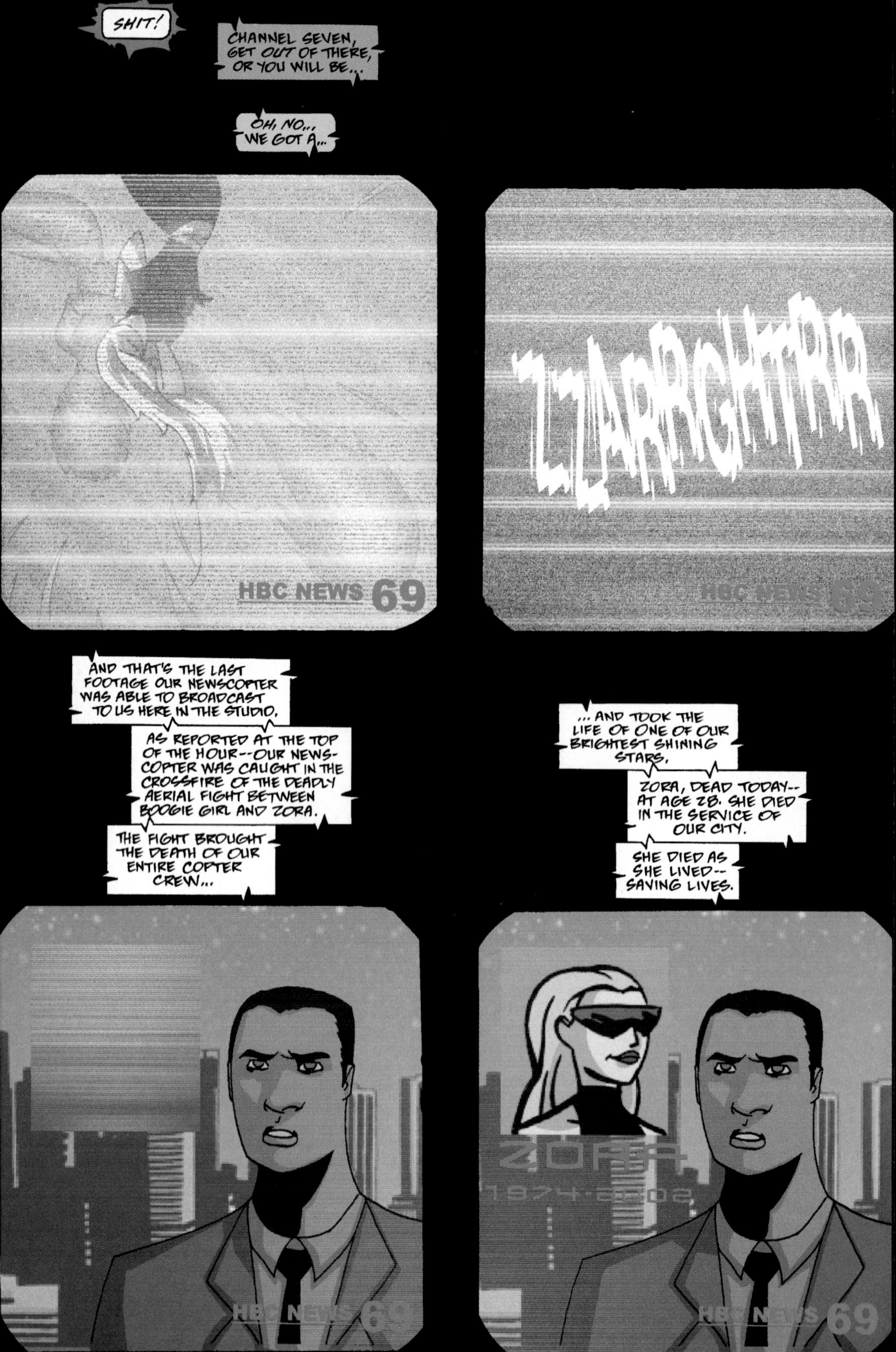
SHIT!
CHANNEL SEVEN, GET OUT OF THERE, OR YOU WILL BE...
OH, NO... WE GOT A...
HBC NEWS 69
ZZARRGHTRR
HBC NEWS 69
AND THAT'S THE LAST FOOTAGE OUR NEWSCOPTER WAS ABLE TO BROADCAST TO US HERE IN THE STUDIO.
AS REPORTED AT THE TOP OF THE HOUR--OUR NEWS-COPTER WAS CAUGHT IN THE CROSSFIRE OF THE DEADLY AERIAL FIGHT BETWEEN BOOGIE GIRL AND ZORA.
THE FIGHT BROUGHT THE DEATH OF OUR ENTIRE COPTER CREW...
...AND TOOK THE LIFE OF ONE OF OUR BRIGHTEST SHINING STARS.
ZORA, DEAD TODAY--AT AGE 28. SHE DIED IN THE SERVICE OF OUR CITY.
SHE DIED AS SHE LIVED--SAVING LIVES.
HBC NEWS 69
ZORA
1974-2002
HBC NEWS 69

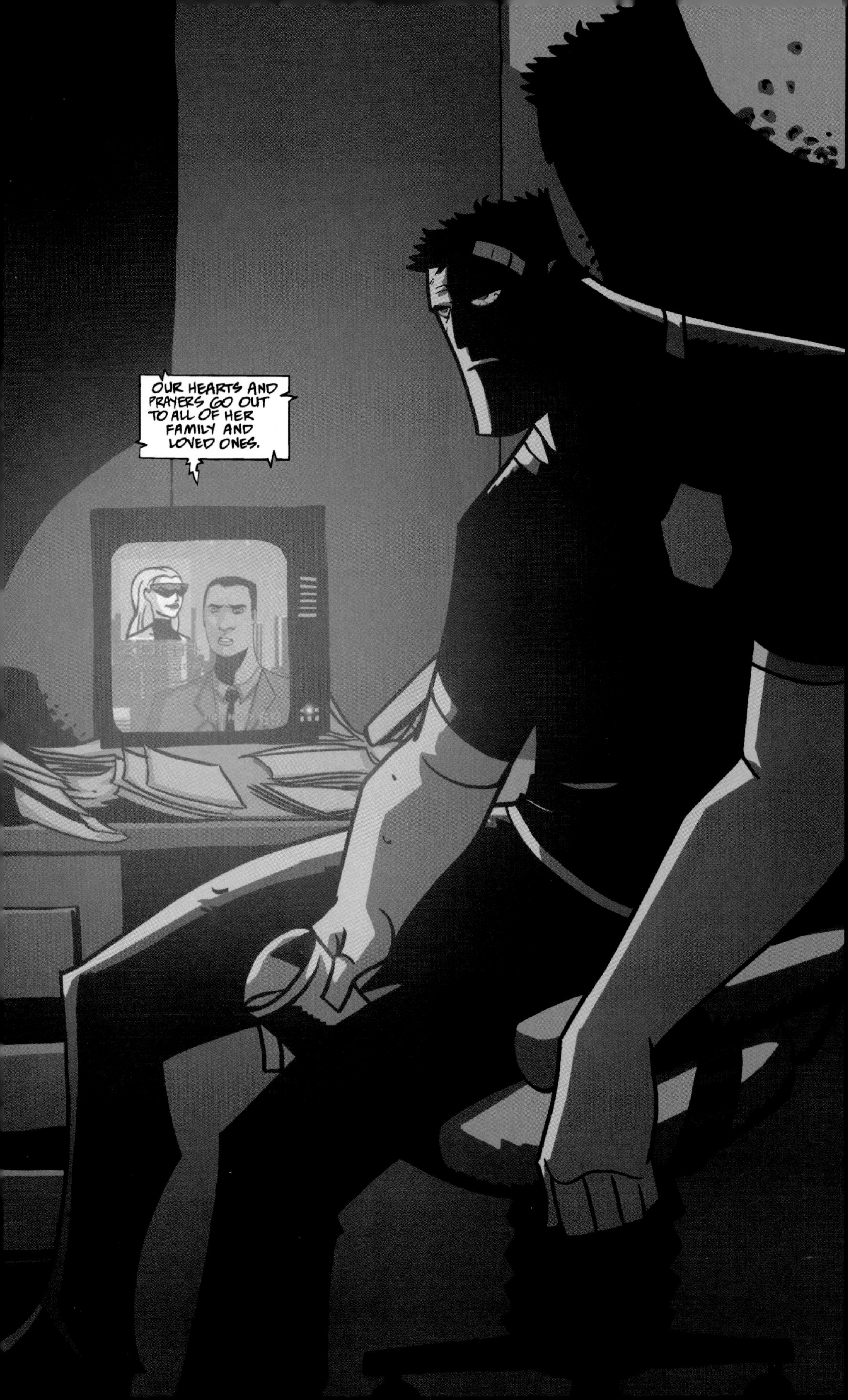
OUR HEARTS AND PRAYERS GO OUT TO ALL OF HER FAMILY AND LOVED ONES.

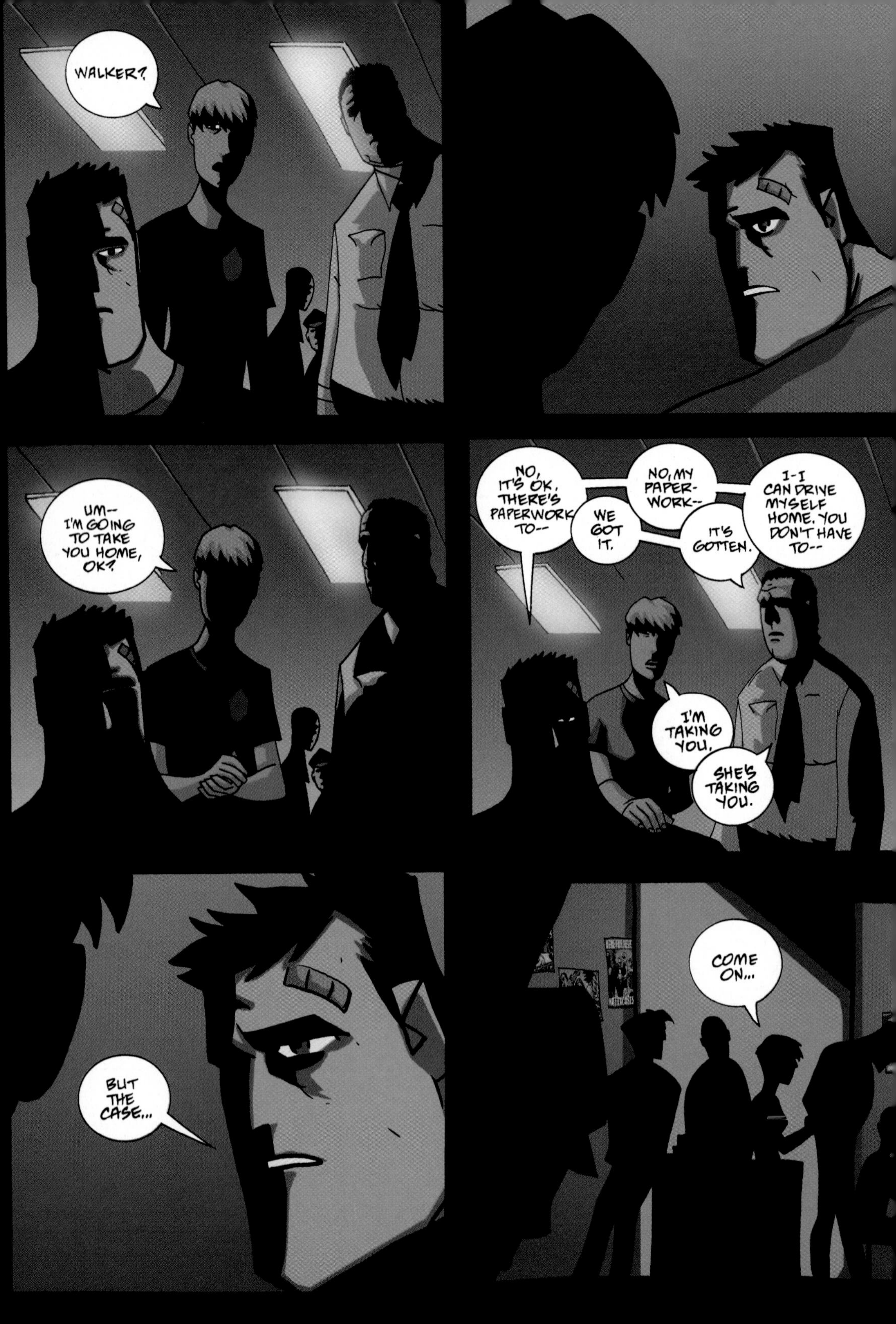
WALKER?
UM-- I'M GOING TO TAKE YOU HOME, OK?
NO, IT'S OK, THERE'S PAPERWORK TO--
WE GOT IT.
NO, MY PAPER-WORK--
IT'S GOTTEN.
I-I CAN DRIVE MYSELF HOME. YOU DON'T HAVE TO--
I'M TAKING YOU.
SHE'S TAKING YOU.
BUT THE CASE...
COME ON...

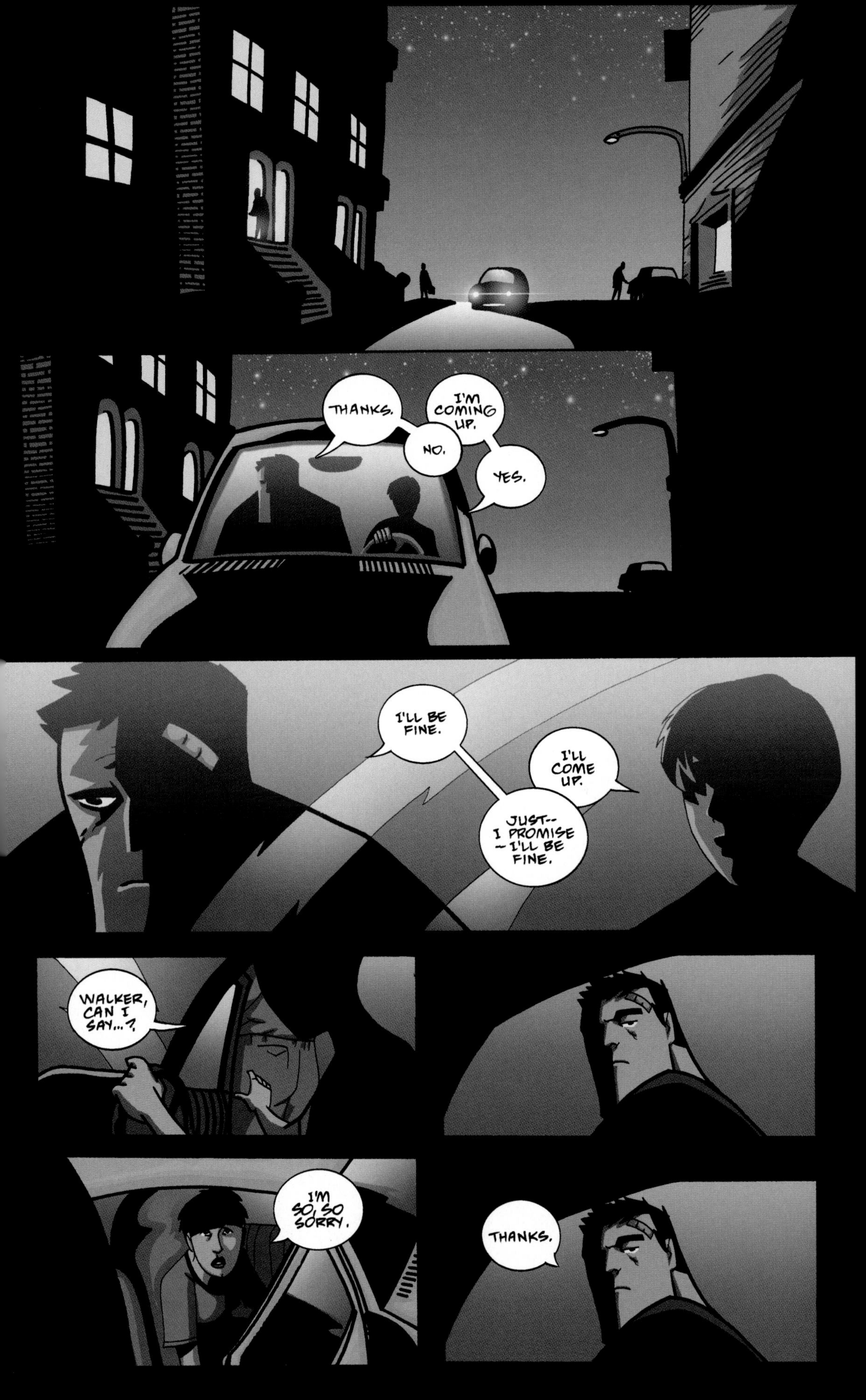
THANKS.
I'M COMING UP.
NO.
YES.
I'LL BE FINE.
I'LL COME UP.
JUST-- I PROMISE -- I'LL BE FINE.
WALKER, CAN I SAY...?
I'M SO, SO SORRY.
THANKS.

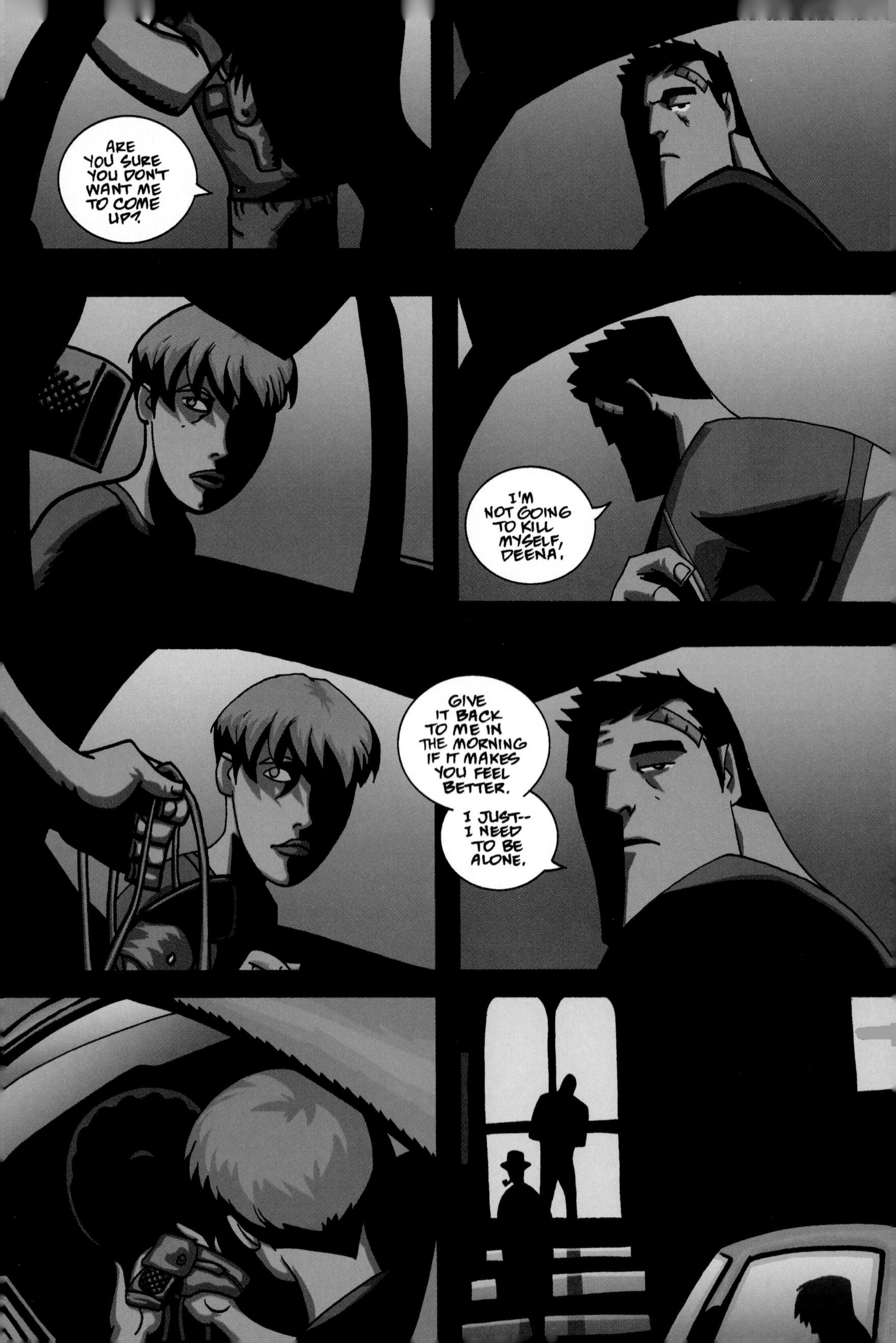
ARE YOU SURE YOU DON'T WANT ME TO COME UP?
I'M NOT GOING TO KILL MYSELF, DEENA.
GIVE IT BACK TO ME IN THE MORNING IF IT MAKES YOU FEEL BETTER.
I JUST-- I NEED TO BE ALONE.

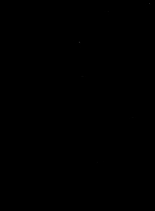

YOU
ALONE?

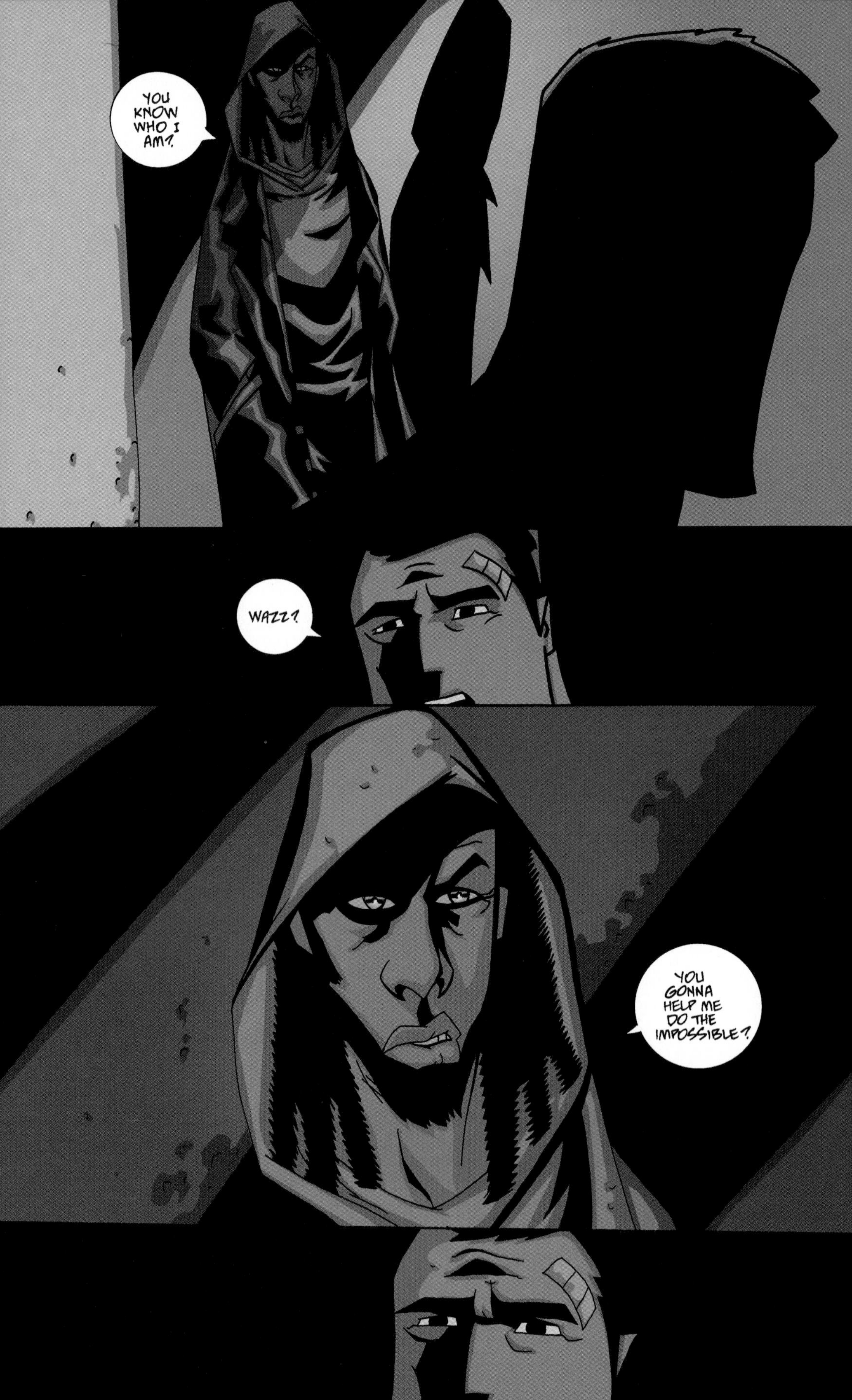
YOU KNOW WHO I AM?
WAZZ?
YOU GONNA HELP ME DO THE IMPOSSIBLE?

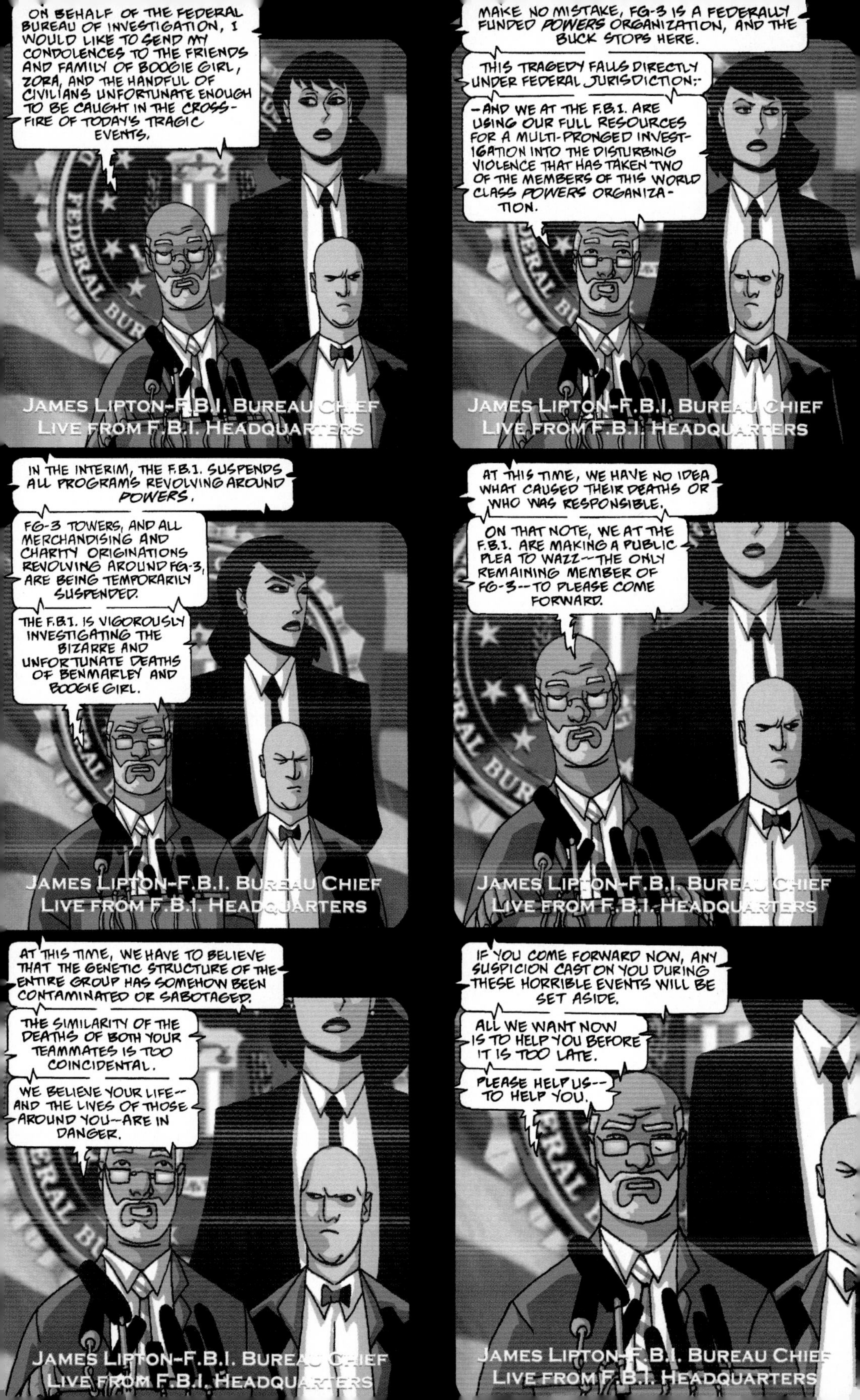
ON BEHALF OF THE FEDERAL BUREAU OF INVESTIGATION, I WOULD LIKE TO SEND MY CONDOLENCES TO THE FRIENDS AND FAMILY OF BOOGIE GIRL, ZORA, AND THE HANDFUL OF CIVILIANS UNFORTUNATE ENOUGH TO BE CAUGHT IN THE CROSS-FIRE OF TODAY'S TRAGIC EVENTS.
JAMES LIPTON-F.B.I. BUREAU CHIEF
LIVE FROM F.B.I. HEADQUARTERS
MAKE NO MISTAKE, FG-3 IS A FEDERALLY FUNDED *POWERS* ORGANIZATION, AND THE BUCK STOPS HERE.
THIS TRAGEDY FALLS DIRECTLY UNDER FEDERAL JURISDICTION:-
-AND WE AT THE F.B.I. ARE USING OUR FULL RESOURCES FOR A MULTI-PRONGED INVESTIGATION INTO THE DISTURBING VIOLENCE THAT HAS TAKEN TWO OF THE MEMBERS OF THIS WORLD CLASS *POWERS* ORGANIZATION.
JAMES LIPTON-F.B.I. BUREAU CHIEF
LIVE FROM F.B.I. HEADQUARTERS
IN THE INTERIM, THE F.B.I. SUSPENDS ALL PROGRAMS REVOLVING AROUND *POWERS*.
FG-3 TOWERS, AND ALL MERCHANDISING AND CHARITY ORIGINATIONS REVOLVING AROUND FG-3, ARE BEING TEMPORARILY SUSPENDED.
THE F.B.I. IS VIGOROUSLY INVESTIGATING THE BIZARRE AND UNFORTUNATE DEATHS OF BENMARLEY AND BOOGIE GIRL.
JAMES LIPTON-F.B.I. BUREAU CHIEF
LIVE FROM F.B.I. HEADQUARTERS
AT THIS TIME, WE HAVE NO IDEA WHAT CAUSED THEIR DEATHS OR WHO WAS RESPONSIBLE.
ON THAT NOTE, WE AT THE F.B.I. ARE MAKING A PUBLIC PLEA TO WAZZ--THE ONLY REMAINING MEMBER OF FG-3--TO PLEASE COME FORWARD.
JAMES LIPTON-F.B.I. BUREAU CHIEF
LIVE FROM F.B.I. HEADQUARTERS
AT THIS TIME, WE HAVE TO BELIEVE THAT THE GENETIC STRUCTURE OF THE ENTIRE GROUP HAS SOMEHOW BEEN CONTAMINATED OR SABOTAGED.
THE SIMILARITY OF THE DEATHS OF BOTH YOUR TEAMMATES IS TOO COINCIDENTAL.
WE BELIEVE YOUR LIFE--AND THE LIVES OF THOSE AROUND YOU--ARE IN DANGER.
JAMES LIPTON-F.B.I. BUREAU CHIEF
LIVE FROM F.B.I. HEADQUARTERS
IF YOU COME FORWARD NOW, ANY SUSPICION CAST ON YOU DURING THESE HORRIBLE EVENTS WILL BE SET ASIDE.
ALL WE WANT NOW IS TO HELP YOU BEFORE IT IS TOO LATE.
PLEASE HELP US--TO HELP YOU.
JAMES LIPTON-F.B.I. BUREAU CHIEF
LIVE FROM F.B.I. HEADQUARTERS

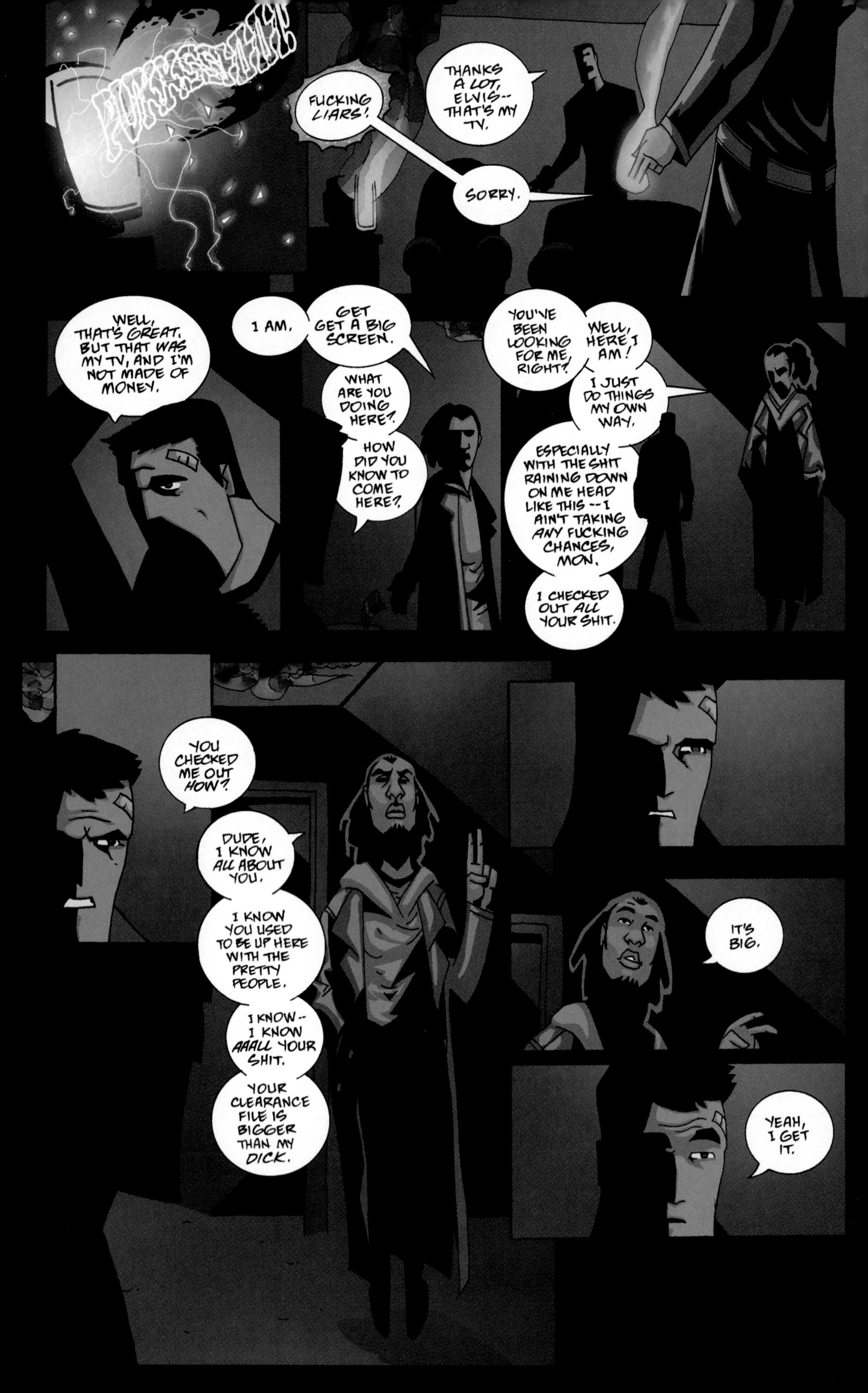
FUCKING LIARS!
THANKS A LOT, ELVIS-- THAT'S MY TV.
SORRY.
WELL, THAT'S GREAT, BUT THAT WAS MY TV, AND I'M NOT MADE OF MONEY.
I AM.
GET GET A BIG SCREEN.
WHAT ARE YOU DOING HERE?
HOW DID YOU KNOW TO COME HERE?
YOU'VE BEEN LOOKING FOR ME, RIGHT?
WELL, HERE I AM!
I JUST DO THINGS MY OWN WAY.
ESPECIALLY WITH THE SHIT RAINING DOWN ON ME HEAD LIKE THIS --I AIN'T TAKING ANY FUCKING CHANCES, MON.
I CHECKED OUT ALL YOUR SHIT.
YOU CHECKED ME OUT HOW?
DUDE, I KNOW ALL ABOUT YOU.
I KNOW YOU USED TO BE UP HERE WITH THE PRETTY PEOPLE.
I KNOW-- I KNOW AAALL YOUR SHIT.
YOUR CLEARANCE FILE IS BIGGER THAN MY DICK.
IT'S BIG.
YEAH, I GET IT.

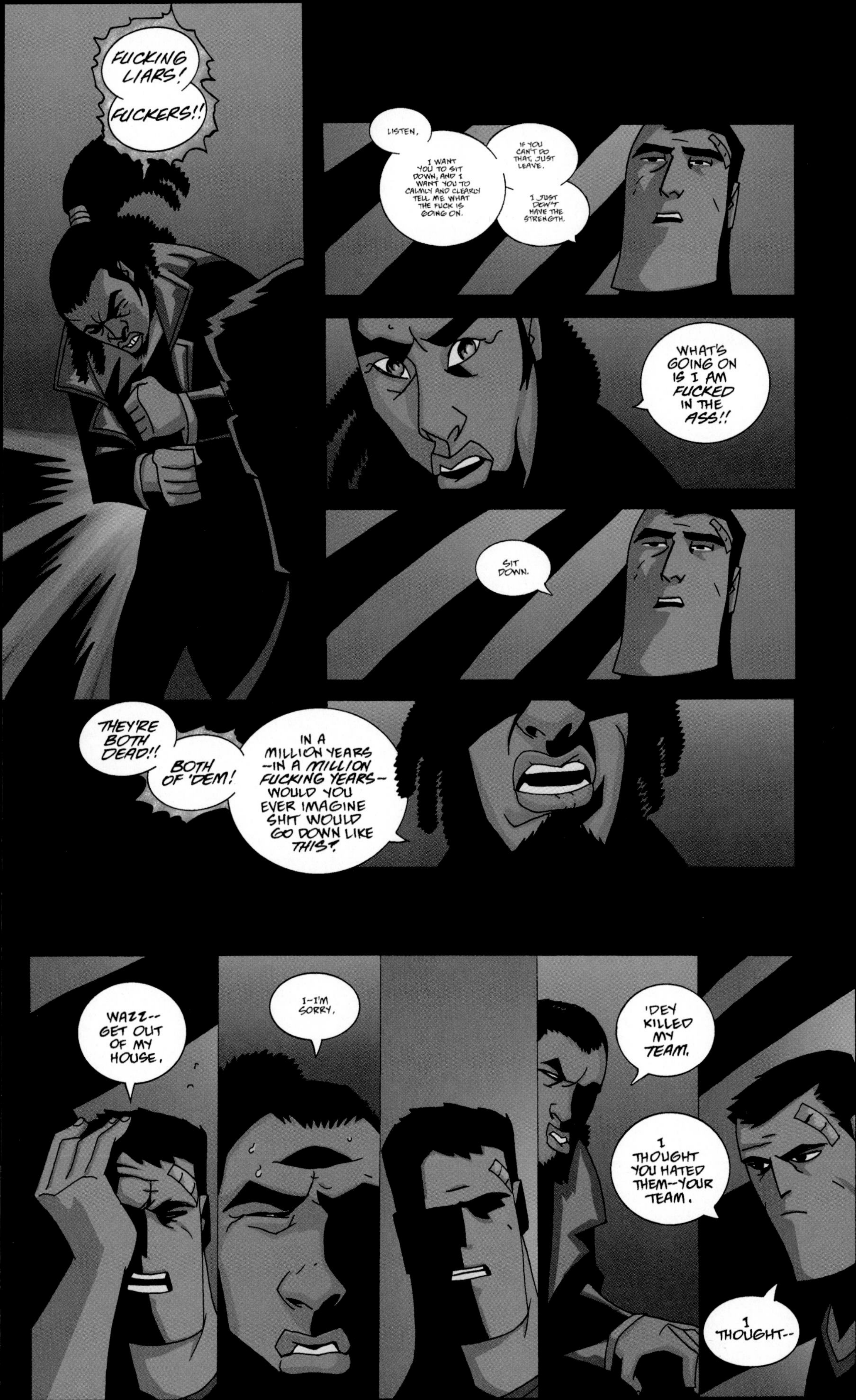
FUCKING LIARS!
FUCKERS!!
LISTEN,
I WANT YOU TO SIT DOWN, AND I WANT YOU TO CALMLY AND CLEARLY TELL ME WHAT THE FUCK IS GOING ON.
IF YOU CAN'T DO THAT, JUST LEAVE.
I JUST DON'T HAVE THE STRENGTH.
WHAT'S GOING ON IS I AM FUCKED IN THE ASS!!
SIT DOWN.
THEY'RE BOTH DEAD!!
BOTH OF 'DEM!
IN A MILLION YEARS --IN A MILLION FUCKING YEARS-- WOULD YOU EVER IMAGINE SHIT WOULD GO DOWN LIKE THIS?
WAZZ-- GET OUT OF MY HOUSE.
I-I'M SORRY.
'DEY KILLED MY TEAM.
I THOUGHT YOU HATED THEM--YOUR TEAM.
I THOUGHT--

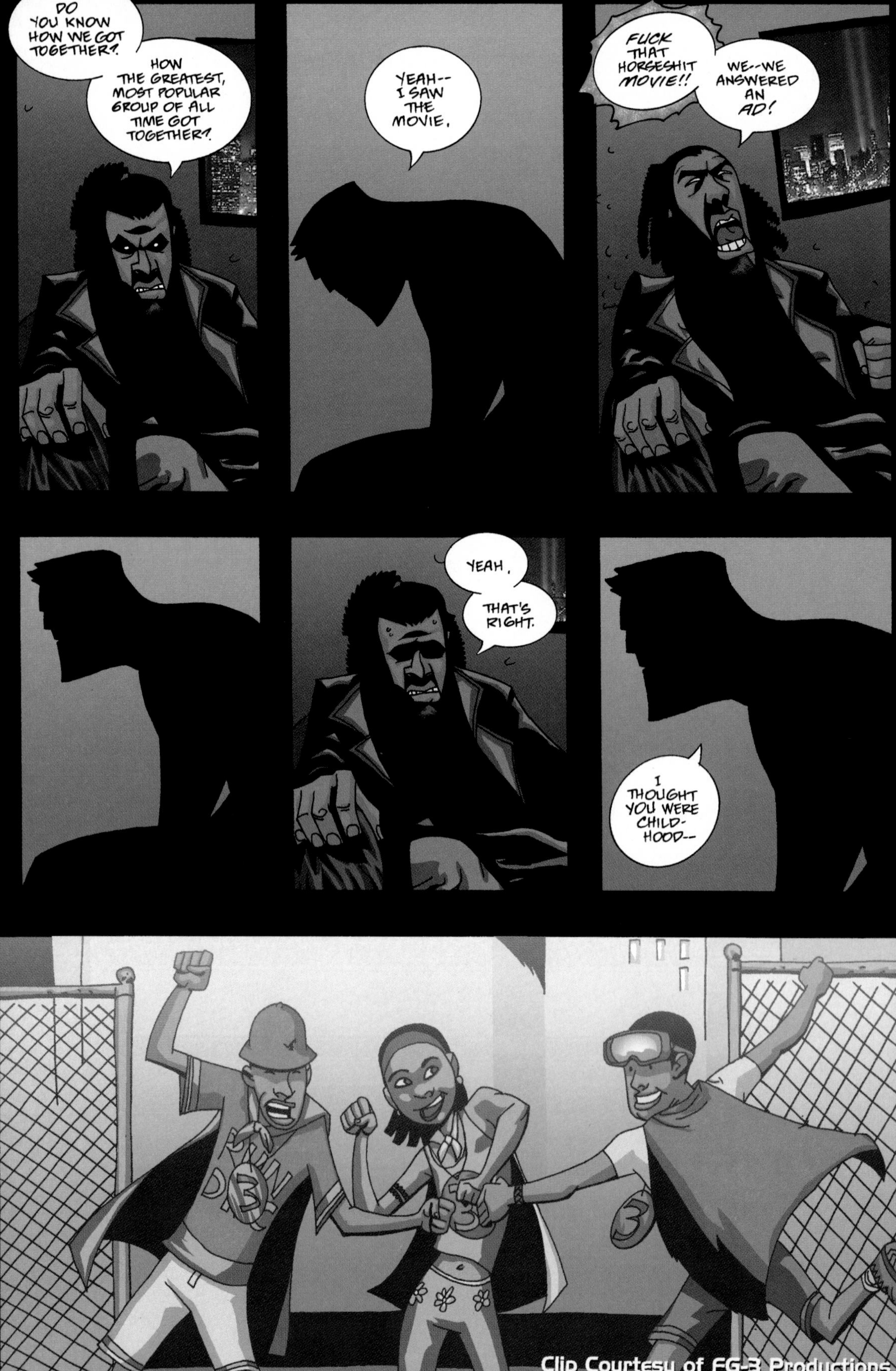

DO YOU KNOW HOW WE GOT TOGETHER?
HOW THE GREATEST, MOST POPULAR GROUP OF ALL TIME GOT TOGETHER?
YEAH-- I SAW THE MOVIE.
FUCK THAT HORSESHIT MOVIE!!
WE--WE ANSWERED AN AD!
YEAH.
THAT'S RIGHT.
I THOUGHT YOU WERE CHILD-HOOD--
Clip Courtesy of FG-3 Productions

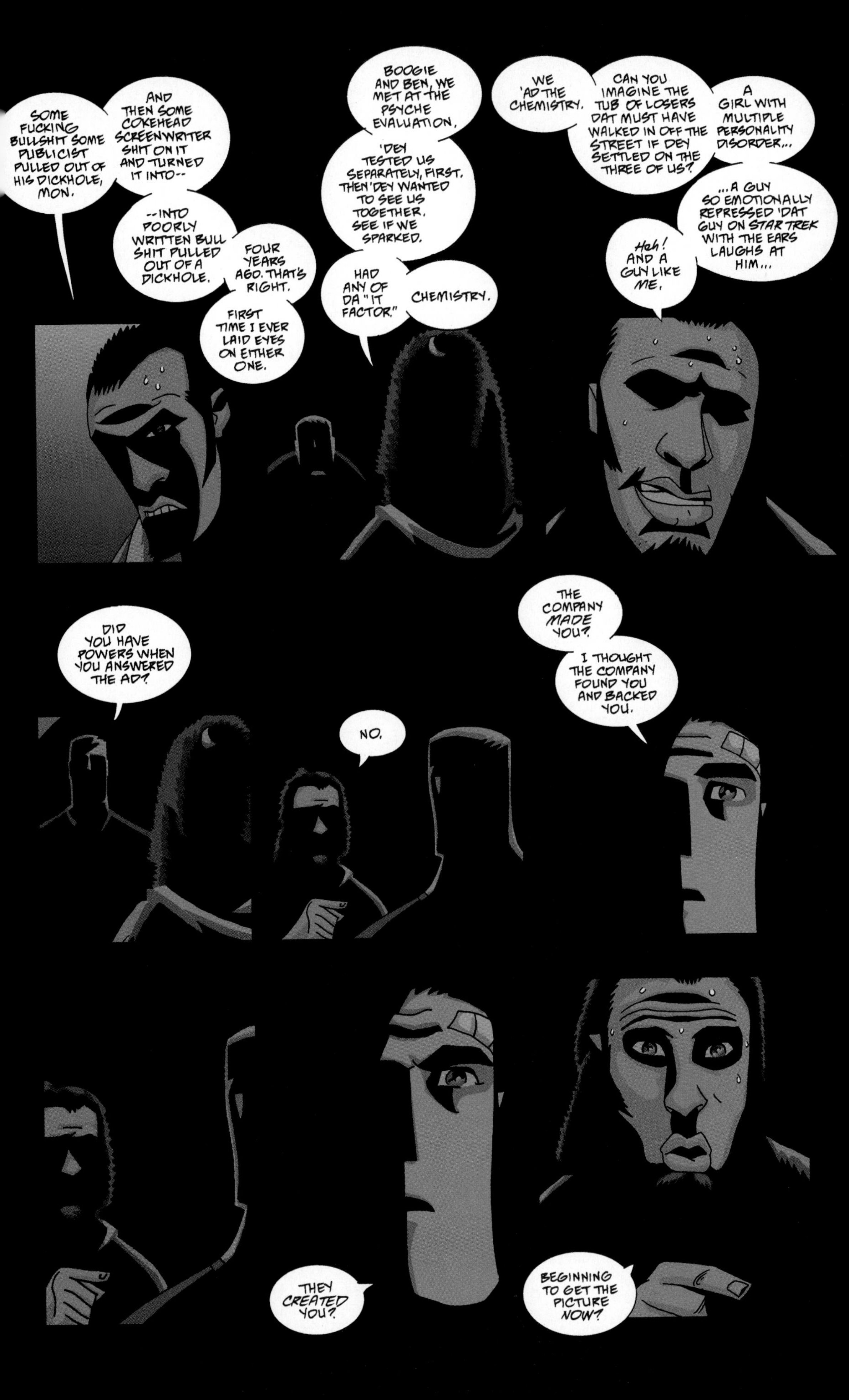
SOME FUCKING BULLSHIT SOME PUBLICIST PULLED OUT OF HIS DICKHOLE, MON.
AND THEN SOME COKEHEAD SCREENWRITER SHIT ON IT AND TURNED IT INTO--
--INTO POORLY WRITTEN BULL SHIT PULLED OUT OF A DICKHOLE.
FOUR YEARS AGO. THAT'S RIGHT.
FIRST TIME I EVER LAID EYES ON EITHER ONE.
BOOGIE AND BEN, WE MET AT THE PSYCHE EVALUATION.
'DEY TESTED US SEPARATELY, FIRST. THEN 'DEY WANTED TO SEE US TOGETHER. SEE IF WE SPARKED.
HAD ANY OF DA "IT FACTOR."
CHEMISTRY.
WE 'AD THE CHEMISTRY.
CAN YOU IMAGINE THE TUB OF LOSERS DAT MUST HAVE WALKED IN OFF THE STREET IF DEY SETTLED ON THE THREE OF US?
A GIRL WITH MULTIPLE PERSONALITY DISORDER...
...A GUY SO EMOTIONALLY REPRESSED 'DAT GUY ON STAR TREK WITH THE EARS LAUGHS AT HIM...
Heh! AND A GUY LIKE ME.
DID YOU HAVE POWERS WHEN YOU ANSWERED THE AD?
NO.
THE COMPANY MADE YOU?
I THOUGHT THE COMPANY FOUND YOU AND BACKED YOU.
THEY CREATED YOU?
BEGINNING TO GET THE PICTURE NOW?

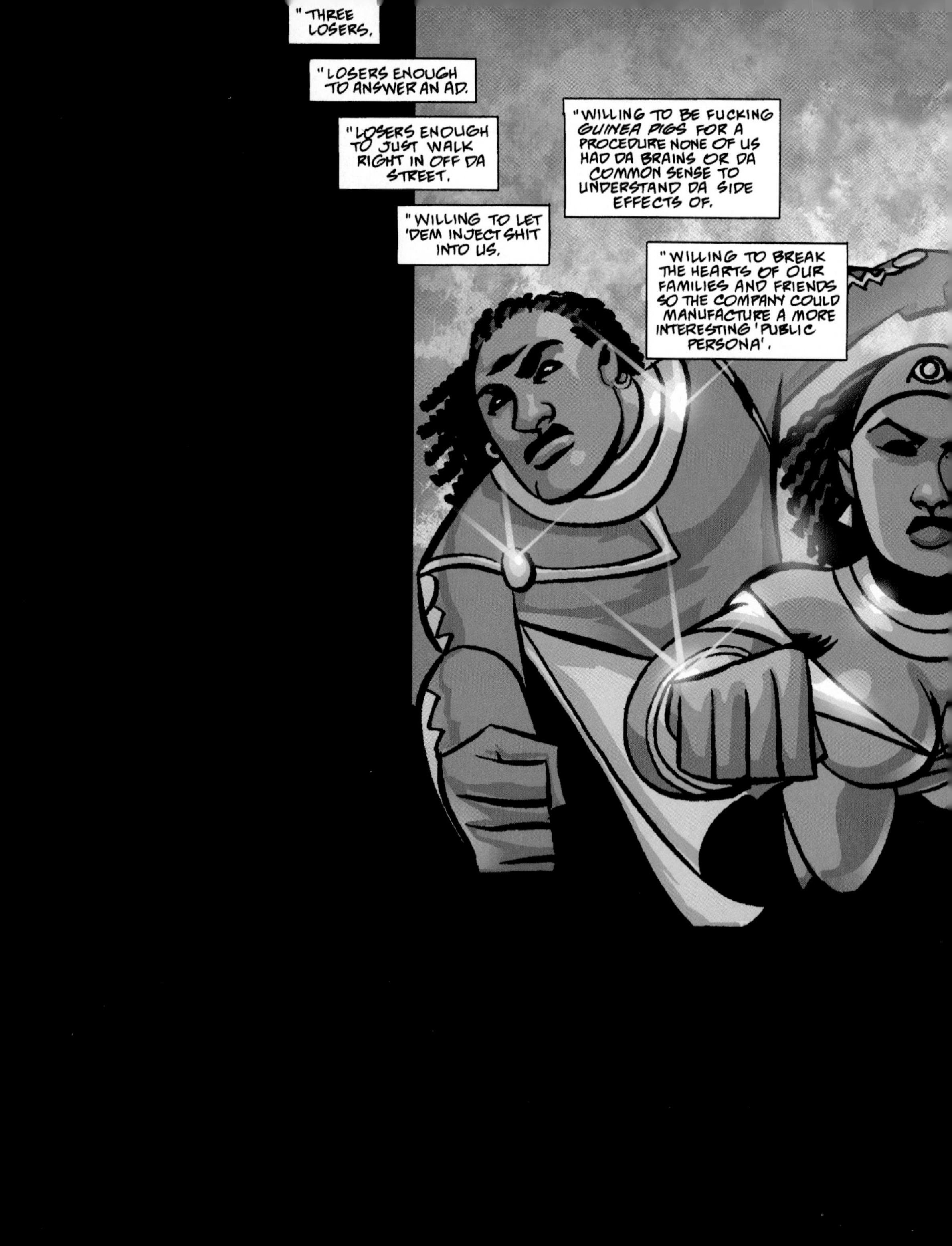
"THREE LOSERS.
"LOSERS ENOUGH TO ANSWER AN AD.
"LOSERS ENOUGH TO JUST WALK RIGHT IN OFF DA STREET.
"WILLING TO LET 'DEM INJECT SHIT INTO US.
"WILLING TO BE FUCKING GUINEA PIGS FOR A PROCEDURE NONE OF US HAD DA BRAINS OR DA COMMON SENSE TO UNDERSTAND DA SIDE EFFECTS OF.
"WILLING TO BREAK THE HEARTS OF OUR FAMILIES AND FRIENDS SO THE COMPANY COULD MANUFACTURE A MORE INTERESTING 'PUBLIC PERSONA'.

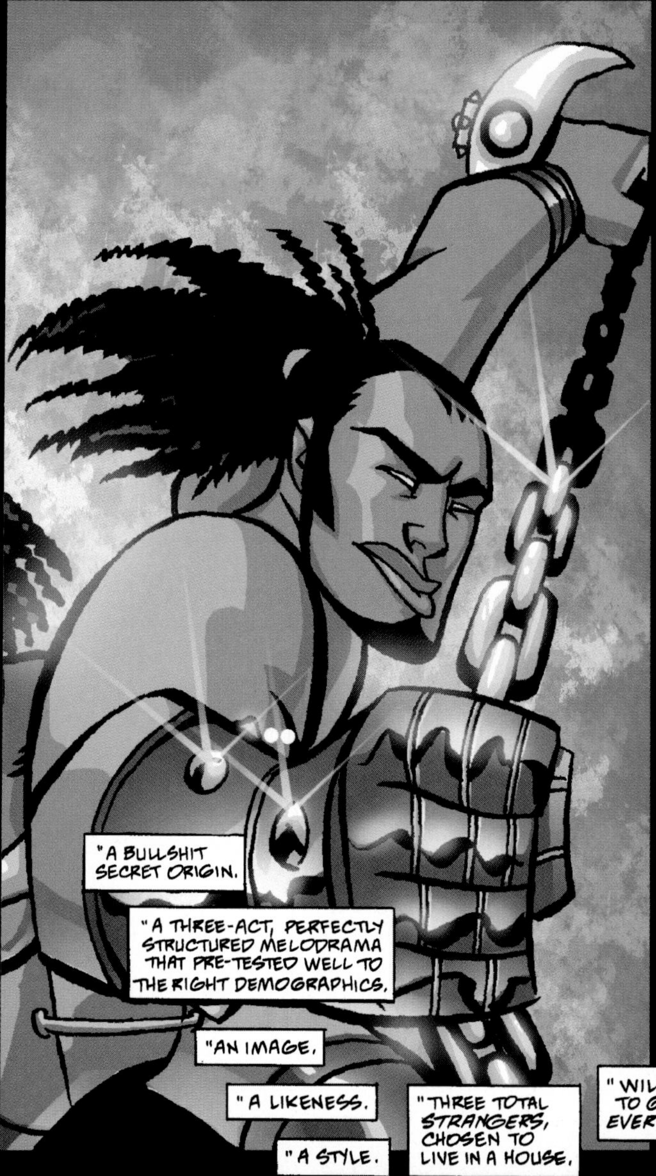
"A BULLSHIT SECRET ORIGIN.
"A THREE-ACT, PERFECTLY STRUCTURED MELODRAMA THAT PRE-TESTED WELL TO THE RIGHT DEMOGRAPHICS.
"AN IMAGE.
"A LIKENESS.
"A STYLE.
"THREE TOTAL STRANGERS, CHOSEN TO LIVE IN A HOUSE.
"WILLING TO GIVE UP EVERYTHING."

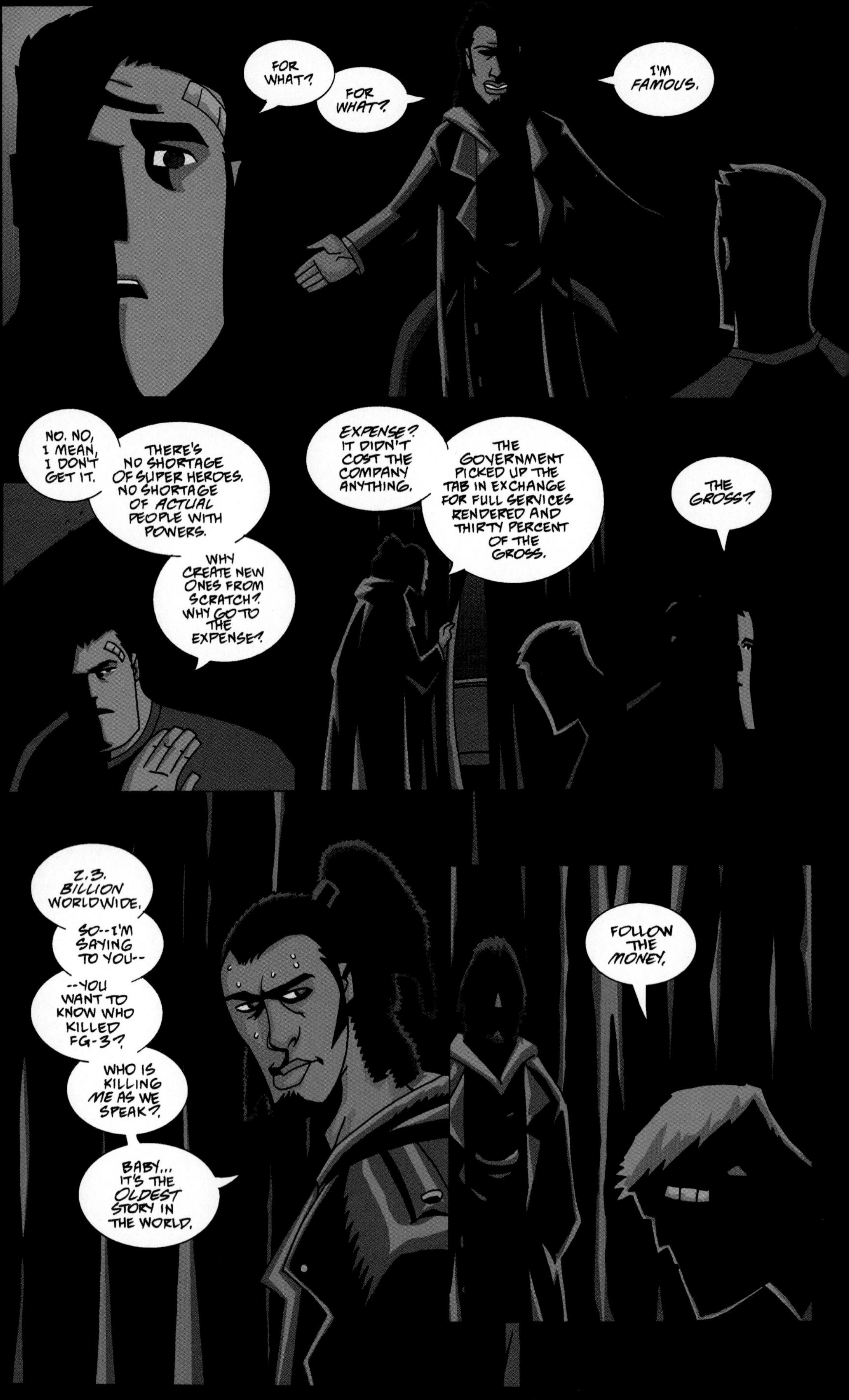

FOR WHAT?
FOR WHAT?
I'M FAMOUS.
NO. NO, I MEAN, I DON'T GET IT.
THERE'S NO SHORTAGE OF SUPER HEROES. NO SHORTAGE OF ACTUAL PEOPLE WITH POWERS.
WHY CREATE NEW ONES FROM SCRATCH? WHY GO TO THE EXPENSE?
EXPENSE? IT DIDN'T COST THE COMPANY ANYTHING.
THE GOVERNMENT PICKED UP THE TAB IN EXCHANGE FOR FULL SERVICES RENDERED AND THIRTY PERCENT OF THE GROSS.
THE GROSS?
2.3. BILLION WORLDWIDE.
SO--I'M SAYING TO YOU--
--YOU WANT TO KNOW WHO KILLED FG-3?
WHO IS KILLING ME AS WE SPEAK?
BABY... IT'S THE OLDEST STORY IN THE WORLD.
FOLLOW THE MONEY.

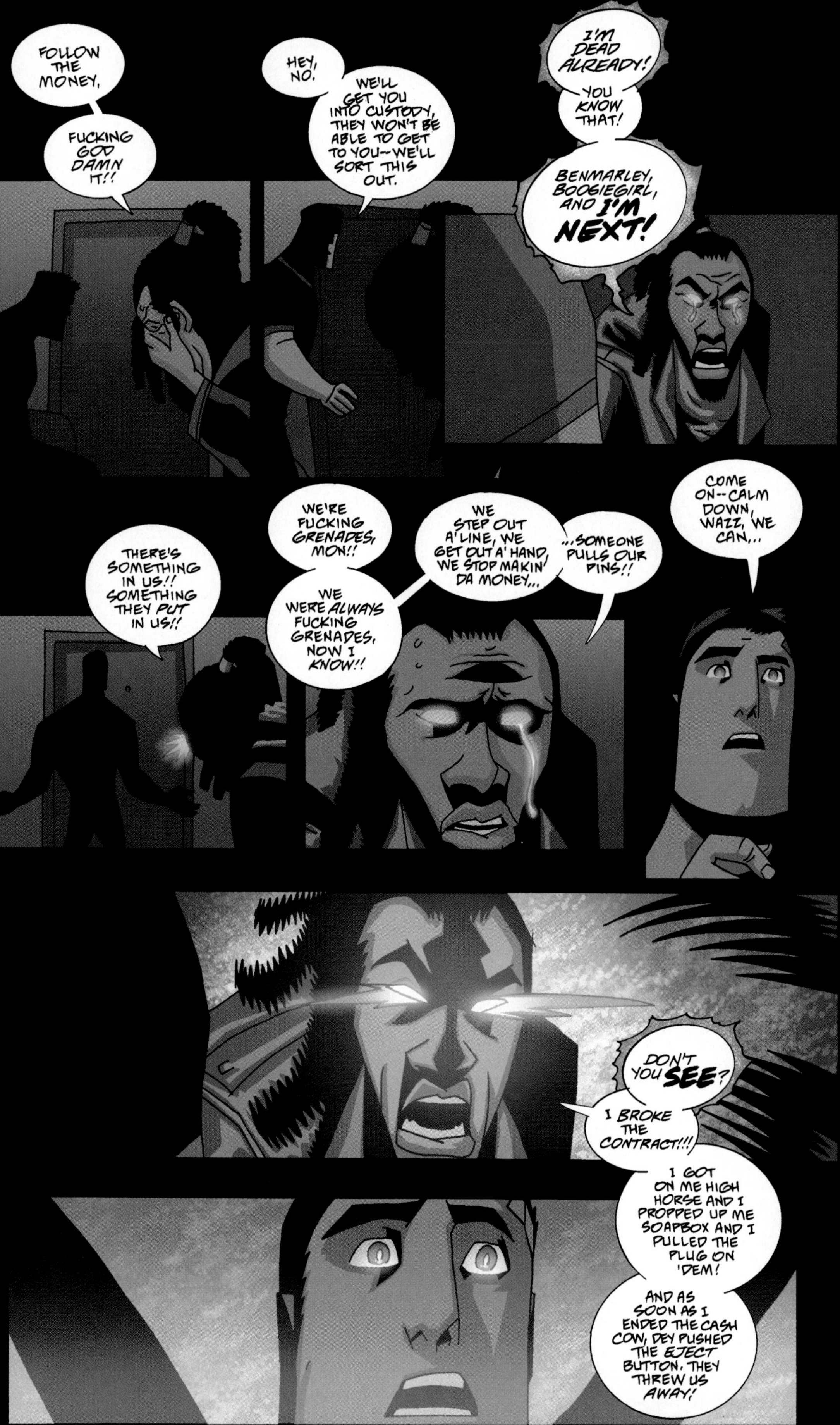
FOLLOW THE MONEY,
FUCKING GOD DAMN IT!!
HEY, NO.
WE'LL GET YOU INTO CUSTODY, THEY WON'T BE ABLE TO GET TO YOU--WE'LL SORT THIS OUT.
I'M DEAD ALREADY!
YOU KNOW THAT!
BENMARLEY, BOOGIEGIRL, AND I'M NEXT!
THERE'S SOMETHING IN US!! SOMETHING THEY PUT IN US!!
WE'RE FUCKING GRENADES, MON!!
WE WERE ALWAYS FUCKING GRENADES, NOW I KNOW!!
WE STEP OUT A' LINE, WE GET OUT A' HAND, WE STOP MAKIN' DA MONEY,..
...SOMEONE PULLS OUR PINS!!
COME ON--CALM DOWN, WAZZ, WE CAN,..
DON'T YOU SEE?
I BROKE THE CONTRACT!!!
I GOT ON ME HIGH HORSE AND I PROPPED UP ME SOAPBOX AND I PULLED THE PLUG ON 'DEM!
AND AS SOON AS I ENDED THE CASH COW, DEY PUSHED THE EJECT BUTTON. THEY THREW US AWAY!

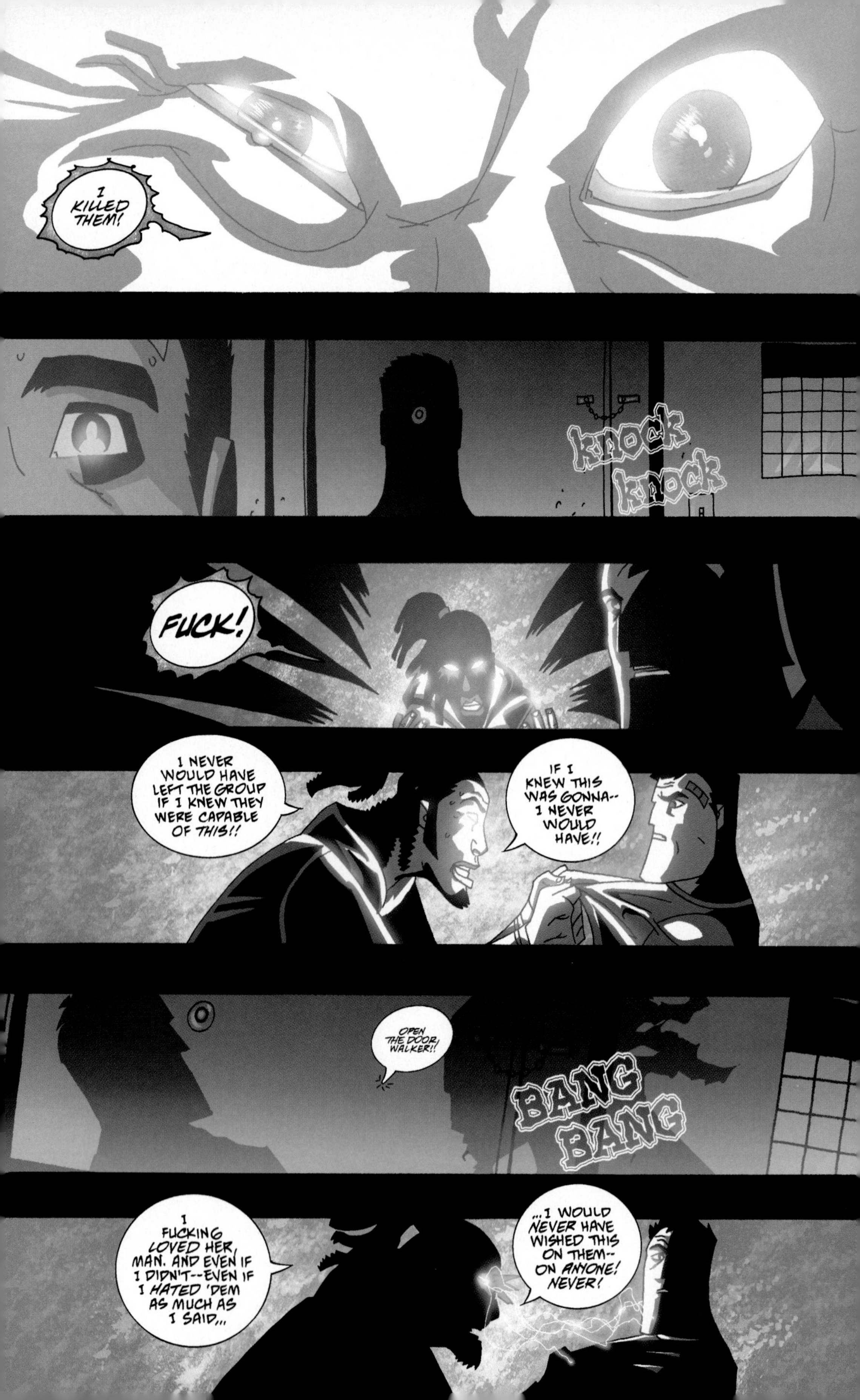
I KILLED THEM!
KNOCK KNOCK
FUCK!
I NEVER WOULD HAVE LEFT THE GROUP IF I KNEW THEY WERE CAPABLE OF THIS!!
IF I KNEW THIS WAS GONNA-- I NEVER WOULD HAVE!!
OPEN THE DOOR, WALKER!!
BANG BANG
I FUCKING LOVED HER, MAN. AND EVEN IF I DIDN'T--EVEN IF I HATED 'DEM AS MUCH AS I SAID...
...I WOULD NEVER HAVE WISHED THIS ON THEM-- ON ANYONE! NEVER!

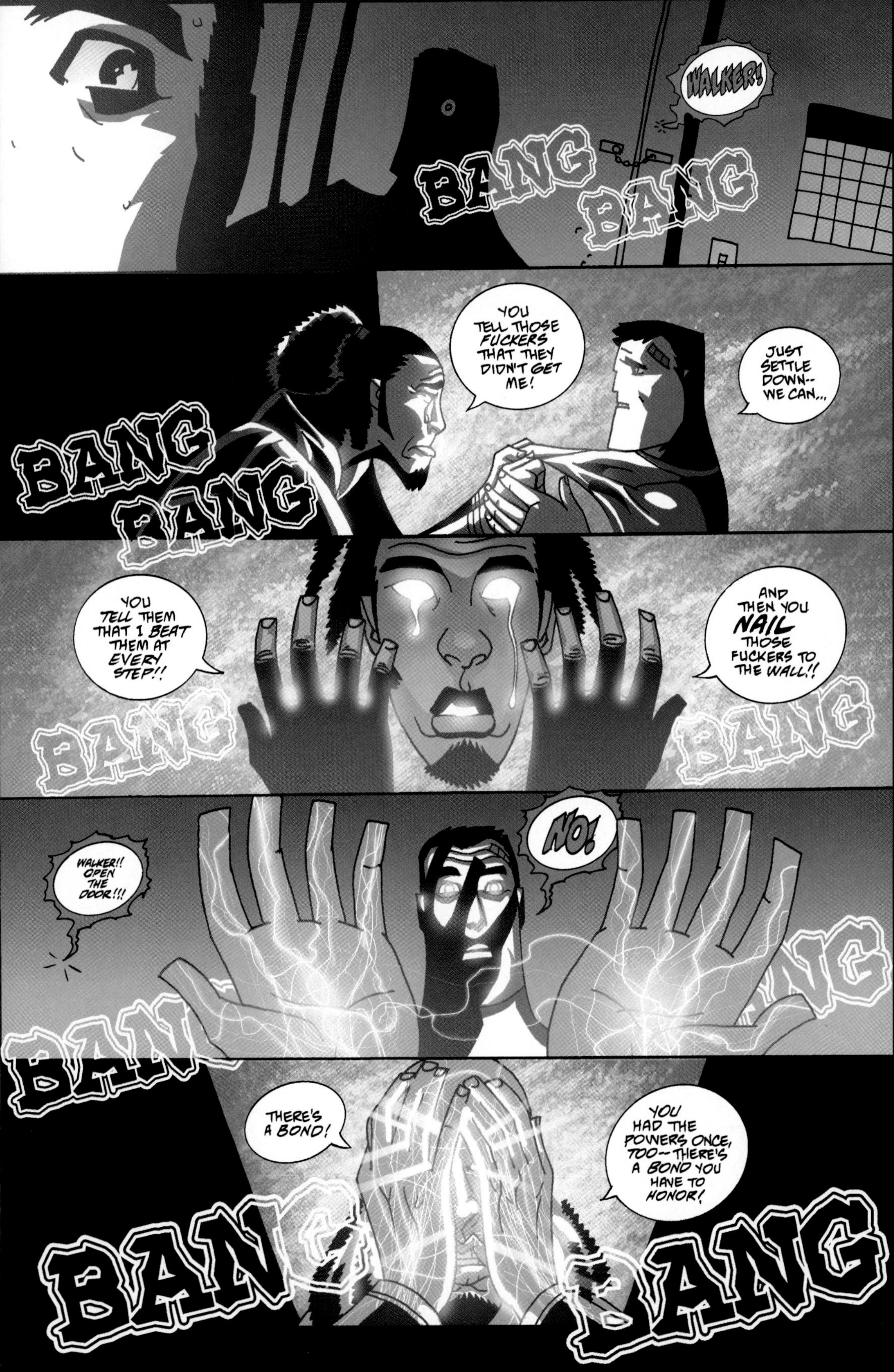

WALKER!
BANG BANG
YOU TELL THOSE FUCKERS THAT THEY DIDN'T GET ME!
JUST SETTLE DOWN-- WE CAN...
BANG BANG
YOU TELL THEM THAT I BEAT THEM AT EVERY STEP!!
AND THEN YOU NAIL THOSE FUCKERS TO THE WALL!!
BANG
BANG
NO!
WALKER!! OPEN THE DOOR!!!
THERE'S A BOND!
YOU HAD THE POWERS ONCE, TOO-- THERE'S A BOND YOU HAVE TO HONOR!
BANG
BANG

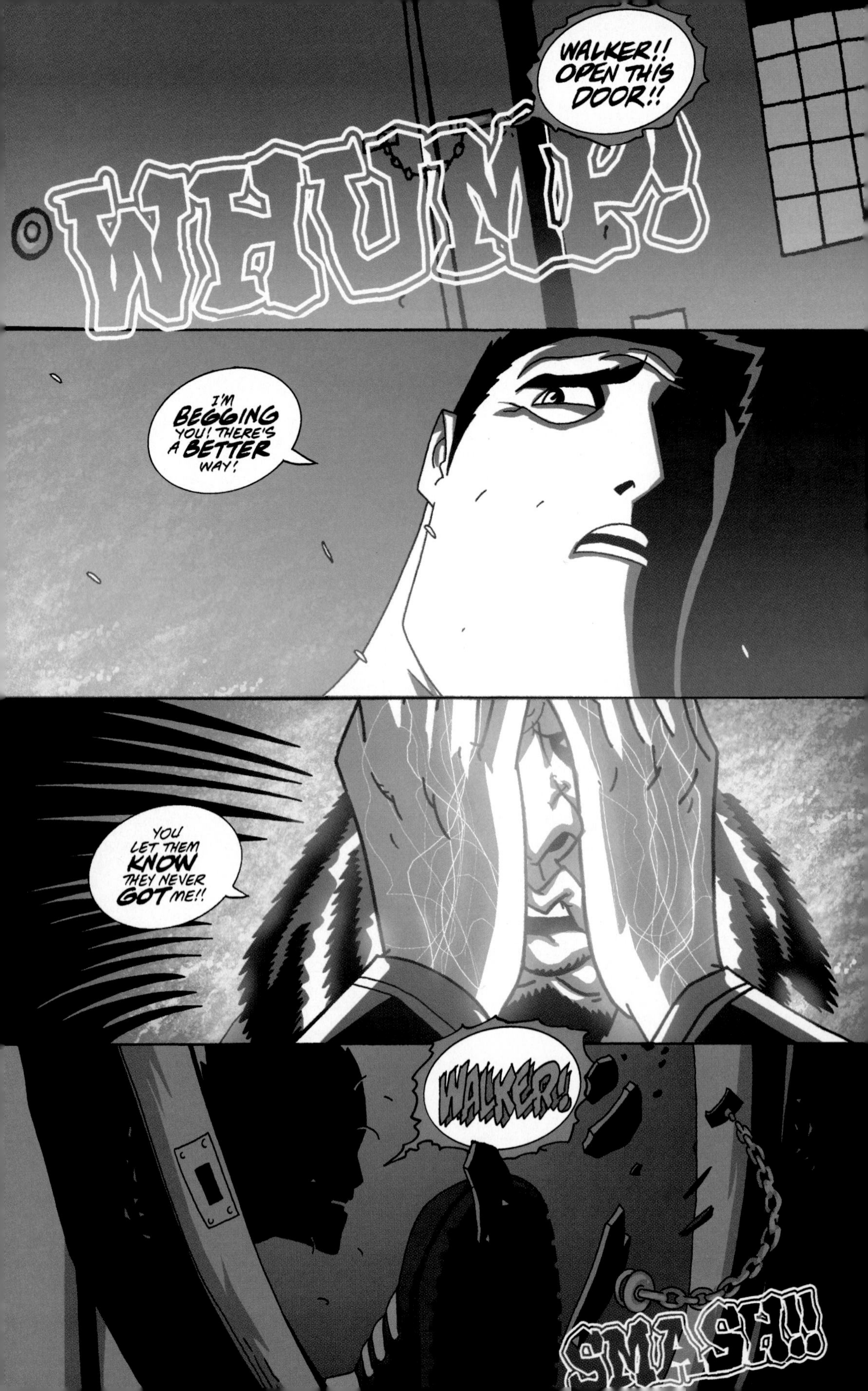
WALKER!! OPEN THIS DOOR!!
WHUMP!
I'M BEGGING YOU! THERE'S A BETTER WAY!
YOU LET THEM KNOW THEY NEVER GOT ME!!
WALKER!!
SMASH!!

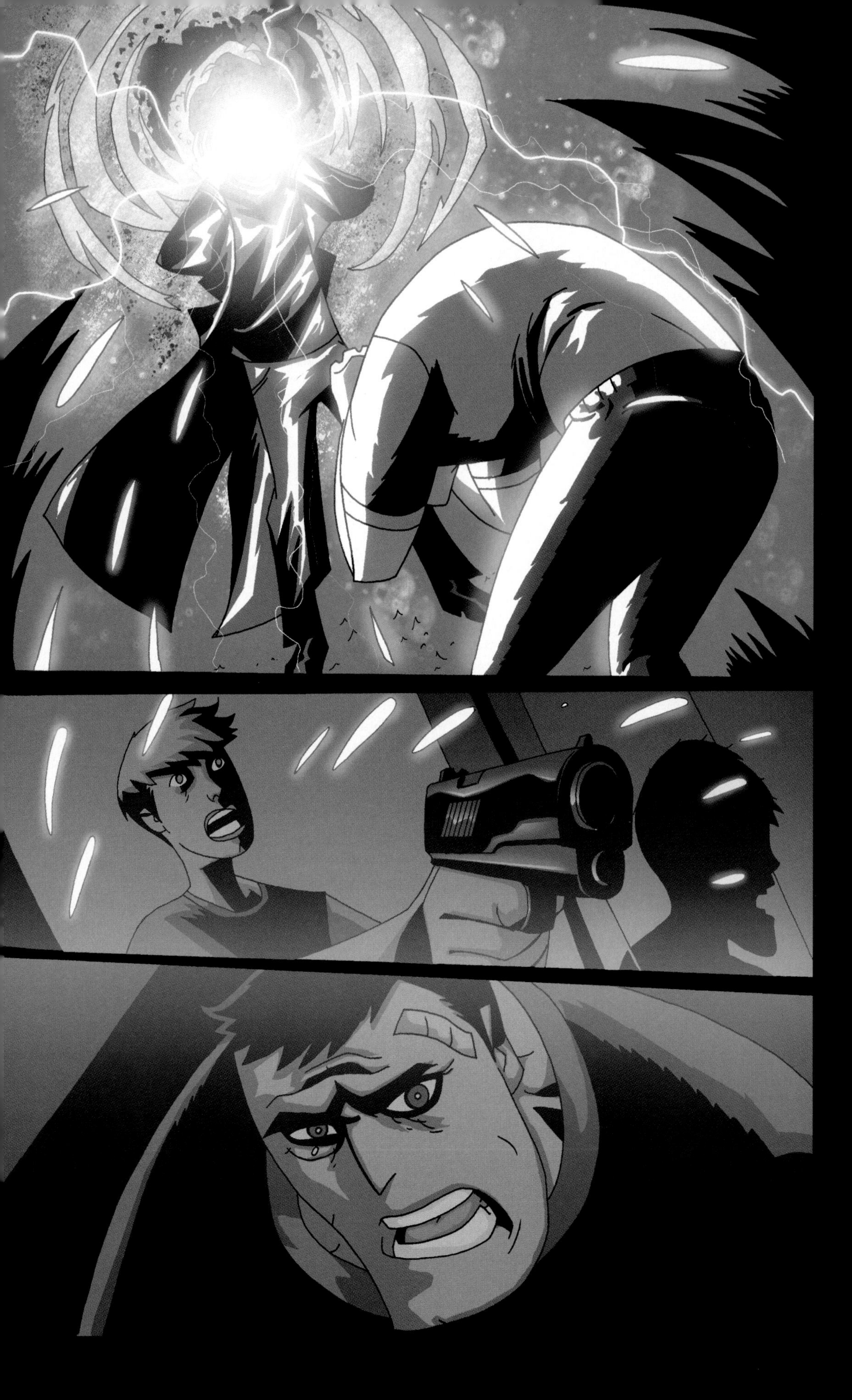

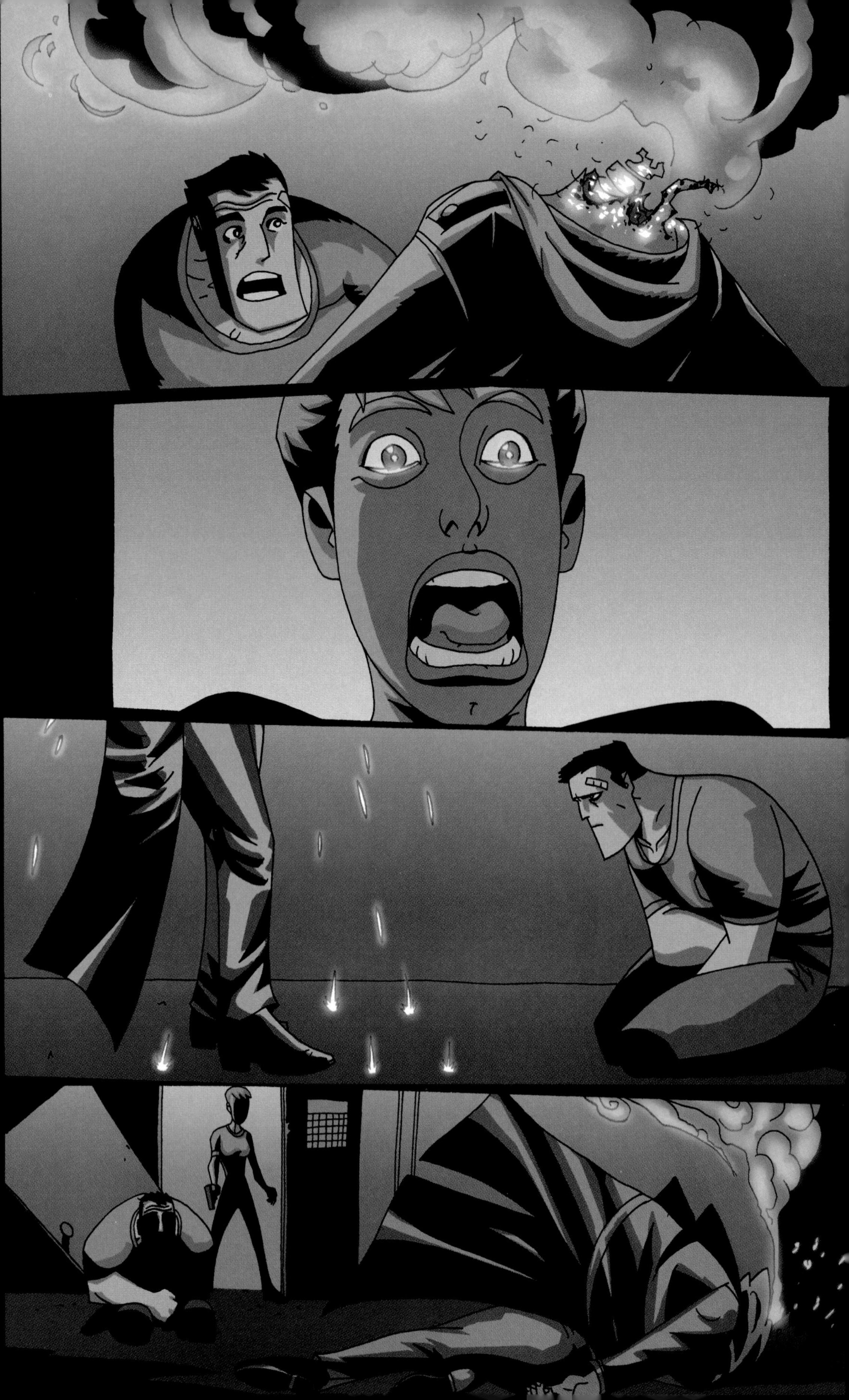

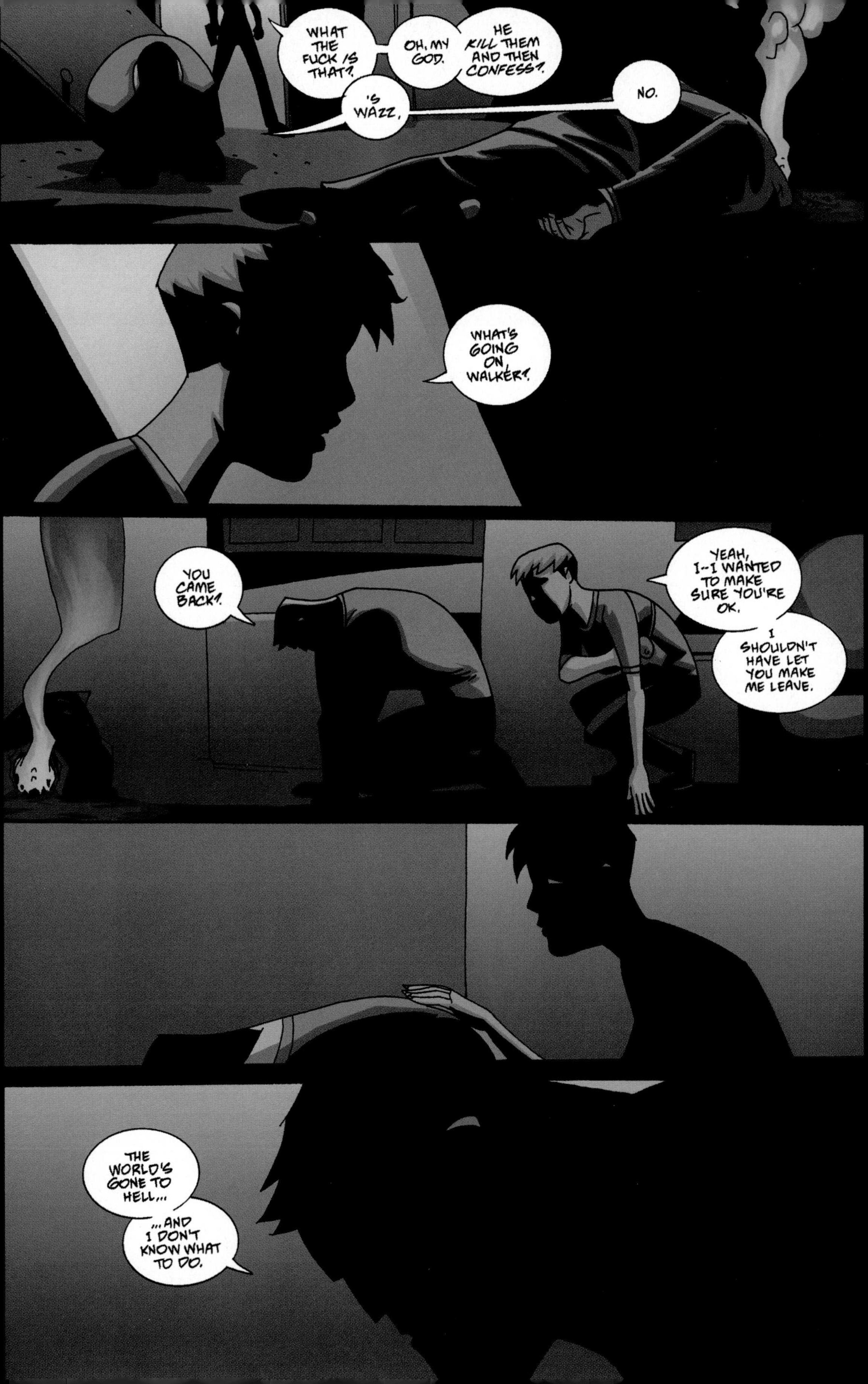
WHAT THE FUCK IS THAT?
OH, MY GOD.
HE KILL THEM AND THEN CONFESS?
'S WAZZ.
NO.
WHAT'S GOING ON, WALKER?
YOU CAME BACK?
YEAH, I--I WANTED TO MAKE SURE YOU'RE OK.
I SHOULDN'T HAVE LET YOU MAKE ME LEAVE.
THE WORLD'S GONE TO HELL...
...AND I DON'T KNOW WHAT TO DO.

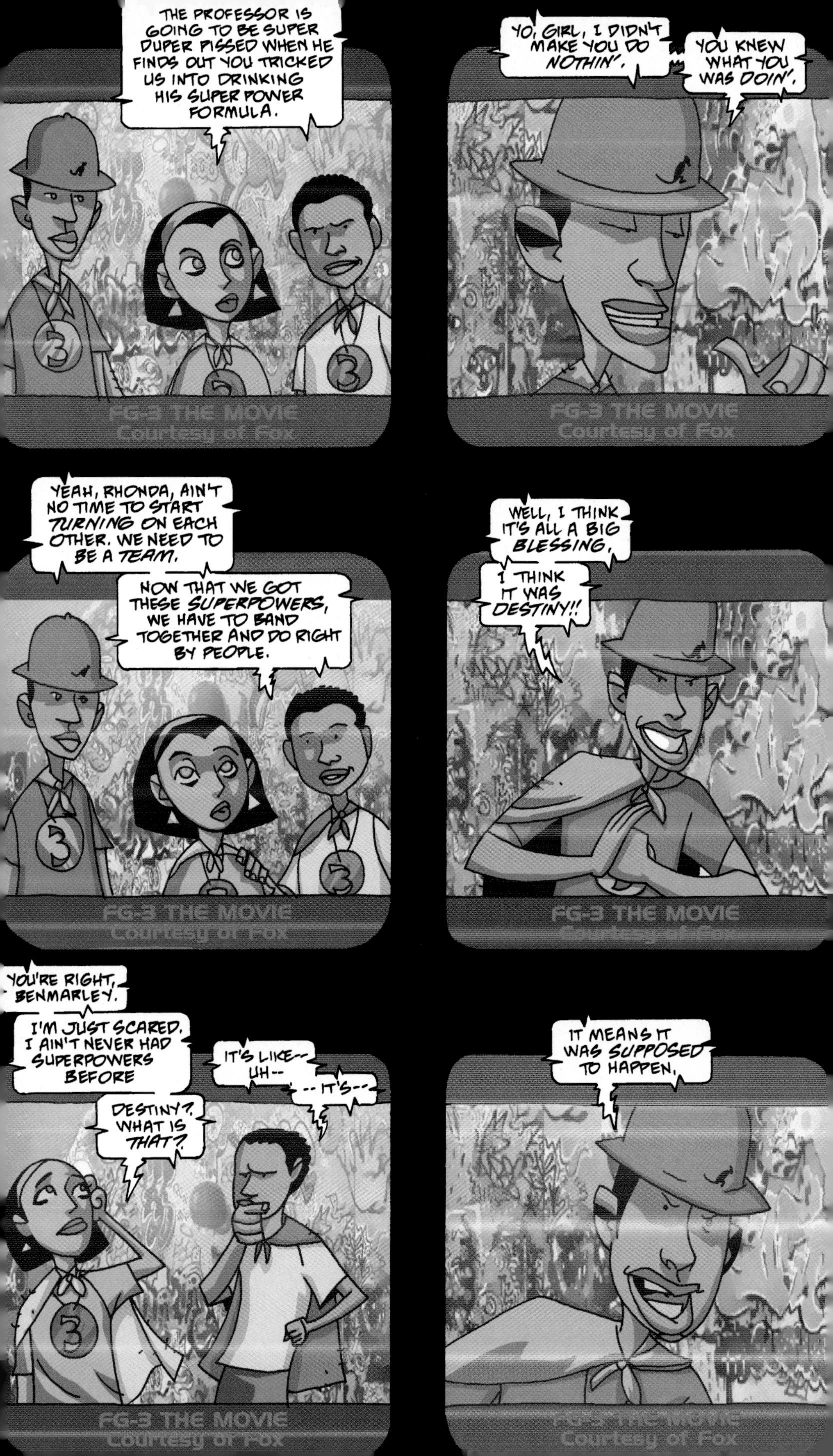
THE PROFESSOR IS GOING TO BE SUPER DUPER PISSED WHEN HE FINDS OUT YOU TRICKED US INTO DRINKING HIS SUPER POWER FORMULA.
FG-3 THE MOVIE Courtesy of Fox
YO, GIRL, I DIDN'T MAKE YOU DO NOTHIN'.
YOU KNEW WHAT YOU WAS DOIN'.
FG-3 THE MOVIE Courtesy of Fox
YEAH, RHONDA, AIN'T NO TIME TO START TURNING ON EACH OTHER. WE NEED TO BE A TEAM.
NOW THAT WE GOT THESE SUPERPOWERS, WE HAVE TO BAND TOGETHER AND DO RIGHT BY PEOPLE.
FG-3 THE MOVIE Courtesy of Fox
WELL, I THINK IT'S ALL A BIG BLESSING.
I THINK IT WAS DESTINY!!
FG-3 THE MOVIE Courtesy of Fox
YOU'RE RIGHT, BENMARLEY.
I'M JUST SCARED. I AIN'T NEVER HAD SUPERPOWERS BEFORE
IT'S LIKE-- UH--
--IT'S--
DESTINY? WHAT IS THAT?
FG-3 THE MOVIE Courtesy of Fox
IT MEANS IT WAS SUPPOSED TO HAPPEN.
FG-3 THE MOVIE Courtesy of Fox

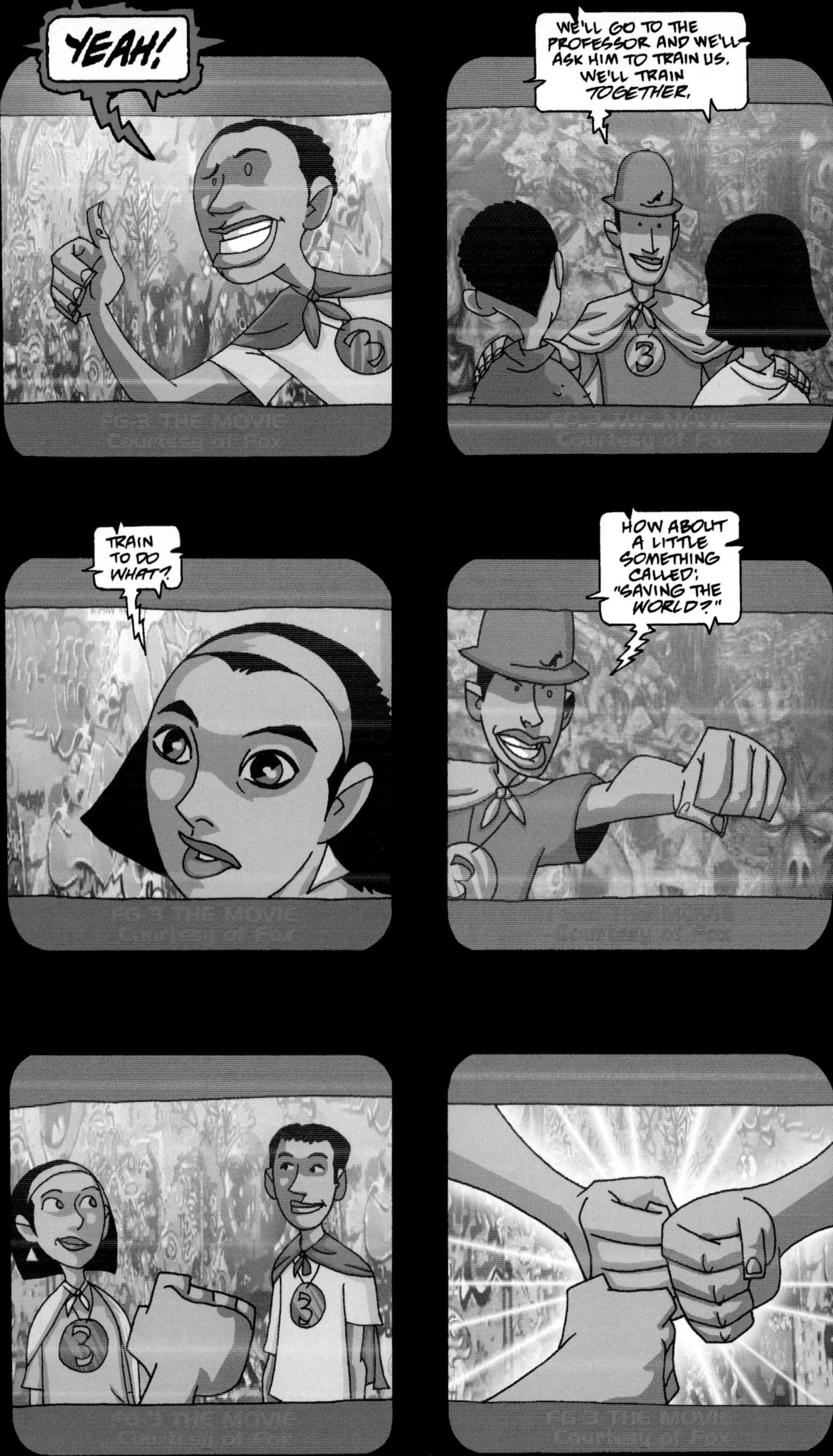
YEAH!
WE'LL GO TO THE PROFESSOR AND WE'LL ASK HIM TO TRAIN US. WE'LL TRAIN TOGETHER.
TRAIN TO DO WHAT?
HOW ABOUT A LITTLE SOMETHING CALLED: "SAVING THE WORLD?"

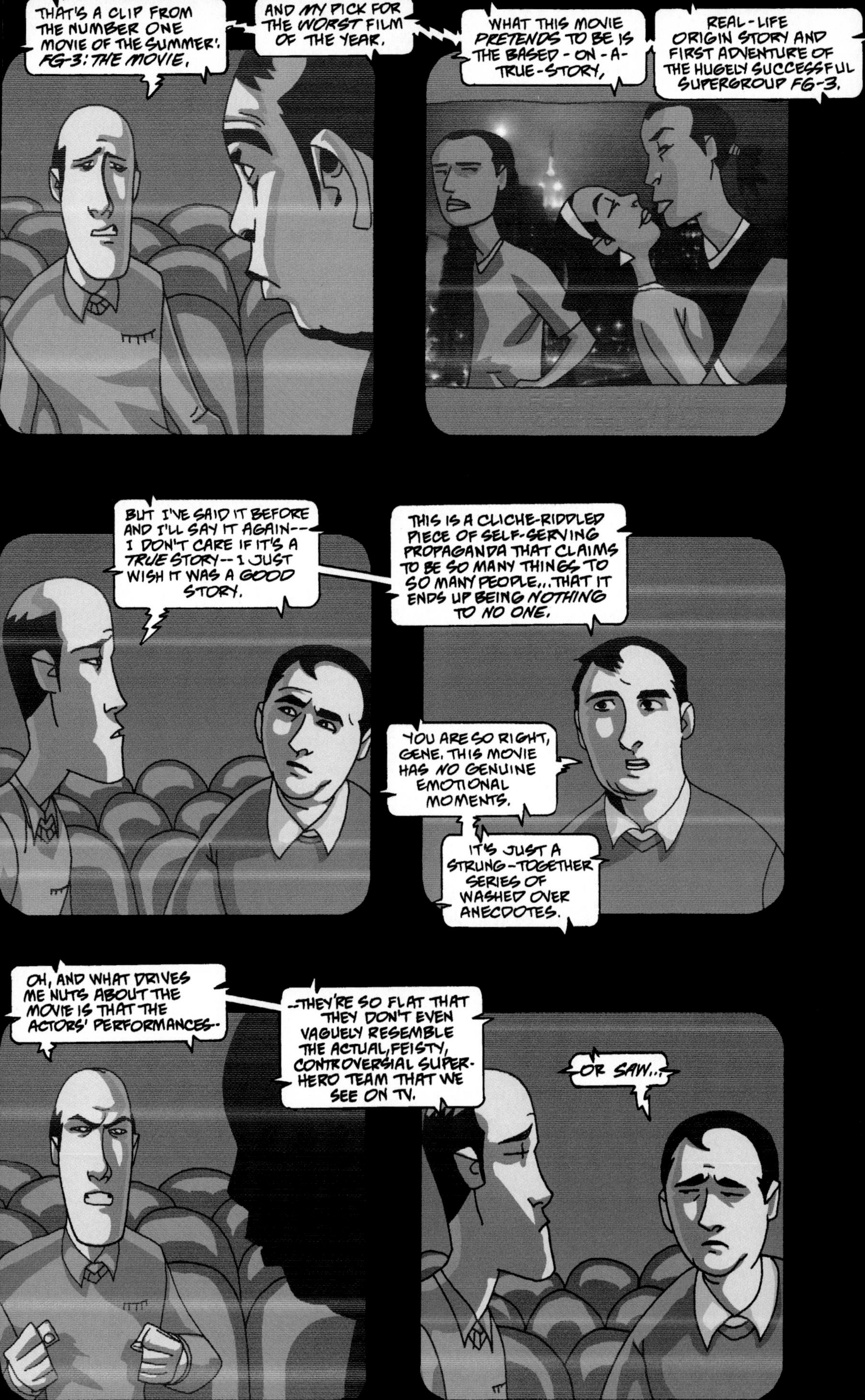
THAT'S A CLIP FROM THE NUMBER ONE MOVIE OF THE SUMMER: FG-3: THE MOVIE.
AND MY PICK FOR THE WORST FILM OF THE YEAR.
WHAT THIS MOVIE PRETENDS TO BE IS THE BASED-ON-A-TRUE-STORY,
REAL-LIFE ORIGIN STORY AND FIRST ADVENTURE OF THE HUGELY SUCCESSFUL SUPERGROUP FG-3.
BUT I'VE SAID IT BEFORE AND I'LL SAY IT AGAIN-- I DON'T CARE IF IT'S A TRUE STORY-- I JUST WISH IT WAS A GOOD STORY.
THIS IS A CLICHE-RIDDLED PIECE OF SELF-SERVING PROPAGANDA THAT CLAIMS TO BE SO MANY THINGS TO SO MANY PEOPLE... THAT IT ENDS UP BEING NOTHING TO NO ONE.
YOU ARE SO RIGHT, GENE. THIS MOVIE HAS NO GENUINE EMOTIONAL MOMENTS.
IT'S JUST A STRUNG-TOGETHER SERIES OF WASHED OVER ANECDOTES.
OH, AND WHAT DRIVES ME NUTS ABOUT THE MOVIE IS THAT THE ACTORS' PERFORMANCES-
-THEY'RE SO FLAT THAT THEY DON'T EVEN VAGUELY RESEMBLE THE ACTUAL, FEISTY, CONTROVERSIAL SUPER-HERO TEAM THAT WE SEE ON TV.
-OR SAW...

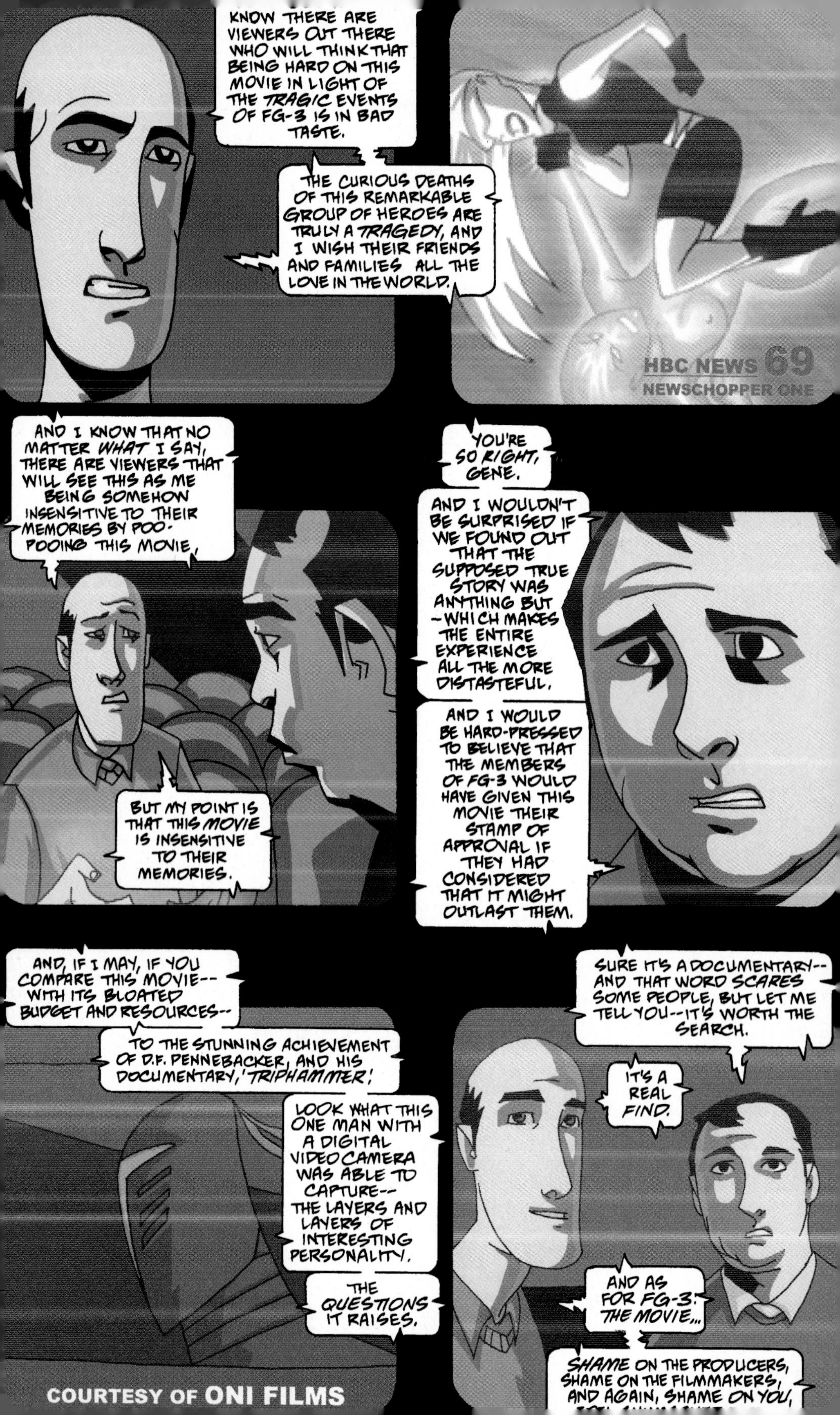

KNOW THERE ARE VIEWERS OUT THERE WHO WILL THINK THAT BEING HARD ON THIS MOVIE IN LIGHT OF THE *TRAGIC* EVENTS OF FG-3 IS IN BAD TASTE.
THE CURIOUS DEATHS OF THIS REMARKABLE GROUP OF HEROES ARE TRULY A *TRAGEDY*, AND I WISH THEIR FRIENDS AND FAMILIES ALL THE LOVE IN THE WORLD.
HBC NEWS 69
NEWSCHOPPER ONE
AND I KNOW THAT NO MATTER *WHAT* I SAY, THERE ARE VIEWERS THAT WILL SEE THIS AS ME BEING SOMEHOW INSENSITIVE TO THEIR MEMORIES BY POO-POOING THIS MOVIE,
BUT MY POINT IS THAT THIS *MOVIE* IS INSENSITIVE TO THEIR MEMORIES.
YOU'RE SO *RIGHT*, GENE.
AND I WOULDN'T BE SURPRISED IF WE FOUND OUT THAT THE SUPPOSED TRUE STORY WAS ANYTHING BUT --WHICH MAKES THE ENTIRE EXPERIENCE ALL THE MORE DISTASTEFUL.
AND I WOULD BE HARD-PRESSED TO BELIEVE THAT THE MEMBERS OF FG-3 WOULD HAVE GIVEN THIS MOVIE THEIR STAMP OF APPROVAL IF THEY HAD CONSIDERED THAT IT MIGHT OUTLAST THEM.
AND, IF I MAY, IF YOU COMPARE THIS MOVIE-- WITH ITS BLOATED BUDGET AND RESOURCES--
TO THE STUNNING ACHIEVEMENT OF D.F. PENNEBACKER, AND HIS DOCUMENTARY, '*TRIPHAMMER*.'
LOOK WHAT THIS ONE MAN WITH A DIGITAL VIDEO CAMERA WAS ABLE TO CAPTURE-- THE LAYERS AND LAYERS OF INTERESTING PERSONALITY.
THE *QUESTIONS* IT RAISES.
COURTESY OF ONI FILMS
SURE IT'S A DOCUMENTARY-- AND THAT WORD *SCARES* SOME PEOPLE, BUT LET ME TELL YOU--IT'S WORTH THE SEARCH.
IT'S A REAL *FIND*.
AND AS FOR *FG-3: THE MOVIE*...
SHAME ON THE PRODUCERS, SHAME ON THE FILMMAKERS, AND AGAIN, SHAME ON YOU,

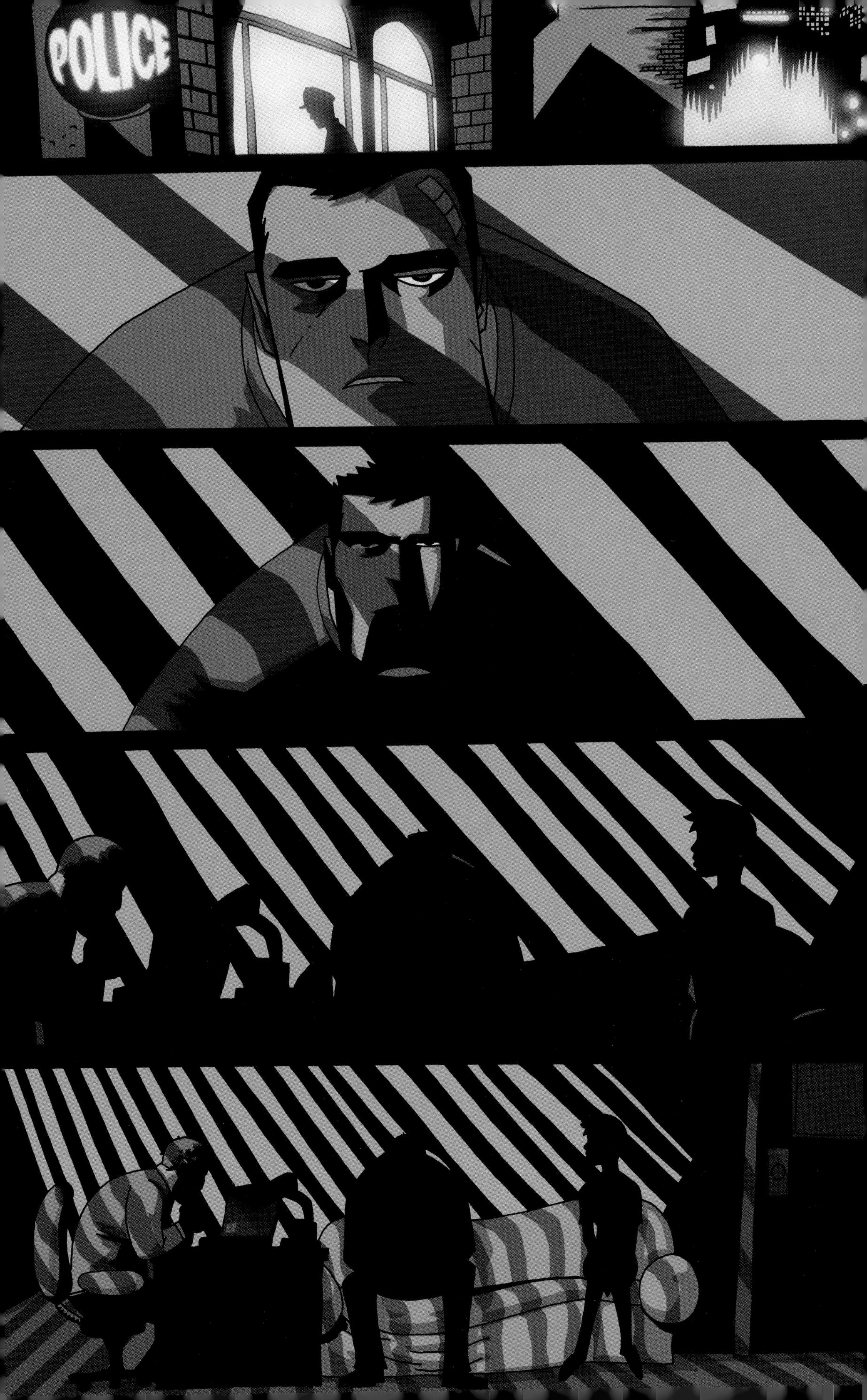
POLICE

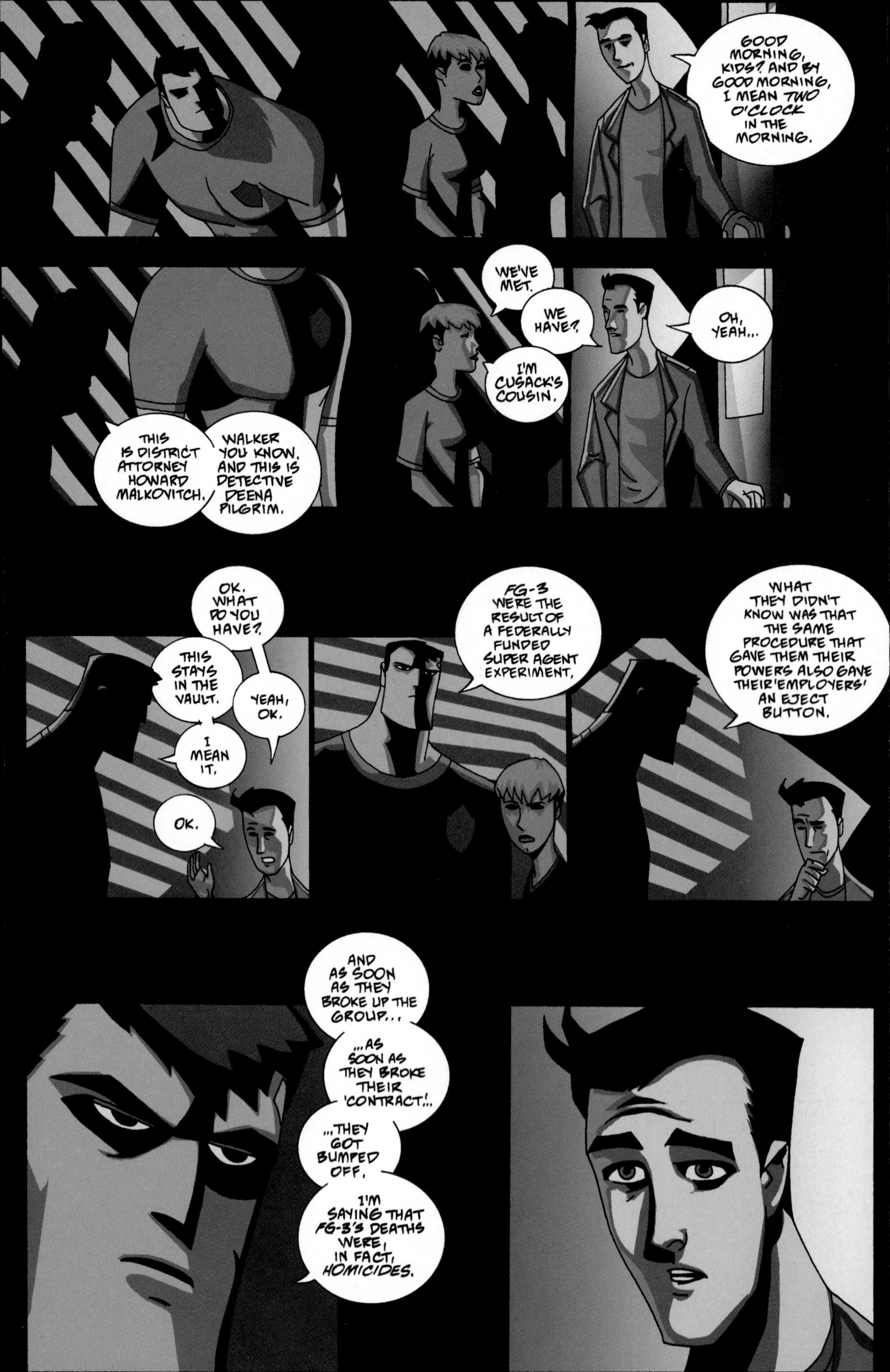
GOOD MORNING, KIDS? AND BY GOOD MORNING, I MEAN TWO O'CLOCK IN THE MORNING.
WE'VE MET.
WE HAVE?
OH, YEAH...
I'M CUSACK'S COUSIN.
THIS IS DISTRICT ATTORNEY HOWARD MALKOVITCH.
WALKER YOU KNOW. AND THIS IS DETECTIVE DEENA PILGRIM.
OK. WHAT DO YOU HAVE?
THIS STAYS IN THE VAULT.
YEAH, OK.
I MEAN IT.
OK.
FG-3 WERE THE RESULT OF A FEDERALLY FUNDED SUPER AGENT EXPERIMENT.
WHAT THEY DIDN'T KNOW WAS THAT THE SAME PROCEDURE THAT GAVE THEM THEIR POWERS ALSO GAVE THEIR 'EMPLOYERS' AN EJECT BUTTON.
AND AS SOON AS THEY BROKE UP THE GROUP...
...AS SOON AS THEY BROKE THEIR 'CONTRACT'...
...THEY GOT BUMPED OFF.
I'M SAYING THAT FG-3'S DEATHS WERE, IN FACT, HOMICIDES.

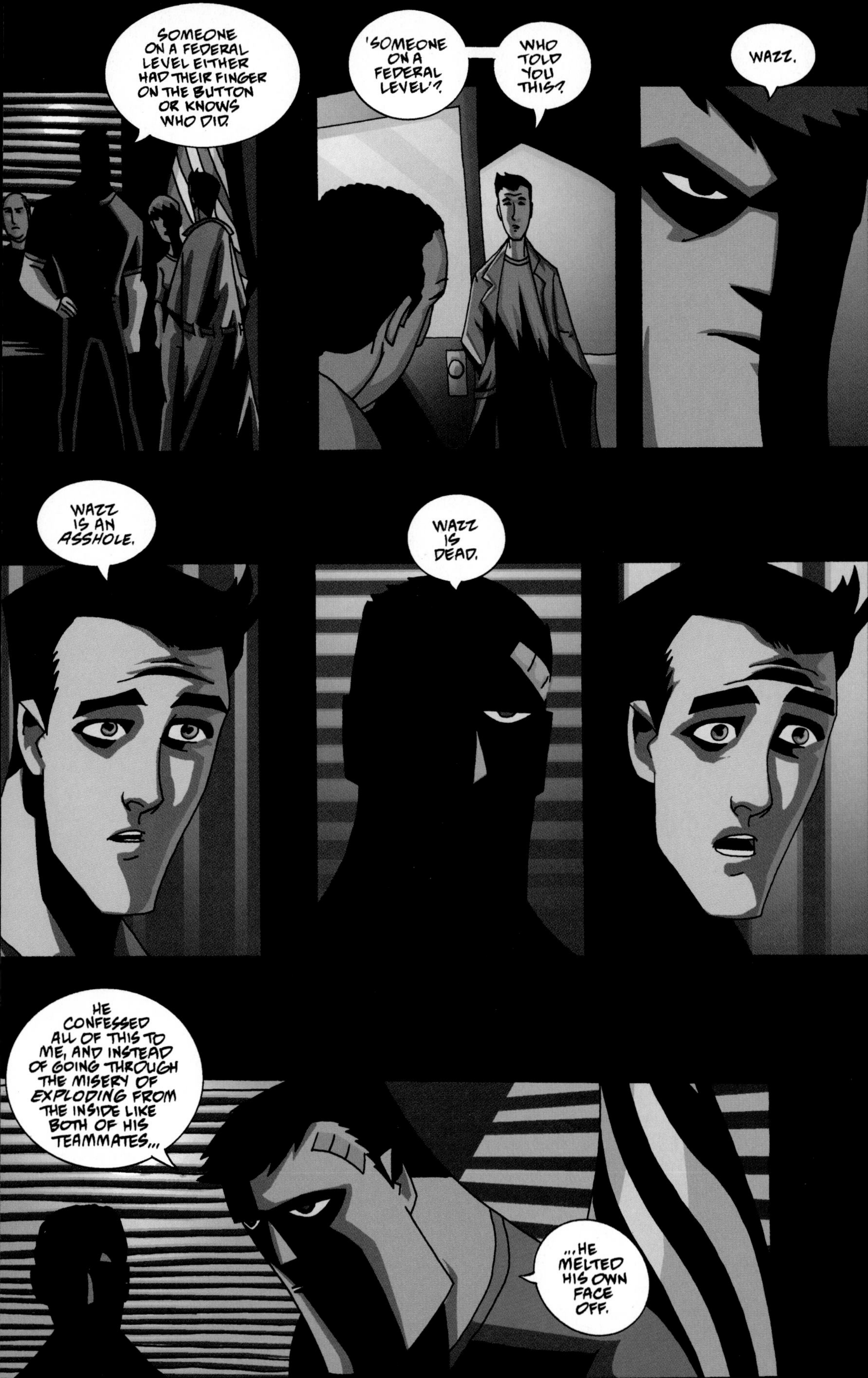
SOMEONE ON A FEDERAL LEVEL EITHER HAD THEIR FINGER ON THE BUTTON OR KNOWS WHO DID.
'SOMEONE ON A FEDERAL LEVEL'?
WHO TOLD YOU THIS?
WAZZ.
WAZZ IS AN ASSHOLE.
WAZZ IS DEAD.
HE CONFESSED ALL OF THIS TO ME, AND INSTEAD OF GOING THROUGH THE MISERY OF EXPLODING FROM THE INSIDE LIKE BOTH OF HIS TEAMMATES...
...HE MELTED HIS OWN FACE OFF.

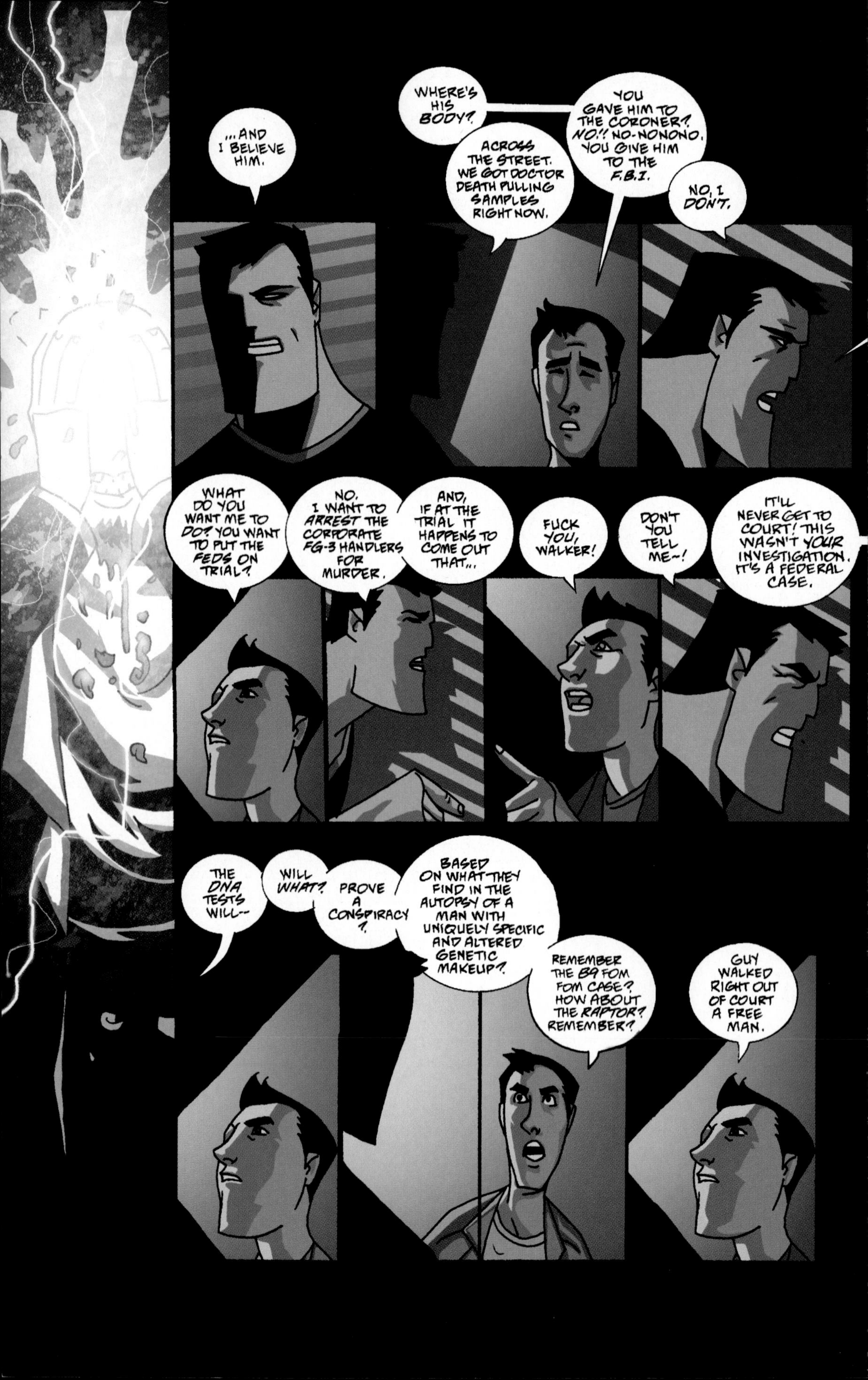
...AND I BELIEVE HIM.
WHERE'S HIS BODY?
ACROSS THE STREET. WE GOT DOCTOR DEATH PULLING SAMPLES RIGHT NOW.
YOU GAVE HIM TO THE CORONER? NO!! NO-NONONO. YOU GIVE HIM TO THE F.B.I.
NO, I DON'T.
WHAT DO YOU WANT ME TO DO? YOU WANT TO PUT THE FEDS ON TRIAL?
NO. I WANT TO ARREST THE CORPORATE FG-3 HANDLERS FOR MURDER.
AND, IF AT THE TRIAL IT HAPPENS TO COME OUT THAT...
FUCK YOU, WALKER!
DON'T YOU TELL ME--!
IT'LL NEVER GET TO COURT! THIS WASN'T YOUR INVESTIGATION. IT'S A FEDERAL CASE.
THE DNA TESTS WILL--
WILL WHAT?
PROVE A CONSPIRACY?
BASED ON WHAT THEY FIND IN THE AUTOPSY OF A MAN WITH UNIQUELY SPECIFIC AND ALTERED GENETIC MAKEUP?
REMEMBER THE B9 FOM FOM CASE? HOW ABOUT THE RAPTOR? REMEMBER?
GUY WALKED RIGHT OUT OF COURT A FREE MAN.

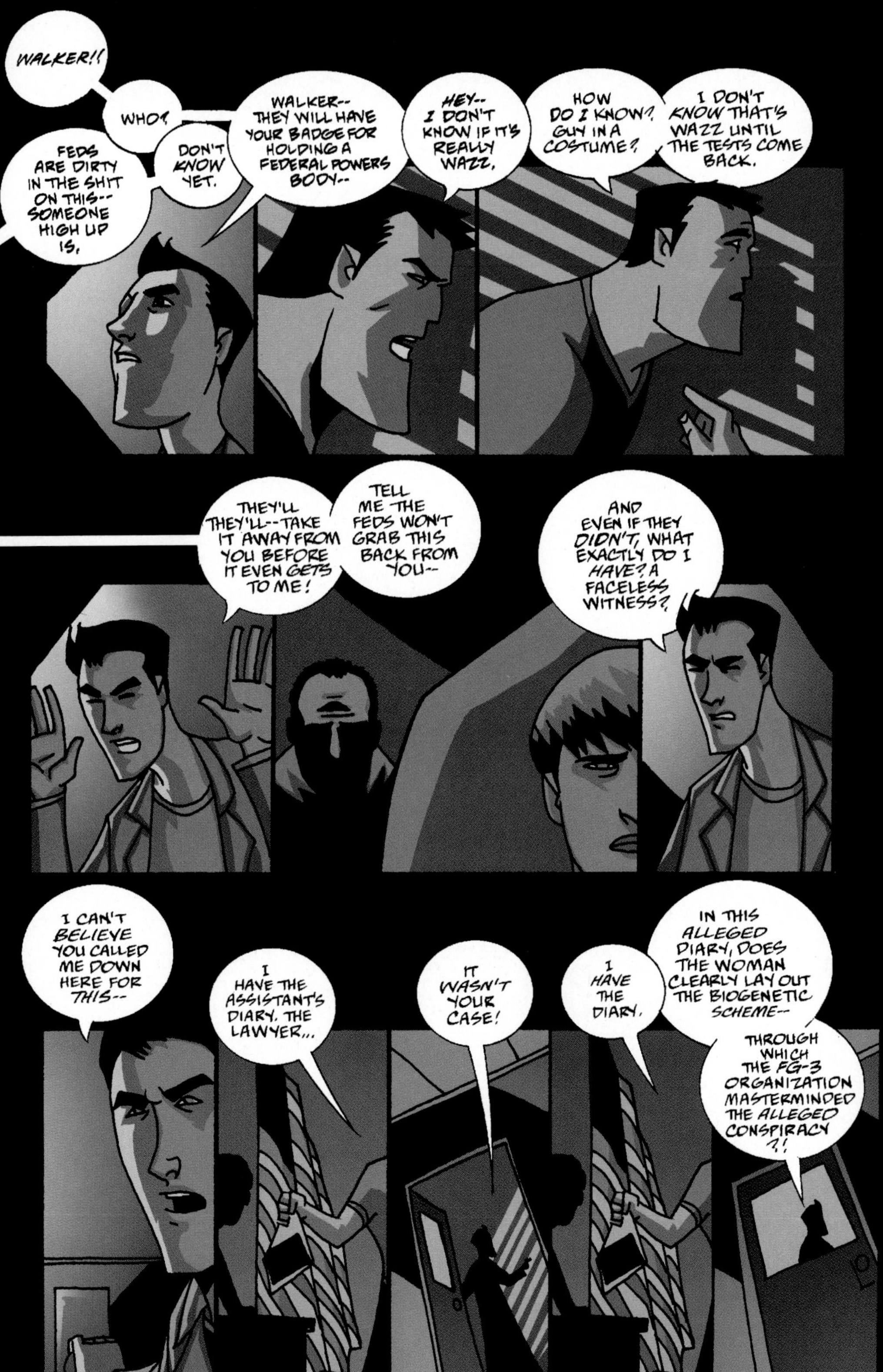
WALKER!!
WHO?
FEDS ARE DIRTY IN THE SHIT ON THIS-- SOMEONE HIGH UP IS.
DON'T KNOW YET.
WALKER-- THEY WILL HAVE YOUR BADGE FOR HOLDING A FEDERAL POWERS BODY--
HEY-- I DON'T KNOW IF IT'S REALLY WAZZ.
HOW DO I KNOW? GUY IN A COSTUME?
I DON'T KNOW THAT'S WAZZ UNTIL THE TESTS COME BACK.
THEY'LL THEY'LL--TAKE IT AWAY FROM YOU BEFORE IT EVEN GETS TO ME!
TELL ME THE FEDS WON'T GRAB THIS BACK FROM YOU--
AND EVEN IF THEY DIDN'T, WHAT EXACTLY DO I HAVE? A FACELESS WITNESS?
I CAN'T BELIEVE YOU CALLED ME DOWN HERE FOR THIS--
I HAVE THE ASSISTANT'S DIARY. THE LAWYER...
IT WASN'T YOUR CASE!
I HAVE THE DIARY.
IN THIS ALLEGED DIARY, DOES THE WOMAN CLEARLY LAY OUT THE BIOGENETIC SCHEME--
THROUGH WHICH THE FG-3 ORGANIZATION MASTERMINDED THE ALLEGED CONSPIRACY ?!

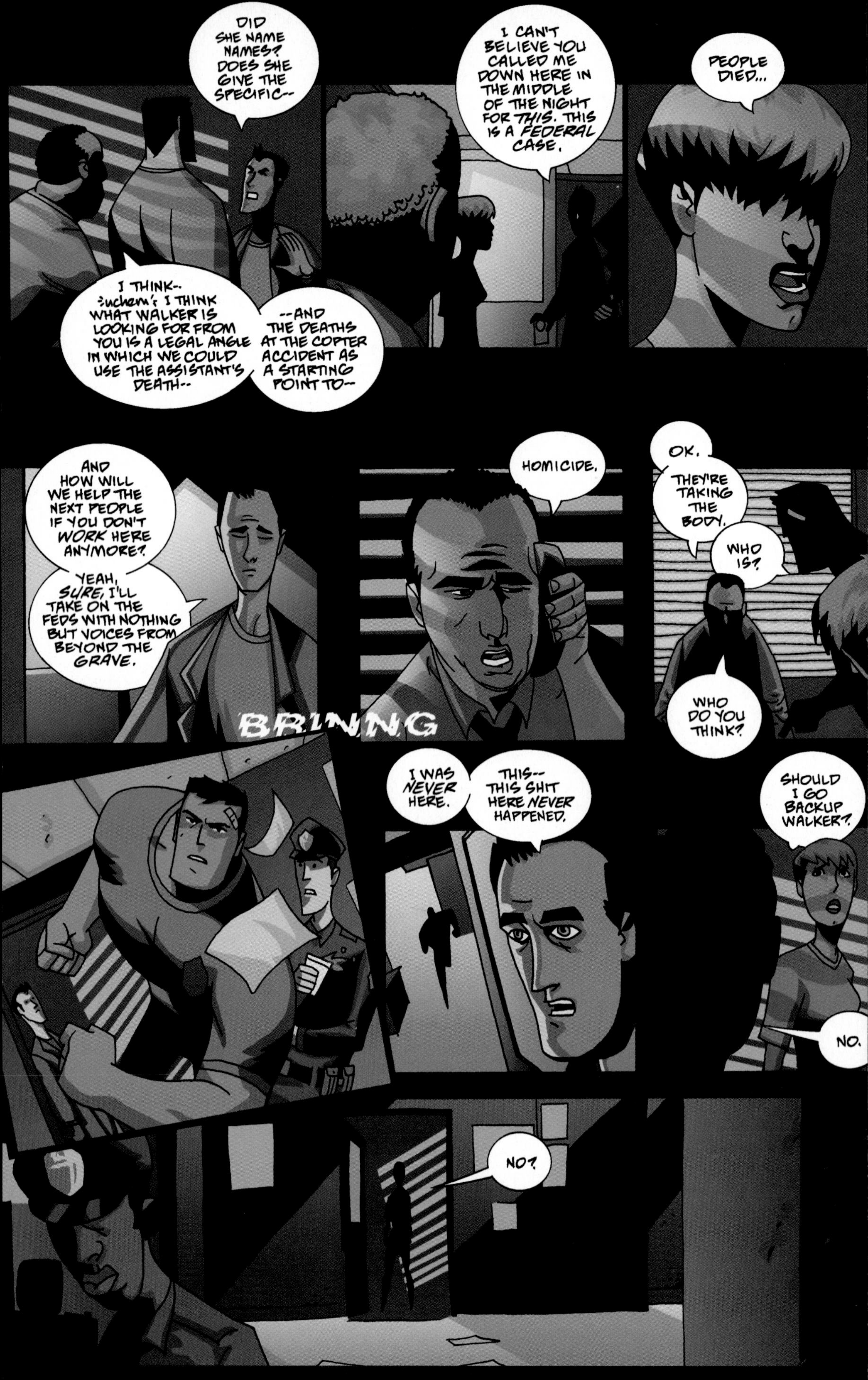
DID SHE NAME NAMES? DOES SHE GIVE THE SPECIFIC--
I CAN'T BELIEVE YOU CALLED ME DOWN HERE IN THE MIDDLE OF THE NIGHT FOR THIS. THIS IS A FEDERAL CASE.
PEOPLE DIED...
I THINK-- *uhem* I THINK WHAT WALKER IS LOOKING FOR FROM YOU IS A LEGAL ANGLE IN WHICH WE COULD USE THE ASSISTANT'S DEATH--
--AND THE DEATHS AT THE COPTER ACCIDENT AS A STARTING POINT TO--
AND HOW WILL WE HELP THE NEXT PEOPLE IF YOU DON'T WORK HERE ANYMORE?
YEAH, SURE, I'LL TAKE ON THE FEDS WITH NOTHING BUT VOICES FROM BEYOND THE GRAVE.
BRINNG
HOMICIDE.
OK.
THEY'RE TAKING THE BODY.
WHO IS?
WHO DO YOU THINK?
I WAS NEVER HERE.
THIS-- THIS SHIT HERE NEVER HAPPENED.
SHOULD I GO BACKUP WALKER?
NO.
NO?

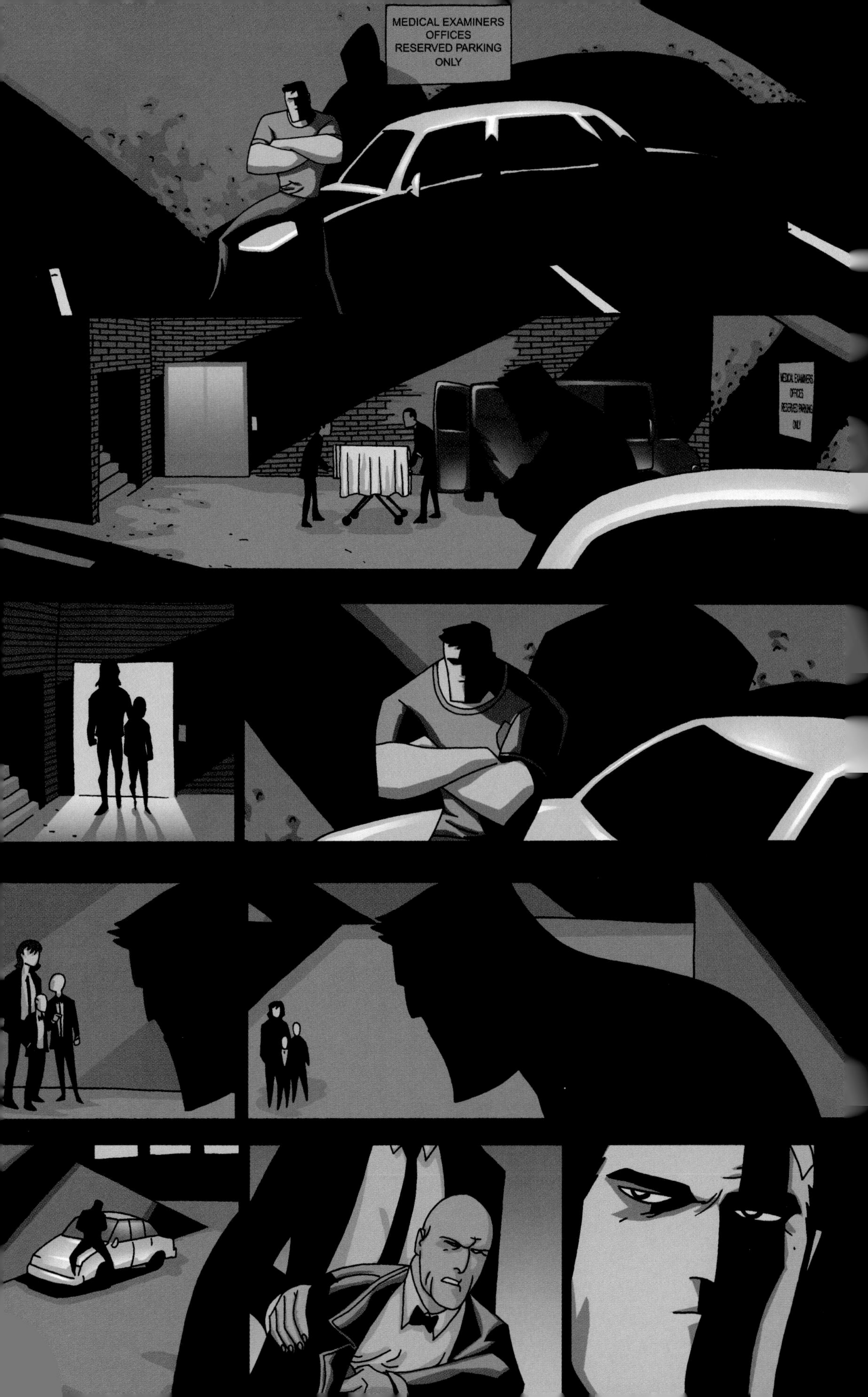
MEDICAL EXAMINERS
OFFICES
RESERVED PARKING
ONLY

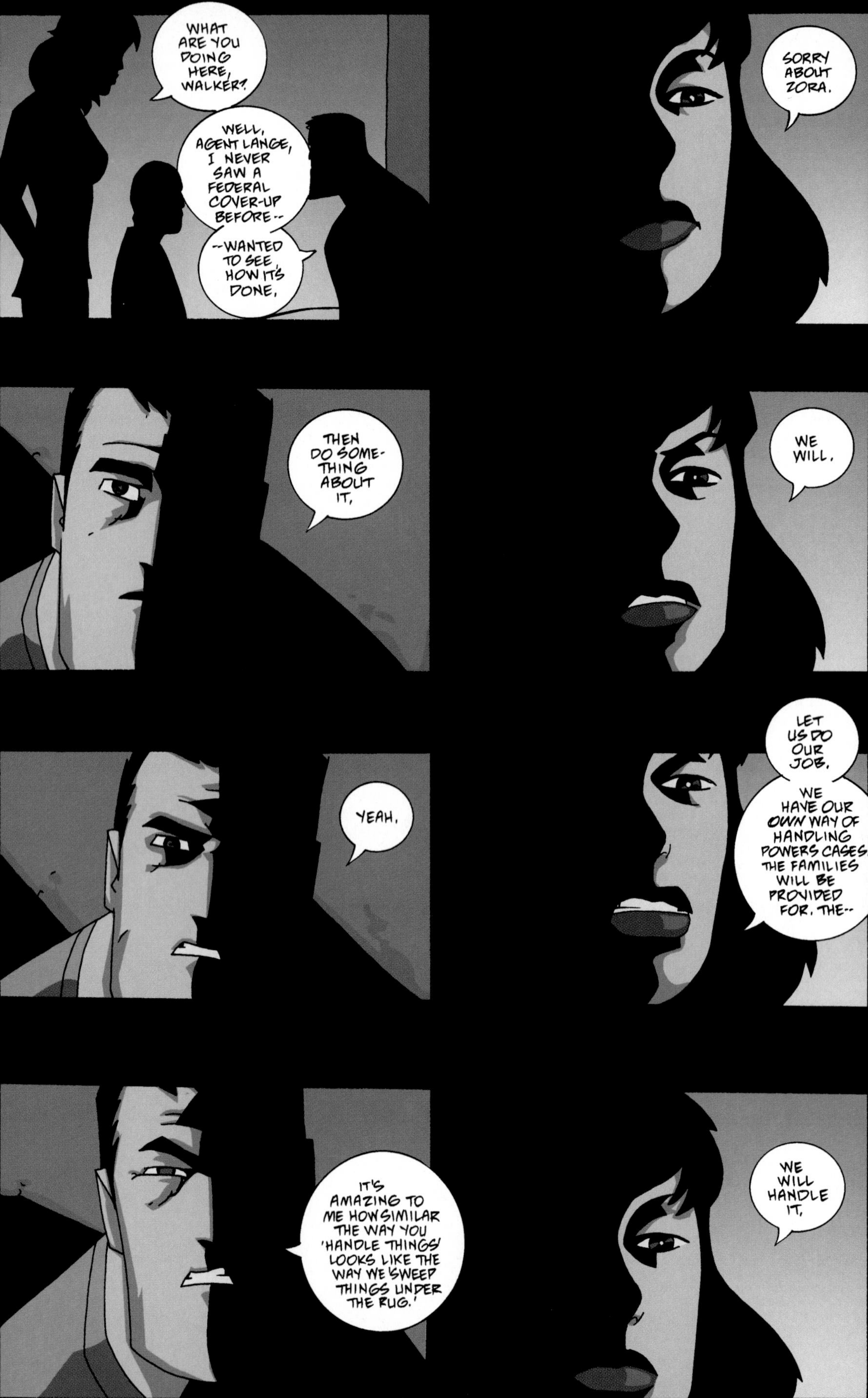
WHAT ARE YOU DOING HERE, WALKER?
WELL, AGENT LANGE, I NEVER SAW A FEDERAL COVER-UP BEFORE--
--WANTED TO SEE HOW IT'S DONE.
SORRY ABOUT ZORA.
THEN DO SOMETHING ABOUT IT.
WE WILL.
YEAH.
LET US DO OUR JOB.
WE HAVE OUR OWN WAY OF HANDLING POWERS CASES. THE FAMILIES WILL BE PROVIDED FOR. THE--
IT'S AMAZING TO ME HOW SIMILAR THE WAY YOU 'HANDLE THINGS' LOOKS LIKE THE WAY WE 'SWEEP THINGS UNDER THE RUG.'
WE WILL HANDLE IT.

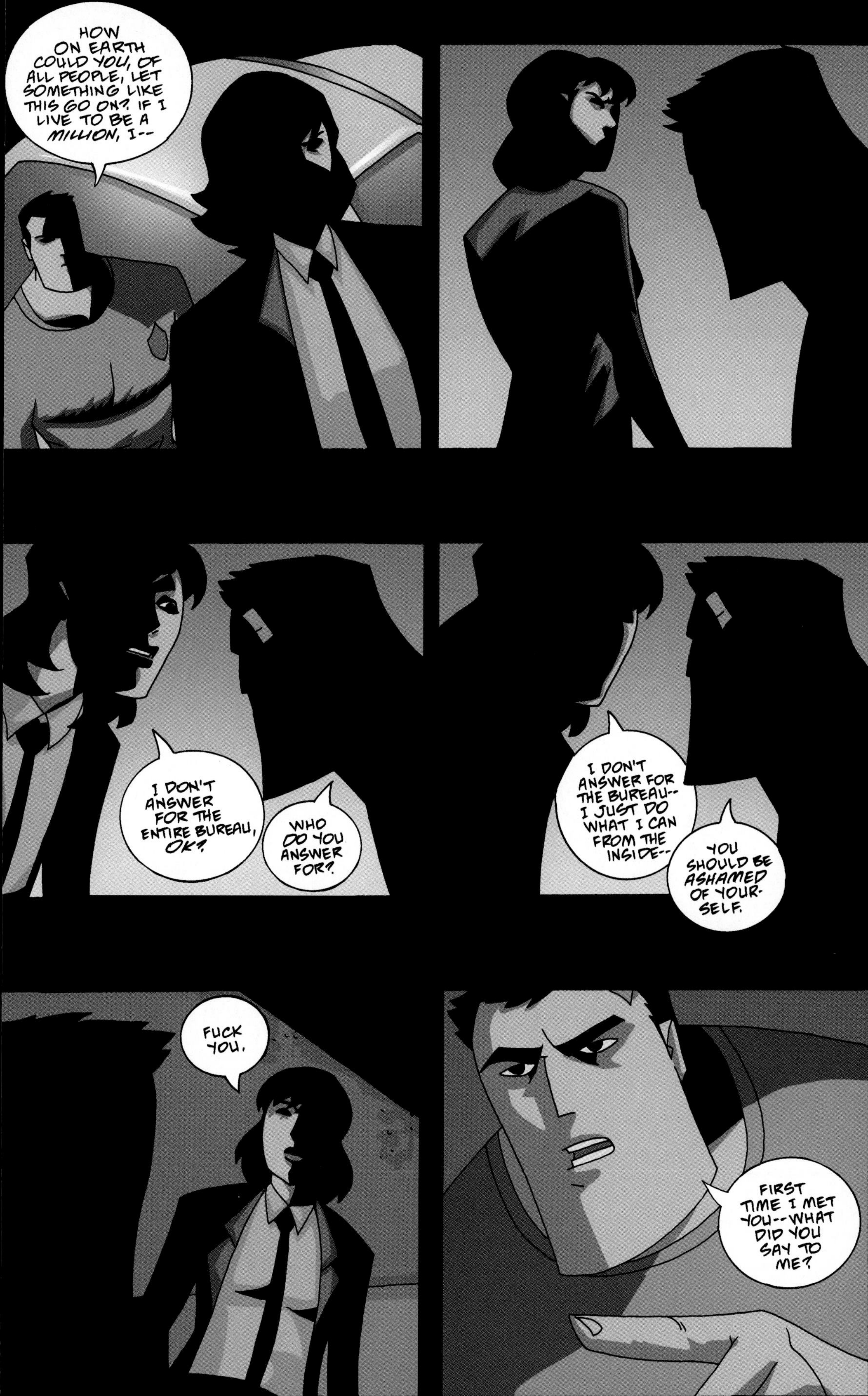
HOW ON EARTH COULD YOU, OF ALL PEOPLE, LET SOMETHING LIKE THIS GO ON? IF I LIVE TO BE A MILLION, I--
I DON'T ANSWER FOR THE ENTIRE BUREAU, OK?
WHO DO YOU ANSWER FOR?
I DON'T ANSWER FOR THE BUREAU-- I JUST DO WHAT I CAN FROM THE INSIDE--
YOU SHOULD BE ASHAMED OF YOURSELF.
FUCK YOU.
FIRST TIME I MET YOU--WHAT DID YOU SAY TO ME?

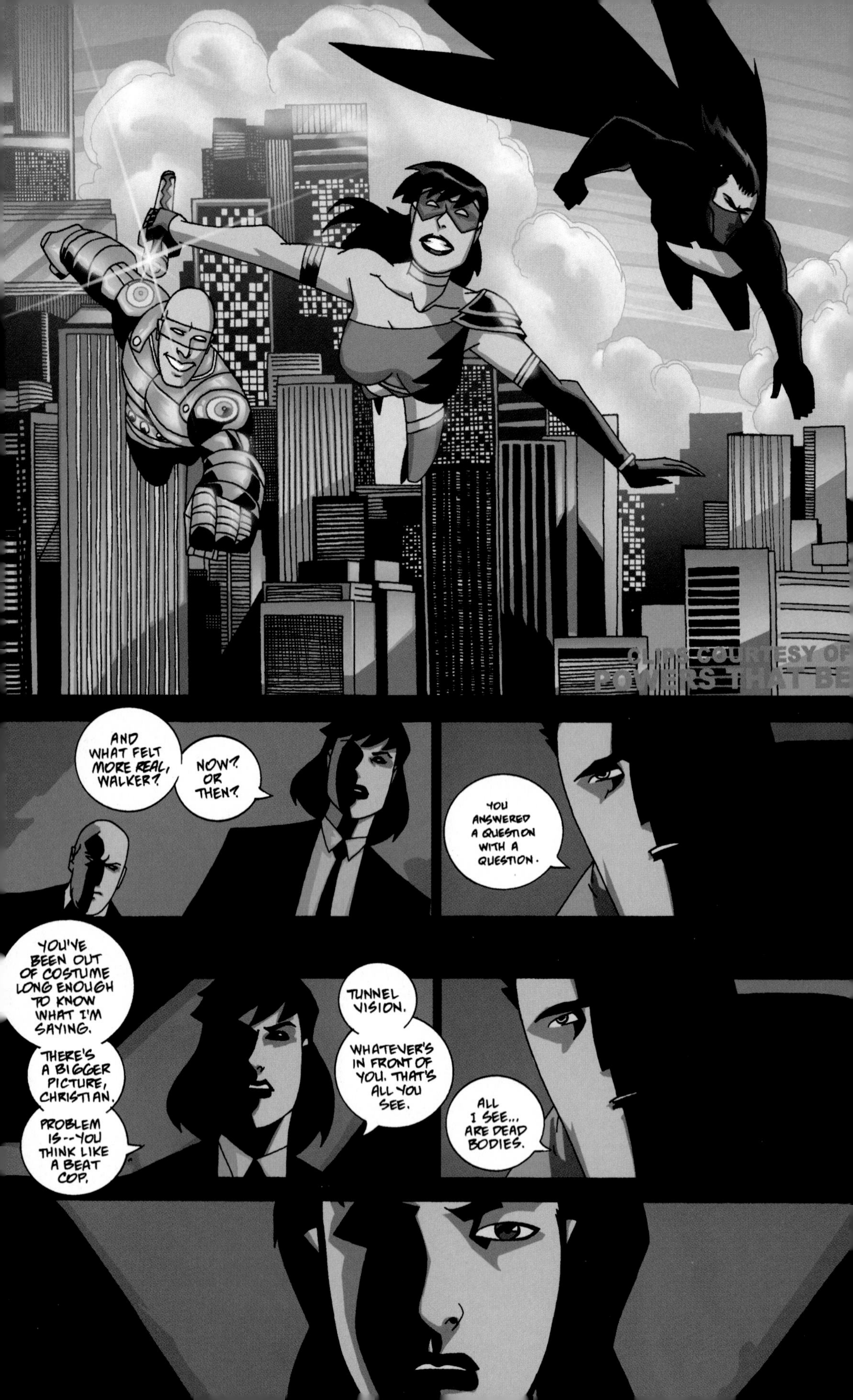
CLIPS COURTESY OF
POWERS THAT BE
AND WHAT FELT MORE REAL, WALKER?
NOW? OR THEN?
YOU ANSWERED A QUESTION WITH A QUESTION.
YOU'VE BEEN OUT OF COSTUME LONG ENOUGH TO KNOW WHAT I'M SAYING.
THERE'S A BIGGER PICTURE, CHRISTIAN.
PROBLEM IS--YOU THINK LIKE A BEAT COP.
TUNNEL VISION.
WHATEVER'S IN FRONT OF YOU. THAT'S ALL YOU SEE.
ALL I SEE... ARE DEAD BODIES.

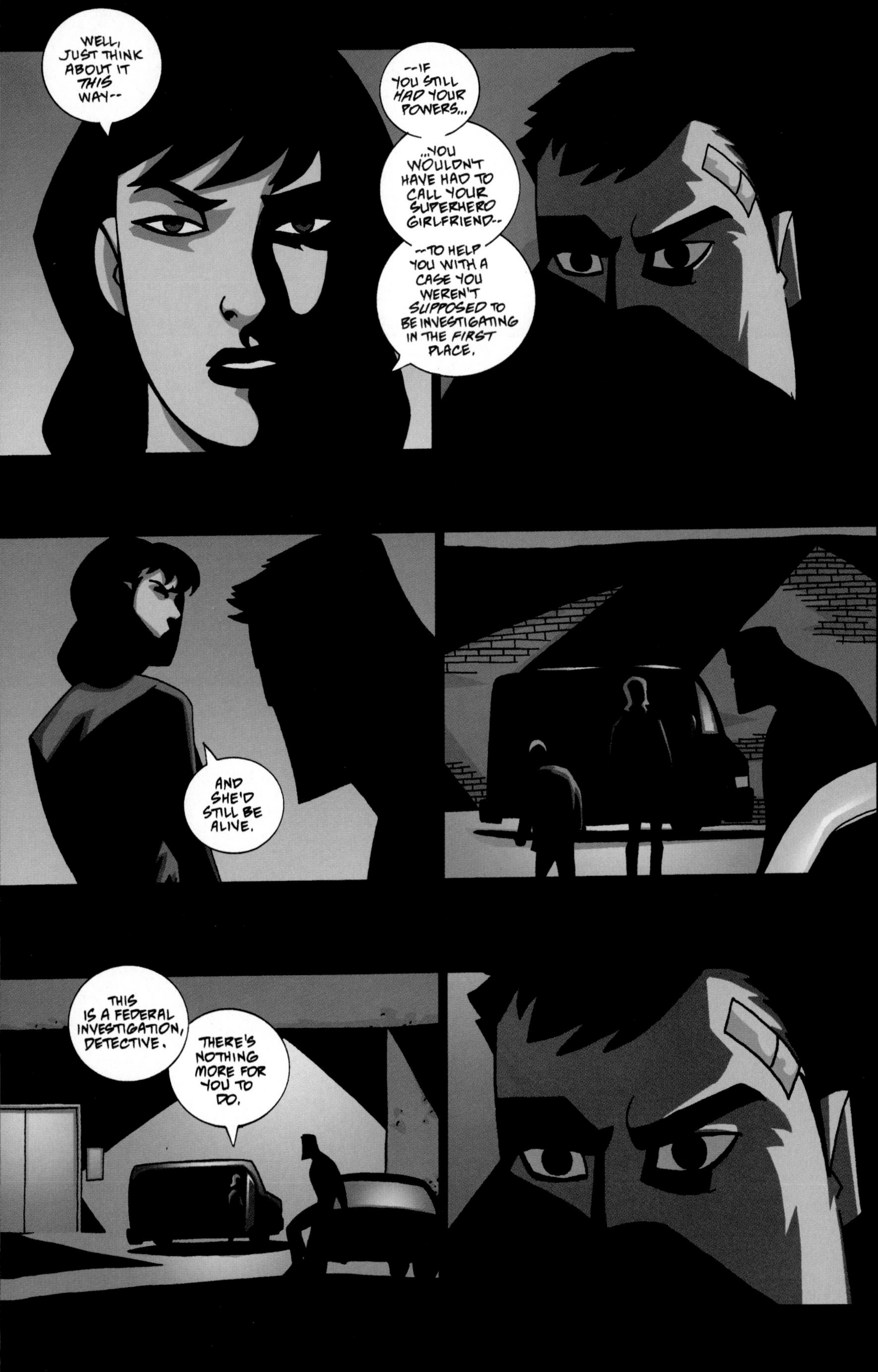

WELL, JUST THINK ABOUT IT *THIS* WAY--
--IF YOU STILL *HAD* YOUR POWERS...
...YOU *WOULDN'T* HAVE HAD TO CALL YOUR SUPERHERO GIRLFRIEND--
--TO HELP YOU WITH A CASE YOU WEREN'T *SUPPOSED* TO BE INVESTIGATING IN THE *FIRST* PLACE.
AND SHE'D STILL BE ALIVE.
THIS IS A FEDERAL INVESTIGATION, DETECTIVE.
THERE'S NOTHING MORE FOR YOU TO DO.

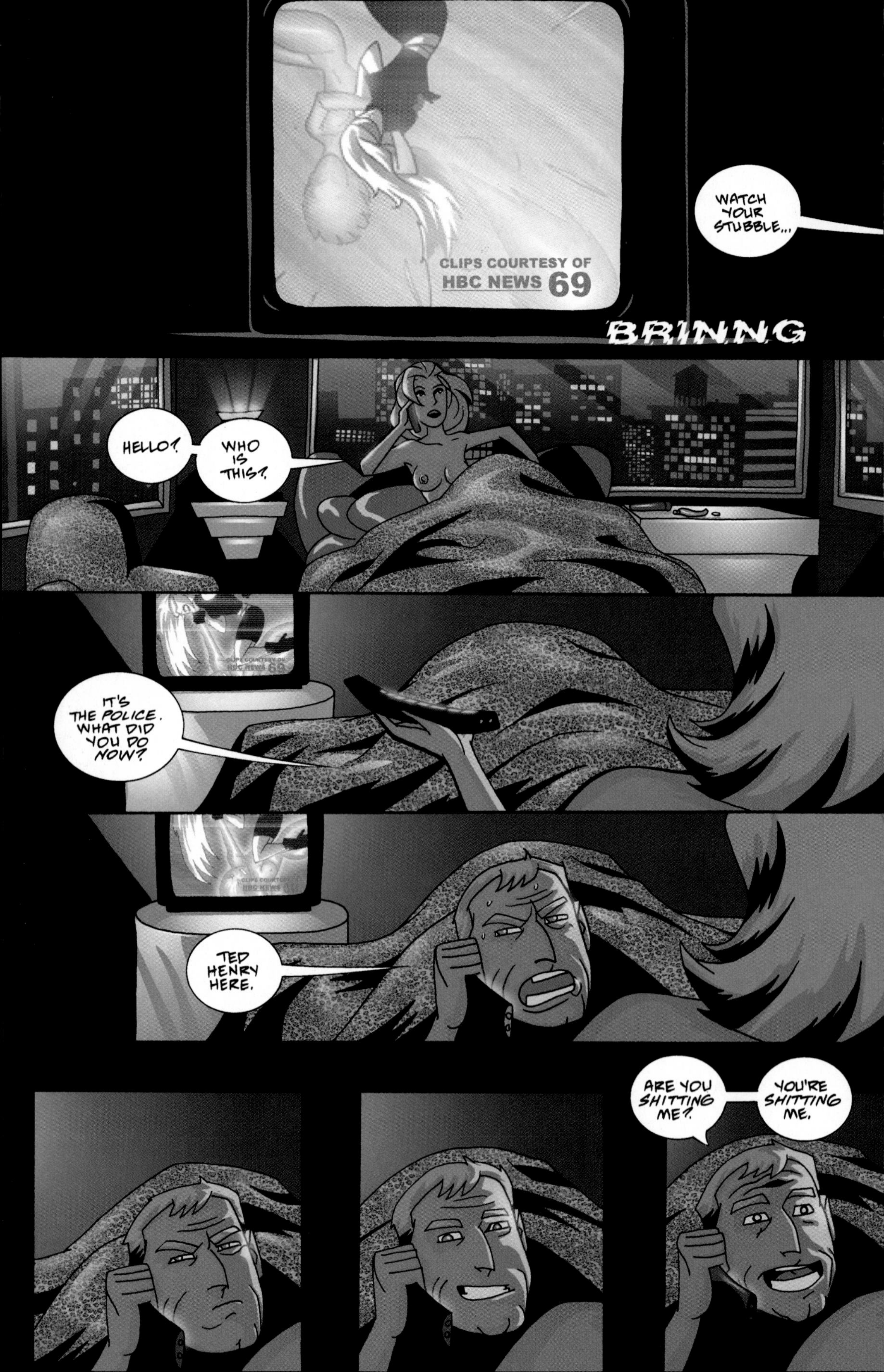

CLIPS COURTESY OF
HBC NEWS 69
WATCH YOUR STUBBLE...
BRINNG
HELLO?
WHO IS THIS?
IT'S THE POLICE. WHAT DID YOU DO NOW?
TED HENRY HERE.
ARE YOU SHITTING ME?
YOU'RE SHITTING ME.

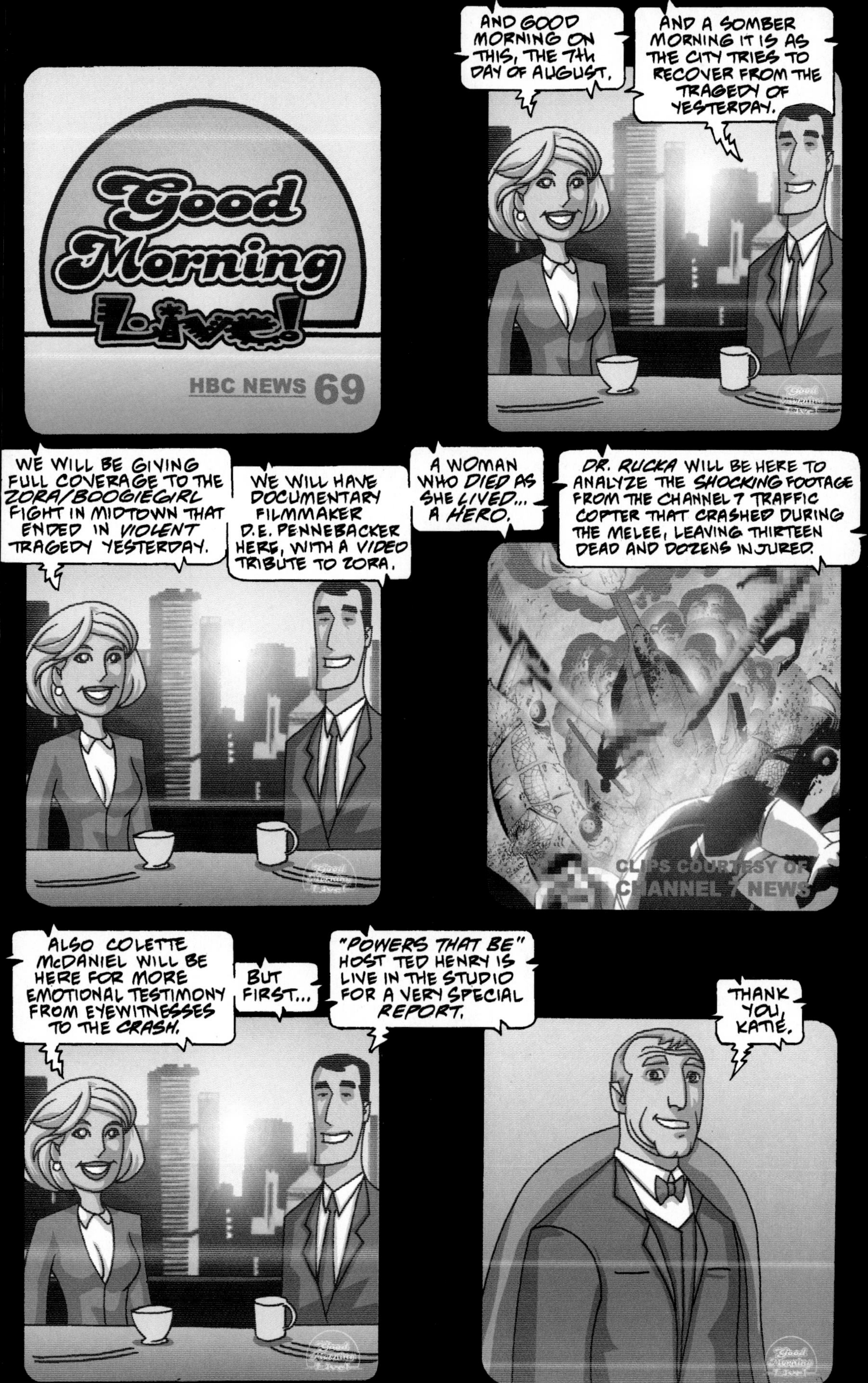
Good Morning Live!
HBC NEWS 69
AND GOOD MORNING ON THIS, THE 7TH DAY OF AUGUST.
AND A SOMBER MORNING IT IS AS THE CITY TRIES TO RECOVER FROM THE TRAGEDY OF YESTERDAY.
WE WILL BE GIVING FULL COVERAGE TO THE ZORA/BOOGIEGIRL FIGHT IN MIDTOWN THAT ENDED IN VIOLENT TRAGEDY YESTERDAY.
WE WILL HAVE DOCUMENTARY FILMMAKER D.E. PENNEBACKER HERE, WITH A VIDEO TRIBUTE TO ZORA.
A WOMAN WHO DIED AS SHE LIVED... A HERO.
DR. RUCKA WILL BE HERE TO ANALYZE THE SHOCKING FOOTAGE FROM THE CHANNEL 7 TRAFFIC COPTER THAT CRASHED DURING THE MELEE, LEAVING THIRTEEN DEAD AND DOZENS INJURED.
CLIPS COURTESY OF CHANNEL 7 NEWS
ALSO COLETTE McDANIEL WILL BE HERE FOR MORE EMOTIONAL TESTIMONY FROM EYEWITNESSES TO THE CRASH.
BUT FIRST...
"POWERS THAT BE" HOST TED HENRY IS LIVE IN THE STUDIO FOR A VERY SPECIAL REPORT.
THANK YOU, KATIE.

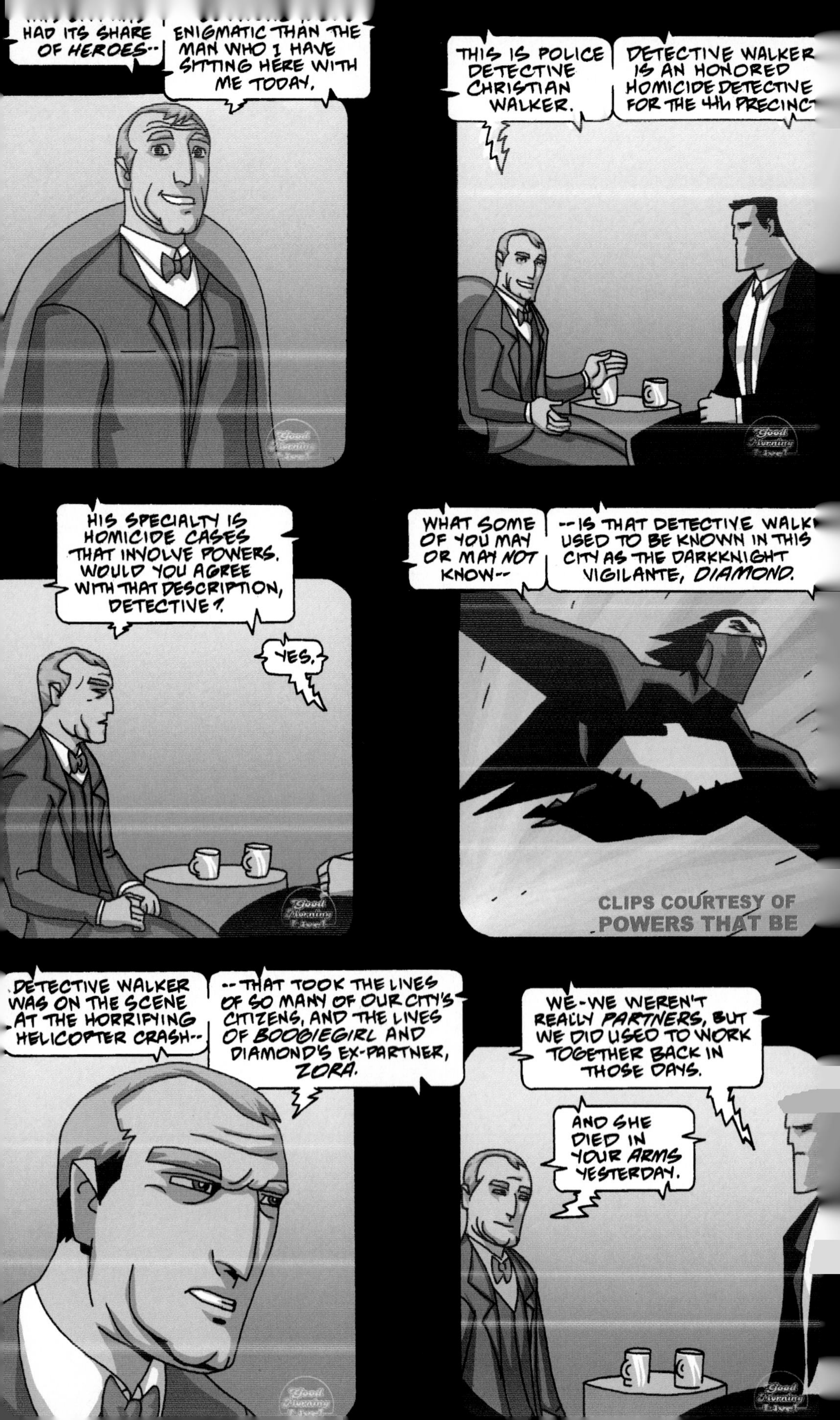
HAD ITS SHARE OF HEROES--
ENIGMATIC THAN THE MAN WHO I HAVE SITTING HERE WITH ME TODAY.
THIS IS POLICE DETECTIVE CHRISTIAN WALKER.
DETECTIVE WALKER IS AN HONORED HOMICIDE DETECTIVE FOR THE 4th PRECINCT
HIS SPECIALTY IS HOMICIDE CASES THAT INVOLVE POWERS. WOULD YOU AGREE WITH THAT DESCRIPTION, DETECTIVE?
YES.
WHAT SOME OF YOU MAY OR MAY NOT KNOW--
--IS THAT DETECTIVE WALK USED TO BE KNOWN IN THIS CITY AS THE DARKKNIGHT VIGILANTE, DIAMOND.
CLIPS COURTESY OF POWERS THAT BE
DETECTIVE WALKER WAS ON THE SCENE AT THE HORRIFYING HELICOPTER CRASH--
--THAT TOOK THE LIVES OF SO MANY OF OUR CITY'S CITIZENS, AND THE LIVES OF BOOGIEGIRL AND DIAMOND'S EX-PARTNER, ZORA.
WE-WE WEREN'T REALLY PARTNERS, BUT WE DID USED TO WORK TOGETHER BACK IN THOSE DAYS.
AND SHE DIED IN YOUR ARMS YESTERDAY.

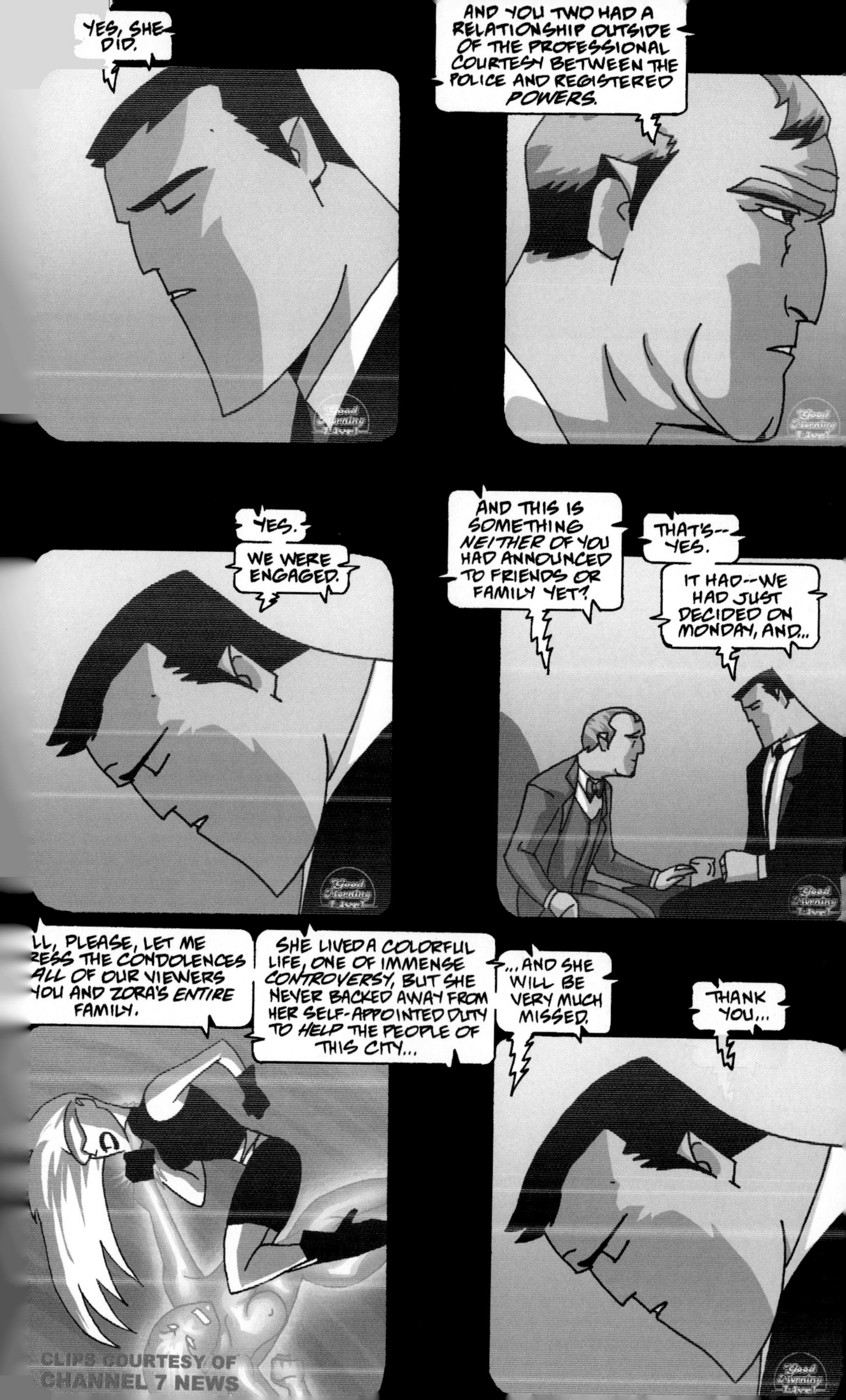
YES, SHE DID.
AND YOU TWO HAD A RELATIONSHIP OUTSIDE OF THE PROFESSIONAL COURTESY BETWEEN THE POLICE AND REGISTERED POWERS.
YES.
WE WERE ENGAGED.
AND THIS IS SOMETHING NEITHER OF YOU HAD ANNOUNCED TO FRIENDS OR FAMILY YET?
THAT'S-- YES.
IT HAD--WE HAD JUST DECIDED ON MONDAY, AND...
LL, PLEASE, LET ME RESS THE CONDOLENCES ALL OF OUR VIEWERS YOU AND ZORA'S ENTIRE FAMILY.
SHE LIVED A COLORFUL LIFE, ONE OF IMMENSE CONTROVERSY, BUT SHE NEVER BACKED AWAY FROM HER SELF-APPOINTED DUTY TO HELP THE PEOPLE OF THIS CITY...
...AND SHE WILL BE VERY MUCH MISSED.
THANK YOU...
CLIPS COURTESY OF CHANNEL 7 NEWS

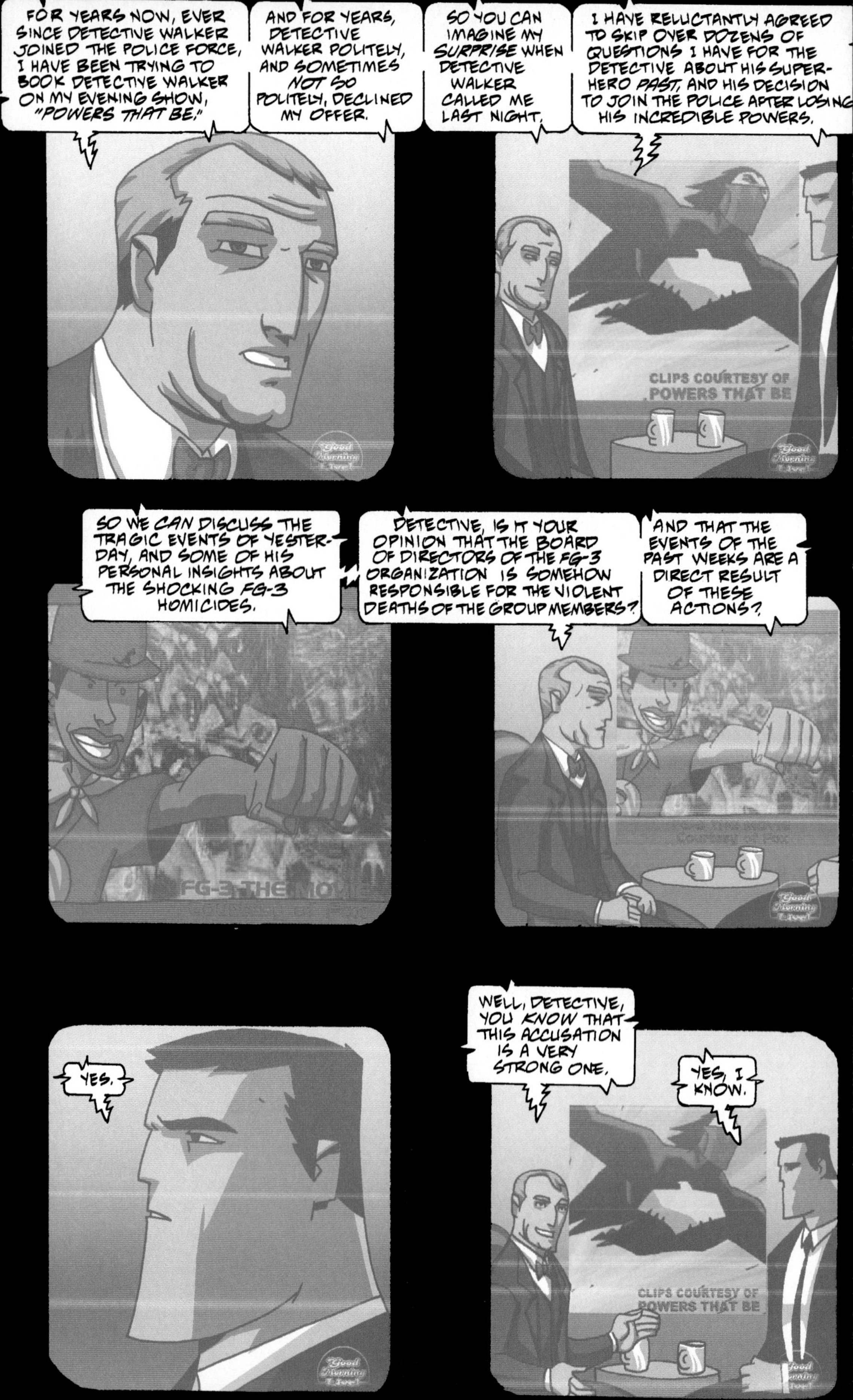
FOR YEARS NOW, EVER SINCE DETECTIVE WALKER JOINED THE POLICE FORCE, I HAVE BEEN TRYING TO BOOK DETECTIVE WALKER ON MY EVENING SHOW, "POWERS THAT BE."
AND FOR YEARS, DETECTIVE WALKER POLITELY, AND SOMETIMES NOT SO POLITELY, DECLINED MY OFFER.
SO YOU CAN IMAGINE MY SURPRISE WHEN DETECTIVE WALKER CALLED ME LAST NIGHT.
I HAVE RELUCTANTLY AGREED TO SKIP OVER DOZENS OF QUESTIONS I HAVE FOR THE DETECTIVE ABOUT HIS SUPER-HERO PAST, AND HIS DECISION TO JOIN THE POLICE AFTER LOSING HIS INCREDIBLE POWERS.
CLIPS COURTESY OF POWERS THAT BE
SO WE CAN DISCUSS THE TRAGIC EVENTS OF YESTERDAY, AND SOME OF HIS PERSONAL INSIGHTS ABOUT THE SHOCKING FG-3 HOMICIDES.
FG-3 THE MOVIE
DETECTIVE, IS IT YOUR OPINION THAT THE BOARD OF DIRECTORS OF THE FG-3 ORGANIZATION IS SOMEHOW RESPONSIBLE FOR THE VIOLENT DEATHS OF THE GROUP MEMBERS?
AND THAT THE EVENTS OF THE PAST WEEKS ARE A DIRECT RESULT OF THESE ACTIONS?
YES.
WELL, DETECTIVE, YOU KNOW THAT THIS ACCUSATION IS A VERY STRONG ONE.
YES, I KNOW.
CLIPS COURTESY OF POWERS THAT BE

YOU ARE POINTING FINGERS AT SOME OF THE MOST PROMINENT BUSINESSMEN OF THE DECADE.

FILE FOOTAGE

I KNOW.

BUT YOU ARE RISKING AN AWFUL LOT BY BREAKING, AS THEY CALL IT, THE BLUE CODE OF SILENCE.

THE CODE OF HONOR HELD BY THE FRATERNAL BROTHERHOOD OF POLICE TO KEEP POLICE BUSINESS POLICE BUSINESS, AND NOT TO--

BUT, UM, I BELIEVE THAT THIS ISN'T POLICE BUSINESS, THIS IS THE BUSINESS OF THE CITY.

OUR INVESTIGATION OF THE MURDERS HAS BEEN HALTED.

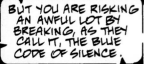

HALTED? HALTED BY WHOM?

THE FEDERAL GOVERNMENT HAS TAKEN JURISDICTION, THEY HAVE ALREADY STATED SO PUBLICLY.

AND YOU BELIEVE THAT BY DOING SO, THEY ARE MAKING WAY TO COVER UP THE TRUE FACTS OF THE CASE?

YES, I DO.

IN OUR SHORT INVOLVEMENT IN THE CASE, CERTAIN TRUTHS HAVE COME TO LIGHT ABOUT THE REAL ORIGIN OF FG-3 THAT ARE BEING IGNORED.

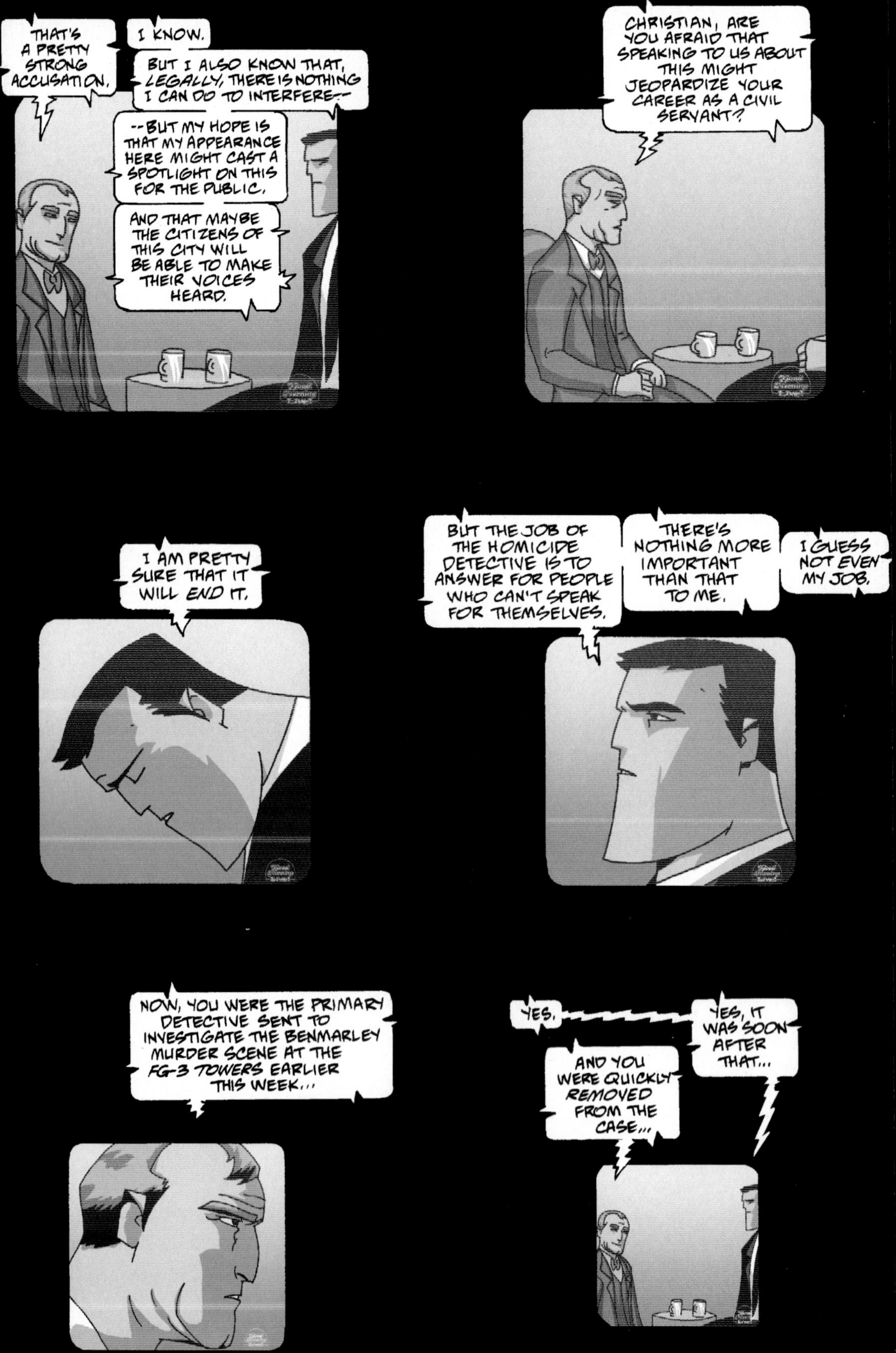
THAT'S A PRETTY STRONG ACCUSATION.
I KNOW.
BUT I ALSO KNOW THAT, *LEGALLY,* THERE IS NOTHING I CAN DO TO INTERFERE--
--BUT MY HOPE IS THAT MY APPEARANCE HERE MIGHT CAST A SPOTLIGHT ON THIS FOR THE PUBLIC.
AND THAT MAYBE THE CITIZENS OF THIS CITY WILL BE ABLE TO MAKE THEIR VOICES HEARD.
CHRISTIAN, ARE YOU AFRAID THAT SPEAKING TO US ABOUT THIS MIGHT JEOPARDIZE YOUR CAREER AS A CIVIL SERVANT?
I AM PRETTY SURE THAT IT WILL *END* IT.
BUT THE JOB OF THE HOMICIDE DETECTIVE IS TO ANSWER FOR PEOPLE WHO CAN'T SPEAK FOR THEMSELVES.
THERE'S NOTHING MORE IMPORTANT THAN THAT TO ME.
I GUESS NOT EVEN MY JOB.
NOW, YOU WERE THE PRIMARY DETECTIVE SENT TO INVESTIGATE THE BENMARLEY MURDER SCENE AT THE *FG-3 TOWERS* EARLIER THIS WEEK...
YES.
AND YOU WERE QUICKLY *REMOVED* FROM THE CASE...
YES, IT WAS SOON AFTER THAT...

67 DAYS LATER

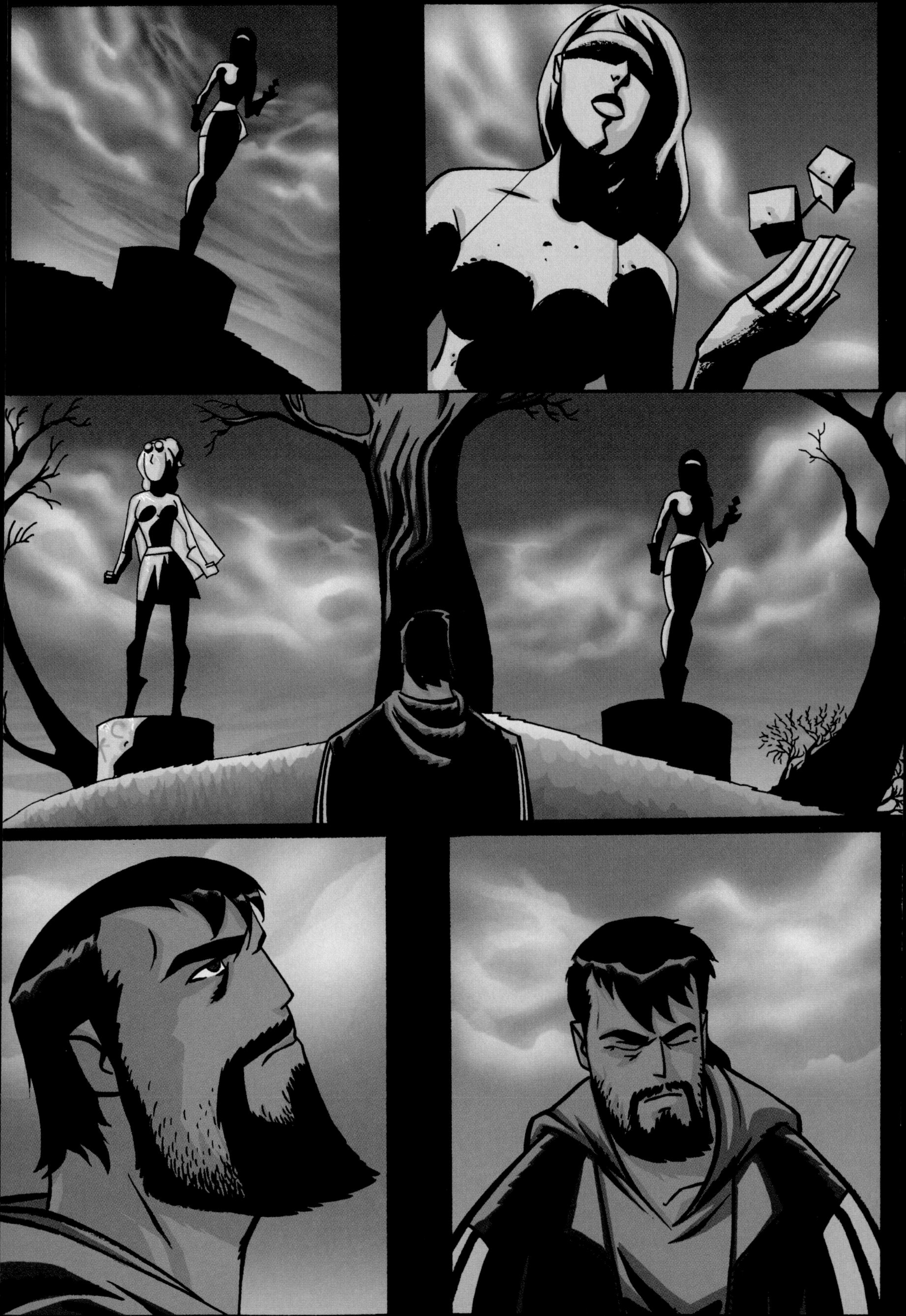

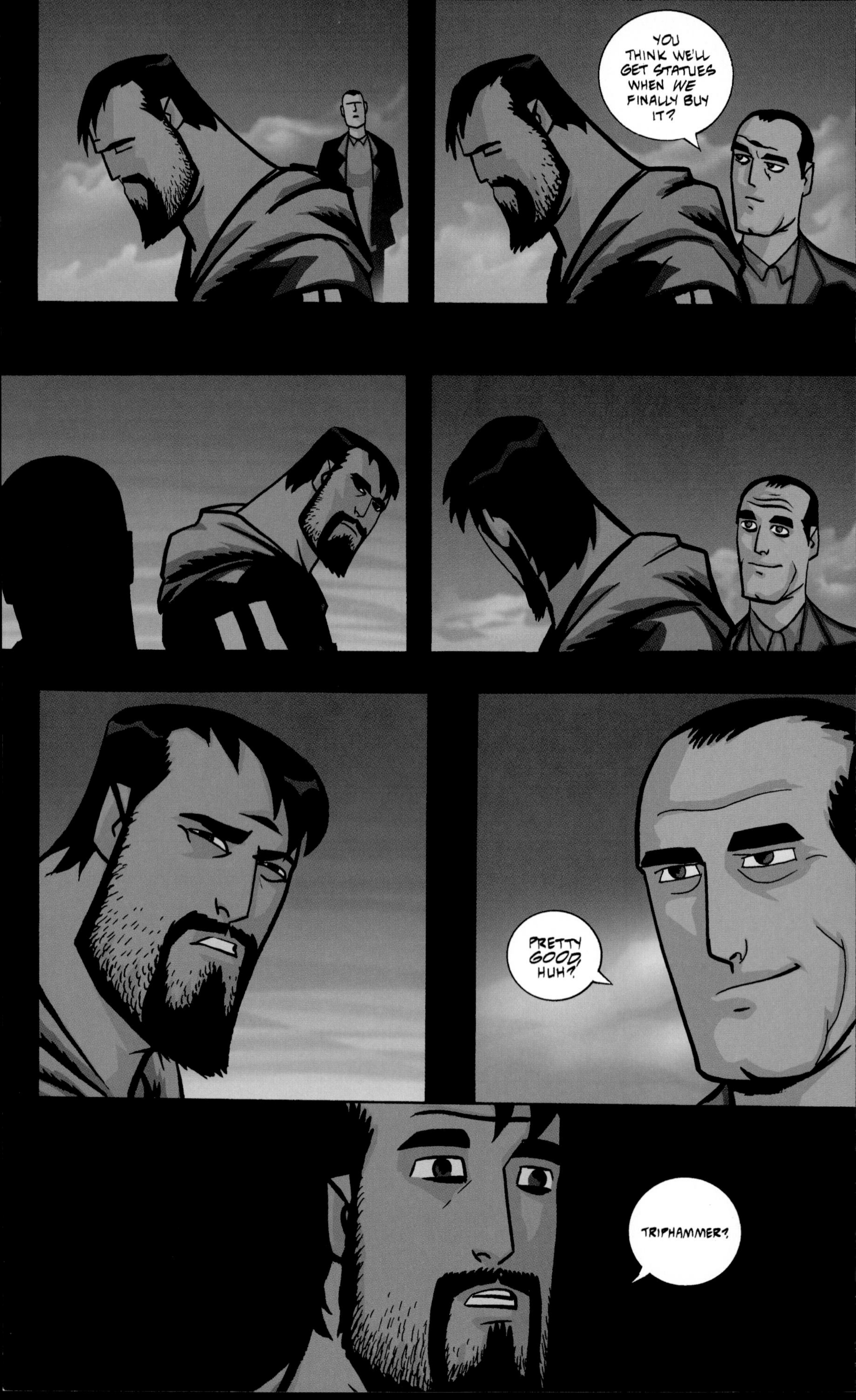
YOU THINK WE'LL GET STATUES WHEN WE FINALLY BUY IT?
PRETTY GOOD, HUH?
TRIPHAMMER?

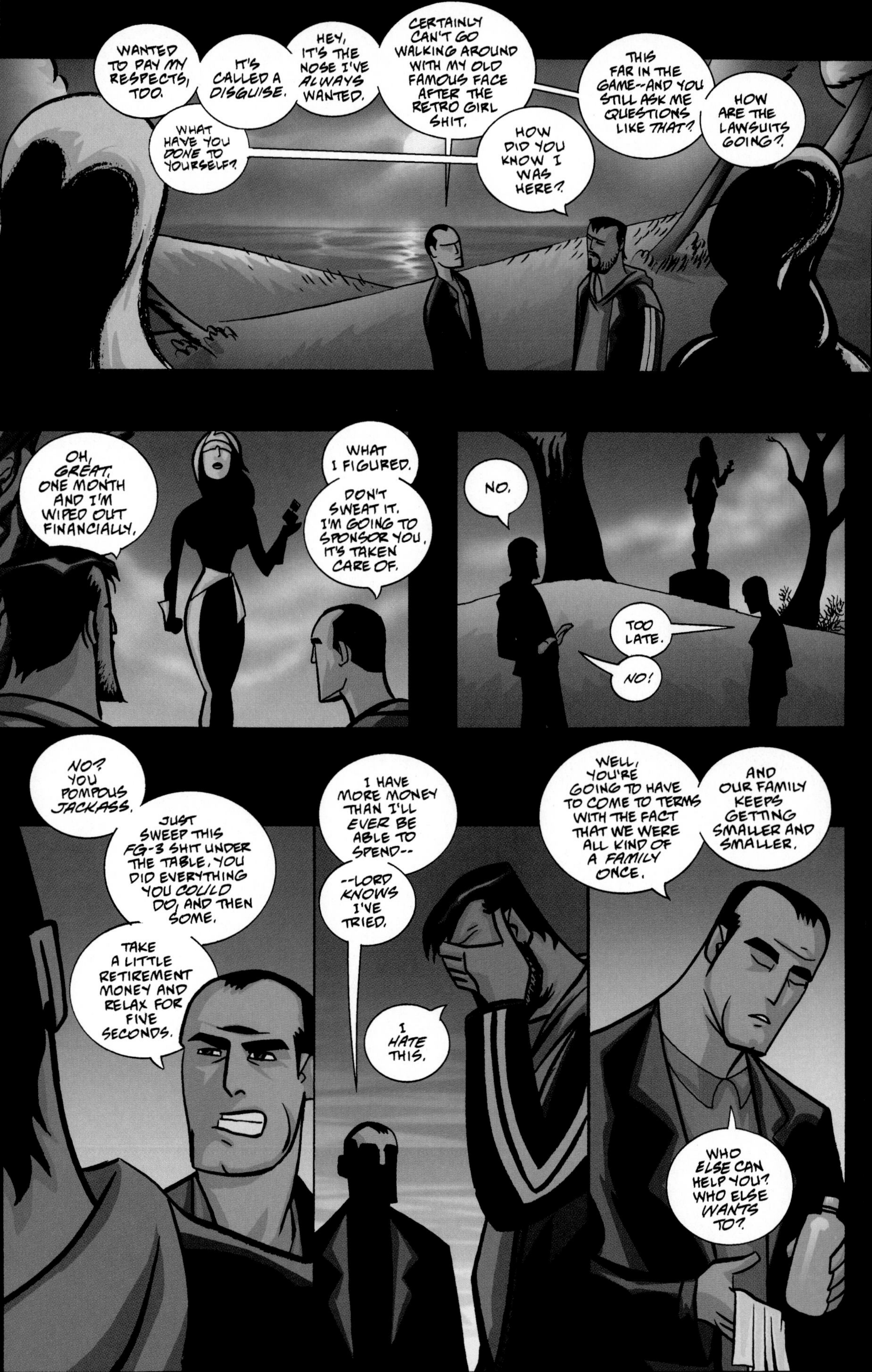
WANTED TO PAY MY RESPECTS, TOO.
WHAT HAVE YOU DONE TO YOURSELF?
IT'S CALLED A DISGUISE.
HEY, IT'S THE NOSE I'VE ALWAYS WANTED.
CERTAINLY CAN'T GO WALKING AROUND WITH MY OLD FAMOUS FACE AFTER THE RETRO GIRL SHIT.
HOW DID YOU KNOW I WAS HERE?
THIS FAR IN THE GAME--AND YOU STILL ASK ME QUESTIONS LIKE THAT?
HOW ARE THE LAWSUITS GOING?
OH, GREAT. ONE MONTH AND I'M WIPED OUT FINANCIALLY.
WHAT I FIGURED.
DON'T SWEAT IT. I'M GOING TO SPONSOR YOU. IT'S TAKEN CARE OF.
NO.
TOO LATE.
NO!
NO? YOU POMPOUS JACKASS.
JUST SWEEP THIS FG-3 SHIT UNDER THE TABLE. YOU DID EVERYTHING YOU COULD DO, AND THEN SOME.
TAKE A LITTLE RETIREMENT MONEY AND RELAX FOR FIVE SECONDS.
I HAVE MORE MONEY THAN I'LL EVER BE ABLE TO SPEND--
--LORD KNOWS I'VE TRIED.
I HATE THIS.
WELL, YOU'RE GOING TO HAVE TO COME TO TERMS WITH THE FACT THAT WE WERE ALL KIND OF A FAMILY ONCE.
AND OUR FAMILY KEEPS GETTING SMALLER AND SMALLER.
WHO ELSE CAN HELP YOU? WHO ELSE WANTS TO?

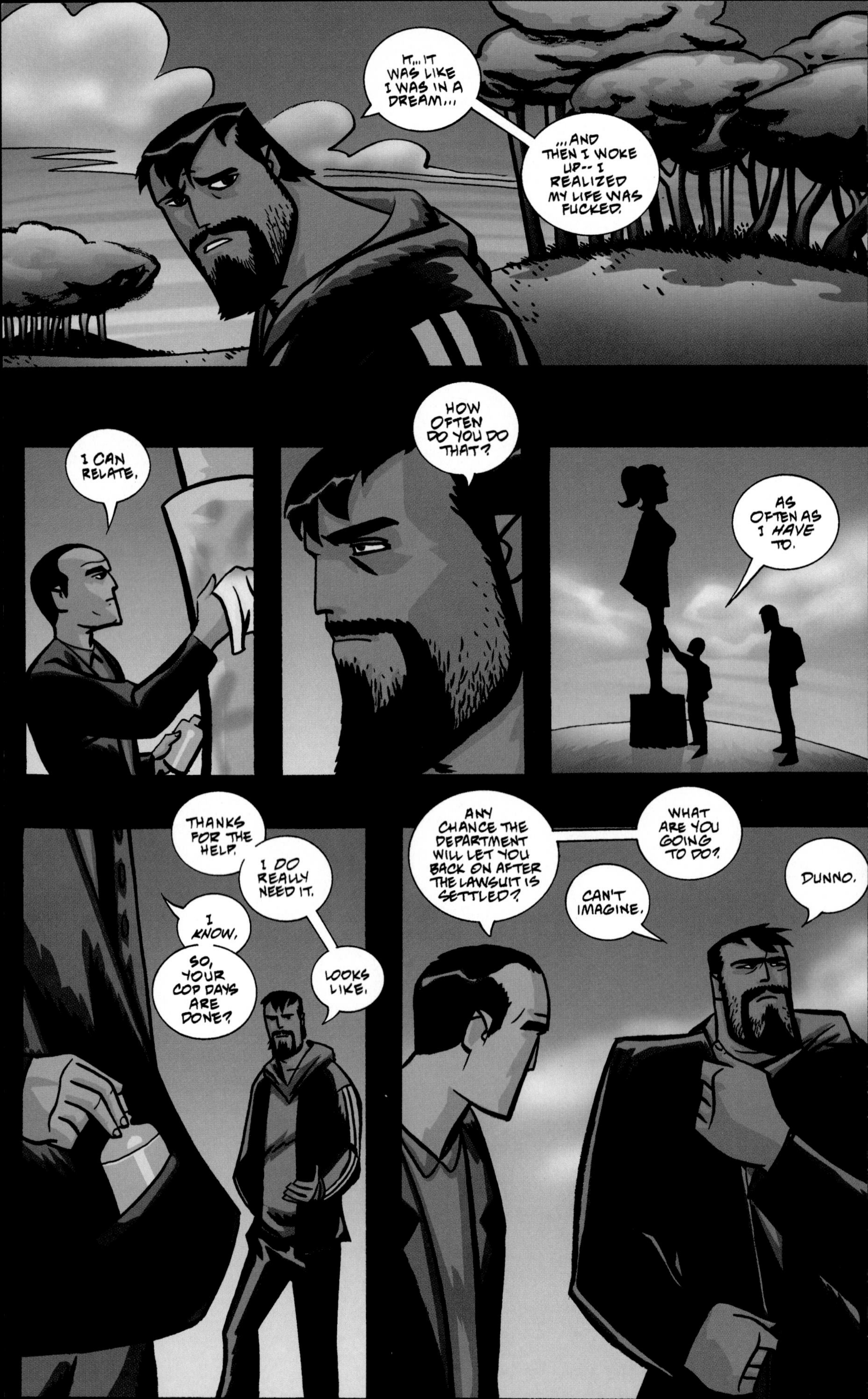
IT... IT WAS LIKE I WAS IN A DREAM...
...AND THEN I WOKE UP-- I REALIZED MY LIFE WAS FUCKED.
I CAN RELATE.
HOW OFTEN DO YOU DO THAT?
AS OFTEN AS I HAVE TO.
THANKS FOR THE HELP.
I DO REALLY NEED IT.
I KNOW.
SO, YOUR COP DAYS ARE DONE?
LOOKS LIKE.
ANY CHANCE THE DEPARTMENT WILL LET YOU BACK ON AFTER THE LAWSUIT IS SETTLED?
CAN'T IMAGINE.
WHAT ARE YOU GOING TO DO?
DUNNO.

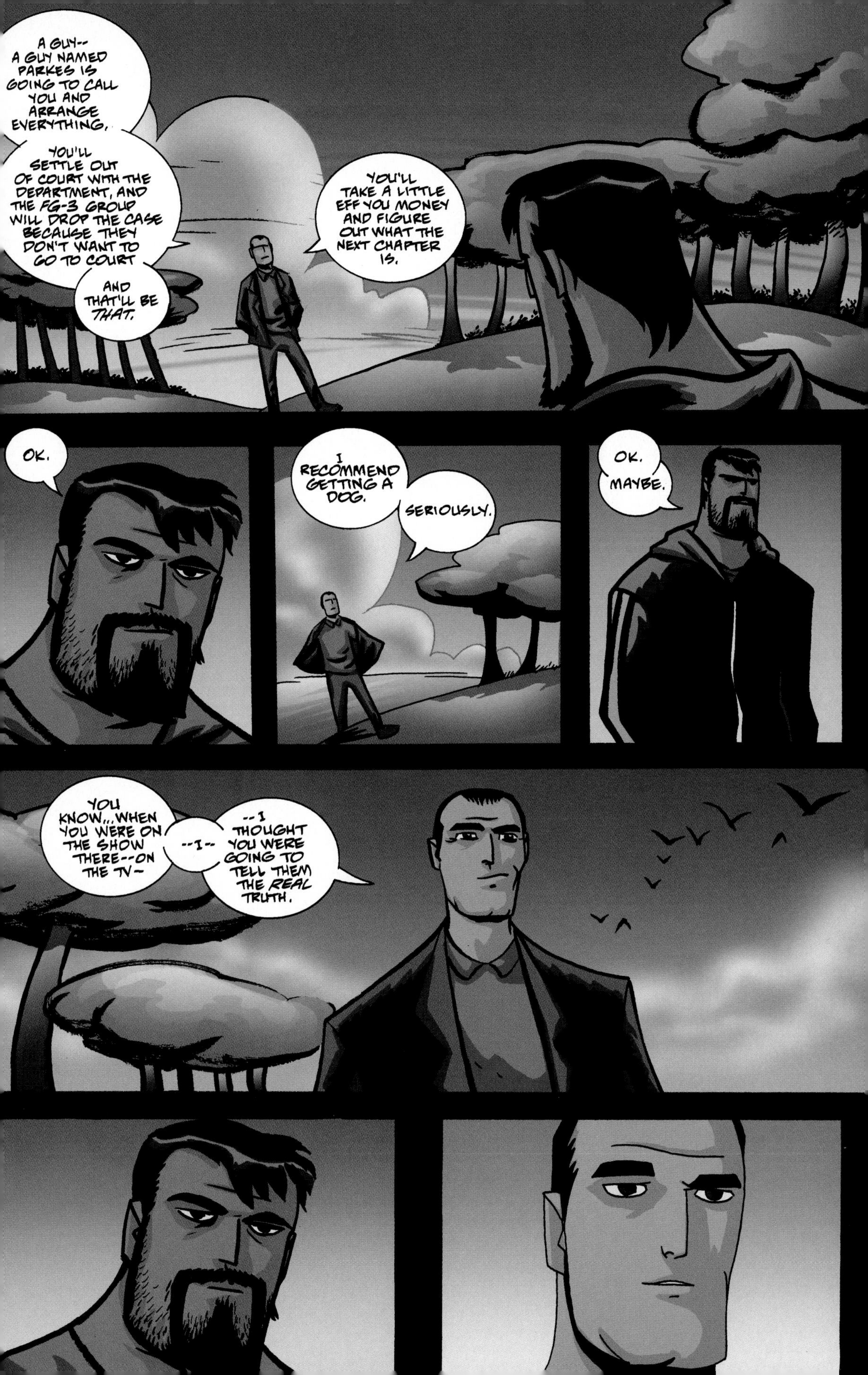
A GUY-- A GUY NAMED PARKES IS GOING TO CALL YOU AND ARRANGE EVERYTHING.
YOU'LL SETTLE OUT OF COURT WITH THE DEPARTMENT, AND THE FG-3 GROUP WILL DROP THE CASE BECAUSE THEY DON'T WANT TO GO TO COURT
AND THAT'LL BE *THAT.*
YOU'LL TAKE A LITTLE EFF YOU MONEY AND FIGURE OUT WHAT THE NEXT CHAPTER IS.
OK.
I RECOMMEND GETTING A DOG.
SERIOUSLY.
OK. MAYBE.
YOU KNOW... WHEN YOU WERE ON THE SHOW THERE--ON THE TV--
--I--
--I THOUGHT YOU WERE GOING TO TELL THEM THE *REAL* TRUTH.

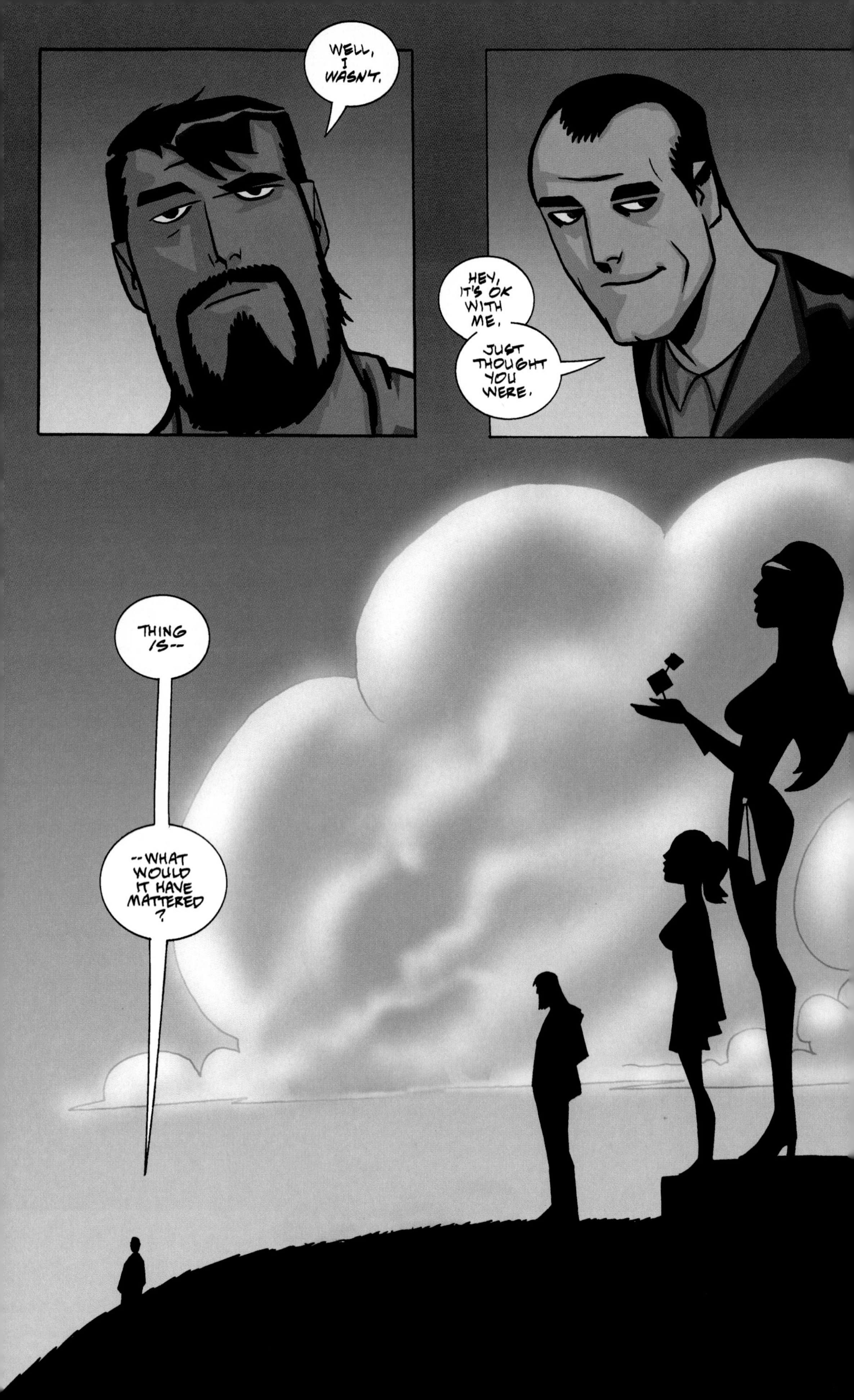
WELL, I WASN'T.
HEY, IT'S OK WITH ME.
JUST THOUGHT YOU WERE.
THING IS--
--WHAT WOULD IT HAVE MATTERED?

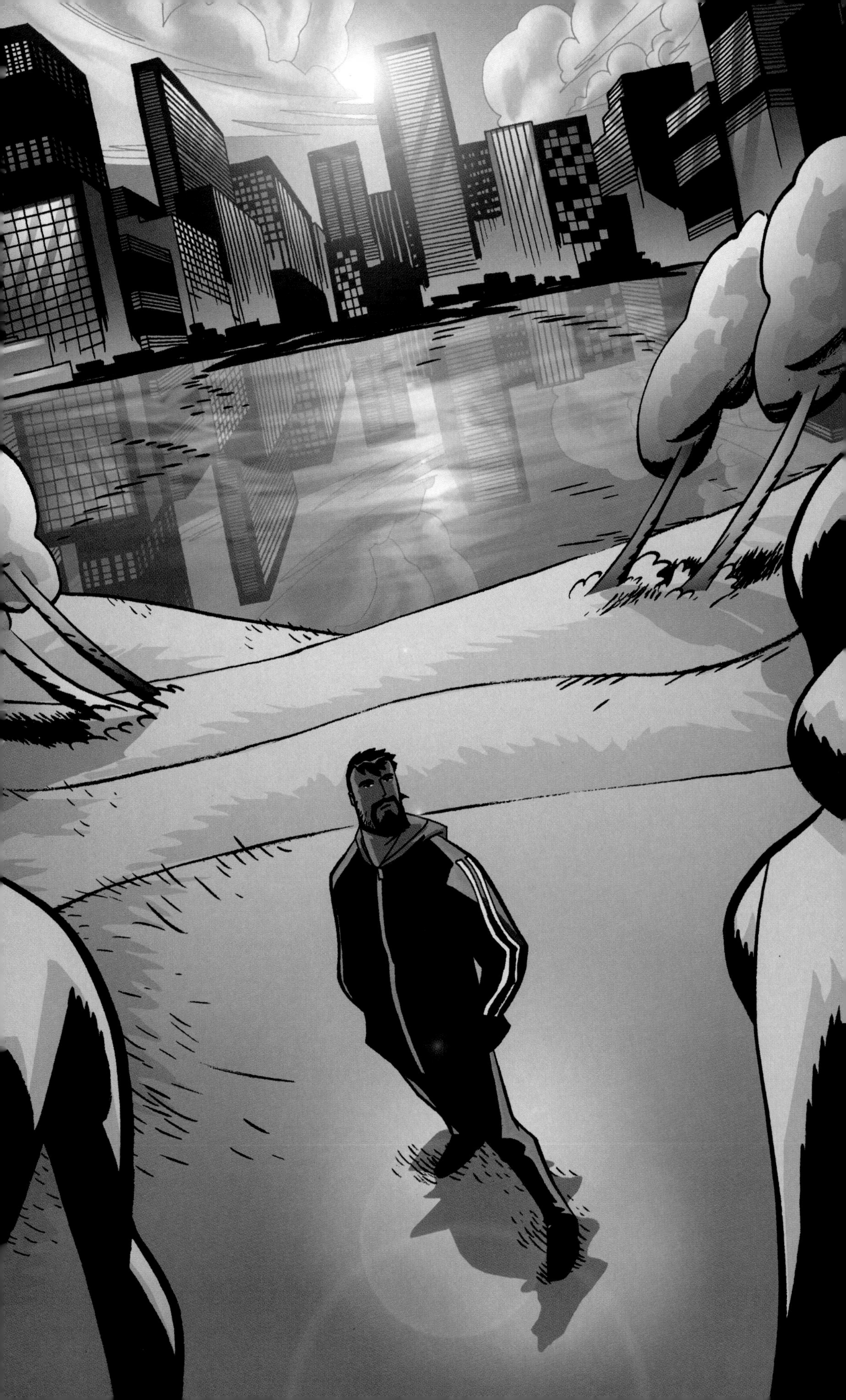

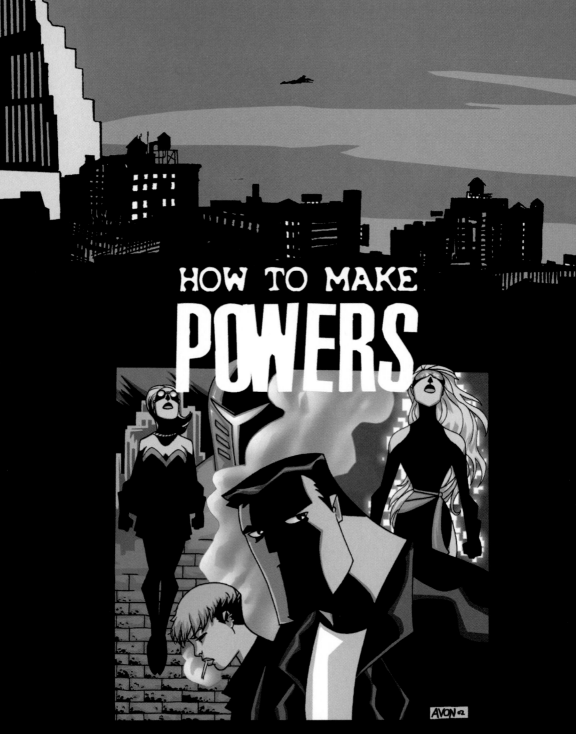

HOW TO MAKE POWERS

The damn fine folks at DRAW magazine asked Mike and the gang to put together this intensive behind the scenes look at the nuts and bolts creation of Powers: the monthly comic. We are presenting it here as it originally appeared in the magazine.

A very special thanks and thank you to DRAW magazine for their attention and generosity.

POWERS: BUILDING THE PAGE

by the Powers team

Wow, DRAW! Magazine is one of the Powers teams' most favorite mags.

In just a short time DRAW! has proven to bring insightful lessons
from the land of comics and animation to the people,
and we hope do the same here, shed a little light
on how we go about our proscess of work.

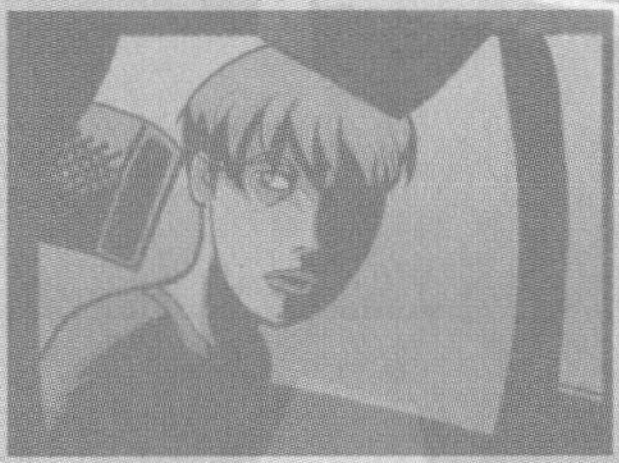

It all begins with the script of Brian Bendis.

So without further hype (doesnt he get enough?)
here is my partner and good friend,
Brian Bendis with a few words on how he builds his scripts.

-Mike Avon Oeming, Powers Artist and co creator

I don't know anything.

I'm not being modest or taking my usual bath in the water of self-loathing.
I really don't know anything. I'm self-taught. I learned as I went.
And what I learned was that there are no hard, set "rules" for writing.
There is no one pearl of wisdom that will open the door to the universe of writing.
Anytime someone tells me what the "rules" are,
my eyes roll up in my head and I lose consciousness.
So, I can't promise you'll find anything even remotely resembling that here.

Any technical writing technique or theory that I hold to -
and I definitely do hold to some vital techniques and theories -
I got from a book called Story by Robert McKee.
Actually, I picked up a lot from pop-culture osmosis,
as I am sure many of you have, but this book put names and labels on it.
It organized what I had learned into a formidable and essential text.
Story is absolutely essential reading for all professed storytellers
and lovers of the craft of storytelling, no matter what medium.
It gets you thinking and keeps you on course,
and really, what's more important than that?

I learned how to write from two things: practice and reading other people's scripts.
I love to read a good script more than I love going to a movie or reading a book or comic.
I love reading scripts to movies before they are released so that when I do get to finally
see them, I can compare the movie I directed in my head to the movie I am watching.

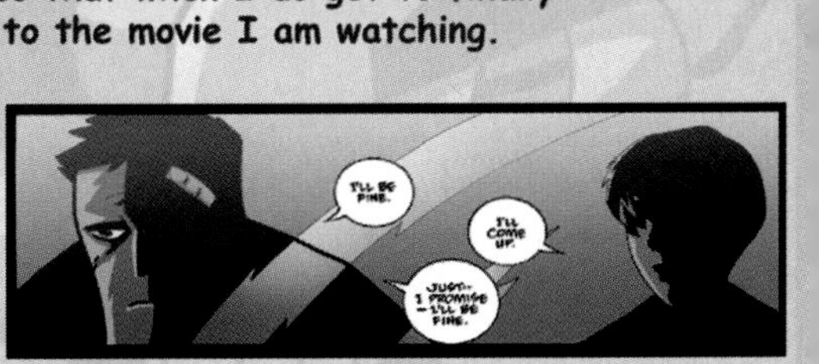
I'LL BE FINE.
I'LL COME UP.
JUST-- I PROMISE --I'LL BE FINE.

The only advice I can give is to write honestly.
Don't write what you think people want.
All people want is not to be insulted.
They want to be entertained.
They want to know that the person writing to them
has something honest and interesting to say.

If you write something you think people want, you will always fail.
Let's say that everyone loves blue this year - blue is all the rage.
So you sit down and write something blue.
Well, by the time you get your blue out for people to see,
people will have moved on to pink and won't want blue anymore.
And now you're stuck with this blue thing that no one wants, including you.

The best thing you can offer the world
as a writer is something you'd like to read,
something that you would buy.

Then, if someone else wants to buy it, too, that's great news for you.
It's all gravy after that. But bare minimum, having something you wrote
be something you would want to read is really the reason anyone in any
medium writes. That's why we made Powers, we wanted to buy the comic.

But - there is no standard script format used in the comic book industry.
People just kind of find their ways around the unique concept of collaboration
with artists to tell a story.

My style is referred to in "The Biz" as full script,
which means there's a panel-by-panel description of the storytelling
with dialogue attached. It's very similar to a movie screenplay,
with each word of scene description is picked for maximum impact.
I'm brief, but I am to the point.

Other styles include the "Marvel-house style", in which the writer gives the artist
a page or two of story description. The artist then interprets the story the way he wants,
and the writer comes back and constructs the dialogue to accentuate the art.
Alan Moore is famous for writing complicated stream-of-consciousness scripts for artists
to approach like cryptographers. Paul Jenkins is known to fill scripts with personal anecdotes
to accentuate the kinds of emotions he wants to convey in his scenes.
Mark Millar drinks himself into a coma and wakes up three days later to find
all of his scripts for the year neatly typed and ready to go.

That last one, of course, is a joke.
Millar doesn't do that - Ed Brubaker does.

Some of the hardest things storytellers have to accept
are that they can't control the environment in which their work
is read or their readers' mindsets, so they have to try to control
the flow and timing as best they can. This is so important to me
and it's probably the thing that drives my editors craziest about me.

This balloon placement and final polish is my favorite part of writing comics.
It's so much fun to have a pile of finished art to craft your words around.
It's a beautiful feeling to see the work of an artist who is on the same page as you.
I imagine it must feel quite similar to a film director and his editor when they have
piles of really good footage to put together.

What I am saying is: I'm a picker. I know some of my peers are not.
Many of them hand in their scripts and look forward. That's fine ... but I pick.
I pick scripts to death, but in doing so I usually find the best one-liners, my best moments.
On the flipside, it's also where I make the most typos.

For the up-and-coming writers out there:
if questions about craft and theory still bounce around your brain,
visit me and my comic-creator peers at the jinxworld.com messageboard.
Feel free to ask any question and discuss it.

Also, for more information, I have a behind-the-scenes look at the creation
of the JINX graphic novel I did for Image both in the graphic novel itself and on my web site.

don't have any advice on breaking into the business.

I'd known how, it wouldn't have taken me forever to get in.
lo know one thing, though: writers write! They don't sit around
hing they were writing or talking about what they're thinking of writing.
ey write! Because while you're sitting around and talking about it,
neone is out there writing their fucking asses off.
neone is out there kicking your ass and stealing your dream job.

read this while you're on the toilet, but when you're done, write something.
vill be.

-Brian Michael Bendis, Powers Writer and co creator

he "Pencils"

ay "pencils" because I rarely do pencil. I go right from my breakdown to inking the page, h as little pencil as possible. When I get Brian's fat (and phat) script, usually scribble a very small panel layout, with no figures or composition. en, I'll use an 11 x 17 photocopy paper and very lightly with pencil, a very loose breakdown. Many of our pages have a good amount of dialogue, I've taken to leaving large tear areas to hold the words, and in this way, an prevent most of my art being covered. From that stage, I break out my pen. ually a bald point pen and thats when most of the drawing actually happens. se as little lines as I can, always thinking of animation, using the "line of action" make figures fluid. Often, I'll even use the much dreaded TANGENT line to move the eye.

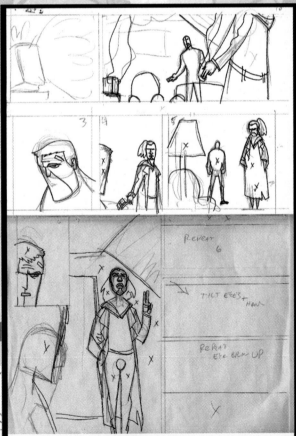

I try and keep a continuous line on the exterrior of figures, imagining each figure as a silhouette, a simple image.

You can see here where I've indicated repeating panels. Even if Im changing a figure or expression within the panel, I will wait to photocopy the finished figure Im repeating and then trace it. I dont paste down the repeats as often as I usually do.

That effect works best when someone is shocked or taken off gaurd. I worry about all the drawn detail until the next stage.

The e..

All my thought process happens in the layout, so now, I can relax, toss on a dvd to listen and half watch while I draw. I work on a light box, lay down the breakdowns and place my drawing paper, wich is not comic paper, but 11x 17 Laser copy paper. Its thicker than photocopy, but thinner than bristol, so its much easier to light box. I use two or three things to ink with- most of the page is inked with a roller ball pen. Just a black pen. I Think it's called UNIBALL and it moves very fast, doesn't fade or change color, doesn't snag the paper or smudge. It's great. I can move really fast with this, and I'd say 90% of the page is done with that. Sometimes, for smaller faces, I use a pigma micron, number 001. I also use the #1 micron which is big and broad, for panel boarders and sometimes close ups, or silhouette outlines like in panel 5.

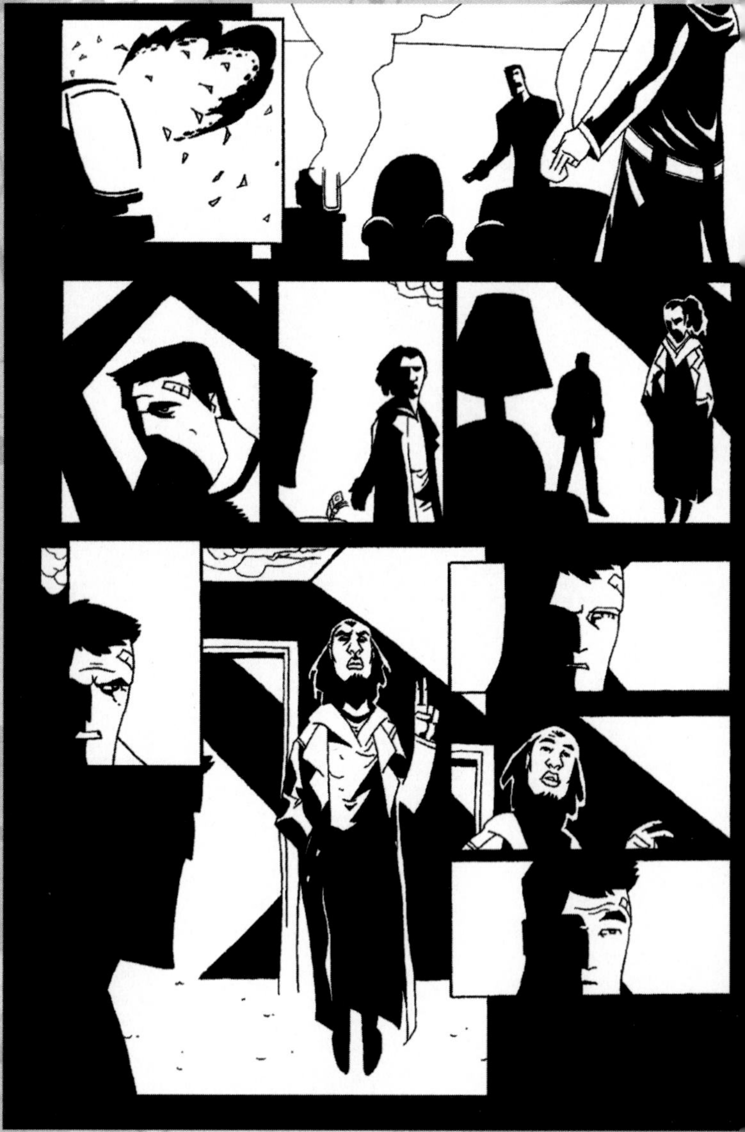

Sometimes, I break out the brush, but the brush has a very distinct look from the pen. You can see the shift in brush to pen in the newer issues of Powers.
Sometimes I will use a combonation of both, and some stories will call just for the brush. You may also notice I dont use a ruler. I only use straight lines for panel boarders, but everything within the panels are freehand to give it loose,alive feeling.
I like the sketchyness of fast inking,for me, it helps give the energy you can find in sketches but rarely in pages.

Check out the repeated panels. You can see where I chose to shift or redraw expressions. I think the "acting" is where my strength is on the page.
When my characters hurt, so do I a little. I love characters like WAZZ or TRIPHAMMER who seem to be one thing, but are truly another. Just like most people you meet, they are not all they seem. This too,I think is the strength in Powers, we show you that everything has a layer, a meaning, everything from story, character, plot, art, colors, letters,all have layers and meaning.

-Mike Avon Oeming, Powers Artist and co creator

Brian emails the script to me a month or two early,

HE LETTERS

Ken Bruzenak, letterer of Powers...

rian emails the script to me a month or two early, but I don't even open ne file until I get the FedEx package of pages from Mike. ince most of the double-page spreads are drawn smaller, at printed size, I pull nd photocopy them larger, to match the rest of the single (11x17") pages. : really can't letter that tiny.)

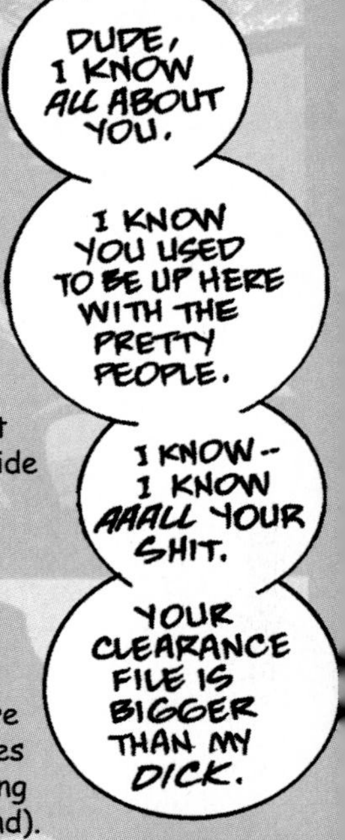
DUDE, I KNOW ALL ABOUT YOU.
I KNOW YOU USED TO BE UP HERE WITH THE PRETTY PEOPLE.
I KNOW-- I KNOW AAALL YOUR SHIT.
YOUR CLEARANCE FILE IS BIGGER THAN MY DICK.

'hen I tape the page to my board and attach an overlay sheet of 14x17" anson Pro Layout Marker paper. Using a non-reproducing blue lead pencil, I make ght circles on the overlay to "spot" the balloons, making sure they all fit, interconnect orrectly, and somehow link to the right characters. Next, I use an Ames lettering guide nd T-square to blue pencil rule my guidelines.

've been working with Fountain Pentels on Powers. An X-Acto cut gives me the slight hisel tip I need--no cut for bold italics. I letter by hand to approximate the innate, rganic handicraft of the comic artwork. Visually repetitive computer fonts are fine or robots, public address announcements and politicians--mechanical constructs--but think real comic people (with two-dimensional black outlines around them) need a more ouncy, quirky freehand approach to simulate human speech. I draw the balloon outlines ith oval templates, and French Curve the tails to complement the geometric formatting f the rectangular page and panels (plus I draw ugly, bumpy, lop-sided balloons freehand).

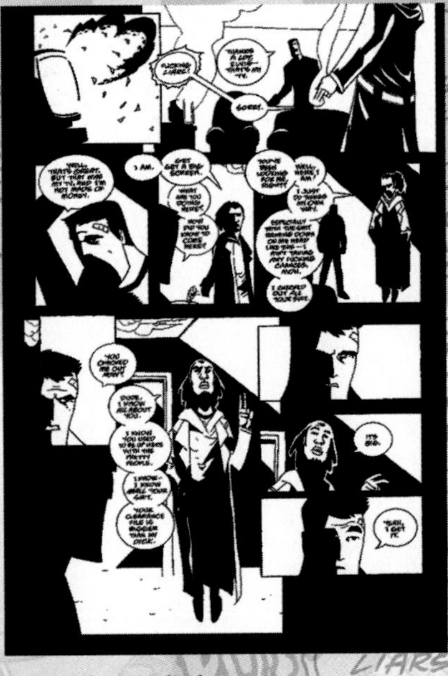

ome pages are silent (God bless you, Brian), ut most are very wordy, and I usually have o completely re-do 2-3 pages per issue to get cleaner fit. I try hard to keep the words ehind the figurework, tracing the overlapping utlines with a red pen, which reproduces s a trap line in scanning and complicates the olorist's job (sorry, Peter). This keeps the focus on the characters, who an struggle through their story without being tabbed in the ear by balloon pointers, or sliced hrough the boobs or forehead by big white llipsis full of dialogue.

ound effects are computer generated for conceptually niform, hard-edged and repetitive sources, like unshots, sirens, helicopters and signage, and I design ll those little TV logos and superscripts. Printed out, hese CG sounds and signs are rubber cemented on the overlay, n position, so that Peter can scan everything in one pass. Death screams, orgasms nd demented laughter--noises made by people, nature and God--get kinetic sfx done y hand directly on the overlay. I may make notes for suggestions about color holds r show-through on the outer edge of the page, then everything gets shipped off to California.

I'm a colorist/inker/letterer...
Let me explain...

-Peter Pantazis,colorist for POWERS

As a colorist, I start the process by first recieving Brians script via e-mail, and Mikes pages with Kens letters attached, from Ken who had his hands on 'em last.

From there, I scan in each page at 300 dpi, and I don't own one of those huge Scanners that take a whole page, so it takes two passes to get one page of Powers actually scanned. I then scan in Kens letters, which also end up in two parts.
After all the scanning is complete, I put all the images together in PHOTOSHOP.

I then proceed into my semi-inking phase, by popping in all the blacks that Mike has nicely marked with an X...I then clean up any specs or marks that possibly appeared in the scan.

Finally the coloring begins, I set up each page with what we colorists call channels, there are a few of 'em: RGB/RED/GREEN BLUE/and LINE ART

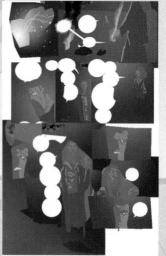

That last one is the key, it acts like an overlay, that channel holds all of Mikes Wonderous art, while I see the art, I am actually working underneath it , not touching a thing..yet..I set up each page with what is called FLATS, and that is a basic color layed down, to separate the skin from clothing, background from foreground ,and all that is in-between.Most of the time, I get the help of my amazing wife for this part. It can be tedious at times...

this is what the color looks like underneath Mikes Lines.

Okay, when all the setup is complete, I can finally get down to rendering each page, I add lighting and shadows as necessary. I closely read Brians script as I color each page,and decide on what the mood of the particular scene would be. For this page, if you've noticed, Walkers' skin tone, (actually throughout the issue) is very muted, almost grey, this is because I chose to reflect the fact that Zora , his ill fated wife to be, has been killed and it has taken it's toll. The scene takes place in Walkers Apt, at night,and pretty much dictates that the colors should also be muted and very downplayed.

I go into special effect mode,

Vell after I'm through rendering the page,
 go into special effect mode, where I go
 and add any type of lighting or glowing
ffects. These are my personal favorite
hings to do. I get to turn on lights,
reate textures for certain powers and
dd stuff into the BG like on Billboards
nd street signs.

here are basically two popular ways of
cheiving these effects, the "normal" way,
nd the "Layers" way. Normal is basically
aking the actual art and pasting it down
o the channel that I have been working
n, and doing the effect right on the art.
he LAYERS way(which I prefer) actually
dds another layer on top of the art,
here I can do any type of effect, and if
ecessary, very easily retouch it.

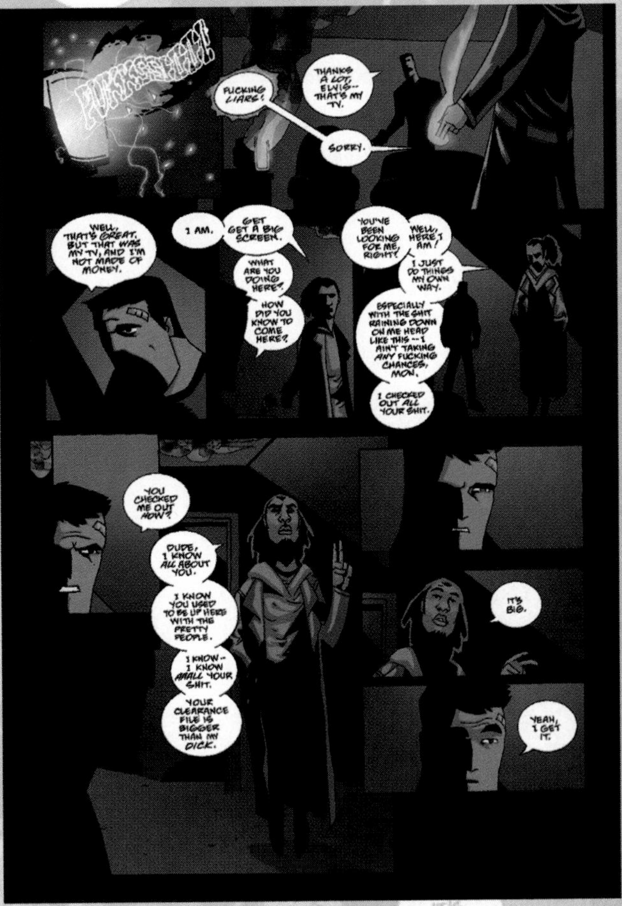
FUCKING LIARS!
THANKS A LOT, ELVIS... THAT'S MY TV.
SORRY.
WELL, THAT'S GREAT, BUT THAT WAS MY TV, AND I'M NOT MADE OF MONEY.
I AM.
GET GET A BIG SCREEN.
WHAT ARE YOU DOING HERE?
HOW DID YOU KNOW TO COME HERE?
YOU'VE BEEN LOOKING FOR ME, RIGHT?
WELL, HERE I AM!
I JUST DO THINGS MY OWN WAY.
ESPECIALLY WITH THE SHIT RAINING DOWN ON ME HEAD LIKE THIS -- I AIN'T TAKING ANY FUCKING CHANCES, MON.
I CHECKED OUT ALL YOUR SHIT.
YOU CHECKED ME OUT HOW?
DUDE, I KNOW ALL ABOUT YOU.
I KNOW YOU USED TO BE UP HERE WITH THE PRETTY PEOPLE.
I KNOW-- I KNOW AALL YOUR SHIT.
YOUR CLEARANCE FILE IS BIGGER THAN MY DICK.
IT'S BIG.
YEAH, I GET IT.

THIS IS PAGE 10 AS IT ACTUALLY APPEARED IN ISSUE 19

Once all the special effects are done, and I'm
appy with the page, I then put on my Letterers
ap, and proceed with placing Kens previously
canned letters exactly where they belong on
he page, Also in Photoshop. Once that is done,
 send off a Jpeg to Brian and Mike, they give
ne their input on anything that might need
weaking, and I go about correcting them .
 also go in and change any noticed typos
hat happen to be pointed out.(we missed
omething on this page see if you can find it)
VHEW!, after all that is done, the page is
eady to be "TRAPPED" which is the word
 use for setting it up for Print. I then
ither Burn the issue onto a CD and Fedex
t to Studio Colour Group or I FTP it via cable
Modem, depending on the amount of time I
ve to get them the pages.
And then I sleep for a week.

Well, that's it, take it as you will- this is how we put Powers together. It's not traditional, it's not the best or right way to do things, but it's how we do it, and how we feel most comfortable with it. Just like art, the process is done in such a way to best please the creators. You've heard from Brian, Myself, Ken and Pete, but there are several other people behind the scenes. The Image Central crew who take care of everything from here, Brian's wife Alisa who takes care of all things legal, Pat Garrahy who colored and did production on the first dozen or so issues, the websites and magazines who promote the book and of course, the readers. Thanks to DRAW! for giving us this chance to show you what's under our skirt.

Thanks,
Mike, Brian, Ken and Pete, the Powers crew.

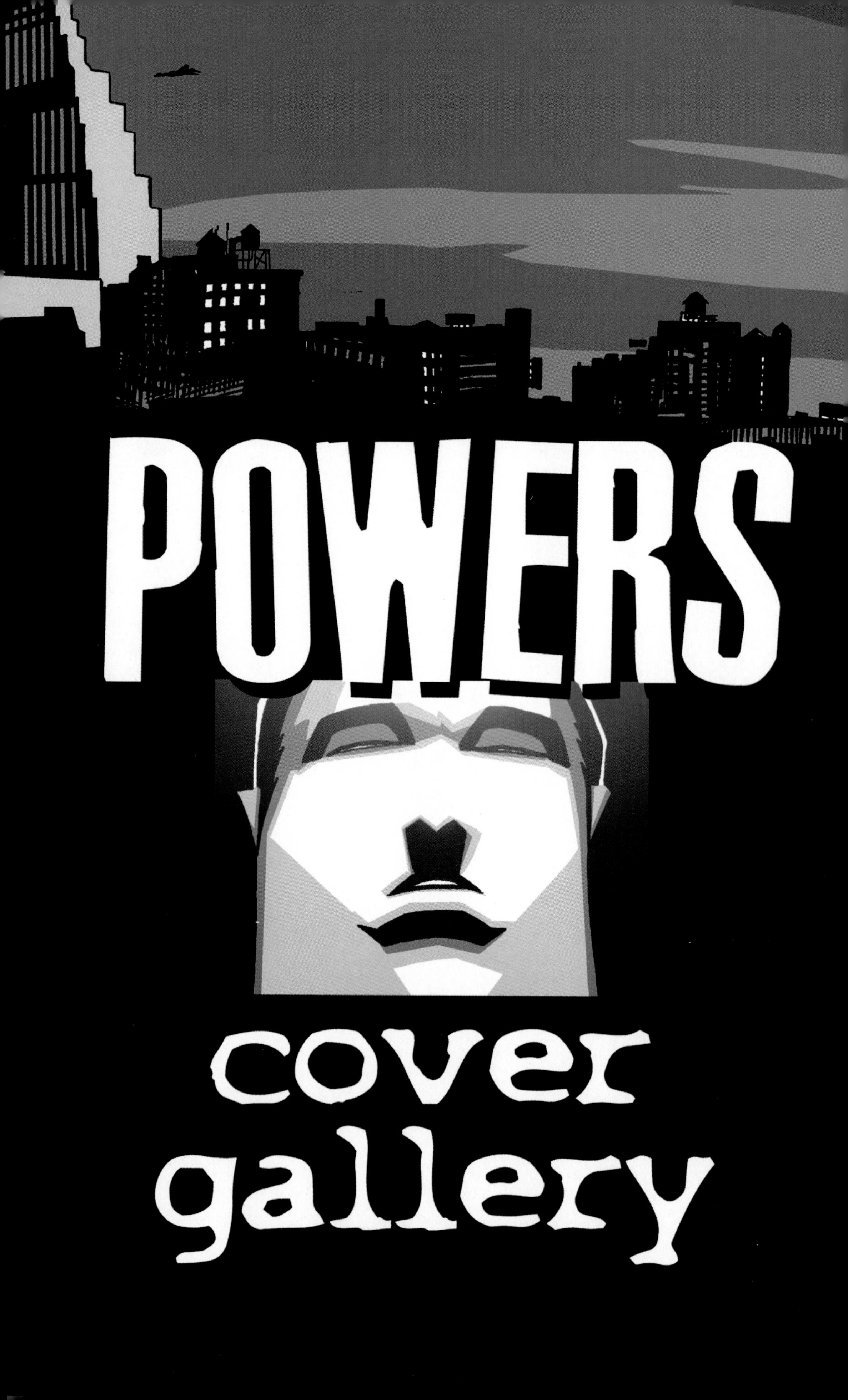
POWERS
cover
gallery

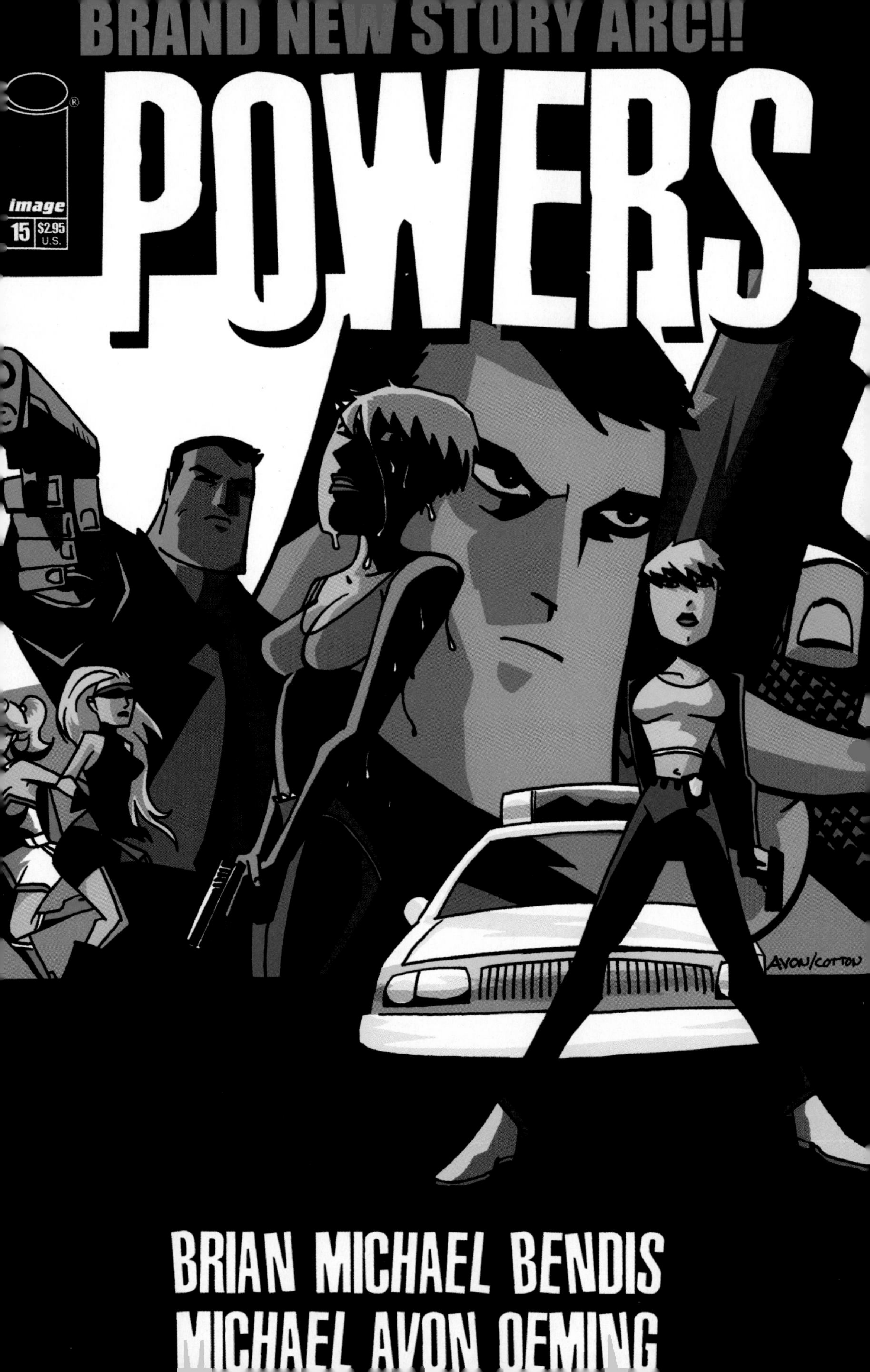
BRAND NEW STORY ARC!!
image
15
$2.95 U.S.
POWERS
AVON/COTTON
BRIAN MICHAEL BENDIS
MICHAEL AVON OEMING

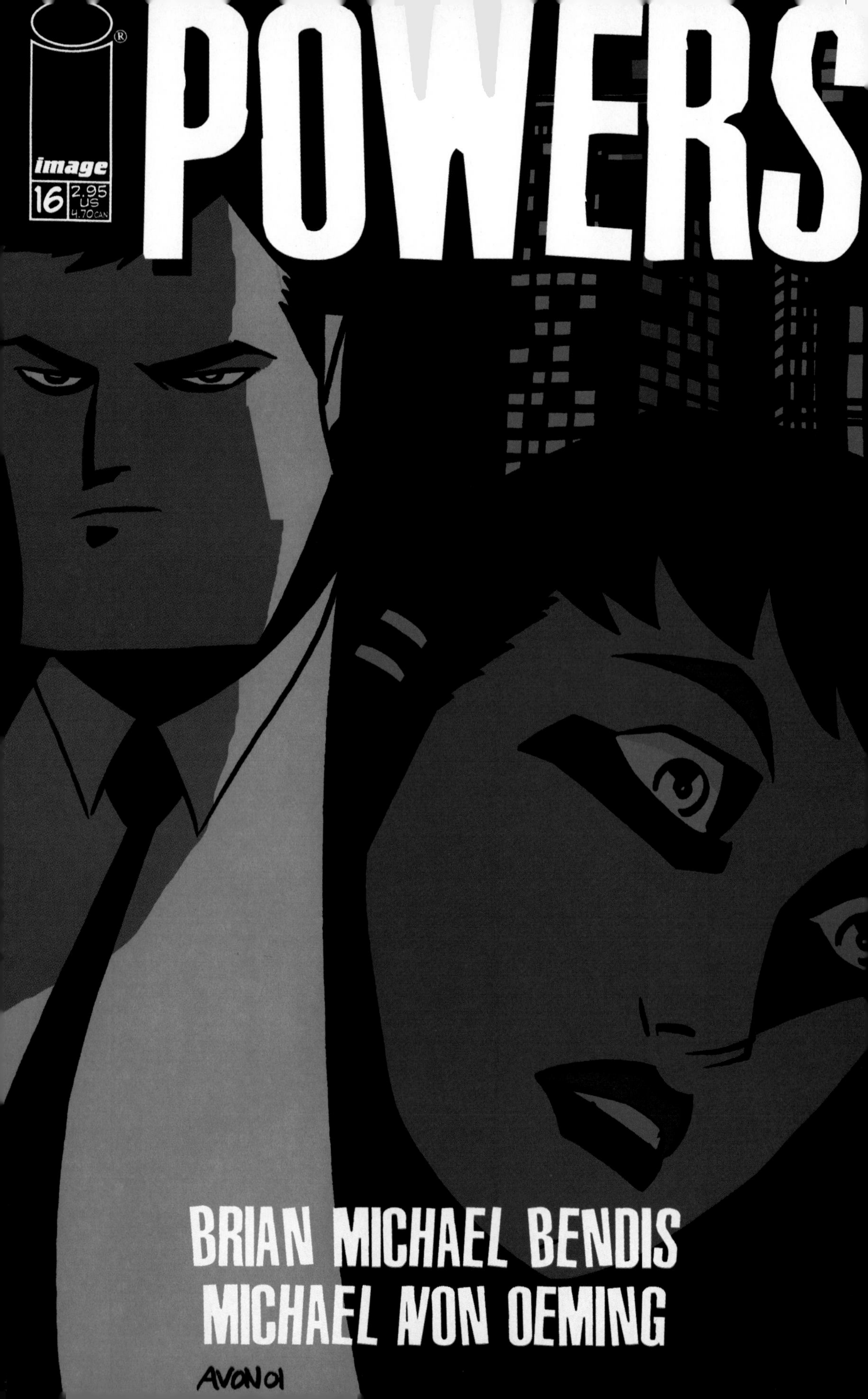
image
16
2.95 US
4.70 CAN
POWERS
BRIAN MICHAEL BENDIS
MICHAEL AVON OEMING
AVON 01

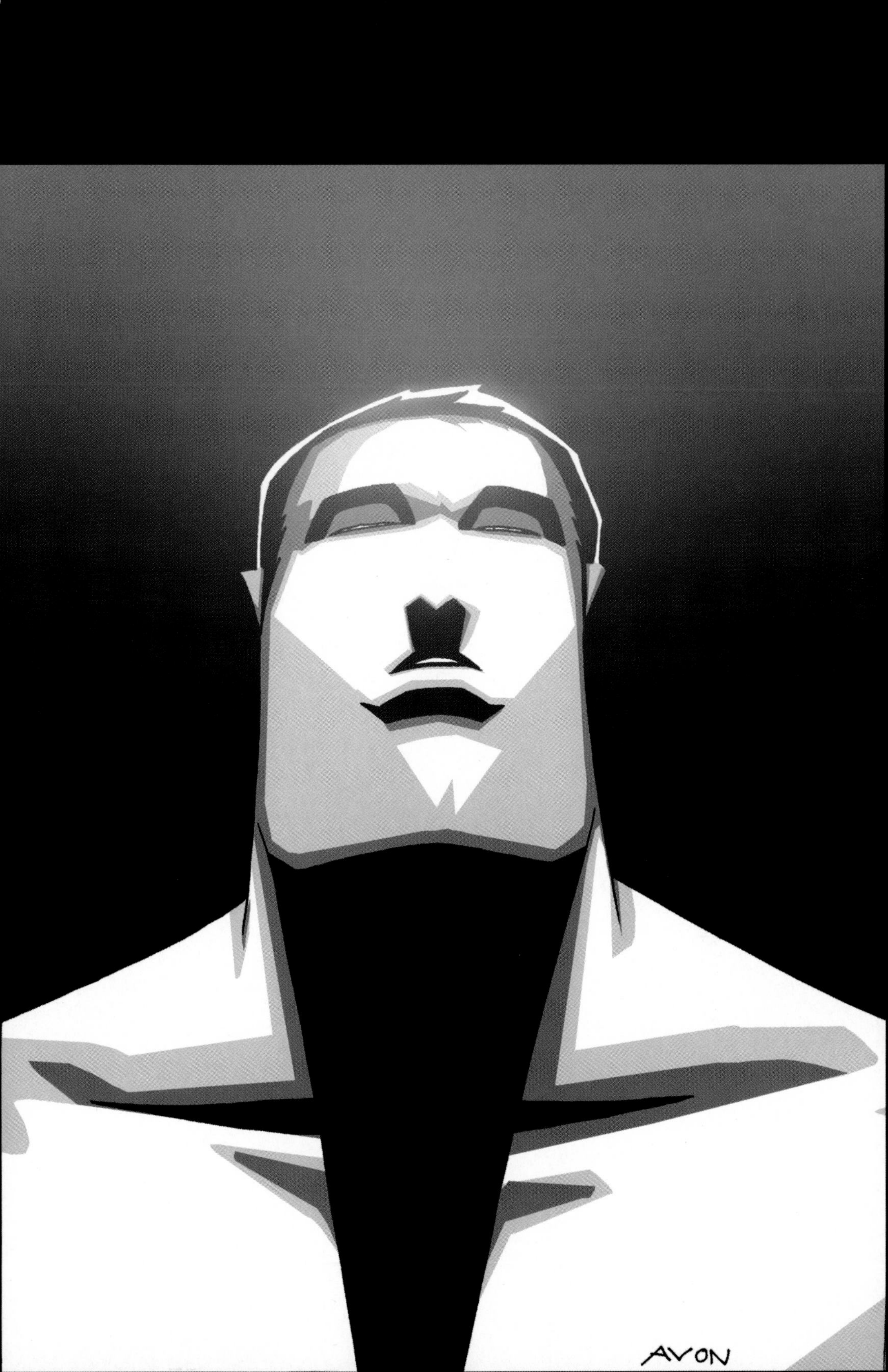
AVON

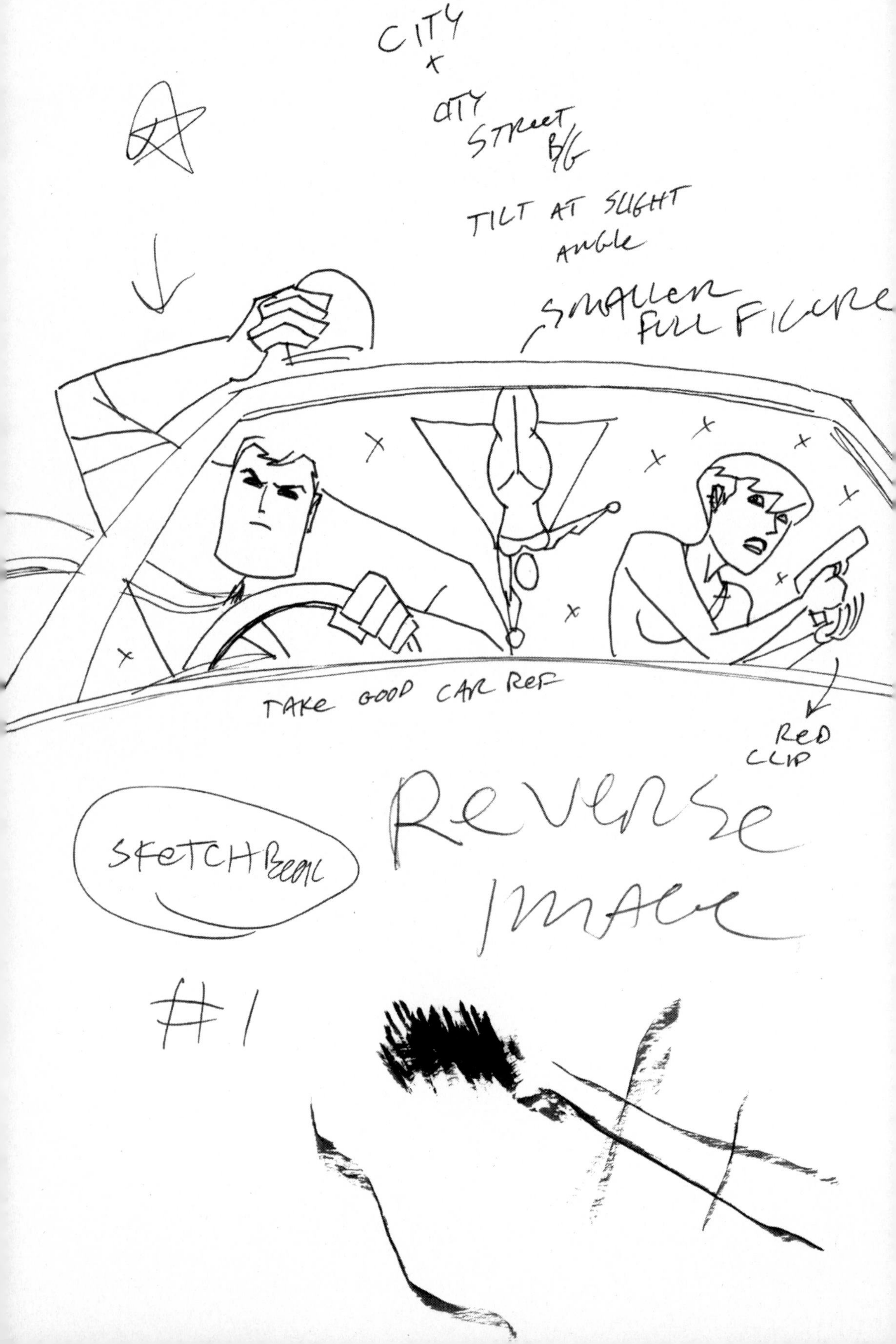
CITY
+
CITY STREET B/G
TILT AT SLIGHT ANGLE
SMALLER FULL FIGURE
TAKE GOOD CAR REF
RED CLIP
REVERSE IMAGE
#1

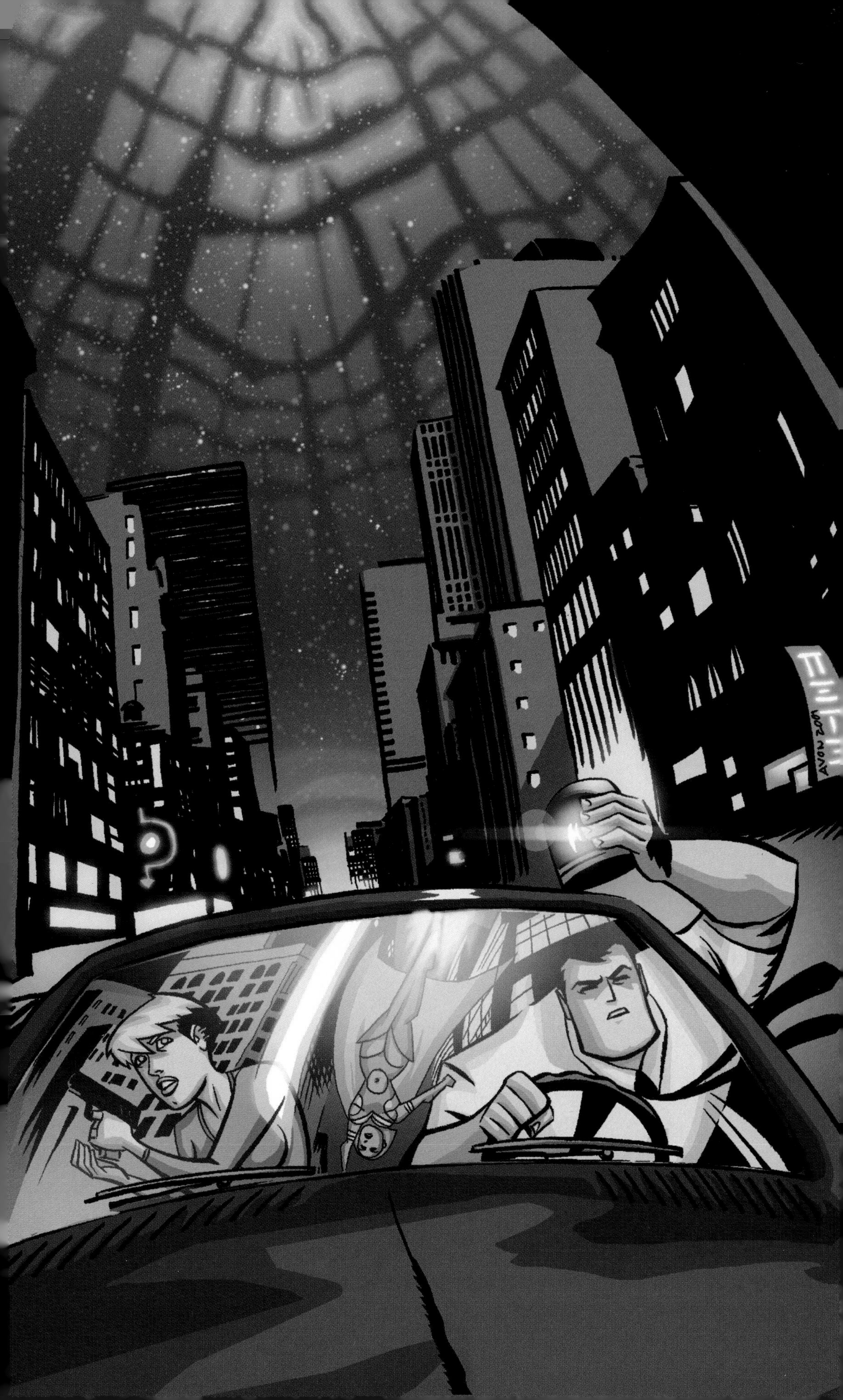
AVON 2001

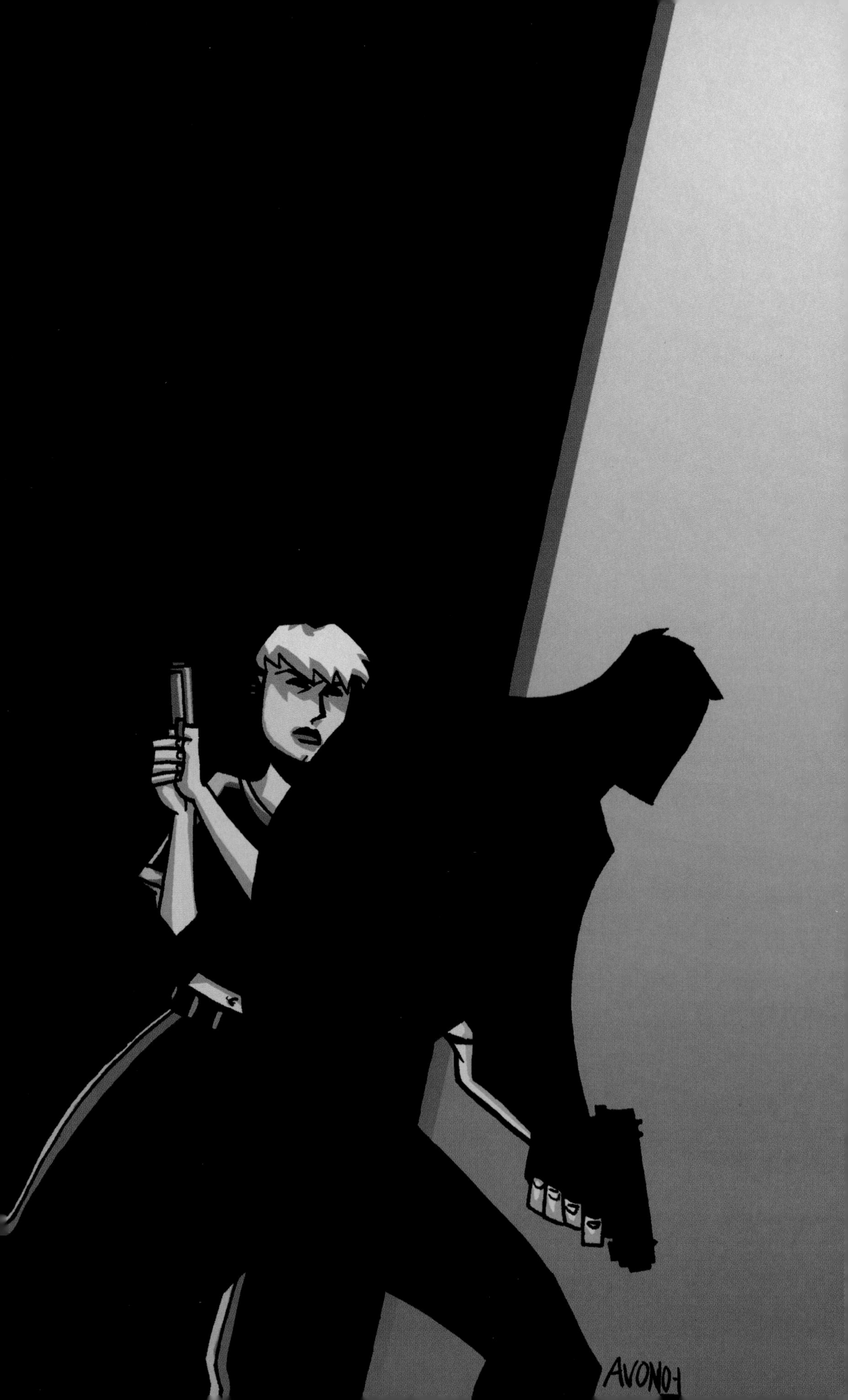

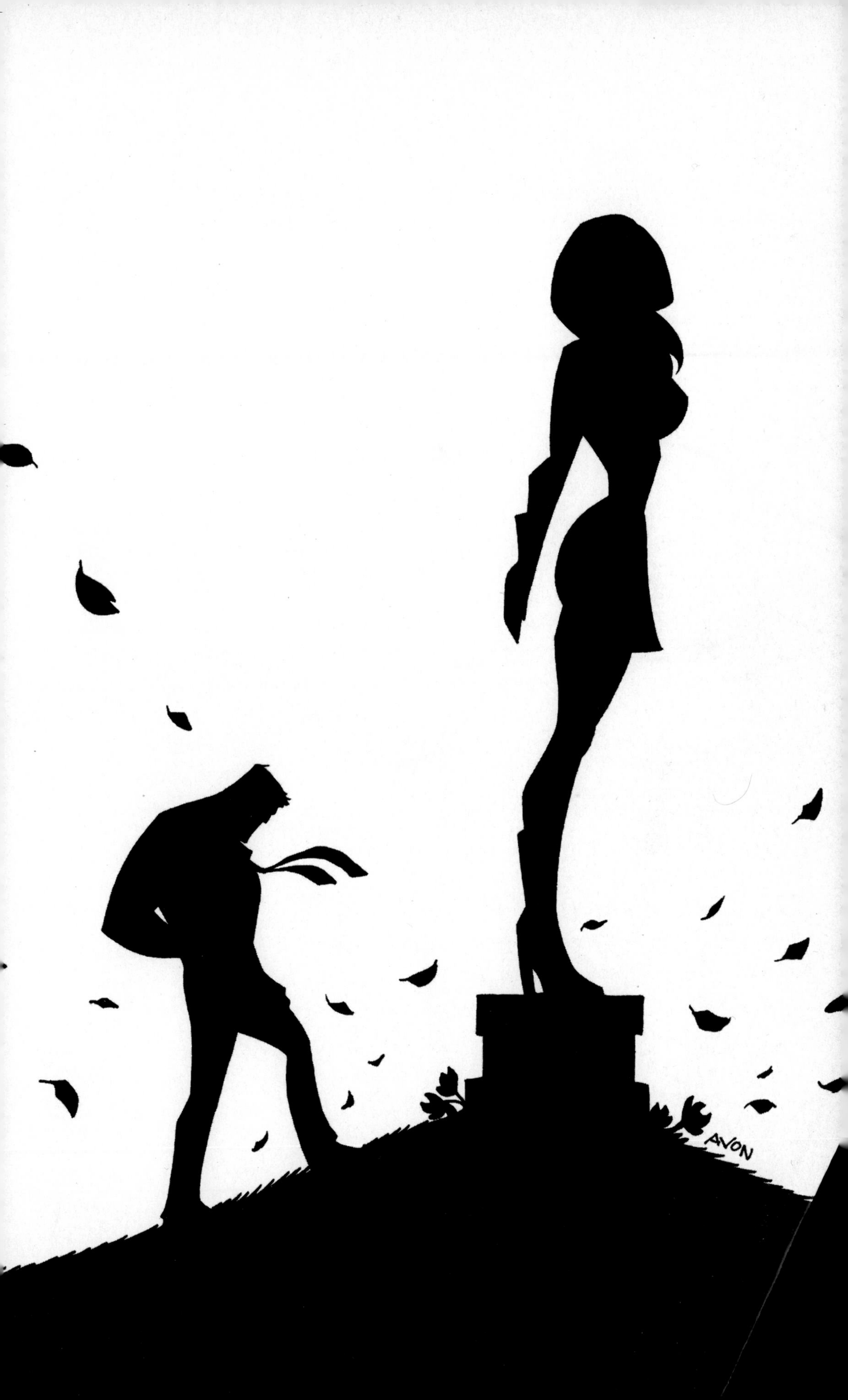
AVON

MORE GREAT BOOKS FROM IMAGE COMICS

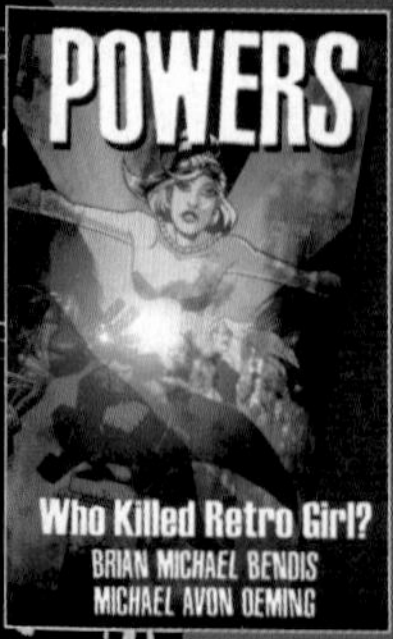
POWERS
Who Killed Retro Girl?
BRIAN MICHAEL BENDIS
MICHAEL AVON OEMING

POWERS, VOL. 1: WHO KILLED RETRO GIRL? TP
ISBN# 1-58240-669-3
$21.99

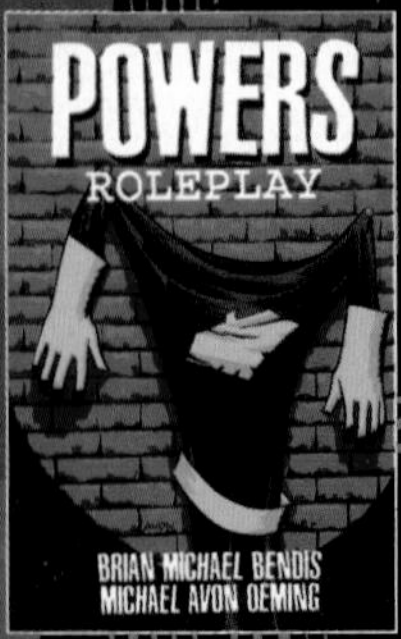
POWERS
ROLEPLAY
BRIAN MICHAEL BENDIS
MICHAEL AVON OEMING

POWERS, VOL. 2: ROLEPLAY TP
ISBN# 1-58240-695-2
$13.99

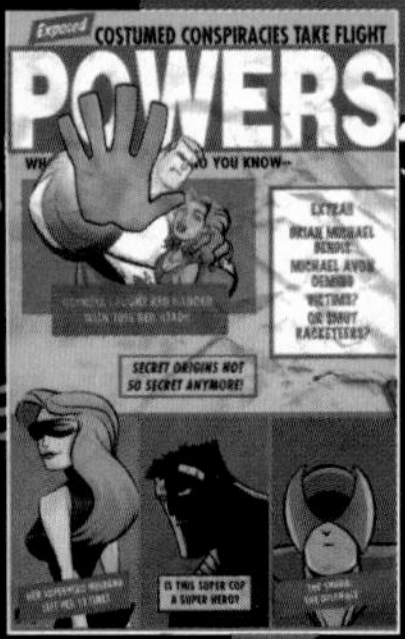
COSTUMED CONSPIRACIES TAKE FLIGHT
POWERS
SECRET ORIGINS NOT SO SECRET ANYMORE!

POWERS, VOL. 3: LITTLE DEATHS TP
ISBN# 1-58240-670-7
$19.99

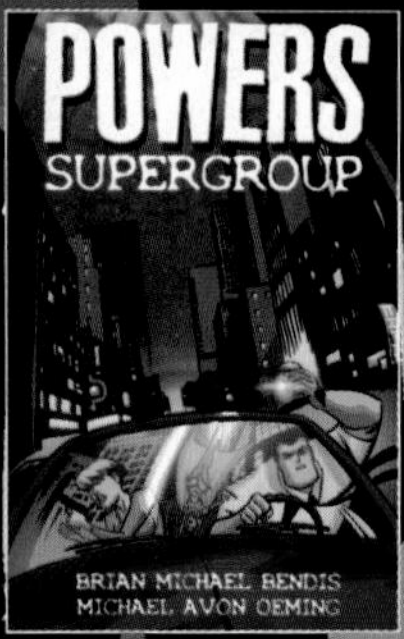
POWERS
SUPERGROUP
BRIAN MICHAEL BENDIS
MICHAEL AVON OEMING

POWERS, VOL. 4: SUPERGROUP TP
ISBN# 1-58240-671-5
$21.99

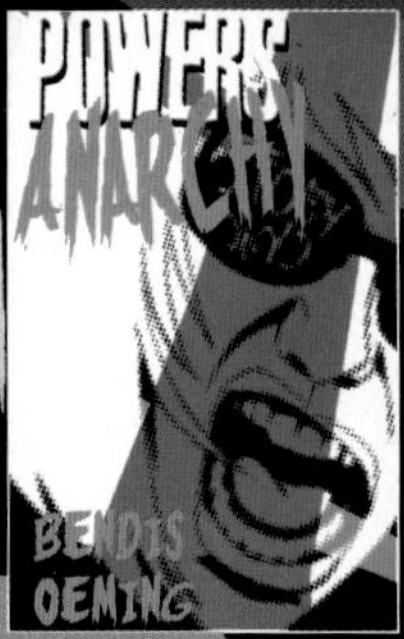
POWERS
ANARCHY
BENDIS
OEMING

POWERS, VOL. 5: ANARCHY TP
ISBN# 1-58240-331-7
$14.95

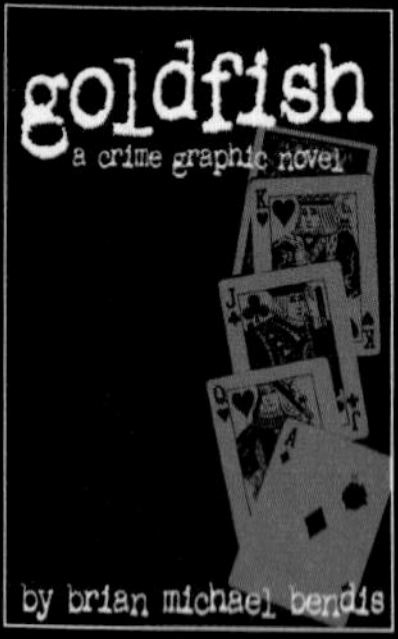
goldfish
a crime graphic novel
by brian michael bendis

GOLDFISH: THE DEFINITIVE COLLECTION TP
ISBN# 1-58240-195-0
$19.95

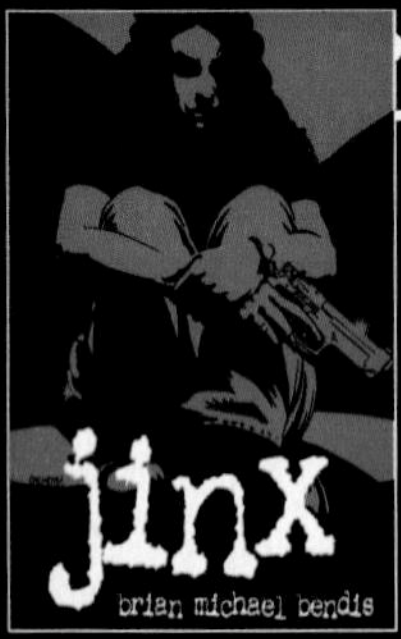
jinx
brian michael bendis

JINX: THE DEFINITIVE COLLECTION TP
ISBN# 1-58240-179-9
$24.95

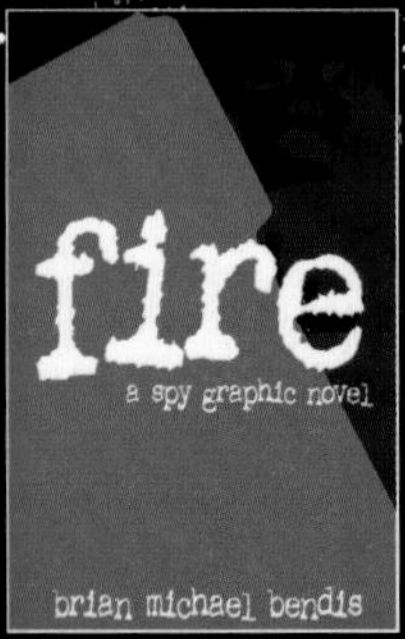
fire
a spy graphic novel
brian michael bendis

FIRE: THE DEFINITIVE COLLECTION TP
ISBN# 1-58240-071-7
$9.95

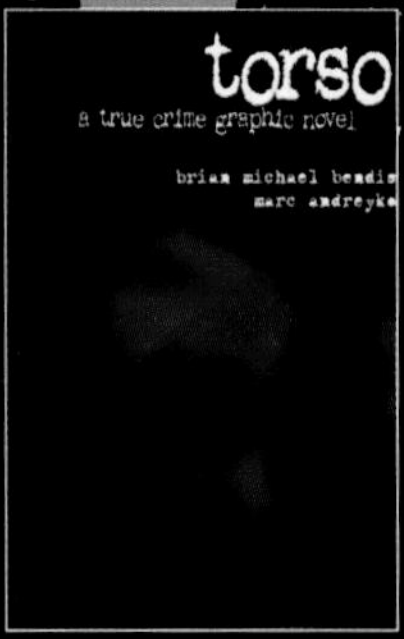
torso
a true crime graphic novel
brian michael bendis
marc andreyko

TORSO: THE DEFINITIVE COLLECTION TP
ISBN# 1-58240-174-8
$21.95

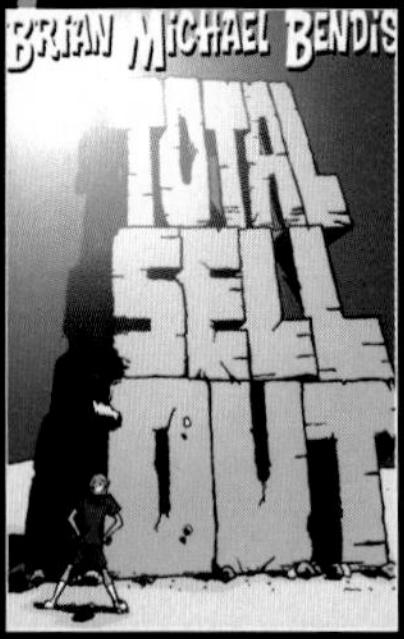
BRIAN MICHAEL BENDIS
TOTAL SELL OUT

TOTAL SELL OUT TP
ISBN# 1-58240-287-6
$14.95

ALSO AVAILABLE

40 OZ. COLLECTED TP
ISBN# 1-58240-329-5
$9.95

BAD IDEAS: COLLECTED! TP
ISBN# 1-58240-531-X
$12.99

CLASSIC 40 OZ.: TALES FROM THE BROWN BAG TP
ISBN# 1-58240-438-0
$14.95

DIORAMAS, A LOVE STORY GN
ISBN# 1-58240-359-7
$12.95

BLOOD RIVER GN
ISBN# 1-58240-509-3
$7.99

WINGS OF ANASI GN
…99

…KI
…OF BLOOD TP

VOL. 2: DREAMS TP
ISBN# 1-58240-277-9
$12.95
VOL. 3: MASKS OF NOH TP
ISBN# 1-58240-108-X
$12.95
VOL. 4: SKIN DEEP TP
ISBN# 1-58240-000-8
$12.95
VOL. 5: METAMORPHOSIS TP
ISBN# 1-58240-203-5
$24.99
VOL. 6: SCARAB TP
ISBN# 1-58240-258-2
$19.95

NIGHT TRIPPERS GN
ISBN# 1-58240-606-5
$16.99

NOWHERESVILLE TP
ISBN# 1-58240-241-8
$14.95

THE FURTHER ADVENTURES OF ONE PAGE FILLER MAN TP
ISBN# 1-58240-535-2
$11.99

GIRLS
VOL. 1: CONCEPTION TP
ISBN# 1-58240-529-8
$14.99
VOL. 2: EMERGENCE TP
ISBN# 1-58240-608-1
$14.99

GRRL SCOUTS
VOL. 1: TP
ISBN# 1-58240-316-3
$12.95
VOL. 2: WORK SUCKS TP
ISBN# 1-58240-343-0
$12.95

HAMMER OF THE GODS, VOL. 1: MORTAL ENEMY TP
ISBN# 1-58240-271-X
$18.95

POWERS SCRIPTBOOK
ISBN# 1-58240-233-7
$19.95

PUTTIN THE BACKBONE BACK TP
ISBN# 1-58240-402-X
$9.95

QUIXOTE NOVEL
ISBN# 1-58240-434-8
$9.95

SAN AND TWITCH: THE BRIAN MICHAEL BENDIS COLLECTION, VOL. 1 TP
ISBN# 1-58240-583-2
$24.95

SIX GN
ISBN# 1-58240-398-8
$5.95

STUPID COMICS, VOL. 1 TP
ISBN# 1-58240-611-1
$12.99

ULTRA: SEVEN DAYS TP
ISBN# 1-58240-483-6
$17.95

WHISKEY DICKEL, INTERNATIONAL COWGIRL GN
ISBN# 1-58240-318-X
$12.95

…near you carrying graphic novels from Image Comics, please call toll free:
…BOOK

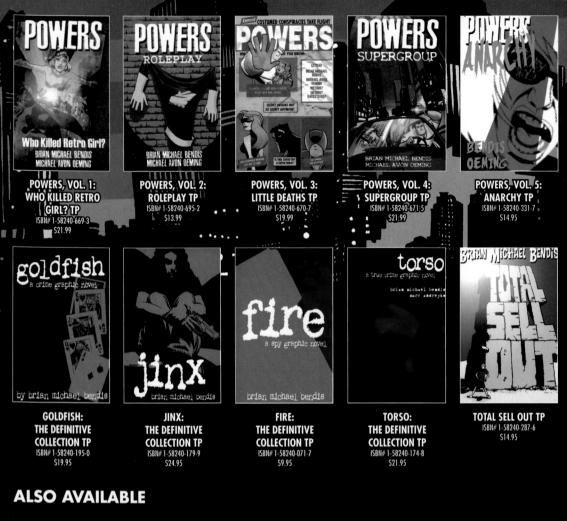